A savage place as holy and enchanted
As e'er beneath a waning moon was haunted
By a woman wailing for her demon lover!
Samuel Taylor Coleridge

BOOKS BY TROY TAYLOR

DEAD MEN SO TELL TALES SERIES
Dead Men Do Tell Tales (2008)
Bloody Chicago (2006)
Bloody Illinois (2008)
Bloody Hollywood (2008)

HAUNTED ILLINOIS BOOKS
Haunted Illinois (1999 / 2001 / 2004)
Haunted Decatur (1995)
More Haunted Decatur (1996)
Ghosts of Millikin (1996 / 2001)
Where the Dead Walk (1997 / 2002)
Dark Harvest (1997)
Haunted Decatur Revisited (2000)
Flickering Images (2001)
Haunted Decatur: 13th Anniversary (2006)
Haunted Alton (2000 / 2003 / 2008)
Haunted Chicago (2003)
The Haunted President (2005)
Mysterious Illinois (2005)
Resurrection Mary (2007)
The Possessed (2007)
Weird Chicago (2008)

HAUNTED FIELD GUIDE BOOKS
The Ghost Hunters Guidebook
(1997/ 1999 / 2001/ 2004 / 2007)
Confessions of a Ghost Hunter (2002)
Field Guide to Haunted Graveyards (2003)
Ghosts on Film (2005)
So, There I Was (with Len Adams) (2006)

HISTORY & HAUNTINGS SERIES
The Haunting of America (2001)
Into the Shadows (2002)
Down in the Darkness (2003)
Out Past the Campfire Light (2004)
Ghosts by Gaslight (2007)

OTHER GHOSTLY TITLES
Spirits of the Civil War (1999)
Season of the Witch (1999/ 2002)
Haunted New Orleans (2000)
Beyond the Grave (2001)
No Rest for the Wicked (2001)
Haunted St. Louis (2002)
The Devil Came to St. Louis (2006)
Sex & the Supernatural (2009)

STERLING PUBLICATIONS
Weird U.S. (Co-Author) (2004)
Weird Illinois (2005)
Weird Virginia (Co-Author) (2007)
Weird Indiana (Co-Author) (2008)

BARNES & NOBLE PRESS TITLES
Haunting of America (2006)
Spirits of the Civil War (2007)
Into the Shadows (2007)

HISTORY PRESS TITLES
Wicked Washington (2007)

STACKPOLE BOOKS TITLES
Haunted Illinois (2008)
True Crime Illinois (2009)

The Haunted & Horrific History of Sex & the Occult

SEX AND THE SUPERNATURAL
BY TROY TAYLOR

- A Dark Haven Entertainment Book from Whitechapel Press -

Sex lies at the root of life, and we can never learn to reverence
life until we know how to understand sex.
Havelock Ellis

ORIGINAL COVER ARTWORK DESIGNED BY
©Copyright 2008 by Michael Schwab & Troy Taylor
With special thanks to Barry Downard for Creative Juice
Visit M & S Graphics at http://www.manyhorses.com/msgraphics.htm

THIS BOOK IS PUBLISHED BY
Whitechapel Press
A Division of Dark Haven Entertainment, Inc.
15 Forest Knolls Estates - Decatur, Illinois - 62521
(217) 422-1002 / 1-888-GHOSTLY
Visit us on the internet at http://www. dark haven entertainment. com

First Printing -- January 2009
ISBN: 1-892523-63-9

Printed in the United States of America

SEX AND THE SUPERNATURAL

I look for ghosts; but none will force
Their way to me. 'Tis falsely said
That there was ever intercourse
Between the living and the dead.
William Wordsworth

Dreaming men are haunted men.
Stephen Vincent Benet

It is with our passions, as it is with fire and water,
they are good servants but bad masters.
Aesop

And it came to pass, when men began to multiply on the face of the earth, and daughters were born unto them, That the sons of God saw the daughters of men that they were fair; and they took them wives of all which they chose. And the Lord said, My spirit shall not always strive with man, for that he also is flesh: yet his days shall be an hundred and twenty years. There were giants in the earth in those days; and also after that, when the sons of God came in unto the daughters of men, and they bare children to them, the same became mighty men which were of old, men of renown.
Genesis, Chapter 6, Verses 1-4

TABLE OF CONTENTS

FOREWORD
BY KEN MELVOIN-BERG
CREATOR OF THE WEIRD CHICAGO RED-LIGHT DISTRICT SEX TOURS

My involvement with both sex and the supernatural started at the tender age of thirteen years. I was going through puberty and I started reading about both subjects voraciously as a young man will do when exploring both his spirituality and his sexuality. I never dreamed that both subjects had any common threads as I was focused on each subject individually.

Sex was the more exciting of the two subjects; it was naughty and forbidden. Like any object that is taboo, I wanted to read about it, fantasized about it and definitely try it. All the different forms of supernatural phenomena were my next greatest love. This was initially sparked in my love of a game called *Dungeons and Dragons*. Reading about the wizards, elves, dragons, warriors and fair maidens was exciting and pretending to be them even more so. This was truly my first taste of how sex and the supernatural were combined, in a subtle way (we pretended). One can hardly think about swords and sorcery literature or games without bringing up the image of a hot babe in chain-mail bikinis.

Folklore has given us a menagerie of mythical beings that try to use sex with unsuspecting humans. Vampires tantalize and have sex with unwilling victims, ghosts drain our energies and might have sex with loved ones that remain alive, witches use sex to raise magickal energy to fuel their spells, succubi and incubi seduce and use sex to steal energies and life force. Not to mention all the demons and devils that have used the enticing offer of sensuality and carnal pleasures to take away souls and free will. Greek mythology gives us a huge body of sexuality; look at the many lovers of Zeus, for example, and the many sexual forms he takes, from that of a swan, a golden shower, a bull and many others. Throughout the recorded history of man, sex has had a place in our hearts and minds that has tantalized us.

But sex has not always been used for pleasure by these entities. In the case of the succubus, sex has been used as a means of control to drain the victim of all his vital energies leaving him drained. The concept of the "energy vampire" comes to mind when discussing these demons.

Since I have grown into an adult I have become heavily involved with many elements of sexuality; bondage, sadism, masochism, sex toys, swinging and open relationships. I have also been a practicing witch for going on twenty years now and have combined sexuality and my religious practices using sex magick to raise energy to heal sick friends and help those with hard financial times to gain prosperity. I have never used this for my own gains, only to help others. To be clear on this point, I do not worship Satan nor do I adhere to any negative energies. The only things I do magickally are to help those in need. I have also taught and written about sexuality, rope bondage, sex tours (our sex tour is rated the best tour in Chicago for the second year running as of this printing), have done networking for kinky people and been involved with Voudoun, Santeria, ghosts, the psychic world, Witchcraft, tarot and the occult.

Weird Chicago's sex tour was my invention around 12 years ago in Chicago. When Troy, Adam and myself joined up to start Weird Chicago I mentioned in passing wanting to do this particular tour. Troy was at first a little hesitant. It's not that he is a prude in any way (as you'll see from the book to follow), he simply didn't want to scare off any long time customers. When we opened up our first sex tour, it sold out faster than any other tour we had done before. We wondered if it was a fluke, so we tried it again -- and again and again. Since that time it has become a regular feature for our company and is still the best selling non-ghost tour we offer at Weird Chicago. In fact some customers have been on as many as four of the sex tours bringing more friends with them each time! The sex tour, combined with our supernatural tours, proved there is a market for the combining of the two, which was one of the many reasons that I loved this book so much.

Troy Taylor has hit on an idea that is a long time in coming. The book you hold in your hands combines my two favorite subjects, sex and the supernatural. Although both of these taboo subjects are something we don't discuss in polite society, they are both ingrained into our American culture. Think of a swear word that does not have some connotation to sex, for example. It's hard to do, isn't it? We take for granted the root of sexuality when we use these words, they have a power over us when we are either angry or amorous. This is the key to the subject of sex and the supernatural. Sex is power both as an act of love and as an act of control over another. Self-proclaimed wizards, witches and magicians have used sex as a way to fuel their magic for centuries. So, it isn't surprising that the two subjects of the paranormal and sex would come together.

Troy has done a great service in writing this book. I can think of no better author to address this subject in a tactful, accurate and informative manner. Troy has accomplished writing so many books on the subject of the paranormal there are few who could be considered his peer by sheer volume alone. He has an exhaustive memory on the supernatural and has forgotten more about the subject than most knew to begin with. I have always been amazed at his knowledge on the subject of both sex and the supernatural and was sorely disappointed by all other books that have come out previously. This book did not disappoint!

So, thank you Troy. You are more than a friend to me, you are a kindred spirit and my brother.

Ken Melvoin-Berg
December 2008

INTRODUCTION

There are two things that every one of us is fascinated, dare I say obsessed, with: sex and death, and by extension, life after death, and the supernatural. Both subjects are usually considered to be taboo, off limits, and not something to be discussed in polite society.

It's easy to understand why sex is something about which most people avoid talking. Growing up in the largely puritanical American society, we are taught from an early age that sex is best kept behind closed doors. We don't talk about it, we aren't supposed to think about it and, of course, it's not meant for public consumption. As small children, we are told that our bodies should always be covered and our sexual organs are given euphemisms to prevent embarrassment when we mention them in front of the wrong people. As we grew older, we were told not to fornicate, masturbate, or engage in any sort of behavior that might give people the wrong impression. We weren't allowed to kiss our girlfriends or boyfriends in the hallways at school, or even hold hands for that matter. Behavior that went beyond that was sure to earn you a detention. When we became adults, we were instructed to abstain from sex before we were married and when we did get married, sex was only something that should be done behind a locked door and with the light turned off. Most religions teach us that sex is a sin, unless it occurs between a married couple. Even then, some faiths have even taught that sex was strictly for procreation, which explains the uptight behavior of many of the members of these faiths and sects.

Of course, those were the rules we were given, but they were flagrantly broken. Sex is a huge part of the American culture, as evidenced by the programs that we see on television, the magazines on the newsstands and the multi-billion dollar pornography industry. We all know about sex, we talk about sex and we constantly think about sex – men and women alike. But deep down, isn't it still a bit taboo? Don't you feel just a little bit dirty when you think about sex with a co-worker, the attractive delivery person who comes into your office, or even your own spouse, especially when you indulge in a position or act that isn't part of your normal bedroom routine?

Sex remains an obsession, but doesn't it remain a bit of a forbidden one?

The same thing can be said for the supernatural. We find ghosts, hauntings, poltergeists, and demons on our television sets nearly every night of the week. Books about ghosts have become standard items on bookstore shelves across the country and in fact, belief in the supernatural is more widely accepted today than in any other time in American history. But just as with our sexual habits, our belief in ghosts and the paranormal is not as widely broadcast as say, our support of a local football team. Our society has ingrained in us the feeling that such beliefs and interests are best kept behind closed doors, so to speak. As children, we were told that ghosts do not exist and that there are no monsters lurking under our beds. Even cartoons like "Scooby Doo" always revealed that the phantom haunting the house was actually just a man in a mask who always cursed "those meddling kids" in the final minutes of the program. Ghost weren't real, we were told, and if ghosts were not real, then neither were demons, vampires, or anything else that went bump in the night. As with our fascination with sex, it was best to keep our proverbial pants up when it came to the supernatural. It was not the sort of thing that people talked about in polite society.

But most of us never stopped thinking about either subject – sex or the supernatural – no matter what we had been instructed to do. Sex became a part of our daily lives, although a carefully hidden one, and our belief or interest in ghosts and the supernatural was either embraced or ignored, depending on the person. Why was this? It's because, as you will see in the page ahead, the combination of the two can often be a pretty nasty mix.

Sex has been with us since the beginning of time. This is an obvious statement considering that you would not be reading these words if not for a sweaty, undignified act that took place between your parents (see, it's not always pleasant to think about sex, is it?) In ancient days, the builders of early civilizations saw sex as a magical, earth-changing event that could be ritualized and used to worship the gods. At times, sexual intercourse with the gods was even possible and when it occurred, it literally gave birth to the great heroes of legend and the mythologies that still shape our world today.

Somewhere along the line, though, sex gained what we might call a bad reputation. It began to be associated with devils, demons, and witchcraft. Many would blame this on the rise of organized religion and the power of the Church during the Middle Ages -- a time of burnings, torture, and that rather unpleasant interlude known as the Spanish Inquisition. Sex was no longer a magical act it was now something evil that was not just an embarrassing subject, it was one that could get you killed. Every so-called witch who was brought before her accusers was not simply believed to have had illicit sex with someone in her town or village, but with Satan himself. And she was supposed to have done so on a regular basis.

Devils and demons ran rampant, appearing in dreams and in ethereal shape in darkened bedrooms, ravishing women and stealing the life force from men. Homes, castles and roadways became unsafe places as residents and travelers began to report their encounters with demonic rapists. But few reported these illicit romps with much enthusiasm because doing so could make them appear to be in league with the devil.

For every action, there is an equal and opposite reaction and in this case, for all of the power given to the Church, a negative force rose to oppose it. When the Church forbade sex, Satanism embraced it and its rituals celebrated the darkest side of human nature and of course, sexuality. Sex and magic once again went hand in hand, but with a diabolical twist. These were not the life-affirming rituals of the old civilizations but a quest to invoke dark spirits and to attain malevolent powers that followers believed only Satan could give them.

During the Victorian era, it was not solely the Church that oppressed the sexual nature of man, but society itself. During this prim and proper age, sex was swept even further under the rug, but the supernatural was openly embraced. People all over the world converted to the practice of Spiritualism, believing that it was possible to contact the spirits of the dead. Not surprisingly, sex became deeply entwined in the Spiritualist movement. In this way, sex became almost acceptable because whatever indiscretions occurred, they could blamed on an outside force. "The spirits made me do it," you might say. For the first time in modern history, women were able to become leaders as mediums and spokespeople for Spiritualism. Soon, séances began to involve scantily clad "spirits" and mediums were quick to disrobe in order to prove that they hid no ghostly stage props under their clothing. Ceremonies to summon the spirits were conducted in lingerie, filmy shifts and, in some cases, nothing at all.

Belief began to develop that the spirits could make intimate contact with the living – not only through messages and the trappings of séances, but with the earthly flesh of the believers. The supernatural side of sex had returned full circle to the beliefs of the early Egyptians and the Greeks, a belief that the spirit world could make sexual contact with our world. And such a belief continues today in the accounts, both terrifying and mundane, of sexual encounters with the beyond.

Sex and death – mankind's greatest obsessions. How closely do they actually interact? It is possible to invoke magic, spirits and demons with sex rituals? Can sexual impulses actually mimic a haunting? Do people really have sex with ghosts? These are all questions that we will explore during the long, strange road ahead. It's not a journey for the faint of heart, or the easily embarrassed. I only ask that you take it along with me and that you do so with an open mind, a lack of inhibition, and a belief that just about anything might be possible.

Troy Taylor
Holidays 2008

1. ANCIENT SOCIETIES
SEX AND THE SUPERNATURAL IN EARLY HISTORY

When first contact may have occurred between ancient man and the supernatural is mystery that will likely always elude us. Although it is known that a creature resembling man was walking upright between one and one-half and two million years ago, he left no traces behind of his interest in the spiritual or the supernatural. Among the only relics ever found were realistic little figures made from clay, confirming beyond a doubt that he had an interest in sex, and he liked his women fat.

Such relics revealed nothing of early man's spiritual beliefs or his connections to what we might consider the occult. It was the fact that such so-called fertility figures stopped turning up in archaeological digs that shined the first light on primitive man's beliefs in magic and superstition. They stopped making the figures because they began to believe they were magical. If you could kill a bison or a deer by making its image and performing magical operations, then you could kill a human just as easily. When it became dangerous to represent the human form, the age of magic officially began.

Among the only relics left behind by ancient man were realistic little figures made from clay, confirming beyond a doubt that he had an interest in sex, and he liked his women fat.

Beyond that, no real proof about man's belief in the occult appeared for some time. The first glimpse into the intricacies of the human mind had to wait until the rise of the civilized societies and the astonishing invention of the written word.

Before that time came, man began to be increasingly obsessed with magic and the number of his gods, and his demons, increased. His belief in the occult took a huge leap forward at about the same time that the human race stepped out of the Stone Age. At some point between 4,000 and 3,000 B.C., the time of stone knives, flint spearheads and wooden tools came to an end and man discovered the use of metals. How this occurred still remains a mystery. Perhaps someone threw a piece of copper into the fire and discovered that a hard, shiny metal flowed out of it, but we'll never know for sure. It was soon learned, though, that the edges of metal could be made much sharper than those of flint and were better for skinning animals. At about that same time, another genius of his day discovered the many uses of the wheel, both for transport and for making pots. Building bricks were invented. Sailing ships were built. Cattle were harnessed to the plough and to the cart. Civilization as we know it came into being.

A few hundred years later, the invention of writing came along. That breakthrough occurred in Sumeria and Egypt about 3,000 B.C. and a new picture of ancient man appeared for modern day archaeologists. In what seemed a short amount of time, he had become inspired, haunted and obsessed by a legion of taboos, superstitions and beliefs, all dealing with ghosts, assorted gods and demons. The new ancient man was now physically and mentally very like ourselves. He was highly socialized, lived in towns, cities and states, practiced complicated rites and maintained armies with which to make war on his own kind. This period signaled an eruption of warfare across the known world, beginning a history of violence and the destruction of civilization that has continued unabated to this day. This was a picture of man as we first came to know him at the beginning of recorded history, and as he remains today.

It is from this early time that our first connections between sex and the supernatural can be made. The worship of gods and a respect for the spirit world was an essential part of the belief system of the ancients and rituals always included sex, the most intimate form of worship that man was capable of offering.

The connections made between sex, the gods and the supernatural began as man started moving into the cities and creating larger, stronger communities. It seemed that the more he expanded his activities, the more gods he needed. When he began to sail the seas, he needed to make sacrifices to the sea gods. When he went on a journey, he needed to feel himself under the protection of the god of travelers, and so on. Every new enterprise needed a new god. Man wanted to gain control of his environment and he believed that he could achieve this control through magic and the supernatural.

During all of the chaos that was occurring, there was little opportunity for the simple kind of worship that had been used by the shamans of the primitive people of centuries before. All religion that came from those earlier times tended to be simple and mystical. The simplistic worship of nature had no place in the new, bustling civilizations that began to spring up and with simplicity and clarity of vision gone hoards of angels, gods and demons came along to fill the gap. Ritualistic sex soon followed.

The ancient hero
Gilgamesh

The primitive people were characterized by what we might consider today to be prudish behavior. Many of the shamans of the past believed that anyone who had sexual relations more than ten or fifteen times a year was a lunatic. Their attitude towards sex was based on the phases of the moon, or upon animals that limited their sexual activity to a brief, annual season. They also believed that sexual indulgence wasted vital powers.

In contrast, the more modern men who came to live in the cities saw sex as a form of recreation rather than merely for procreation. The natural outlets for male dominance were hunting and fighting. As those were reduced, the interest in sex naturally replaced them with the penetration of the female as the act of supreme dominance. The act of making love to a placid, domesticated woman was less satisfying than making love to a woman who was independent and challenging. When a type of person is demanded by circumstances, it soon appears. The ancient city culture produced glamorous, intelligent women for whose attention men competed and it became a challenge to dominate them. Sex began to become a part of human life in a way that it had never been before, including in the stories, poems and songs of the time.

The Babylonian epic of Gilgamesh began by describing how the insatiable sexual appetite of the warrior and king Gilgamesh "leaves no virgin to her lover, neither the warrior's daughter nor the wife of the noble." His fellow citizens realized that the king's rabid lust was taking the place of his urge to conquer and they begged the gods for a man strong enough to be his downfall. They created the man-god Endiku, who first had to be "humanized" by a courtesan who attended to his sexual education. Endiku's eagerness for her was so great that he made love to her for an entire week, at the end of which time he was so enfeebled that his former companions, the beasts of the forest, were unable to recognize him. Later, when Endiku and Gilgamesh have fought, and then sworn friendship, Endiku finds the debauched life in the city to be a drain on his powers, so he and Gilgamesh went in search of adventure. When they returned, the goddess Ishtar tried to seduce Gilgamesh, but he rejected her since his heroic energies were now diverted into the proper channels and he wanted nothing more to do with seduction. Many see the entire poem as a protest of the old tribal morality against the sexuality of the city. The author of it was pointing out the lack of challenge that man had in the urban life, causing him to become bored, slack and demoralized. The sexual instinct remained as strong as ever, though, and with no other channels, became a fascination, even an obsession.

Gilgamesh, one of the earliest written tales in history, deals with sex in a frank, graphic manner but there is no mention of two types of sexuality that became rampant in the ancient world, homosexuality and incest. Many authors have noted that homosexuality does not seem to appear in any records of the primitive world, but only began to appear after ancient men gravitated to the cities.

The same can be said for incest. Primitives had strong incest taboos, even believing that engaging in it could make a man become sterile. Ancient men seemed to instinctively know that incest could weaken the purity of the tribe. Every child takes half its genes from its father and half from its mother. It may receive a recessive gene from one parent, like color-blindness or some other defect, but this may be counteracted by a healthy gene from the other parent. If blood relatives mate, the chances are higher that the child will get two recessive genes, so that in the long run, incest will breed weaker specimens and than the offspring of unrelated parents.

When man began to live in the city, the incest taboo was weakened. The brother-sister marriages of the ancient Egyptian rulers were slightly outside of this example, because they were the result of the belief that the kings and queens were gods and were unable to mate with mortals. However, it has been recorded that some of the Caesars indulged in incest purely for pleasure. Was this merely a sexual indulgence to stir appetites that had become jaded by repetitive sex?

Primitive magic was basically the use of man's hidden power to influence the hunt, or perhaps the battle. Under the new, urban conditions, it inevitably became more closely connected with sex. Sexual frustration was common in the cities. The rulers could enjoy their harems and the concubines, but the poor man still had his overworked wife and his large family, and he only had to turn his head to see bare-breasted women passing by him in the street. Men were inclined to die younger than women, leaving behind many sexually frustrated widows. Such times likely gave birth to the sexual origin of the fear of witches. It was believed that if a girl wanted to prevent her lover from being unfaithful, she should bake a cake containing her menstrual blood, which, after eating it, would make him impotent with other women. The young man who wanted to win over a woman had to induce her to drink a potion into which his semen had been mixed.

Magic, as it became urbanized, was that it began to be infused with a hysterical element of nonsense. It was widely believed that if women could drink the urine of mules and use it as a contraceptive, because mules are sterile. Obviously, this was as about effective as most "love potions." On the other hand, it would be incorrect to assume that all sexual magic was mere superstition. Sex is one of the most basic human functions and while civilization managed to rob modern man of many of his deeper powers, sex has remained unaffected. If anything, it has become stronger. Subconscious powers can still be unleashed by sex, as the later chapter on poltergeist phenomena will reveal.

Researchers believe that primitive man once

The ancient art of making love potions

possessed the instincts of telepathy and the intuition of danger – a sixth sense that led him to places where the hunting was good but where death awaited. After hundreds of thousands of years of evolution, those instincts were lost and were replaced by the magic of ancient man and soon, sorcery came into existence. Unlike ordinary witchcraft, which used a form of extrasensory power, sorcery was an attempt to use spells, potions, rituals, and sex, to manipulate the surroundings of the sorcerer. Men lived in small villages and tribes when this type of magic came into existence and it soon replaced the shamans and natural magic of old. From that point on, magic and sex remained in close association, which would eventually lead to the persecution of witches, the growth of Satanism and sex cults of the late 19th century.

SEX AND THE SUPERNATURAL IN EGYPT

By 5,000 B.C. the fabled land of Egypt already possessed many of the luxuries of modern life. In addition, she had assembled an entire pantheon of gods, a universe of spirits from its primitive past, and a complex methodology of religious practices and rituals. But Egypt was not alone. Her distant Mesopotamian neighbor, Sumeria, also possessed an extravagant worship system of its own gods. Nearly 2,000 years later, Egypt invented writing with the hieroglyph method and Sumeria followed soon after with cuneiform. While Egypt has long held an honored place in history, Sumeria all but disappeared. It vanished so completely that even 150 years ago its name was virtually unknown in the world. Cuneiform had survived, borrowed in the writings of some of the Babylonians, but the clay tablets of its inventors were gone. As luck would have it, Egypt's dry climate miraculously preserved the written records of her supernatural beliefs, both on papyrus and on stone.

Because Egyptian religious thinking was based on the absolute conviction of spirit survival in the after-life, it is not surprising that many consider the Egyptians to be the true creators of the Spiritualist movement. As a source for many supernatural beliefs, Egyptian influence is still seen today in New Age movements, shamanistic cults and in witchcraft practices. The names of Egyptian gods appear in symbols and in the literature of groups like the Rosicrucians, the Golden Dawn, and in dozens of other religious and semi-religious orders.

There is no denying that Egypt's material achievements at the dawn of history are a monument to human progress. But in certain spheres, despite the multitude of gods and the superstitions that surrounded the demonic underworld, her religious practices were constricted by the rigid control of the priesthood. As the centuries passed, they became increasingly obsessed with the preservation of the physical body for its owner's use in the world to come. Temple rituals were not altogether joyless affairs, but the religious atmosphere and the nature of the Egyptian gods contrasted sharply with the lustily sex-conscious beliefs and cults of the Greeks. There are few Egyptian deities of a predominantly sexual nature and although highly erotic practices emerged during several popular festivals, it seems that these sprang originally, perhaps even with no planning, from the people rather than the priests, who were wise enough to accept and ritualize the proceedings, which would have been nearly impossible to stop.

The Egyptian ruling class, which by 1500 A.D., had reached the peak of its power and influence, governed a land of plenty that was ruled by a pharaoh, who was considered a god, and his priests. The empire was based on conquest and slave labor and it was also an efficient bureaucracy. The priests were seen as the nation's intellectual elite and were of great importance to the temple, which was a repository of the country's learning and the center of its religion. Egypt's material success was built on the backs and ideas of its practical leaders, the engineers, mathematicians, and the civil servants. None of these professions were emotional ones and none of the gods, except for Osiris and Isis, could be closely identified with human sensibilities. Had the priesthood wished to do so, they could have created a sexual god, or perhaps presented Isis, the mother-god, as an Egyptian love goddess, a counterpart to such gods in other lands, whose worship was accompanied by sexual excitement, orgies, and ecstasy.

But Egypt was above all a practical empire, and the priests may have preferred to avoid such distracting interruptions of the nation's working life and military ventures. The people themselves were generally peaceful, tolerant, energetic, and placed great importance on family life, in which the wife was a respected figure. Polygamy was not unknown but the sex life of the average Egyptian, neither stimulated by the open sensuality of the Greeks nor provoked by the repression of the Christian Church, was nothing out of the ordinary.

But sex was a major part of the festivals of Isis, sister-wife of the great Osiris, who was identified with goodness and charity, love and resurrection. He was murdered by his jealous brother, Set, who cut his body into pieces and cast them into the Nile. After a tragic search, Isis found the pieces scattered throughout the land and buried them where they were found, each grave being honored as a part of the god himself. The only part that she had failed to find was his penis, so she made an image of it, which was then used in all of her festivals.

The people's sympathy for the beloved Isis, mourning her lost love, made her anniversary one of the most important events in the country and perhaps the most sexual in the way that it was celebrated. It was during these events that the cult of the phallus was most prominently displayed in Egypt. The Greek historian, Herodotus, reporting on these phallic festivals described the women's role in one of the processions. He wrote, "In place of the phallus they have created figures about one

Osiris and Isis in Ancient Egypt

and a half feet high, which are carried by the women. These are equipped with phalluses of great size, scarcely smaller than the figures themselves and which move in a life-like way when operated by the bearer with a string."

The festivals mostly involved women and were by no means orgies. They were instead an attempt to console the goddess for her dead lover in a tender, realistic way.

The feast for Osiris was a more male-oriented affair. Osiris was portrayed during these events with a whip in his hand and rigidly erect penis. The Sacred Bull of Apis was regarded as an incarnation of Osiris and when the animal that represented it died, a successor had to be found for it immediately. The choice followed a battery of stringent tests, which were known only to the priests. When a bull with the proper qualifications was found, it was brought to the temple with great ceremony and then was put on display for forty days so that it could be inspected by women only. According to tradition, they opened their clothing, displayed their genitals and offered themselves to the bull as an incarnation of the god. The purpose was not an erotic one, though; it was actually believed that by offering themselves to the sacred bull, they would be assured of fertility.

The legends of Isis and Osiris deeply influenced Egyptian life and custom. The grief that Isis suffered over Osiris' dismembered body became the model for all Egyptian funeral lamentations. And from the other gods, who helped Isis to find and piece the body parts together, wrapping them in linen bandages, the Egyptians learned the art of making mummies. There was something both emotional and human about the story of Isis and Osiris that appealed to the common people and their sense of the romantic, sexual and otherwise, although most aspects of the worship of the story were never officially encouraged.

For the most part, Egyptian art remained cold, formal and obsessed with power, as it had been for thirty centuries. Only once, for a short period of just eleven years, the pattern was broken by a pharaoh called Amenophis, otherwise known as Akhenaton. This young man, ruling jointly from Thebes with his father, was twenty-one years old when he married the beautiful Nefertiti, his father's daughter and his own half-sister. It was said to be a union of love, not mere politics. A few years later, he made a startling decision: he was going to build a new capital at Tel-el-Amarna, two hundred miles down the Nile River. Two years later, he entered this new and city with his wife and daughters and in defiance of the Egyptian establishment, changed his name to Akhenaton and the religion for all of the country from worship of Amon-Ra, the Sun God and the God of Thebes combined, to the Aten, god of the sun alone. For the first time in Egyptian history, not only Amon-Ra but the entire pantheon of minor gods, was cast aside.

Akhenaton, who changed the entire face of Egyptian religion for a very short time.

In his new capital, he received the envoys of kings from most of the known world, but his main preoccupations were the palaces and gardens of his city, its temples to Aten and the encouragement of a new concept of truth in art and life. He introduced a new and informal style of royal behavior, which was shocking and almost inconceivable to people who were accustomed to the ritualized formality of the previous pharaohs, considered gods on earth. He and his family traveled freely about the city and for the first time in twenty centuries, the members of the royal household were portrayed as human beings. The enjoyment of life and love was an essential part of worship of Aten, so Akhenaton and Nefertiti were often pictured embracing, kissing one another, and holding their children. Surprisingly, Akhenaton ordered that he be depicted as he really was – an unattractive, frail epileptic with a limp. He also ordered that Nefertiti be portrayed in terms of equality with himself and as his close and constant companion. He believed that women were "as of equal worth as all alike were blessed by the rays of the sun."

Akhenaton's beliefs, and these words, which came from his Hymn to Aten, were revolutionary for the time and place and prove him to have been one of the first visionaries of equality for all mankind under God and the law. Unfortunately, he failed to do anything to bring this ideal into being. To make matters worse, his pacifism caused him to neglect his military, which brought the empire dangerously close to collapse.

Akhenaton nearly vanished from the pages of history. Whether or not the dispossessed priests of Amon brought about his downfall, as some have suggested, eleven years after his move to the new capital, Akhenaton and Nefertiti disappeared and their tombs have never been discovered. Amon-Ra and the other gods were soon back in power at Thebes, bringing with them the demons and monsters of the underworld to hold sway over Egyptian superstitions.

This ended the one attempt in Egypt's history to provide the ethical foundation lacking in the worship of the legendary gods. Whatever his shortcomings, Akhenaton was a leader who managed to start a religious revolution and had dreams of a social one. He attempted to show that equality could, and did, exist between the sexes and his failed attempt still managed to change history. He is one of the few pharaohs that modern people recognize, for both his religious changes and as the husband of Nefertiti, Egyptian queen and mother of Tutankhamen, the boy king who captured the world's imagination.

What impact has Egypt left behind on the study of the spirit world? It's nearly impossible to say because many believe that the visual impact of Egyptian art has stirred the imagination of the modern world in ways that their pantheon of gods never could. Their lives and culture remain for us to see, in paintings, carvings, and in massive stone works, thousands of years after their empire vanished, making more of an impression that their gods ever have. The depictions of their lives and worship have inspired many researchers throughout history, seeking to make contact with the spirits of the dead, to turn to Egypt and her ancient mysteries. Few answers are found, however, leading, perhaps, to more unanswered questions than startling revelations.

SEX AND THE SUPERNATURAL IN ANCIENT GREECE

There is a vast difference between the cultured, stiff occultism of the Egyptians and the passionate, almost frenzied worship of the Greeks. The Greeks not only adored the material things in life, they had a deep devotion to beauty in all its forms and of love itself in every known variety. Their passion and fervor for life, and for their gods, created the concept of intellectual and artistic freedom that would eventually inspire the entire western world.

The Greek culture managed to change history, even though it was a much younger civilization that others that existed around the same time. In Akhenaton's time, nearly 2,000 years after Egypt had been united, the Greeks were a nomadic tribe grazing their herds north of the Balkans. They had no written language, but their tribal dialects were sufficiently alike to make them realize, mostly from the heroic tales of the past that had been told over and over again, that they shared a common heritage. The early Greeks eventually drifted southward in search of better grazing. In the valley of the Euphrates and the Tigris Rivers, they encountered the highly civilized Sumerians, Babylonians, and Assyrians, who had developed social and religious systems, with temples for the worship of their various gods.

The Greeks were still divided by their tribal differences, but they managed to unite together as one vast force. They had come to the region to graze their herds, but became conquerors, first of the promontory of Hellenes, then taking to the sea, taking over parts of Asia Minor, Crete, the many surrounding islands, and even southern Italy. These once-nomadic people inhabited the cities they had taken and later began to create a civilization of their own.

From the beginning, the Greek civilization was different than that of their conquered enemies. A strict organized religion of the state had no place in the Greek concept of government and worship. The most startling difference, however, was that the Greeks believed in the full pursuit of happiness, in life and most especially, in love. Their beliefs covered every possible form of pleasure, ambition and material achievement and allowed love to be interpreted in any number of ways, according to the innermost longings of the individual.

The Greeks conceived their gods in human form, although immortal, with all of the vices and virtues of human beings, yet possessing supernatural powers and influence. They were human-like beings that had attained divinity and whose origins and exploits had been long part of Greek culture, dating back to the stories and songs of their nomadic days. It was probably around 900 B.C. when the first of these stories were preserved in *The Iliad* and *The Odyssey* of Homer. These great works, and others, attributed to the poet provided the mythology, interwoven with history, which became the basis of Greek religion and an essential part of their daily lives and customs.

To the gods, and by extension to the Greeks, sex was never anything to be ashamed of. On the contrary, it was to be exalted and the power to enjoy it was one of the greatest gifts that the gods had given to the people. Even the beginning of the world was represented as a sexual act. According to Aeschylus, the semen of the sky (Uranus) penetrated the warm-breasted earth (Gaea), from which every living thing was born and sustenance was provided for mortals and the animals of all of the lands. Gaea gave birth to several children, one of whom (Cronos) hated his father. Waiting until Uranus was visiting Gaea for their nightly copulation, Cronos sprang upon him, cut off his giant penis and flung it into the sea. As it happened, some of the drops of semen remained in the penis and when it fell into the sea foam, it created the lovely form of Aphrodite.

Aphrodite became one of the most beloved of the Greek goddesses, but she was not above the occasional lapse in virtue. The sensuality of the gods was a mere extension of their human qualities, which made them understandable to all and made them sympathetic figures to everyone who loved them. Aphrodite was

Aphrodite -- the birth of Venus from the foam of the Sea

one of the most appealing. She was the wife of the god of fire, Hephaestus, who, while being the son of the mighty Zeus, was no heroic figure. Hephaestus was lame, hairy and overly preoccupied by his smoky forge, so it was no surprise when Aphrodite was led astray by the young, vigorous and handsome Ares, the god of war. The lovers were witnessed in an act of passion by Helios, the sun god, and he carried his tale to Hephaestus, who promptly reacted to the news. He went to his forge and made a net so fine that it was invisible to mortal and immortal eyes alike. He attached it above the bed he shared with his wife and then told her that he had to go away for a short trip. His plan worked and the two lovers were ensnared on the bed and exposed to the mockery of the gods, who Hephaestus had called upon this witness the grievous outrage that he had suffered.

This would not be Aphrodite's last affair. Her tragically brief fling with Adonis, who was killed by a boar during a hunt, was followed by her flight to Paphos, in Cyprus, which became one of her most celebrated shrines. Worshippers came to Paphos by the thousands. Woman and girls were required to enter before marriage and offer themselves to any stranger on demand. They were repaid with a handful of gold coins. The same rite was practiced at Byblos, Malta, Alexandria and other great cities of the time and was sometimes mandatory for every woman once in her life. After this encounter, the woman could return home and thereafter, no amount of money could buy her.

The ruins of the Aphrodite shrine at Paphos

A trip to Paphos, or some other shrine, was considered a sacred duty and it was not something the women had to be forced into doing. They made the journey, and carried out the act, by choice. Sexual intercourse in honor of Aphrodite was something to be cherished, hence the importance of this part of the temple duties. Being chosen as a priestess for the temple was an even greater privilege. Women of all classes, whether cultured or simple, rich or poor, came to seek this honor. To be among the chosen meant that a woman became one of the few who had the necessary character and sexual attributes to serve. The grounds of the temple contained a wide assortment of women who were dedicated solely to the glory of sensual love. Special quarters and privileges were afforded to those with high standing in the cult and each of the women had a small statue of Aphrodite in their quarters, where they could worship in their own tongue.

The women apparently came from all over the world, but were not slaves. They lived their life in service to Aphrodite, giving a large proportion of their earnings to the temple. Any children that were born from their services were brought up in the sanctuary. If a woman bore a son, he was dedicated to the service of his divinity. A girl was symbolically married to the son of Dionysus and deflowered with a little golden knife, because virginity displeased Aphrodite. The girls became neophytes whose education, including training in the erotic arts, began at the age of puberty. She would be taught the method of the gaze, the clasp, movements of the body, complication of the caress, biting, kissing and more. The girl was allowed to choose the day when she would first experience a man because Aphrodite commanded that only desire would allow this act to occur and no woman would ever be forced.

The festivals of Aphrodite were always popular, especially with sailors, who had a fondness for a goddess who had born from sea foam. Trouble and disorderly conduct rarely occurred during these events, but the same could not be said for the festivals of Dionysus, equally well known as Bacchus. As the god of wine, he was always associated with drunkenness and excess, notably sexual, which were crucial to the celebration of his rites. Dionysus was portrayed as a handsome, virile figure, often nude or covered with a convenient fig leaf, always with a glass of wine in his hand and a jovial smile on his face. He had a large and varied band of cohorts, who were largely responsible for the practices associated with his cult and which brought it into disrepute.

The most attractive of his retinue were the nymphs, friendly spirits of nature that danced, played and roamed around, making love freely with the gods they liked. They delighted in teasing the lustful satyrs and, when tricks failed and they were captured and possessed, submitted to their advances with obliging readiness. Human men and boys who were attractive enough to catch their fancy found themselves the recipients of ecstasies of the kind they could never imagine.

The most attractive of the sex spirits were the nymphs, shown here luring a young man in a painting by John William Waterhouse

The satyrs were less attractive than the nymphs, but were also nature spirits. They had pointed ears, flat upturned noses, bristly hair and a goat-like tail. They were addicted to every form of sensual pleasure, but mainly to wine and sex. They spent most of their time sleeping, drinking, dancing, playing music or having sex with nymphs, humans and animals – whoever or whatever was available.

The three best known of the satyrs were Silenus, Priapus and Pan. They were an unruly crew that was always ready and willing for whatever sexual escapades that came their way. Silenus was a habitual drunk while Pan, a mountain spirit, was an amiable, peaceful fellow with horns, a beard and the legs and hooves of a goat. He was a bit of a romantic, who spent much of his time playing music on his pipes. He was always a great companion for the nymphs because he could always be relied upon to be willing to engage in intercourse on demand. Priapus was the crudest and coarsest of the three. His name was turned into the word "priapism" (which is a potentially harmful and painful medical condition in which the erect penis does not return to its flaccid state, despite the absence of either physical or psychological stimulation, within four hours) and this said a lot about his demeanor. He was in a constant state of arousal and was not above taking a partner by force. Eventually,

A Greek satyr and a collection of nymphs

Priapus was punished for attempting to rape a goddess and was cursed with a huge, but useless, wooden penis.

The strange appearance and lusty vitality of Dionysus' questionable followers were irresistible subjects for

Dionysus, the god wine, sex and debauchery. His festivals were among the most popular in ancient Greece.

stories and artwork in ancient Greece. The festival for Dionysus in Athens had a civic significance and therefore became even more important to the people. It included a lavish banquet that was provided by the government, but the real climax of the proceedings was the annual marriage of Dionysus to the wife of the Archon, the chief magistrate. This enhanced the prestige of the Archon as it was expected to produce practical returns that would benefit the city. The wedding party was followed through the streets by crowds of revelers but only the participants were allowed to witness the actual rite, which took place in a building near the Acropolis. It was said that the consummation of the union was enacted, although whether or not the part of the god was played by his image or a man is unknown.

Athens was perhaps the most reserved and conservative of the Grecian cities, but its Dionysian celebrations were allowed great license. In the procession were phallus-carriers and costumed satyrs, leading a drunken Silenus on a donkey. The *ithyphalle*, men with gigantic genitals in female clothing, were accompanied by half-naked nymphs who waved torches and provoked the crowds into a frenzy. These portrayals of Dionysian characters were followed by the *kanephores*, young girls of character and purity who were carefully chosen from among the noblest families in Athens. These girls carried various symbolic objects in the procession and were not part of the general licentiousness and sexual freedom that prevailed in the streets.

It was among the rough and warring Thracian people of Greece that the worship of Dionysus reached its wildest and most ecstatic form. Delirious dancing, thrumming music and the consumption of vast quantities of wine were just the start of the most extreme form of worship in the region. The women, referred to as Dionysus' "coursing bitches," were as given to drunkenness as the men and, inspired by the same devotion to the god, danced with frenzied abandon before the men departed for a wild nocturnal hunt on the nearby hillsides. With spears and blazing torches, the hunters ran down game and then devoured it alive in a bloody, thrashing feast that turned into a brutal orgy before the night was over. Such a celebration was outside the nature of the generally more levelheaded Greeks, but word of it reached other parts of the country and variations of the bloody hunt soon became a part of Dionysian rites in other places, as well.

The phallic element so prominent with the satyrs was not confined to the worship of Dionysus. Phallus worship was also part of a festival called Targelia, devoted to Apollo. The cult of Priapus himself was celebrated in many of the larger cities, with portraits of the god affixed high atop pillars that had huge penises jutting out of them at a lower level. The most devoted worshippers kissed the sacred phallus or hung images of their own genitals upon it as a way of asking for the god's favor or protection.

With Greece being a place where worship of the penis was widely accepted, it is likely unnecessary to note that homosexuality was never regarded as being reprehensible by the Greeks. In fact, homosexual relationships were regarded with respect. It is less generally known that while sensuality was an important element in such relationships, there was also a religious and spiritual basis for the practice. Spiritually speaking, the Greeks believed that during the sexual act, the virtues of the lover were transferred to his beloved, whether male or female. It was believed this occurred physically through the transmission of semen, which contained the essence of the soul. This metaphysical explanation lent, in the eyes of the Greeks, a dignity to homosexual relationships that would not be ascribed to them in the prudish centuries to come. It refutes the suggestion that to the Greeks it was solely a form of sexual self-indulgence.

There were, of course, many less admirable aspects to homosexuality in Greece. It could be vicious, debauched and commercialized with boy prostitutes and brothels. And it was not unknown for religious feasts to be misused for devotions of a very ungodly kind.

The Greek's love of male beauty is easier to understand when it's noted that, as with most ancient civilizations, the Greek world was essentially a male creation in which the ideal of womanhood was being a devoted mother and wife. When the Greeks maintained that the naked human body was the most beautiful object in creation, the body they had in mind was male. Their art, writing and poetry made it clear that their ideal of beauty was a splendid masculinity, combined with grace.

A nude Greek foot race is depicted on this ancient vase

But it was not just the bodies of young men that they loved and admired. Women were just as revered and since the Greeks not only extolled beauty but did their best to make it a part of daily life, athletics and gymnasiums were important institutions. They constructed extensive buildings, baths, training grounds and other facilities use by the young men. This combination of athletic prowess and beauty was a subject of constant debate and gossip among the poets, philosophers and the common people.

Although athletics were not practiced by girls in Athens, almost everywhere else in Greece, the young women competed and exercised as freely as the boys and in the same state of nakedness. Nudity was not a general state of affairs but athletics, dancing, religious rituals and processions, and the theater were all occasions where nudity was appropriate. When clothing was a hindrance, such as during games, the Greeks preferred nothing at all to a mere self-conscious covering of the genitals. Where nudity enhanced, as it usually did, the aesthetic value of the occasion, it was encouraged. But nudity for purely erotic effect was not approved of in ordinary life and always frowned upon.

It is curious that while people were familiar enough with the sight of beautiful bodies on the appropriate occasions, women and girls, who could share in the games and run and wrestle naked with the young men, were forbidden from watching the males at exercise in Athens and from attending the great Olympiad. This could have been due to the religious significance of the occasion, for it was a truly a national event, lasting for five days during which a Truce of God was declared. Quarrels and even wars were suspended while men competed for simple crowns of olive leaves, a predecessor for the gold medallions used today.

Female homosexuality occupies a minor place in the records of Greek life. Although Aphrodite considered lovers to be in love, no matter what the nature of the pairing, there was little attention paid to the lesbians of the era. The position of women, from whom little was expected beyond the wifely virtues, made their relationships of comparatively small importance in that there seemed to be no high ethical purpose to justify a lesbian relationship as beneficial for the individual or the state. While female relationships were never regarded as a vice, the general attitude of men seems to have been a rather patronizing indulgence or worse, a tendency to equate it with prostitution.

There is much written and pictorial evidence to show that lesbianism did exist at the time. Illuminating scenes are shown on bowls and vases that portray women with phalluses and other accessories and make clear that the manner of their use was for dual pleasure. However, it was the poetic genius of Sappho that presented homosexuality in women as a deeply emotional, as well as a sensual type of relationship.

Sappho was an Aeolian of Lesbos, an island where women were respected and enjoyed a greater freedom than in any other part of Greece. Sappho herself was born into a wealthy family in 612 B.C., a time of political

Sappho on the island of Lesbos by Lawrence Alma-Tadema

upheaval and war, and was twice exiled for her political associations. She was a delicately small, dark-haired woman who wrote extensively, although only a small amount of her writings survived later destruction by the Christian Church. The opinions of her contemporaries state that she was one of the greatest lyric poets of her time. There has been much controversy about her "morals" since direct evidence of her love for other women is stated clearly in her writings. Her poetry made it clear that the love of a woman for a woman could be passionately sensual and yet retain its delicate femininity. Her writings often described, in lyrical, sensuous details, her relationships with other women, which she referred to as "vagrant friendships."

At the age of twenty-six, Sappho returned to Lesbos after her second exile and opened an academy for girls, the House of Muses. Her poetic fame had spread and she carefully chose her students, including many from abroad, and offered them the chance to study music, dancing, and the literary arts. She had the ability to recognize and nurture talent and the school became very successful. It was also quite luxurious and no doubt, expensive. In the sexual atmosphere of Greece in those days, it was no surprise that Sappho took many of her students as her lovers. Many of their names are mentioned in the fragments that remain of her writings. Her most famous love was for Atthis, with whom she knew the greatest happiness. When Atthis' passion for her cooled, Sappho knew her greatest suffering. One of her most famous poems has been called "her immortal song to Aphrodite," a desperate cry for help from the goddess to return Atthis' love to her. Unfortunately, Aphrodite never responded and Atthis was lost to her, although a close friendship between the two women endured for quite some time.

Sappho's chosen divinity was, of course, the warm and loving Aphrodite. As a true believer, she diligently served her temple and the "House of Muses" composed and provided music that was used in the festivals and provided dancers for all of the festival processions.

There were critics of Sappho who appeared in her own time, but most would come later during the years of oppression and censorship by the Church. Most of her contemporary critics feared that she was tutoring her students to turn from the love of man and therefore imperiling the institution of marriage. But there is little evidence to show this fear was justified. Returning to their homes, Sappho's young women undoubtedly behaved as young women of the time usually did, as models of Greek propriety and as good wives. One has to wonder, though, if some unsuspecting husbands may have found, in addition to their social and cultural accomplishments, a surprising amount of sexual awareness in their seemingly innocent young brides.

As we can see, sex and the supernatural combined in ancient Greece in a way that no other culture has ever achieved. The worship of their mysterious gods used so many sexual elements that it was hard to tell where the needs of man ended and the demands of the gods began. Regardless of the individual beliefs of the reader, there is no denying that the Greeks managed to give us two of the most powerful images of supernatural sexuality -- in Aphrodite and Dionysus -- that mankind has ever known.

SEX AND THE SUPERNATURAL IN INDIA

In the Hindu pantheon of India, one of the most revered gods is Krishna, who came to earth in human form and whose stories have been told and re-told in art and literature for centuries. It may come as no surprise to learn that his adventures among humans are filled with an astonishing array of sexual encounters.

To appreciate the popularity of Krishna, we have to understand the basic conception of the Hindu gods. The universal spirit is envisioned as a trinity of three gods, Brahma, Shiva, and Vishnu. Brahma is the creator of heaven, earth, man, and the underworld. Shiva is the terrible destroyer and the bringer of calamities, but also a source for renewal and regeneration. Vishnu is the preserver and loving protector of mankind. In the Hindu tradition, the gods could descend to earth to intervene in the affairs of men. Demons, who manipulated men and unleashed evil, were intent on viciously destroying the human race. The sole defense for man was the goodwill of the gods, especially the protection of Vishnu.

An ancient Indian phallic symbol

It was believed that righteous living provided some protection against demons, often through a series of lifetimes. By the transmigration of souls (reincarnation), which was fundamental to the Hindu belief system, man's existence was continued over a number of lifetimes during which his conduct determined his chances of progression towards a spiritual reward. Good deeds and righteous living could mean a more favorable life in the next incarnation and through a succession of virtuous lives, man might qualify for a place in heaven. But the ultimate goal was Nirvana, a blissful identification with the universal spirit. It was only then that the cycle was complete and man's spirit was released from earthly living. Many failed to achieve such a goal. For those whose conduct was unworthy or wicked, the next life would begin at a lower level, perhaps even as an animal. The climb back to redemption would be long and arduous. Or he might become one of the demons, bringing evil to men, though even then there was still a chance of eventually earning salvation.

Good works alone could not achieve Nirvana. With self-discipline and meditation, a man gained strength but only along the path of the *bhakti*, complete devotion to the gods, could a man win the favor of Vishnu and the union with the spirit. The *bhakti,* with its sense of personal attachment to a great and beneficent god like Vishnu, evoked the most widespread and deeply felt response in Hindu hearts. Worshippers of every kind and from every social standing worked to achieve this close connection with the spirit world.

The fierce devotion that Hindu followers felt toward the path of the *bhakti* was inspired through Krishna, whose story first began to be told around 600 B.C. in oral stories that were passed along to students by learned Hindus known as the Upanishads. From these tales, the Krishna story was developed through the centuries and was ultimately told in a connected form in the *Bhagavata Purana* centuries later. Krishna's exploits, mighty in battle and perhaps even mightier when it came to erotic love, created an image that was soon admired and venerated by the Hindu people. Krishna was the earthly incarnation of Vishnu himself, which made a devotion to him one more step down the path of *bhakti*. Followers could not only celebrate the life of Krishna, but their love for him also made it possible for them to be closer to heaven, as well.

A large part of the Krishna story concerns the conflicts of two aristocratic families until Kansa, a demonic personage, wins power, overthrows the reigning king, and not only commits a series of atrocities and crimes, but also bans the worship of Vishnu, who naturally undertakes the task of ridding the earth of such an evil being. He came to earth in the living form of Krishna with a plan to destroy the tyrant, but he arrived as a child. Krishna was brought up from birth at the home of his foster-father, Nanda, a wealthy cattleman. As a baby, he was threatened by many perils devised by his enemy Kansa, but his divine nature protected him and he managed to escape from the dangers that were sent his way. One of the most dangerous attempts to kill Krishna came as a demon who took the form of a beautiful young woman. She came to Nanda as a wet nurse and tried to suckle the infant with poison smeared on her breasts. Krishna, however, was unaffected by the poison. Instead, he sucked the life force out of the demon through her breast milk and the creature died.

As Krishna grew into a young man, alongside his friend Balarama, he was a very exuberant, high-spirited boy. He managed to both infuriate and captivate the local people with his laughter and his pranks, which were carried out with all of the mischievous ingenuity of a clever young man gifted with supernatural powers, which he used without scruples to shift blame and escape from the consequences of his actions. At the age of five, he was allowed to help with the herding of young calves, which put him in the right place to prevent a demonic attack on the herd. Even though he was considered the son of the owner, he took to the fields at the age of eight and helped their cattle-herders and their wives with the livestock. He grew into a handsome, courageous man, garnering respect from his friends and co-workers and proving his mettle during several attacks by demons. He was regarded as a brilliant leader and led the way through a number of natural and unnatural disasters, the latter of which were caused by demons. His companion's strange unawareness of his supernatural powers is explained by Krishna using an ability to create a sort of amnesia in the minds of those concerned in the hair-raising events. In this way, their relationship remained that of simple people towards a compassionate, higher-born friend.

But as Krishna grew out of adolescence, the love and admiration of the women on his foster father's farm began to take a different turn. Krishna began to inflame the passions of these young women, even though most of them were already married. But moral precepts and duty to marriage vows were simply not enough to keep the striking young man from their thoughts. They spoke and gossiped about him endlessly and the girls spied on him in the fields and forests as often as they dared. Such intense, overwhelming passion usually leads to action and the women began bathing in the river Jumna, since it was believed that its waters could bring the fulfillment of the heart's desire. The women gathered at the river every day, praying to Shiva to make Krishna look on them with favor.

Krishna's attraction to young women is shown in this painting

A group of young women were in the river one day when Krishna, grazing the cattle, came upon their clothing scattered on the bank and spotted the naked girls in the river. He quietly gathered up their clothing, rolled up their dresses, and climbed into a nearby tree. As the women emerged from the water, they saw him watching them from his vantage point. They ducked back down under the water and demanded that he give them their clothes. Krishna laughed and began to argue with them. He insisted that each of them come out of the river, one by one, and ask him politely for their dresses. They protested that they were naked, but Krishna was unmoved by this. The girls complained that he was being unfair and admitted to bathing in the water in hopes that he might fall in love with them. Krishna shrugged and asked them why they should be bashful under those circumstances. The girls reluctantly agreed to his terms and each emerged naked from the river and Krishna handed them their clothing. He did so with the implausible explanation that he was trying to teach them a lesson – that to go naked into the water was to lose one's character. He consoled the girls with a promise. Because he loved them, he would dance with them if they returned to the spot in early autumn. The women accepted this and ran away, their love for Krishna now wilder than ever.

Months later, the women were living in eager hope for the fulfillment of Krishna's promise. As autumn approached, Krishna was moved by the beauty of the cool night to think of the girls again. Late one night, the sound of his flute was heard in the forest and news spread quickly among the young women that Krishna was calling to them. They dressed in their finest clothing, abandoned their families and homes and found Krishna waiting in a forest clearing, his body shining in the moonlight. He greeted them with fondness and pretended to be surprised by their arrival – then mysteriously questioned them about their homes and families. Why had they left those things behind? He teasingly urged them to hurry back and make their peace at home while there was still time.

The girls recoiled from him, shocked, and then felt embarrassed and ashamed. They began to cry and one of them demands of Krishna why he would call to them if he does not want to be with them. It was his flute, she said, that called them to come. They lived for his love and left their husbands to be with him. They had nowhere else to go.

Krishna calmed the women, saying that if they loved him, they would dance and sing with him. Elated, their sorrows were forgotten and the girls were joyous once more. They moved with him to the riverbank, which had been magically transformed into a golden terrace, glittering with jewels and precious stones in the moonlight. They joined with Krishna in a frenzied episode of song and dance during which all restraint was cast aside. The dance became a seething orgy with Krishna in the center, but when their excess caused them to go too far, Krishna disappeared. The confused young women anxiously searched the forest for any sign of him and soon discovered a set of footprints. Krishna's tracks were accompanied by the smaller footprints of a girl. The trail led to a bed of leaves upon which a small hand mirror was left behind. Someone suggested its purpose; Krishna had used it so that while he braided his lover's hair, she could still see his face.

Unknown to them, the favored girl, Radha, had also earned his disapproval. Believing that she had enslaved Krishna, she complained that she was tired of walking and asked to be carried on his shoulders. Krishna sat down and invited her to climb onto his back, but when she reached out to do so, he vanished under her touch. The others arrived to find her weeping bitterly – not because Krishna had wronged her, but because she had foolishly tried to take advantage of her lover.

The women continued to search for Krishna and when he could not be found, they collapsed in the grass, weeping and moaning in anguish and unsatisfied lust. Krishna saw their suffering and returned to them, appearing as mysteriously in their midst as he had disappeared. He told them that he had left them to test their strength of their love for him and they had passed the test. The girls accepted this explanation without question and began to smother him with their kisses and caresses. Krishna's body began to descend upon each of the women simultaneously, making love to each of them at the same time. To accomplish this, he apparently used his supernatural powers to be with all of the women at once. The coupling was said to be so amazing that the gods in the heavens looked down on the scene and all of the goddesses longed to join in. The winds were still and the waters ceased to flow until the night was concluded. When morning came, Krishna bathed the women in the river and sent them home. They continued to love him, occasionally returning to his embrace for another night of passionate lovemaking.

After this resounding, erotic event, Krishna turned to his real task on earth, the defeat of Kansa and his demons. Krishna was barely able to act before Kansa began to launch his own attacks against the man who was born to destroy him. A number of horrific incidents followed and after several murderous attempts against Krishna at a great sports festival, Kansa and his cohorts are annihilated by Krishna and his friend, Balarama.

This would seem to be the end of Krishna's journey, but he did not return to heaven. With wrongs to be righted and still other demons to be destroyed, his task on earth continued. He was forced to leave his childhood home, where he spent a happy boyhood and made love to local girls, and assume his rightful place in the world but he did so with mixed feelings. The farm women could not be consoled and he promised to return and visit them again someday.

Krishna took his place as the ruler of the country and became involved in the politics and military strategy after the death of the demon tyrant, Kansa. He soon took his first queen, a woman with whom he fell in love named Rukmini. She had been promised to a disreputable man by her father but Krishna rescued her on her wedding day and she became the first of his wives. Seven more consorts added to his bevy of queens were later augmented by an array of distressed virgins, daughters of various kings. These young women, imprisoned for various complicated reasons, became inflamed with love for Krishna and begged to be allowed to give themselves to him. Krishna rescued each of them and brought them all to the capital, marrying all of them as he continued to display unceasing love for his eight queens. No matter the inexhaustible powers of a divinity, the queens were merely human and were not immune to the occasional twinge of jealousy. Krishna did all that he could to keep them satisfied. When one queen became upset that he had given another a flower from a certain heavenly tree, he consoled her by promising to bring her the tree itself. Krishna took the tree by force from heaven when the gods refused to let it go.

As time passed, Krishna's personality began to change. His youthful, audacious charm was gone and it was replaced with a grave, formal dignity that was in keeping with the princely figure that he had become. When by chance he encountered the women from his foster father's farm at a festival, they rushed to him and smothered him with kisses and adoration, but he only gave them words of wisdom in return:

Whoever believes in me shall be fearlessly carried across the sea of life. You gave me your bodies, your minds and wealth. You loved me with a love that knew no limit. No one has been so fortunate as you – neither Brahma nor Indra, neither any god or any man. For all along I have been living in you, loving you with a love that never faltered. I live in everyone. What I say to you cannot easily be understood, but as light, water, fire, earth and air abide in the body, so does my glory.

Krishna never saw the young women again, but his words seemed to suggest that it was Vishnu himself that was speaking directly via his earthly form and they painted a vivid picture of Krishna's dual character. Although he was generally regarded as a man, there were moments when those around him seemed to be aware that he was something much more than a mere mortal.

Krishna continued to bestow passionate pleasures of the flesh on the women in his life, but even that had changed. Gone was the dangerous, illicit lover who engaged in orgies in the woods with farm girls, but Krishna was no less ardent as a husband and he continued to bestow even greater, more sensuous pleasures upon his many wives. His dismissal of the farm women, while enjoying the love of his wives, was consistent of his new, reserved personality. The charming young man who had abetted and enjoyed the pleasures of their adultery had become a figure of respectability, careful to uphold the sanctity of a marriage in which 16,108 women were his legal wives!

Aside from continually satisfying his wives, Krishna's task on earth, beyond righting wrongs and protecting the righteous from evil-doers, seemed to have been hunting demons and aiding the causes of certain noble families. He never seemed to be concerned with ethics or religious observances and only asked, as the human incarnation of Vishnu, for the enduring love of his followers and their proper appreciation of their good fortune as the recipients of his love, which put them on the path of *bhakti*.

In later centuries, following a revival in Hinduism more than 1,000 years ago, Vishnu and Krishna began to be firmly established at the forefront of Hindu gods, an importance challenged only by the fervent worshippers of Shiva. The popularity of Vishnu and Krishna began to be reflected in the literature and art of India, especially when it came to the erotic love affairs of Krishna. Many followers used his sexual encounters as an allegory for his divine love for mankind and his passion as a symbol of the ecstasy of final reunion with the universal spirit. This belief systems remains in place today, making it a true example of the supernatural, erotic love of a god that has literally changed a religion and in many aspects, the faith, of a large portion of the eastern world.

2 SEX MAGIC
RITUAL SEX, THE ORDO TEMPLI ORIENTIS AND "THE WICKEDEST MAN IN THE WORLD"

Throughout history, there have generally been two kinds of sexual magic: sexual acts aimed at achieving magical ends and magical acts aimed at achieving sexual ends. While the former category certainly had its place in early witchcraft, it has certainly become a more common practice of modern times. Magical acts aimed at affecting sexual behavior were a mainstay of the medieval witch or sorcerer.

Most witchcraft was used not merely for sexual gratification, but for reproduction, as well. Magic was used to inflame passions, or to suppress them; to cause impotence and frigidity; and to cause sterility, abortions or to make a baby stillborn. Witches could also disrupt the passage of urine and feces from the body, causing great pain. One of the techniques used by witches to prevent men from urinating was the same used to make men impotent: the tying of knots in a rope. Many men, unable to pass urine because of these spells, reportedly suffered excruciating pain and died. The witches accomplished this by making the rectum or urethra clench, or even by causing flesh to grow over the openings. In certain cases, a bewitched person might be forced to vomit up his or her own excrement, as well as peculiar objects like stones, balls and the hair of animals. In one famous case in France, a young boy was said to have "urinated" a half dozen pieces of paper inscribed with "strange characters," along with some peas. This incident followed the exposure of homosexual activities between the boy and his schoolmaster, who was then branded a witch.

While most spells of this nature targeted people, animals were sometimes also affected. Witches dried up the udders of cows and also stopped the flow of milk in young mothers who were trying to breastfeed, which starved both calves and infants alike.

That witches concocted love potions (using semen, menstrual blood, human and animal genitalia, among other ingredients) is well known. But there were other methods of arousing lust, some by means of witchcraft and others by the alleged intervention of demons. For example, some believed that demons could awaken strong sexual desire by introducing aphrodisiacs directly into the human bloodstream. They might also do the opposite, causing a man to become impotent, or a woman to be repulsed by sex.

It is almost certain that by the 12th century, witches were using wax effigies in their spells, as the pagans before them had done. The figures were used to incite passion in men and women, and sometimes to injure them, a purpose we are more familiar with today. Spells were pronounced over the wax images, caresses lavished upon them, and in a variety of other ways, they were manipulated to produce the desired effect – which sometimes included unflagging erections and nymphomania, depending on the sex of the intended victim.

Sexual bewitchments sometimes took on bizarre forms. One strange case was recounted in the book called

Malleus Maleficarum, the infamous witch-finder's manual that literally meant "a hammer with which to strike witches":

There is in the town of Coblenz a poor man who was bewitched in this way. In the presence of his wife he is in the habit of acting in the manner of men with women, that is to say, practicing a coition, as it were, and he continues to do this repeatedly, nor have the cries and urgent appeals of his wife any effect in making him desist. And after he has fornicated thus two or three times, he bawls out, 'We are going to start all over again'; when actually there is no person visible to mortal sight lying with him. And after an incredible number of such bouts, the poor man at last sinks to the floor utterly exhausted. When he has recovered his strength a little and is asked how this happened to him, and whether he has had a woman with him, he answers that he saw nothing, but that his mind is in some way possessed so that he can by no means refrain from such priapism. And indeed he harbors a great suspicion that a certain woman bewitched him in this way, because he had offended her, and she had cursed him with threatening words, telling him what she would like to happen to him.

Legends of witchcraft also told of spells that had the ability to change the gender of a man or beast, always with the intervention of demons. There were also claims that witches possessed a drug that had the capacity to reverse the sex of those who swallowed it. Some said that males could be transformed into females and females into males, but it was also argued that the sex change only worked in one direction. It was stated that the Devil could make women into men, but could not transform men into women because it was the rule of nature to add on rather than to take away.

But the greatest sexual magic of the witches was said to be ligature, the production of impotence by magical means. During the Middle Ages (and later), the fear of impotence was widespread, which likely indicates that many men experienced impotence at one time or another. This is not surprising when one considers how available sex was on one hand and how universally condemned it was on the other, not to mention contributing factors like poor diet and lack of hygiene.

Catholic clergymen began addressing the problems of ligature in the 12th century, but medieval executions of witches for the offence went back much earlier. In France of the 7th century, a renowned witch was executed, a witch who was specially feared for her ability to inflict impotence in men. Clergymen of the time believed that witches achieved impotence with the cooperation of demons. St. Thomas Aquinas wrote: "Demons can do harm by their operations and impede carnal copulation." He noted various methods by which demons produced impotence and various forms that impotence might take. One procedure, he said, is to make a particular woman, perhaps a wife, so unattractive to a man that he loses his desire for her and hence is unable to copulate with her. Aquinas' statement was often cited by subsequent authorities on the subject. These Christian authors believed that impotence was a characteristic of Satan and many tales of the Devil involved symbolic attempts to castrate him, or at least affirm his impotence. His inability to achieve an intended goal is a hallmark of stories about the Devil. As an architect or an engineer, he was never able to complete his bridges or buildings. His plans and projects were never finished. His deals usually fell through and even

A witch works her craft in this old woodcut

when he contracted for a soul, he was often denied payment. It was alleged that he had no semen and if he wanted to have sexual intercourse, he had to do so by stealing the penis of a man or a beast.

Some Christian authors saw impotence as more of a blessing than a curse, declaring that angels could take away man's virile powers, although this was usually something they only did on request. It was considered a token of divine esteem for the individual to be unsexed. St. Gregory told of the Blessed Abbott Equitius, incessantly distracted and tormented by temptations of the flesh, who called upon God to set him free from his evil thoughts. An angel came down one night and removed all of the sensation from his genitals, which allowed him to focus more intently on spiritual matters rather than earthly ones. God also answered the similar prayer of St. Serenus, sending down an angle who "seemed to open his belly and take from his entrails a burning tumor of flesh, and then to replace all his intestines as they had been; and said, Lo! The provocation of your flesh has been cut out, and know that this day you have obtained perpetual purity of your body, according to the prayer which you prayed, so that you will never again be pricked with that natural desire which is aroused even in babies and sucklings."

These castrating angels (angels really did do all of God's dirty work) took away not only the capacity for sex but also all desire for it. Witches and demons were less kind. They made it impossible for men to have sex, but they left the lust for it intact. An unsatiated hunger for sex would allegedly rage in those who were bewitched, driving men to insanity and even suicide.

Four Witches by Durer

Writers theorized about the various ways that demons inflicted impotence. Peter Paludanus (Petrus de Palude), the French theologian and archbishop, wrote that demons had five ways of preventing husbands from having intercourse with their wives: they could interpose themselves between the man and women so that no contact was possible; they could "freeze" desire, or make the woman appear loathsome to the man; they could act directly on the penis, making an erection impossible, or even prevent the flow of "vital essence," making the erect penis unable to perform.

The one technique that Paludanus neglected to mention was the one that was the most feared and drastic of all: the literal "theft" of the penis, the testicles, or both, causing the organs to disappear. Whether demons and witches were able to steal a man's private parts, and whether or not they could restore what was taken, was a subject in great dispute by theologians. According to contemporary accounts, it was commonplace during the Middle Ages for sex organs to turn up missing. Priests wrote of witnessing with their own eyes faithful church members who had been mutilated in this manner. Some held that demons could in fact rob a man of his genitals, but that God would usually forbid such degradation. Those who believed this could not deny that penises and testicles still sometimes vanished anyway, leaving shamed and grieving men as eunuchs, but they claimed that the mysterious vanishings were only an illusion. The priests might sometimes restore the "missing" organs through prayer and by the goodness of God. Penis thefts were, in this way, merely an object lesson of sorts.

Witches too, some maintained, could create the illusion that a penis had disappeared, but demons could truly snatch it off. Demons were able to cloud the victim's senses of sight and touch and then cause the penis to vanish, leaving only smooth skin behind. Others argued that this was not true – witches could also steal a man's penis and cited numerous "case histories" to substantiate their claims. On case involved a man who prevailed upon a witch to return the penis that she had taken. She took him into the woods and led him to a large nest containing a dozen or more male organs. The man, whose own instrument had been of average size, saw his opportunity and identified his as the largest of the lot, which later turned out to be the much-used property of the local priest.

In addition to theft, a man's penis might be made to shrivel up (or a woman's cleft might close up so tightly that penetration was impossible). A man's organ might also draw up into his belly, where it might, with luck, be recovered by medical rather than magical means.

Although there were a number of ways to inflict impotence, the most common method was by tying a knot in a cord. Women were made frigid in the same way, and there were dozens of knots that were possible, each inflicting a different degree or form of frigidity or impotence. One knot was designed to prevent conception, and also to keep the witch advised on how things were going; each time the women had sex and a pregnancy was averted, a "wart" would appear on the knotted cord.

Impotence would be enacted permanently, or on a temporary basis. In the past, divorces and annulments were usually only granted after a considerable passage of time, often three years, at the conclusion of which the impotence was presumed to be permanent. Frigidity of wives, even though caused by witchcraft, was usually not a basis for terminating a marriage since sex could still occur. However, many women managed to get out of loveless marriages by paying a witch to make her husband impotent for a set length of time. In other situations, a woman whose lover was going to marry someone else might pay a witch to prevent the marriage or its consummation. The penalty for soliciting a witch was usually forty days on bread and water, but stiffer sentences were imposed on those who hired a witch to prevent a man and woman from conceiving a child. This type of crime was often classified as murder and the penalty could often be death.

Of course, what one type of magic carried out, another type of magic could cure. There was an abundance of remedies and preventives for impotence, frigidity, and sterility caused by the influence of witches. Sometimes, God himself would step in and restore a man's potency when it had been taken from him by ligature. This could be accomplished by a fervent prayer, in which the afflicted promised never to engage in adultery, sodomy or any other sexual practice that might offend God. His problem part could then be returned to working order. The afflicted party might also go to confession, shed many tears, meditate, plan a pilgrimage to a holy shrine or – especially popular with many clergymen – make a large contribution to the local church.

There were other methods to end the enchantment, most of which hearkened back to pagan days. This including having a man urinate through his wife's wedding ring or finding a magpie's nest in the woods. Those who preferred prevention to a cure fell back on pagan amulets and charms, which usually represented the sexual organs. They included an upright knife or broomstick, a horse's skull, a pentagram, horseshoes and hag stones, which were rocks with a hole bored into them to represent a vagina.

Witches themselves could also, in most cases, nullify a spell by supplying an antidote or a love potion that was powerful enough to override the affliction. It was also said that a man could spend the night in the bed of the witch who hexed him and that she could restore his potency in order for him to make love to her. He would then be able to retain his prowess, as long as his performance measured up.

How much truth was there to the accounts of witches affecting the sex lives of men and women? We'll likely never know which stories were fanciful tales and which began with a kernel of truth. The important point is that people of the time believed them to be true. There was little question that witches could make their victims believe that they were impotent or frigid – a method that became essential to the practice of witchcraft and voodoo. The mind is a powerful tool and getting someone to believe in something is always the greater part of the battle. Once they truly believe, they can be convinced of almost anything – including sexual problems brought about by magical means.

And these are not merely the beliefs of the superstitious times of the Middle Ages. Even today, it is a common occurrence among voodoo practitioners to make people believe that spells have caused them to become sick, bewitched and impotent. In a 1950 case in Shreveport, Alabama, a man was sentenced to jail for attempting the murder of another who had allegedly put a hex on him. The assailant stated that he believed that he could recover his lost potency by killing the witch and he was arrested after beating a sorcerer nearly to death with a wooden board.

MODERN SEX MAGIC

Modern sex magic (beginning in the latter part of the 1800s) more often than not falls into the category of sexual acts that are aimed at achieving magical ends. The fundamental premise of sex magic is the belief in the sexual energy of the human body as a most potent force, and harnessing that force through sexual activity provides a special conduit for the transcendence of normal reality.

Two fundamental applications of sex magic concern the use of the orgasm. Some practitioners base their use of sex on the power that the orgasmic release of sexual energy contains. An example of this type of sex magic is the "Great Rite" of Wicca, a neo-pagan, nature-based religion that was first popularized in 1954 by Gerald Gardner, a retired British civil servant. He stated that the religion was a modern survival of an ancient witchcraft religion that had existed in secret for hundreds of years, originating in the pre-Christian paganism of Europe. Wiccans typically worship a Horned God and a Triple Goddess, which represent nature. Their practices include the ritual use of magic, a liberal code of morality and the celebration of eight seasonal-based festivals.

The Wiccans' Great Rite is either sexual intercourse, or a ritual, symbolic representation of it. In the symbolic version, the High Priest plunges the *athame*, or ritual knife, (the male symbol) into a cup (the female symbol), which is filled with wine. The Great Rite symbolizes creation in the union of the Maiden Goddess with the Lover God and is also used as a fertility rite. The Great Rite is performed on a variety of occasions, including the festival of Beltane, which is usually held on May 1 in the northern hemisphere.

Another school of thought holds that "sexual sublimation" should be used to transform sexual energy into creativity, thereby facilitating a mystical awakening. In psychology, sublimation is the transference of sexual energy into a physical act or a different emotion in order to avoid confrontation with the sexual urge. It is based on the belief that sexual energy, the creative function of the human being, can be used to create a spiritual nature. This method of sexual magic was popularized by Samael Aun Weor, an occultist and author who created a method of teaching that he called "Gnosis," the Greek word for knowledge, from which is derived the term Gnosticism, designating a sect that appeared at the beginning of the Christian Era and was considered heresy by the Church fathers.

Some of the earliest sex magic theories and techniques were formed from the teachings of Paschal Beverly Randolph, an American medical doctor, writer and occultist. Born in 1825, Randolph was perhaps the first person to introduce the principles of sex magic to North America. He established the earliest-known Rosicrucian order in the United States.

Randolph was a free man of mixed-race ancestry who became an outspoken opponent of slavery. He trained as a doctor of medicine and traveled widely as a young man, becoming fascinated with mysticism and the occult. He worked on a sailing ship, journeyed through Europe and as far east as Persia (present-day Iran). Back at home in America, he lived in New Orleans, New York, San Francisco and Toledo, Ohio. He also worked as a trance medium during the early days of the Spiritualist movement, lectured in favor of the abolition of slavery and taught reading to freed slaves.

Randolph was the founder of the Fraternitas Rosae Crucis, the oldest Rosicrucian organization in the United States, which today avoids mention of his interest in sex magic. His magical-sexual theories formed the basis of much of the teachings of the Hermetic

Pascal Beverly Randolph

Brotherhood of Luxor, a ritual sex organization that was formed in 1884, although it's never been clear whether or not Randolph himself was ever actually associated with the sect.

In 1851, Randolph became friends with Abraham Lincoln and their relationship was close enough that, when Lincoln was assassinated in 1865, Randolph accompanied Lincoln's funeral procession by train to Springfield, Illinois. He was later removed from the train when some objected to the presence of a mixed race man in the funeral party.

Randolph died at the age of forty-nine in 1875, under mysterious circumstances. The coroner in Toledo, Ohio stated that he had died from a self-inflicted gunshot to the head, even though his many writings expressed his aversion to suicide. Years later, a deathbed confession from a former friend of Randolph admitted that, in a state of jealousy and temporary insanity, he had killed Randolph, bringing an end to the man's strange and fascinating life.

One of the most famous organizations to be influenced by Randolph's teachings was the Ordo Templi Orientis (O.T.O.), which was founded by Carl Kellner, a wealthy paper chemist and occultist. Kellner was a student of Freemasonry, Rosicrucianism and Eastern mysticism, and traveled extensively in Europe, America and Asia. During his travels, he claimed to come into contact with a trio of ancient masters or adepts, consisting of a Sufi and two Hindu Tantrics, and an organization called the Hermetic Brotherhood of Light.

In 1885, Kellner met the Theosophical and Rosicrucian scholar Dr. Franz Hartmann and the two men later collaborated on the development of an inhalation therapy for tuberculosis. During the course of his studies, Kellner believed that he had discovered a "Key" that offered a clear explanation of all of the complex symbolism of Freemasonry and, Kellner was convinced, opened the mysteries of nature.

Kellner soon began working to found the Academia Masonica, which would enable all Freemasons to become familiar with all existing Masonic degrees and systems. In 1895, he began to discuss this idea with his friend and associate, Theodor Reuss, and decided that the Academia Masonica should be called Ordo Templi Orientis (Oriental Templar Order). The inner circle of the order would be organized parallel to the highest degree of the Masonic Rite of Memphis and Mizraim and would teach the mysterious Rosicrucian doctrines of the Hermetic Brotherhood of Light and Kellner's "Key" to Masonic symbolism. Both men and women were to be admitted to all levels of the O.T.O., but possession of the various degrees of Craft and High-Grade Freemasonry would be required in order to be admitted to the inner circle. Unfortunately, due to regulations of the established Grand Lodges, which governed regular Freemasonry, women could not become Freemasons and therefore, would be excluded from the O.T.O. This may have been one of the reasons that Kellner and his associates decided to try and obtain control over one of the many rites, or systems, of Freemasonry and reform the system so that women could be admitted.

Despite plans and lengthy discussions between Kellner and Reuss, nothing came of their attempts to launch the O.T.O. Reuss was busy at that time trying to revive the 18th century Order of the Illuminati with his friend Leopold Engel, a sect that Kellner did not approve of. The revival of the Illuminati failed and in 1902, Kellner

(Left) Carl Kellner and (Right) Theodor Reuss

contacted Reuss again and they agreed to proceed with the establishment of the Ordo Templi Orientis by seeking authorization to work the various rites of Freemasonry. Kellner and Reuss prepared a manifesto for the Order in 1903 that was published the next year in the obscure Masonic periodical, *The Oriflamme*. Before the group could really get started, Kellner died on June 7, 1905, leaving it in the hands of Theodor Reuss. In 1912, he announced, "Our Order possesses the key which opens up all Masonic and Hermetic secrets, namely, the teachings of sexual magic, and this teaching explains, without exception, all of the secrets of Freemasonry and all systems of religion."

Reuss undoubtedly felt that the Ordo Templi Orientis was one of the most important movements in the history of the world, especially when it came to the use of sexual magic, but he would soon have another personage to deal with who would threaten the status of the O.T.O. and gain a worldwide following that endures to this day.

ALEISTER CROWLEY

The most infamous practitioner of sex magic in history was undoubtedly Aleister Crowley. Through his carefully cultivated reputation as "the wickedest man alive" and his identification with the Anti-Christ (he adopted the moniker "Great Beast 666"), Crowley developed his own magical system, which he termed "magick." He explained that the "k" stood for *kteis*, meaning "vagina" in Greek. Seemingly obsessed with sex, Crowley regularly practiced rites with both male and female acolytes (the females being known as his "Scarlet Women") that included fellatio, cunnilingus, the drinking of menstrual blood, sodomy, and even bestiality. Crowley

Aleister Crowley as a young magician. He became fascinated with the occult as a young man and became involved in the new Order of the Golden Dawn before striking out on his own. He would later be dubbed "the wickedest man alive".

was even in the habit of eating his own semen, which he regarded as a potent magical elixir. Cynics claimed that Crowley's claims to be a seeker of occult wisdom were entirely fabricated to enable his debauchery, while others regard him as a true visionary of the early 20th century. Either way, he remains a remarkable and fascinating figure whose views on sex and magic permanently changed the occult world.

He was born Edward Alexander Crowley in England on October 12, 1875 – that much we do know. Beyond that, much of Crowley's life remains shrouded in mystery. This is not because documentation of his life does not exist, but because most of that documentation was provided by Crowley himself. As a shameless self-promoter, Crowley undoubtedly "invented" whole sections of his life, magnifying the occult aspects of his existence to appeal to his followers and devotees. We'll never know for sure just how much of his biography is fact, and how much is fancy, but the following has been pieced together from the most reliable sources that could be found.

His father, Edward Crowley, had made his fortune from Crowley's Ales, and had retired to become a minister, preaching the conservative evangelical doctrine of the Plymouth Brethren. The family lived in Leamington, a small peaceful town, and Crowley made it clear that his "diabolism" later in life was a revolt against the religious repression of his childhood. However, his youth was not a bitter one and his parents were very affectionate and indulgent, spoiling their son. Crowley admired his father and imitated his leadership abilities, a skill that would

A young Aleister Crowley

serve him well as an adult. His father died when Crowley was eleven and the boy began getting into trouble. He was sent to a private, religious school and it was here that his seeds of rebellion began to be sown in earnest.

As Crowley became a teenager, his interest in sex began to grow. His mother was a puritanical woman and so straitlaced that she once argued violently with Crowley's cousin Agnes because the younger woman had a book by Emile Zola in her house. As an outright revolt against such attitudes, Crowley lost his virginity to a servant girl on his mother's bed when he was fourteen years old.

Just a year later, Crowley's career almost came to a premature end on Guy Fawkes Night in 1891. Guy Fawkes Night (or Fireworks Night) is an annual celebration on the evening of November 5 to celebrate the foiling of the Gunpowder Plot in which a number of Catholic conspirators, including Guy Fawkes, attempted to blow up the Houses of Parliament in London. As Crowley tried to light a ten-pound, homemade firework, it exploded, knocking him unconscious for ninety-six hours. His followers believe that the accident may have awakened some sort of latent psychic abilities, which they use to explain the dark career of his adulthood and the powerful influence that he obtained over the occult community of the day.

After recovering from the fireworks accident, Crowley began attending public school at Malvern, and then went on to Oxford, where he lived lavishly on his inheritance and published his own poems. Crowley was not a poet, but he certainly believed that he was. At one point, he referred to the small town where he grew up and its proximity to Stratford-on-Avon and noted that it was "a strange coincidence that one small county should have given England her two greatest poets – for one must not forget Shakespeare." He discovered rock climbing while in college and for many years, this satisfied his adventurous nature. But the lure of the occult continued to call to him.

As a student, he discovered *Kabbalah Unveiled*, which fascinated him because it was all so incomprehensible. It was perhaps at this time that the first inklings of what lay ahead of him in life began to surface, especially after his discovery of A.E. Waite's compilation on ceremonial magic, *The Book of Black Magic and of Pacts*. Crowley continued to pen his own poetry, including a cycle of poems about a sexual psychopath who becomes a murderer, but his writings began to take on a more supernatural feel. But sex was never far from his mind and he also wrote a short sadomasochistic novel called *Snowdrops from a Curate's Garden*.

Through a fellow student, Crowley was introduced to an "alchemist" named George Cecil Jones, and through Jones to the Order of the Golden Dawn, a magical cult that practiced arcane rituals for spiritual development. The Order had been founded by retired physician Dr. William Robert Woodman; Dr. William Wynn Westcott, a London coroner, and Samuel Liddell MacGregor Mathers. They were Freemasons who were also members of the Societas Rosicruciana, an offshoot of the Masons. Westcott, also a member of the Theosophical Society, appears to have been the initial driving force behind the establishment of the Golden Dawn.

The Golden Dawn was formed along the lines of a Masonic Lodge, however women were admitted on an equal basis with men. The Golden Dawn is technically only the first or "outer" of three orders, although all three are often collectively described as the "Golden Dawn." The First Order taught esoteric philosophy based on the Kabbalah, as well as the basics of astrology and tarot reading. The Second, or "Inner," Order, the Rosae Rubeae et Aureae Crucis (the Ruby Rose and Cross of Gold), taught magic proper, including scrying, astral travel, and

The Order of the Golden Dawn was founded by (Left to Right) retired physician Dr. William Robert Woodman; Dr. William Wynn Westcott, a London coroner, and Samuel Liddell MacGregor Mathers.

alchemy. The Third Order was that of the "Secret Chiefs," who were said to be powerful adepts no longer in human form, but who directed the activities of the lower two orders through spirit communication with the Chiefs of the Second Order.

In October 1887, Westcott began working to translate the legendary Cipher Manuscripts, which allegedly gave the specific outlines of the Grade Rituals of the Order, and organized a curriculum of specifically graduated teachings that encompassed the Kaballah, astrology, occult tarot, geomancy, and alchemy. He wrote to a woman in Germany named Anna Sprengel, whose name and address he said he received through the decoding of the Cipher Manuscripts. Sprengel was said to be an adept of the Order of the Golden Dawn. She reportedly replied to Wescott's letter with a letter of her own that contained much in the way of supernatural wisdom and also bestowed honorary titles on Westcott, Mathers and Woodman. She also supposedly gave Wescott the task of establishing the first Golden Dawn temple in England.

In 1888, the Isis-Urania Temple was founded in London and the order's myriad of rituals began to be developed and practiced. The original lodge did not actually teach magical practices, except for basic "banishing rituals" and meditation, but was rather a philosophical and metaphysical teaching group. This was called the "Outer Order," but the "Inner Order" became active in 1892 and it was comprised of a circle of adepts who had completed the entire course of study and initiations of the "Outer Order," detailed in the Cipher Manuscripts. This group eventually became known as the Second Order.

A short time later, the Osiris Temple in Weston-super-Mare, the Horus Temple in Bradford, and the Amen-Ra Temple in Edinburgh were founded. A few years after this, Mathers started the Ahathoor Temple in Paris.

In 1891, correspondence with the mysterious adept Anna Sprengel suddenly stopped, and Westcott allegedly received word from Germany that she was either dead or that her companions did not approve of the founding

Crowley in the Golden Dawn

of the order and demanded that she cut off contact with them. If the founders were to contact the Secret Chiefs, they would have to do it on their own, without the help of their benefactor. It was about this time that Woodman died, never having seen the Second Order come into being. In 1892, Mathers (not surprisingly) claimed that a link to the Secret Chiefs had been formed and supplied the rituals for the Second Order.

By the middle 1890s, the Golden Dawn was well established in England, with membership rising to over one hundred from every class of Victorian Society. This was considered the heyday of the order and many celebrities of the time boasted membership within its ranks, including actress Florence Farr, Annie Horniman (who sponsored the Abbey Theatre in Dublin), occult novelist Arthur Machen, William Butler Yeats, Evelyn Underhill, and many others.

After Aleister Crowley's introduction to the Golden Dawn during this period, he found himself disappointed with the mediocrity of most of the members and found the ceremonies boring and commonplace. Nevertheless, he was admitted to their ranks and was given the name Brother Perdurabo (one who endures to the end). He was among the lowest of the order's levels and he began working hard to rise in status.

Around 1897, Westcott broke off all ties to the Golden Dawn, leaving Mathers in complete control. It was speculated that Wescott left the order after some papers were found in a hansom cab, outlining his connection to the Golden Dawn. His affiliation came to the attention of his superiors and he was told to either resign from the Order or be relieved from his position as a coroner. Rumors claimed that Mathers planted the papers to drive Westcott out, but there has never been any proof offered of this. It was noted that any public relationship between the two men ended at this point, although it's possible that Westcott continued with the order in secret. Lodge documents bearing his signature have since been found, dated years after his "resignation." After Westcott departed, Mathers appointed Florence Farr to be Chief Adept in Anglia. This left Mathers as the only active founding member and in charge of the order. Thanks to personality clashes with other members, and his frequent absences from the center of order activity in England, challenges to Mathers' authority as leader began to develop among the members of the Second Order.

By late 1899, leaders of the Isis-Urania and Amen-Ra Temples had become very unhappy with Mathers' leadership, as well as his growing friendship with Crowley, whom they saw as a disturbing influence in the order. They were anxious to make contact with the Secret Chiefs on their own, instead of receiving their wisdom through Mathers. To make matters worse, when Crowley was denied entry into the Second Order by London officials, Mathers overrode their decision and initiated him at the Ahathoor Temple in Paris on January 6, 1900. For the London leaders, this was the last straw. Crowley's initiation led to a general meeting that called for Mathers' removal as chief and his expulsion from the order. A committee of three was formed to temporarily govern the order, which included P.W. Bullock, M.W. Blackden and J. W. Brodie-Innes. After a short time, Bullock resigned, and Dr. Robert Felkin took his place. In 1903, A.E. Waite and Blackden joined forces to retain the name Isis-Urania, while Felkin and other London members formed the Stella Matutina. J.W. Brodie-Innes continued the Amen-Ra Temple in Edinburgh.

Once Mathers realized there would be no reconciliation among the members of the order, he began trying to establish himself again in London. Members of the Bradford and Weston-super-Mare temples remained loyal to him, but their numbers were few. He appointed Edward Berridge as his representative, who proceeded to begin working the ceremonies and rites of the Golden Dawn in West London in 1903.

Brodie-Innes, who had continued the Amen-Ra Temple, eventually reached the conclusion that the revolt against Mathers was unjustified. By 1908, the two men were again in complete accord. Brodie-Innes assumed command of the English and Scottish temples, while Mathers concentrated on building up the Ahathoor Temple and extending his connections in America. The first Golden Dawn temple had been established in Chicago around 1900. It was located in a small building on Halsted Street, which is now home to a bar. Renovations in the building in recent years revealed ritual paintings in the basement and a dagger that had been buried under the floor to purify the location.

The Order of the Golden Dawn (at least in its original incarnation) eventually faded out of existence. Most of the temples closed down by the 1930s, with the exception of the Hermes Temple in Bristol, which operated sporadically until 1970. The group has been revived several times over the years and a modern version still survives today.

Crowley abandoned the Golden Dawn after Mathers' falling out with them and after a public disagreement that Crowley had with W.B. Yeats -- who Crowley maintained hated him because Crowley was a much better poet. The problem emerged over money, of which Crowley had plenty, thanks to his inheritance. However, Crowley shared with Mathers a curious habit of pretending to be an aristocrat. Mathers was given to dressing in kilts and calling himself the Chevalier MacGregor or the Comte de Glenstrae, both of which were titles he created himself. Crowley rented a flat in London shortly after joining the Golden Dawn, started using Russian accent, and called himself Count Vladimir Svareff. He explained later that he did this in the interests of psychological observation. He had observed how tradesmen deferred to his because of his wealth and he wanted to see how they behaved with a Russian nobleman. This may, or may not have been the case because Crowley continued such charades long after the "experiment" in London.

When he moved to a house that overlooked Loch Ness, he dubbed himself Lord Boleskine, or the Laird of Boleskine, and imitated Mathers by adopting a kilt. While living in the house, he concentrated on the magic of Abra-Melin the Mage, whose ultimate aim was to establish contact with one's guardian angel. Crowley claimed that in London, he and George Cecil Jones, his alchemist friend, succeeded in materializing the helmeted head and left leg of a spirit called Buel, and that on another occasion, a group of semi-formed demons spent the night marching around

Crowley's Boleskine House on the shores of Loch Ness. The house was later owned by Led Zeppelin's Jimmy Page, who maintained that it was still "tainted" by Crowley's tenancy in the mansion

his room. At Loch Ness, the lodge and terrace of his house allegedly became haunted by shadowy shapes and the lodge keeper went mad during Crowley's tenancy and attempted to kill his wife and children. Crowley claimed that the ritual room of the house became so dark while he was trying to copy magical symbols that he would have to light lamps, even when the sunshine was blazing outside.

After his quarrel with Yeats, Crowley went to Mexico, where he claimed that his concentrated effort almost made his reflection vanish from a mirror. In the dry, hot climate of Mexico, Crowley continued to work to create his own mystical religion, greater than any that he had encountered before, but he was at a loss as to how to continue. He said that he put out a great call for help from the Masters and a week later, he received a letter from George Cecil Jones, suggesting a new course of study. Oddly enough, it was an old mountain climbing companion of Crowley's who suggested his next move. He advised him to give up magic and simply develop a power of intense concentration. Crowley followed his friend's suggestion and spent months involved in what constituted yoga training.

More mountain climbing followed, as well as travels to San Francisco, and Ceylon (now Sri Lanka), and a love affair with a married woman that resulted in his book *Alice, An Adultery*. In Ceylon, he found his close friend Allan Bennett, a colleague from his Golden Dawn days and a student of Buddhism. Crowley's generosity to his friend had resulted in Bennett's trip to Ceylon. Bennett later became the founder of the British Buddhist movement, and he was one of the few people of whom Crowley remained consistently fond. He spent months teaching Crowley all that he knew of Eastern mysticism, and after his recent period of intense thought control, Bennett's teachings came as a revelation to him. Crowley now believed that he could harness all of his psychic energies and do

Crowley's friend, Allan Bennett

amazing things with such a force.

Meanwhile, Bennett, who had been working as a private tutor to the solicitor-general in Ceylon, decided that he was going to renounce the world and become a Buddhist monk. With his friend out of commission, Crowley went on a big game hunt, penetrated a secret shrine at Madura, explored the Irrawaddy River in a canoe, and finally visited Bennett at his monastery, where he claimed to see Bennett levitating in the air during a period of intense meditation.

Crowley, now in his middle twenties, was still basically a rich playboy and sportsman, not much different from the Golden Dawn members whom he held with such disdain when he first joined the order. In 1902, he was one of the party that attempted to reach the summit of the Chogori (now known as K2), the world's second-highest mountain, (after Everest) in India's Karakoram range. Bad weather and illness prematurely ended the expedition.

Crowley returned to Paris and called on Mathers, hoping that his mental accomplishments would earn his respect. Mathers was not in the least bit interested in yoga and dismissed his one-time ally, which greatly cooled Crowley's respect for him. Crowley set about becoming an eccentric character in the artistic circles of Paris and W. Somerset Maugham wrote about him in his 1908 novel, *The Magician*. In this tale, the magician, Oliver Haddo, a caricature of Aleister Crowley, attempts to create life. Crowley wrote a critique of this book under the pen name Oliver Haddo, where he accused Maugham of plagiarism.

After a time in Paris, he returned to Boleskine House at Loch Ness and became friendly with a young painter named Gerald Kelly (who later became Sir Gerald Kelly, president of the Royal Academy). Crowley soon met Kelly's unstable sister, Rose, an attractive young woman with a score of emotional issues. Already a widow, she had involved herself with a number of men who wanted to marry her, and she encouraged them all. Crowley's odd sense of humor offered her a solution to her dilemma: marry him and she could leave the marriage unconsummated if she wished. She could have his name and be free of her admirers. They were married by a lawyer the next morning.

Crowley had pretended to be uninterested in sex with Rose, but he could not pass up the opportunity to work his "sexual magic." In addition, there was something about Rose's mental weakness that appealed to the sadist in him and he couldn't help

In 1903, Crowley married the unstable sister of his friend George Kelly. Rose became pregnant a short time later, beginning a strange new era in Crowley's life.

but take advantage of her. Their decision to keep the marriage platonic lasted for only a few hours. He ravished her over and over again, much to his new bride's delight. However, Kelly and the rest of Rose's family were not happy about the marriage, which delighted Crowley, who loved drama of any sort. He took Rose to Paris and then they traveled on to Cairo, where they spent a night inside the Great Pyramid. In Ceylon, Crowley took his new wife hunting and he shot a bat, which fell onto Rose's head and dugs its claws into her hair. That night, Rose had a nightmare in which she was the bat, and clung to the frame of the mosquito netting over the bed. When Crowley tried to detach her from it, she howled, spat, scratched and bit at him. He later described it as "the finest case of obsession that I have ever had the good fortune to observe."

Soon after occurred the event that Crowley would call the most important in his life: Rose became pregnant. Her behavior, already bizarre, became even stranger. Crowley didn't blame hormones on her personality change, but stated that the spirits of the air that he had invoked for her benefit put her into a peculiar mood. She told him that she had offended the Egyptian god Horus, of whom, Crowley said, she knew nothing. In a museum, she showed him a statue of Ra-Hoor-Khuit, one of the forms of Horus, and he was impressed to find that the number of the exhibit was 666, the number of the Beast in the Biblical Book of Revelation. Rose, whom he began calling Ouarda, now began to instruct him on how to invoke Horus. The ritual did not seem to make sense, but he tried it anyway, and later claimed that it was a complete success. Horus allegedly told him that a new epoch was beginning, a statement that many other occultists also believed. Crowley was ordered to write and a "musical voice" from out of the corner of the room dictated *The Book of the Law* to him, assuring him that the volume would solve all religious problems and would be translated into many languages.

The Book of the Law, with its fundamental theme of "Do What Thou Wilt," became what Crowley considered one of his central pieces of writing. He attached enormous importance to it. It was his own bible and he was the chosen prophet. For the rest of his life, he began all of his letters with the assertion "Do what thou wilt shall be the whole of the Law." He believed that the old era of gods and demons was over and that a new epoch was beginning that would force man to stand on his own and come into his own power. Crowley saw himself as a potential new god, gradually coming to understand his own powers. The book became Crowley's major achievement, and when he had finished it, he likely felt that he had at last produced his masterpiece, a work that towered above everything that he had previously written, and one that was worth devoting his life to making known.

The next portion of Crowley's life was filled with anger and perhaps even madness. After he completed *The Book of the Law,* he wrote Mathers from Paris and told him that the Secret Chiefs had appointed him the head of the Order of the Golden Dawn. The letter was obviously meant to antagonize Mathers (Crowley said that he "declared war on him") and it succeeded. According to Crowley, malevolent magical currents swept from Mathers in Paris to Loch Ness, where he had taken Rose to give birth to their child. He believed Mathers was out to get him and was responsible for killing off his dogs and causing a workman to go insane and try to attack Rose. In response, Crowley invoked forty-nine demons, which Rose allegedly saw, and sent them off to torment Mathers. Soon, Rose gave birth to their daughter, who Crowley named Nuit Ma Ahathoor Hecate Sappho Jezebel Lilith.

After his daughter was born, Crowley returned to traveling. He took on another mountaineering expedition, this time to Kanchenjunga in Nepal, at 28,160 feet the world's third-highest mountain. In 1905, he led the group that attempted to scale the peak. His personality soon set the others on edge. After the party had reached a height of about 24,000 feet on the main peak, a conference was called to formally deposed Crowley as the leader of the team, thanks to his sadistically cruel treatment of the porters. One of the expedition members, noticing the porters were climbing the icy mountain barefoot, accused Crowley of failing to provide them with shoes, as he had agreed. Crowley insisted that he had given the "economical natives" footwear but they preferred to pack them away for future use rather than wear them "unless there is some serious reason for putting them on." Crowley refused to accept the demotion and the expedition was called off. Everyone but Crowley and a Swiss climber named Reymond started down the mountain toward the lower camps. There was a slip that set off an avalanche and all of them were swept down the mountain and buried under the snow. A few of the men managed to dig themselves out and called to Crowley to come and help as they searched for the porters and the other climbers, who later turned up dead. Reymond ran to help, but Crowley refused to leave his tent, where he was drinking tea.

Crowley traveled widely around the world, climbing mountings, experimenting with drugs and creating his unique magical philosophy.

That evening, he wrote a letter, which was later printed in English newspapers, commenting that he "was not over-anxious in the circumstances to render help. A mountain accident of this kind is one of the things for which I have no sympathy whatever." The next morning, he ascended the mountain, avoiding his former companions, and proceeded to Darjeeling by himself.

He went on to Calcutta, where he described an incident in which he was attacked in the street by a gang of thieves. Crowley claimed that he fired his revolver at them and then "made himself invisible." He explained that this was not literally true; it was simply that he possessed an odd power that caused a blank spot in the minds of those who were looking at him.

The next day, Rose and the baby arrived in India. Crowley had fallen out of love with her, he said, and had little interest in the child. Regardless, he took his family with him to China, where he tried opium for the first time. After four months, he sent Rose back to England by way of Calcutta, so that she could pick up some luggage they had left there. Crowley, meanwhile, returned through New York. When he arrived back in Liverpool, he learned that his daughter had died of typhoid in Rangoon.

Rose gave birth to another child not long after, Lola Zaza, who almost died of bronchitis soon after she was born. The birth and illness caused a permanent falling out with Rose's family and shortly after, his marriage to Rose came to an end. Rose became an alcoholic and later went insane. Strangely, this was a pattern that seemed to occur over and over again with people who became too intimate with Crowley.

Left to his own devices, Crowley began seeking disciples. His first was a man named Lord Tankerville and together, they traveled in Morocco and Spain. Tankerville footed the bill for these trips because Crowley's fortune was finally beginning to run out. They parted ways, but Crowley soon found another follower, a poet named Victor Neuberg. Crowley published more of his own poetry, a book praising himself called *The Star in the West*, and started a bi-annual journal about magic called *The Equinox*. Crowley also decided to start his own magical society, which he called the Silver Star and made use of some of the rituals from the Golden Dawn. He knighted himself, claiming that he had received the title in Spain and shaved his domed head. Rose was, by now, completely insane, and he divorced her.

In 1910, he discovered the use of mescalin and, probably with assistance from the drug, devised a series of seven rituals, which he called the Rites of Eleusis. He hired a hall for their performance on seven successive Wednesdays. Admission was five guineas and the aim of the rituals, he said, was to induce religious ecstasy. Crowley's mistress, Austrian violinist Leila Waddell, provided musical accompaniment for them. Newspapers and magazines were harshly critical of the performances and one magazine even devoted three

As Crowley began attracting disciples, he shaved his head to attain a more sinister air.

issues to attack Crowley personally. This was the beginning of what Crowley referred to as the "persecution" that plagued him until his death in 1947.

At the same time, he began having trouble with his former friend Samuel Mathers again. Crowley was being sued to try and stop the publication of the third issue of his magic journal, *The Equinox*, because it contained a full description of the secret rites of the Golden Dawn, which Crowley had taken an oath never to reveal. The judge found in favor of Mathers but Crowley later claimed that he performed a series of magic rituals and appealed the case. This time, he won. The issue was published and Mather's secrets were revealed, affording Crowley a small bit of revenge.

Crowley was now beginning to fear that the high point in his life was over. His existence was becoming a series of repetitive events – magical ceremonies, mistresses, frantic efforts to raise money, and newspaper attacks on him, followed by attempts to justify himself in the press. But everything changed in 1912, when Crowley met German occultist and Ordo Templi Orientis leader Theodor Reuss. At first, Reuss was angry with Crowley because he had revealed in his *The Book of Lies* that sex could be used magically. When he realized that Crowley's revealing of the secret had been inadvertent, he authorized him to set up his own branch of the O.T.O., an idea that Crowley heartily embraced. He launched his branch of the order by sodomizing disciple Victor Neuberg as part of a magical ceremony in 1913.

Crowley's need for debauchery now had an outlet and he began practicing sex magic (or "magick" as he began to call it) with a new diligence. One of his companions in this was a friend of Isadora Duncan's, Mary D'Este Sturges. They rented a villa in Italy for a lengthy bout of rituals. He also took a troupe of chorus girls, the Ragged Ragtime Girls, to Moscow and became involved in a violent affair with a young woman who needed to be beaten in order to achieve sexual satisfaction. Crowley claimed this was his first relationship of this kind, but it was not the last. He developed a taste for sadism and began incorporating it into his rituals.

He continued to irritate the British press and opened a Satanic Temple in a studio on London's Fulham Road. The newspapers had a field day, especially after an American journalist was allowed to visit the Temple and wrote an article about the number of rich British women who frequented it. Crowley had filed his two canine teeth to a sharp point and when he met women, he was inclined to give them the "serpent's kiss," biting them on the wrist, and occasionally the throat, with his fangs. He also developed a new kink: defecating on carpets. He explained to one man, who was offended that Crowley had done this in his home, that his waste was sacred, like that of the Dalai Lama.

When World War I broke out, Crowley, now age thirty-nine, was caught in Switzerland. He claimed that he tried to get the British government to employ him as a spy, but was refused. He decided to go to America and after a year of unsuccessful magical activities (apparently the Americans were not yet ready for Crowley's version of weird), he developed a new role: the anti-British Irishman. He was not, of course, Irish, and had never been to Ireland, but this didn't matter to him. He made a speech at the foot of the Statue of Liberty and tore up what he claimed was his British passport. After this, he began to write anti-British propaganda for a German-leaning newspaper; a bit of treason that he later explained was actually to help the British cause during the war. He said that he tried to make his propaganda so absurd that it would provoke the opposite effect. The British were not impressed, but dismissed Crowley as a man looking for attention who would do anything to keep his name before the public. But was this the truth? Some researchers don't think so, nor do they accept Crowley's later version of events. They believe that he was becoming increasingly disgusted with England, a country from which he felt that he had been exiled and rejected. He had never

Crowley and his magical symbols

been given any recognition at home and he struck out in the only way that he could.

Crowley described his period in America as a time of poverty and humiliation. Humiliated or not, he managed to live quite well in the states. A report in a New York newspaper, *The Evening World*, described a fairly luxurious studio in Washington Square, most likely provided for him by his followers. Crowley was an expert at cadging money from his disciples. American writer on witchcraft and voodoo, William Seabrook, who was introduced to Crowley, said that Crowley had a retinue of followers and disciples around him at all times. He witnessed several of the group's rituals and admitted that some of the invocations were "quite beautiful." Seabrook also remarked that Crowley seemed to be a "man of power" and a person of great inner strength. He recalled that Crowley would eat and drink until he became bloated and then starve himself down to a healthy weight again. Seabrook recounted an amusing story of how Crowley one day announced that he was going off to spend forty days and

Author William Seabrook

nights in the wilderness. Seabrook and some other friends decided to fund his trip, since Crowley was broke. They gave him some money and found him a canoe and a tent. When they went to see him off, they discovered that he had spent all of the money they had given him on huge cans of red paint and rope. He told them that, like the prophet Elijah, he would be fed by the ravens. Crowley spent the forty days and nights painting in huge red letters on the cliffs south of Kingston the inscriptions EVERY MAN AND WOMAN IS A STAR and, of course, DO WHAT THOU WILT SHALL BE THE WHOLE OF THE LAW. He was fed by local farmers, who periodically brought him eggs, milk and sweet corn. He returned to New York after his time in the "wilderness" looking healthy and well.

Seabrook told another story about Crowley, an incident that marked one of the strangest examples of his powers. After his return to New York, Crowley told Seabrook that he had gained strength during his time away and Seabrook asked for a demonstration of this. Crowley took him along Fifth Avenue, on a sparsely populated stretch of the sidewalk, and fell into step with a man, walking behind him and imitating his walk. Suddenly, Crowley buckled at the knees, squatted on his haunches for a moment and then stood upright again. At the same time, the man in front of him collapsed onto the pavement as his own knees gave out. Seabrook and Crowley helped him to his feet and the man nervously went on his way, unable to explain why he had fallen. Was this a real example of Crowley possessing a supernatural power? Was it merely the power of suggestion? Or did Crowley imply stage the event for the benefit of Seabrook, who he knew would write about it and generate publicity for the charismatic cult leader?

Towards the end of his time in America, Crowley discovered yet another "Scarlet Woman." An acquaintance named Renata Faesi called on him one day in the company of her younger sister, Leah, a thin, not very attractive girl with a wide mouth, strangely sharp teeth, a bony, angular body and no breasts to speak of. But something almost magnetic occurred when she and Crowley saw one another. Crowley immediately seized Leah and began to kiss her violently, much to Renata's astonishment. Within hours, Leah was agreeing to be painted in the nude and Crowley created a ghoulish picture that he called "Dead Souls." In due course, Leah, whom Crowley called Alostrael and The Ape of Thoth, in reference to the companion of the god Tahuti, who enabled his ideas to become reality, became pregnant.

In December 1919, Crowley finally returned to England, but was not happy there. He now suffered from asthma and bronchitis every winter and his periodic indulgence in all kinds of drugs, from mescalin to hashish, cocaine and opium, had lowered his physical resistance to the British cold and dampness.

He had lost many of his English friends and contacts during the war. His former disciple, Victor Neuberg, had married and settled down, but he remained obsessed with Crowley for the rest of his life. Crowley had cursed him when they separated before the war and Neuberg was very nervous for years after, blaming a number of health problems on Crowley's incantations. There was no one else in London from whom Crowley could get money, but as luck would have it, he received a fairly large sum of money around this time and decided to leave England for a warmer climate. Crowley and Leah found a farmhouse in Sicily and were accompanied there by a Ninette Shumway, who doubled as a nursemaid and also Crowley's mistress; Ninette's young son, Hermes, and two children that Crowley had with Leah: a boy named Dionysus and a newborn girl named Anne Leah. Crowley, now in his middle forties, seemed to have developed a few normal human feelings. He wrote of his family: "I love Alostrael; she is all my comfort, my support, my soul's desire, my life's reward..." He also expressed deep affection toward Anne Leah, whose health had been feeble since the time she was born.

One of Crowley's "Scarlet Women"

At first, life in Sicily was idyllic, with swimming in the ocean, long hours of meditation and magical sex rituals. Crowley covered the walls of the farmhouse with paintings of people having sex in every position, and painted his studio, which he called the Chamber of Nightmares, with pictures of demons. He became convinced that one could only free one's self from the need for drugs by taking them freely so piles of cocaine were left around the house for anyone to take and Crowley arranged for opium was supplied to him by a trader from the mainland.

The only thing that seemed to spoil the scene was the jealousy of his two "Scarlet Women." One peace-shattering incident occurred on the day that the sun entered the sign of Taurus (April 20, 1920). Crowley celebrated the event with a sex ritual in which both women participated. In the middle of the proceedings a violent argument broke out between Leah and Ninette and the latter, bursting into tears, snatched up a cloak to cover her nakedness and ran out into the dark, rainy night. Crowley wandered all over looking for her, afraid that she had fallen over one of the nearby cliffs. After calling her name for almost an hour, he found her and dragged her back to the house. Meanwhile, Leah had opened a bottle of brandy and was now raging drunk. She cursed at Ninette when Crowley brought her back and the fight started all over again. Crowley managed to get Ninette to go to bed and then Leah, as if to have the last word, vomited and passed out.

Crowley tried hard to convince the two women that possessiveness was an evil, and that they should rise above such a trivial thing, but they were unconvinced. However, they continued to take part in his magic sex rites, including one ceremony when Leah allowed herself to be penetrated by a goat. The animal's throat was then cut as a sacrifice.

Visitors, both disciples and curiosity-seekers, began to arrive at the Sicily farmhouse, which Crowley had dubbed the Abbey of Theleme. American film star Elizabeth Fox was among the first visitors. Crowley looked forward to introducing her to sex magick, but she turned out to be a disappointment. The mathematician J.N.W. Sullivan arrived with his wife, Sylvia. He found he liked Crowley and staying up talking with him all night. Sylvia liked him too and stayed on for another day to practice sex rituals after her husband left. But life at the Abbey was becoming too complicated with personal issues, arguments and tragedies – something that visitors were becoming aware of. Crowley's daughter, Anne Leah, died after a long illness and Crowley was shattered. Soon after, a young American, an ex-naval officer named Godwin, arrived and Crowley named him Brother Fiat Lux. The strain of life around Crowley and his mistresses became too much for him after another disciple, Australian businessman Frank Bennett, arrived at the Abbey. Crowley asked Godwin to let Bennett have his room. This resulted in a violent argument. Godwin returned to America with the sanity that he had left and in 1931, he founded the Chortonzon Club, which was named for a demon. Godwin rejected Crowley's magic rituals and invented his own type of sex magic, which involved sexual intercourse that would be continued indefinitely without orgasm. The aim of it was to produce long and drawn-out ecstasy and intoxication. Godwin operated in California for many years.

Another rebellious Crowley disciple was Jack Parsons, a brilliant rocket scientist who was obsessed with the sexual side of ritual magic. He was an early follower of Crowley but went on to become fascinated with the idea of incarnating the Whore of Babylon, described in the Book of Revelation. He believed this creature would be the bride of the Antichrist and the Mother of All Abominations. His chosen method of doing this was known as "Babylon Working," which essentially involved him impregnating his mistress, the actress Marjorie Cameron, under occult conditions. Parsons hoped that the resulting "moonchild" would be the Whore's incarnation on earth. Parsons collaborated with L. Ron Hubbard, the founder of Scientology, in the magical exercises that followed, which included Parsons having sex with Cameron while Hubbard "magically" described what was happening on the astral plane. Parsons claimed that his "Left-Hand Path" magic had been successful in creating the child, but there is no evidence to substantiate this claim. Increasingly identified with the Beast 666, in his later years Parsons legally changed his name to Belarion Armiluss Al Dajjal Antichrist. He was killed in a mysterious lab explosion in 1952.

Crowley disciple, Frank Bennett

But Crowley did succeed with some of his disciples, especially Frank Bennett. Like Crowley, Bennett had lived through a repressive childhood. When Crowley explained to him that the sexual organs were the image of God, and the best way to free the hidden powers of the subconscious mind was through sexual magic, Bennett found the revelation so startling that he ran out into the ocean and began to swim frantically up and down the beach. After further discussion that same night, he walked barefoot into the mountains. Then, after a day of bewilderment, he lapsed into a trance-like state of pure delight as he began to grasp the idea of allowing the subconscious to free itself. After all of this, Bennett departed and went back to Australia, filled with the gospel of the "Beast."

Crowley's health and financial status began to suffer. The doses of heroin that he had begun to take would have killed a normal man. Periodically, he would force himself to go "cold turkey," going without all drugs for days. After a period of intense depression and misery, he would begin to paint and write again with his old excitement. He always returned to the drugs, though, claiming that he could take them or leave them however he wanted. The result was long periods of listlessness and increasing insomnia, which troubled him for years. In addition to his drug problem, he was broke again. In Sicily, there were no rich disciples to sponge off; on the contrary, his steady stream of visitors sapped his finances. J.N.W. Sullivan suggested that he write his memoirs, but Crowley wanted to write a novel first and managed to get a small advance for a book called *Diary of a Drug Fiend*. The novel was about an aristocratic couple that became slaves to heroin, met Crowley, retired to his Abbey, and were miraculously cured. The book appeared in 1922 and was violently attacked by newspapers that revealed that the Abbey was a real place and denounced Crowley as a seducer of young people. Crowley was not entirely displeased by the publicity, but the publisher allowed the book to go out of print and balked at the idea of publishing Crowley's autobiography, even though he had been given a good-sized advance.

While in London for the release of his book, Crowley met an enthusiastic, but slightly unbalanced, young man named Raoul Loveday, who was married to a pretty model. Loveday had read Crowley's works, and within hours, he was an enthusiastic disciple. When Crowley returned to Sicily, Loveday and his wife, Betty May, followed. Loveday's wife had strong misgivings about Crowley. She hated the Abbey, hated the food, the lack of bathrooms, the obscene paintings, and most of all, her husband's total infatuation with Crowley.

Loveday's stay at the abbey lasted three months – and ended with his death. Both he and Crowley came down with the same ailment, similar to hepatitis, caused by bad water. In February 1923, Crowley decided that a cat should be sacrificed. He hated cats and chose one to kill that had scratched him badly when he threw it out of a room. Allegedly, he found the animal in a pantry and made the sign of a pentagram over it with his staff, and ordered it to stay there until the hour of sacrifice. Crowley claimed that the animal never moved. Even when Betty May took it somewhere else in the house, it came back to the same spot, petrified and refusing food. Loveday was selected to perform the sacrifice. The cat was placed on an altar, incense was lit, and incantations

Raoul and Betty May Loveday

were performed for two hours. Finally, Loveday slashed the animal's throat with a knife, but the cut was too shallow and the cat ran from the room. It was captured and slain and then Loveday was made to drink a cup of its blood. He subsequently collapsed and was taken to his bed. Crowley consulted his horoscope and predicted that Loveday was going to die, on February 16.

A number of terrible arguments with Betty May followed. One day, she stormed out of the Abbey after calling Ninette a whore, but returned the next day at her husband's request. On February 16th – the day that Crowley had predicted – Loveday died. Betty May was stunned and recalled that on their wedding day, he had dropped the ring as he was about to put it onto her finger, a bad omen. She also remembered a photograph of the two of them that had been taken at St. John's College, Oxford, in which the ghostly outline of a young man appeared, his arms stretched out over his head. This was the same position that Loveday had been in when he died.

Betty May departed Sicily and returned to England, where she gave newspaper interviews about her disastrous visit to the abbey. The British public was both shocked and delighted with more gossip about the infamous Crowley. More newspaper attacks followed and by the time they appeared, Crowley was also taken ill with the same sickness that had killed Loveday. He was semi-conscious for three weeks before slowly recovering. But the adverse publicity over Loveday's death had its effect on the new ruler of Italy. A short time later, Mussolini ordered Crowley to vacate the abbey and leave the country.

Once again, a strange turn of events saved Crowley from poverty and homelessness. Norman Mudd, a young man who had known Crowley since 1907 at Cambridge came back into his life. Mudd had been introduced to the Beast through Neuberg but when Crowley's unsavory reputation and pornographic books got him kicked out of the college where he was a student, their friendship cooled. Mudd had become a professor of mathematics in South Africa, but was unable to forget about Crowley. As Crowley was being attacked by the British press, and being kicked out of Sicily, Mudd appeared at the abbey, presented Crowley with his life savings, and begged to be accepted as his disciple.

Crowley moved to Tunis, hoping that the Italian government would change its mind. Leah went with him, as well as his five-year-old son, who reportedly smoked cigarettes all day long and declared that he would become the Beast when his father died. Ninette had borne Crowley another daughter, and Crowley's horoscope for the child ended with the prediction, "She is likely to develop into a fairly ordinary little whore." Norman Mudd accompanied the party and he and Leah became lovers, a development that Crowley did not mind. He was too preoccupied with recovering his health, and with his drug addiction, which he realized he was unable to shake.

When Crowley became bored, he abandoned the group and went to Paris, leaving Leah and Mudd to starve in Tunis. Crowley was faring no better in the City of Lights. He was drug-addled and wandered the city in a daze.

Eventually, he was kicked out of the hotel where he was living on credit. Leah and Mudd followed him to Paris and then Mudd moved on to London, where he took refuge at the Metropolitan Asylum for the Homeless Poor. Crowley and Leah stayed together for a few months, but Crowley was growing tired of her and her inability to survive under any conditions, as he was able to do. When a rich American woman named Dorothy Olsen fell under his spell, Crowley named her his new "Scarlet Woman," and deserted Leah. Leah's sister, Renata, had already taken her son from her to America. Instead of being grateful, Leah was furious and hysterical. Mudd returned to her and they lived on the streets of Paris together while Crowley and his new mistress traveled in North America.

Both Leah and Mudd became bitter about Crowley, although there was nothing to stop them from finding work and continuing a life together. But Crowley's abandonment of them seemed to break something inside of the pair. Leah worked as a prostitute for a while, then as a waitress. Mudd remained in a state of despair but even after all that had happened his main concern seemed to be whether or not Crowley would remain faithful to *The Book of the Law*. Crowley's new lover soon ran out of money after a few months of supporting him in the luxurious style to which he was accustomed and had to write to friends in America to borrow money.

But Crowley, once again, had another stroke of incredible luck. Theodor Reuss, his old friend from the Ordo Templi Orientis, died and his successor turned to Crowley as one of the elite members of the Order. The O.T.O. paid off all of Crowley's debts in Paris, and even gave money to Dorothy Olsen, Mudd and Leah. Both Mudd and Leah eventually grew to hate Crowley, and Leah wrote him a letter renouncing her vow of obedience to him. What eventually happened to her is unknown. In 1934, Mudd committed suicide by drowning himself in the Channel Islands. He closed the bottom of his pants with bicycle clips and then filled them with rocks as he walked into the sea.

Crowley still enjoyed his reputation as the "wickedest man in the world", but this was a double-edged sword for him. He loved the infamy, but it meant that no major publisher would touch the autobiography that he had been working on. Eventually, a small press put out the book, but they were unable to get bookstores to place orders for it.

Crowley and Maria Teresa de Miramar, who he married in 1929. She, like so many others who passed through his life, later went insane.

In 1929, Crowley was ordered to leave France. He tried to go back to England but his two chief disciples, an American secretary that he called "The Serpent" and his latest mistress, Maria Teresa de Miramar, were not allowed to enter Britain. It was to get Maria into England that Crowley took the startling step of marrying her in August 1929. He was due to lecture at Oxford in early 1930, but found himself banned from the college. He tried to present an exhibition of his paintings at a rented house in Langham Place, but bad newspaper publicity caused the owner to cancel his lease. His marriage to Maria became a series of vicious arguments and was soon fell apart, but there were plenty of other women who wanted to be his "Scarlet Woman."

Crowley took a new mistress, a 19 year old German girl named Hanni, which he called "The Monster". They went to Lisbon together but Hanni soon became disenchanted with Crowley and his sex magic rituals. She deserted him and returned to Berlin. To be abandoned was a new, and shattering experience, for the Beast. He pursued the girl to Berlin and a reconciliation took place. Before leaving, he left a suicide note at the top of Hell's Mouth, a high cliff, and the result was a flattering uproar in the world's press, which delighted in the fact that the "world's wickedest man" had taken his own life. But after lying low in Berlin for a few days, Crowley attended the opening of an exhibition of his paintings, ending the speculation about his "death". Hanni became Crowley's magical assistant and Crowley maintained that she became a skilled "scryer" and once saw the Devil's face looking up at her from inside of a crystal. Their sex magic was so successful that she became pregnant, but she left him soon after.

Crowley's wife, Maria, went insane and was hospitalized for the rest of her life. At least one Crowley biographer claims that Hanni also went insane. While some might claim a supernatural cause behind the reports of insanity and suicide connected to those who were close to Crowley, there is a simpler explanation. Crowley's powerful, dominant personality attracted people to him who were much weaker than he was, and in many cases, already mentally unstable. Crowley's rejection and abandonment, or perhaps simply their exposure to his magical rituals, often sent them over the edge and drove them to suicide and into asylums.

As far as magic is concerned, the remainder of Crowley's life was anticlimactic. In the 1930s, Crowley became involved in a court case against his old friend Nina Hammett. He got a taste for litigation when he saw a copy of his novel *Moonchild* displayed in a bookstore window with a sign next to it stating that an earlier novel (*Diary of a Drug Fiend*) had been withdrawn from publication after a newspaper attack. This was not true, it had simply gone out of print. Crowley sued the bookseller and received a small settlement.

This legal victory gave him the idea to raise money by suing Nina Hammett, a Soho personality who had referred to Crowley as a "black magician" in her autobiography. She had raised the idea, only to dismiss it and hinted that a baby (possibly used as a sacrifice) had disappeared from the Abbey. Crowley knew that Hammett had no money, but her publisher, Constable & Co., certainly did, and they would have to pay. Whether he expected to win the case, or merely thought that it would garner him more publicity remains a matter for speculation but he hired the lawyers to pursue it. Unfortunately, none of his friends would appear for the defense and his attorneys warned him that if the courts got a look at any of his pornographic writings, the case would be thrown out of court. As it turned out, things never got that far. When several witnesses appeared on the stand and described Crowley's magical activities, the judge halted the case and declared that he had "never heard of such dreadful, horrible, blasphemous and abominable stuff as that which has been produced by a man who describes himself as the greatest living poet in the world." The jury found against Crowley and he was bankrupted, although he really had no assets anyway. The publicity for the case, though, was absolutely tremendous – and that might have been just what Crowley wanted in the first place.

Crowley spent his last days living in a boarding house called Netherwood at the Ridge, Hastings. Photographs of him from the years after World War II show a thing old gentleman, dressed in tweeds, smoking a pipe and looking more like a retired British military man than one of the infamous men in history. He was a bored, lonely old man who was more interested in heroin than food. He lived until 1947 on the generosity of old friends and fading disciples, who couldn't bear to see the Great Beast starve during his final days on earth. He continued, as he had throughout his life, to impose on the kindness of friends, taking whatever he desired from them. The irate wife of one of his disciples pointed out to him in a letter that he had spent £15,000 of her money on expensive cigars, cognac, cocktails, taxis, dinners, and mistresses and concluded "God Almighty himself would not be as arrogant as you have been, and that is one of the causes of all of your troubles". And she was right. Until the very end of his life, Crowley possessed a withering arrogance, a lofty view of his own value that paled in comparison to the admiration that even his most devoted followers felt toward him. This explained why he could so easily turn on faithful disciples like Norman Mudd and his mistress, Leah, totally convinced in his own mind that some action of theirs had forfeited their rights to his divine presence.

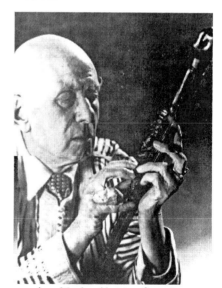

An elderly Aleister Crowley

But there were positive aspects to Aleister Crowley, as well. It cannot be denied that, no matter what his shortcomings, his over-the-top self-promotion, his haughty arrogance and his exaggeration (or perhaps outright lies) about his true magical abilities, Crowley managed to change the entire course of occult history with his ideas, theories, sex rituals and by the fact that he existed at all.

It seems almost tragic to say that he died from something as common as pneumonia on December 5, 1947. He was seventy-two years old at the time and unrepentant about his life of sin and scandal. The novelist Louis Wilkinson read aloud Crowley's *Hymn to Pan* at the funeral service, as gleefully and shamelessly as Crowley might have expected it to be read for such an occasion. According to author Colin Wilson, the Brighton City Council angrily stated that it would take steps to see that such an incident was never, ever repeated again.

It was a fitting, scandalous end for the "wickedest man in the world."

AUSTIN OSMAN SPARE

Less known than Aleister Crowley, but equally respected in some sexual occult circles, was the artist Austin Osman Spare. Spare's particular brand of sex magic centered largely around masturbation, which would summon forth "sigils," elemental spirits who would copulate amongst themselves, breeding more astral beings. Many of his techniques involved the use of automatic writing and automatic drawing, which captured the relationship that he believed existed between the conscious and unconscious self.

Spare was born in Snow Hill, London, on December 30, 1886. He was the son of a retired London policeman and the fourth of five children. According to his mother, he began to develop his artistic abilities when he was only four years old. His parents enrolled him in evening classes at Lambeth Art School and at fourteen, he won a county council scholarship and one of his drawings was selected for inclusion in the British Art Section at the Paris International Exhibition of 1899. A year later, he left school and began designing advertising posters and working in stained glass. One of his glass designs led to his being recommended for a scholarship at the Royal College of Art, where he began his formal studies. Shortly thereafter, his father convinced him to send two of his drawings to the Royal Academy for consideration and one of them was accepted. At the age of only sixteen, an exhibition of his work at the academy created something of a sensation.

Austin Osman Spare

In October 1907, Spare had his first major commercial exhibition at the Bruton Gallery in London's West End. The content was striking, but arcane and grotesque, causing great controversy. These elements in his work appealed to the British intellectual set and brought him to the attention of the infamous Aleister Crowley. The two became acquaintances and Spare was named as a probationary member of Crowley's Silver Star order, which had been founded by Crowley and George Cecil Jones. Spare contributed several drawings to Crowley's periodical, the *Equinox*, and at least one photograph exists that shows a young Spare with his hands held parallel at the sides of his face in the same pose that Crowley himself adopted in the famous 1910 photo with book, hat and robe. Whatever the nature of the two men's relationship, it was apparently short-lived.

In September 1911, Spare married the actress Eily Gertrude Shaw, but the union did not last long, although it was never formally dissolved. Around this same time, Spare began to grow more interested in the esoteric and the occult. A self-published book that appeared in 1913, called *The Book of Pleasure*, was conceived initially as a pictorial allegory but quickly evolved into a deeper work, drawing inspiration from Taoism and Buddhism, and from Spare's own experiences as an artist.

In 1917, during the World War I, Spare was conscripted into the British army, and served as a medical orderly for the Royal Medical Corps in London Hospitals. In 1919, his notoriety as an artist earned him a commission as an official war artist. In this capacity, he visited the battlefields of France and created a number of striking pieces of art depicting the horrors of war. Spare later said that his stint on the battlefields "pushed me into the abstract world --- and there I have more or less remained."

After the war, Spare began to develop his sex magic system, which he called Kiaism. The ideas for it were unique and could not be traced back to other traditions. The system first appeared in his book *Earth Inferno* and involved masturbation rituals that could be used to summon male and female earth spirits who would have intercourse with one another. By binding these elementals, Spare could "activate" them and give them a specific purpose. Spare stated that the supreme state of "kia" was "the absolute freedom which being free is mighty enough to be "reality" and free at any time: therefore is not potential or manifest (except as its instant possibility) by ideas of freedom or "means," but by the Ego being free to receive it, by being free of ideas about it and by not believing." Unfortunately, his definition makes little sense – something that Spare seemed to be aware of. He continually insisted that "kia" was indefinable and any definition would make it even more obscure.

Spare also designed a set of hieroglyphic-like letters that he called the "Sacred Alphabet," simplified forms of the sigils used in his sex magic that could be composed for expressing a desire. This first appeared in his volume, *A Book of Satyrs,* and he later designed a pack of playing cards in which each card in the deck bore a variation of one of the letters of the "Sacred Alphabet."

Some of Spare's techniques, particularly the use of sigils and his alphabet system became the cornerstone of the movement that is loosely referred to as "Chaos Magic." This type of magic was first formulated in the 1970s. Through a variety of techniques of ceremonial magic, practitioners believe that they can change both their subjective experience and objective reality. Although there are a few techniques unique to chaos magic, it is often highly individualistic and borrows liberally from other belief systems. The only thing about that never changes is that central belief that the power of the magic is the most important tool.

In the years that followed, Spare became increasingly unhappy with society and by 1927, had taken a public stance about his disgust with human nature. Many believe that his exposure to the brutality of war, combined with his financial instability, failing ventures, and hostile reviews for his work led to this state of affairs. Whatever the cause, Spare's loathing for humanity was clearly expressed in his final book, in which he railed, "Dogs, devouring your own vomit! Cursed are ye all! Throwbacks, adulterers, sycophants, corpse devourers, pilferers and medicine swallowers! Think ye Heaven is an infirmary?"

In 1941, a fire caused destroyed Spare's apartment, leaving him injured and deprived of his home and his studio. For the next three years, he struggled to regain the use of his arms until finally, in 1946, in a cramped basement flat, he was able to paint again. At the time, he could not even afford a bed to sleep on. He worked strictly for cash, charging only £5 per picture, his former fame and notoriety forgotten.

Spare was sixty-nine when he died in 1956, a lonely old man whose real fame was to come nearly two decades later when his techniques for sex magic were adopted by a popular form of magic that is still in use today.

SAMAEL AUN WEOR

Another type of sex magic, which differs from that performed by Aleister Crowley, Jack Parsons and others states that "sexual sublimation" should be used to transform sexual energy into creativity and a mystical awakening. In psychology, sublimation is the transference of sexual energy into a physical act or a different emotion in order to avoid confrontation with the sexual urge. It is based on the belief that sexual energy, human beings' creative function, can be used to create a spiritual nature instead of being unleashed.

The best-known proponent of this type of magic was Samael Aun Weor and the main objective of his teachings, which he called "white sexual magic," was to conclude the act of intercourse without an orgasm or

Samael Aun Weor

ejaculation from either the man or the woman. That way, instead of sexual energy being released in a spasm, the energy would transform through will power and the sacrifice of desire. According to Weor, the magnetic properties created by crossing the active and passive creative organs (the penis and the uterus) could cause lunar, solar and paranormal currents to flow through the couple. The current would then provide an active connection between the magnetic center at the root of the nose and solar and lunar principals located within the "chakras" of the human body. The energy, through will power, would ignite and cause the crystallization of the "solar bodies" that were formed due to the transformation that occurred through the white sexual magic. The "solar bodies" were the vehicles of emotion, mind and will. Weor taught and believed that, through sexual magic, the radical removal of one's ego could be achieved. By eliminating the ego, which contained the inferior and animalistic vehicles of emotion, mind and will, a person could be elevated to the angelic state and beyond.

Weor asserted that when a person reached orgasm, his atoms were expelled and replaced, via "genital orgasmic contraction," with impure atoms of fornication. Those atoms would be rejected by the higher powers and would be forced downward into the human body, replicating the fail of Satan. The repetition of this act would cause a person to become disconnected from the formation of "solar bodies." Weor referred to any type of sexual magic that used orgasm for spiritual or magical purposes as black sexual magic, and those that performed it as black magicians, intent on acquiring negative powers.

Samael Aun Weor was born on March 6, 1917 as Victor Manuel Gomez Rodriguez in Bogota, Columbia. His childhood and family life are mostly unknown, although he was known to have had at least one brother. Weor would later claim that he was born with an awakened consciousness and that he was analyzing his previous lives before he was able to walk. At the age of seventeen, he was asked to lecture at the local chapter of the Theosophical Society, and a year later was admitted into the occult society Fraternitas Rosicruciana Antiqua. Weor methodically studied the entire Rosicrucian library and it was during this time that he allegedly learned the secret of white sexual magic, the profoundly veiled sexual key which, according to Weor, underpins all of the world's great religions.

From the middle 1930s to 1950, little is known about Weor. It is believed that he became a spiritual vagabond of sorts, having no home or income. During this time, he claimed to live with a tribe of Indians in Northern Columbia, learning the healing secrets that later formed the theories behind his medical book, *Occult Medicine and Practical Magic*. It was at this point he claimed to first become aware of his "Inner Being," called "Aun Weor," a name that he would later adopt.

Although he was briefly married once before, in the early 1940s he met Mistress Genie Litelantes (the chosen name of Arnolda Garro Mora), who, during their thirty-five years of marriage, became his collaborator and the mother of his four children.

In 1948, Weor began teaching to a small group of students and in 1950, under the name "Aun Weor." he published *The Perfect Matrimony of Kinder, or The Door to Enter into Initiation*. The book, later called *The Perfect Matrimony*, claimed to unveil the secret of sexuality as the cornerstone of the world's great religions. In the book, Weor wrote of subjects like sexual transmutation, sex magic and tantra. The candid manner of his writing was met with disdain by the general public at the time and the book was seen as both immoral and obscene. Weor was incarcerated several times but while in jail, he continued to write books, eventually completing more than 60 volumes. Around this same time, he and his growing number of followers built the Sumum Supremum

Sanctuarium, an "underground temple" in the Sierra Nevada Mountains of Mexico.

By 1960, Weor had developed the Universal Gnostic Movement, based on "Gnosis," the Greek word for knowledge. The movement was not a new one, but the resurgence of a very old sect that had appeared at the beginning of the Christian era and was considered heresy by the Church fathers. The movement struggled for many years after attacks by evangelical Christians and others. Branches of it still remain active today.

Weor continued to publish new books throughout the 1960s, offering a wide range of topics like astrology, the Kaballah, flying saucers and esoteric symbolism that could be found in Wagner's operas. He also wrote a number of sociopolitical commentaries in book form on Marxism, Leninism and on conspiracies involving large corporations, crime organizations, the anti-Jewish "*Protocols of the Elders of Zion*" and a volume on Gnostic anthropology that attacked Darwin and his "henchmen."

In the early 1970s, he began work on one of the most important vehicles of his doctrine, *The Pistas Sophia Unveilved*, in which he studied, verse by verse, the extremely esoteric Gnostic text, *The Pistas Sophia*. Despite the many titles that he wrote, Weor never received any income from his work. In 1976, he renounced all of the copyrights on them in an effort to make them more widely available to the public. Although copyrights were later restored to his wife to prevent bad translations, Weor always wanted them to be sold very cheaply so that even the poorest people would be able to afford them.

Weor developed stomach cancer in 1977, but he continued to speak at events and give radio and television interviews for several months after he was diagnosed. Eventually, he had to stop due to severe pain. He died on December 24, 1977, bringing an end to the sex magic philosophies of this unique and brilliant man.

3. SEX AND THE DEVIL
THE SUPERNATURAL SIDE OF SATANISM AND BLACK WITCHCRAFT

Sex, Satanism and witchcraft have been closely tied to together for centuries. Dating back to the trials of the Middle Ages, accused witches were often said to have had intercourse with the Devil as part of their pact with Satan, who gave them their evil powers. In most cases, though, it should be noted that witchcraft and Satanism are two very different things. While they have become synonymous in popular culture over the years, they actually constitute two vastly divergent philosophies. It cannot be denied that the two have been blended in many ways over the years, but their respective practitioners are well aware of the distinction between the two.

Witchcraft had its origins in primitive nature worship and was a means by which man sought to control the forces of nature and the elemental forces of both the visible and invisible world. In essence, the power of witchcraft had always been the effective exercise of mind over matter, although it was often carried out by way of potions, spells, rituals and ceremonies, which were used to focus the energy in achieving the wants and needs of the witch.

ANTON LAVEY'S SATANISM

Satanism has always been something else entirely from witchcraft, although one recent form of Satanism is much closer to the practice of witchcraft than it is to traditional satanic worship. This recent type is usually referred to as "Laveyan Satanism" and its followers are generally atheists or agnostics who believe that Satan is simply a metaphor for the natural urges of mankind. The name for these symbolic Satanists is taken from that of Anton LaVey, the founder of the Church of Satan, who began publicizing the old Crowley motto of "Do What Thou Wilt" in the 1960s.

The Church of Satan was built entirely by the sheer force of LaVey's dynamic personality. He was a writer, occultist, musician, actor, and bona fide showman. He was brilliant, always controversial, and, in the end, more than a bit of a mystery since his autobiography was so mixed with legend that it's almost impossible to separate fantasy from the truth.

He was born Howard Stanton Levey in Chicago on April 11, 1930. His father, Michael Levey, was a liquor distributor from Omaha. His mother, Gertrude, was a homemaker. The family later relocated to the San Francisco Bay area and young Levey spent most of his early life in California. From his Eastern European grandmother, young Howard learned much about the superstitions that were rampant in her part of the world, which led to his interest in vampires, witchcraft and the occult. He became an avid reader of dark literature and pulp magazines and later befriended writers of the day, like Clark Ashton Smith, Robert Barber Johnson and George Hass. According to his biography, he began developing his musical skills at an early age and tried his hand at various instruments, including the pipe organ and the calliope.

Anton LaVey

LaVey dropped out of high school and began working in circuses and carnivals, first as a roustabout and cage cleaner, and later as a musician. He learned the ropes in the spook shows and became well versed in the rackets to separate the rubes from their money. He played the calliope for the "grind shows" on Saturday nights and played the organ on Sunday mornings for the tent revivals. He later noted seeing many of the same men attending both the strip shows on Saturday night and the church services on Sunday mornings, which reinforced his cynical view of religion.

When the carnival season ended, LaVey began earning a living playing the organ in Los Angeles bars, lounges, nightclubs and burlesque theaters. It was during this time that he claimed to have a brief affair with then-unknown actress Marilyn Monroe.

Moving back to San Francisco, LaVey worked as a police photographer for a time and a short time later, met and married Carole Lansing, who bore him his first daughter, Karla Maritza, in 1952. They divorced in 1960 after LaVey began seeing Diane Hegarty. They never married, but she was his companion for many years, and bore his second daughter, Zeena Galatea LaVey in 1964. LaVey's final companion was Blanche Barton, who gave him his only son, Satan Xerxes Carnacki LaVey in 1993. Barton became the head of the Church of Satan after LaVey's death, but later stepped down to be replaced by Peter H. Gilmore.

During the 1950s, LaVey dabbled as a psychical investigator, looking into what his friends on the police force referred to as "nut calls." LaVey soon became known as a San Francisco celebrity. Thanks to his paranormal research and his live performances as an organist (including playing the Wurlitzer at the Lost Weekend cocktail lounge), he attracted many California notables to his parties. Guests included Michael Harner, Chester A. Arthur III, Forrest J. Ackerman, Fritz Leiber, Dr. Cecil E. Nixon, and Kenneth Anger. He began presenting lectures on the occult to what he called his "Magic Circle," which was made up of friends who shared his interests. A member of the circle suggested, perhaps jokingly, that he could start his own religion based on the ideas that he was coming up with.

LaVey took this seriously and on April 30, 1966, he ritualistically shaved his head, declared the founding of the Church of Satan and proclaimed 1966 as "the Year One," Anno Satanas - the first year of the Age of Satan.

To create his version of Satanism, LaVey mixed together writings of Ayn Rand, Friedrich Nietzsche, Aleister Crowley, H.L. Mencken, and Jack London with the ideology and ritual practices that he created for the Church of Satan. He wrote essays that re-worked books on philosophy and "Satanized" versions of John Dee's Enochian Keys, turning them into books like *The Satanic Bible*, *The Compleat Witch* (re-released in 1989 as *The Satanic Witch*), and *The Satanic Rituals*.

Media attention soon followed, leading to coverage in newspapers all over the country and the cover of *Look* magazine. The *Los Angeles Times* and the *San Francisco Chronicle* were among those that dubbed him the "Black Pope." LaVey performed Satanic weddings, Satanic baptisms (including one for his daughter Zeena) and Satanic

LaVey poses during a Satanic Mass with one of his female "living altars".

funerals, and released a record album entitled *The Satanic Mass*. He appeared on talk shows with Joe Pyne, Phil Donahue, and Johnny Carson, and in feature length documentaries like *Satanis* in 1968 and *Speak of the Devil* in 1993. Since its founding, LaVey's Church of Satan has attracted scores of followers who shared a jaded view of organized religion, including celebrities like Jayne Mansfield, Sammy Davis, Jr., Marilyn Manson, director Robert Fuest, ufologist Jacques Vallee, author Aime Michel and many others.

The Church of Satan was based at LaVey's home in San Francisco's Richmond District, where its purple and black façade stood out on the residential street. The interior was painted in glossy black and red and was fitted with secret passages and rooms. Grotesque paintings, created by LaVey, were on display throughout the house, as were huge murals that depicted the Devil in action. The fireplace had a trapdoor that led to the "Den of Iniquity," where Satanic rituals allegedly took place.

Hegarty and LaVey separated in the middle 1980s, and she sued for palimony. The claim was settled out of court. LaVey's next and final companion was Blanche Barton.

Anton LaVey died on October 29, 1997, in St. Mary's Hospital, San Francisco of pulmonary edema. For reasons open to speculation, the time and date of his passing were listed incorrectly on his death certificate - stating that he died on Halloween. His estranged daughter, Zeena, took credit for his demise, claiming that she had put a "death curse" on him. LaVey's funeral was a secret, by invitation only Satanic service that was held in Colma, California. His body was cremated, with his ashes eventually divided among his heirs as part of a settlement. The ashes allegedly possessed occult powers that could be used for Satanic ritual magic.

The type of Satanism created by LaVey is the most accepted form among the general public today, but it's certainly not the only one. In fact, practitioners of traditional Satanism see it as a watered-down, mainstream version of what they truly believe in – the literal worship of Satan.

TRADITIONAL SATANISM

Traditional, or theistic Satanism, is essentially a perversion both of witchcraft and formal, orthodox church worship, especially and specifically Christianity. This type of Satanism mocks the rituals, priesthood, dogma and liturgies of the Church and over the centuries has created its own rituals of sex and orgies to take the place of the form of worship practiced by Christians. This movement has never pretended to be anything other than an enemy of civil and religious establishment, a sworn enemy of the Church and the antithesis of the precepts of nature-based witchcraft. These types of Satanists are often referred to as "reverse Christians" because they practice what would be the opposite of the teachings of the Christian church. Satan is not a figure that is meant to be feared, but one that is embraced and upheld as the enemy of God.

The first appearance of Satan (also known as Lucifer or simply, the Devil) in history seems to be in the Christian Bible, when he was identified as one of God's favorite angels. His name literally mean "Bringer of Light" and he was regarded as a Prince among the angels. But Lucifer was unhappy with God placing the importance of his human creations above that of the angels and he led a rebellion in heaven that eventually caused him to be cast down onto the earth with the other angels that followed him. These other angels became Lucifer's, or Satan's, demons and brought terror and despair to the people of the world. This is the traditional view of Satan, largely from the Christian and Jewish faiths, and enhanced in works like Milton's *Paradise Lost*.

The name Satan actually means "the accuser" or "to overcome" and stands for one who challenged the religious faiths of humans. He has long been regarded as a demon, a rebellious angel, or as an allegory for knowledge and the enlightenment of mankind. He is believed to have been the spirit who brought death into the world and to have appeared in the form of a serpent to induce Eve to eat the fruit from the tree of knowledge in the biblical Garden of Eden. For this reason, he has long been seen as an evil spirit who knew the difference between what was "righteous" and what was "sinful" – and gleefully tried to send humans down the wrong path.

For the Christian church, Satan has always been seen as the angel who rebelled against God and his ultimate goal has always been to lead people away from the love of God --- and into activities that God opposes. Satan appeared many times in the Bible, including as the figure who tried to force Job to curse God after being afflicted with all manner of tragedies

Satan, or Lucifer, depicted as a fallen warrior angel. Cast out of heaven, he made the earth his home, destined to plague God's creation by offering sin and iniquity.

and torments. He also appeared in the New Testament attempting to convince Jesus not to go through with the crucifixion that ended his human life. Needless to say, he has always been the most feared, and most reviled, character in the scriptures – a monster that many fundamentalist Christians believe would try and drag them kicking and screaming into the bowels of hell if given half a chance.

Most "Satanic" lore does not originate from actual Satanists, but from Christians, as will become increasingly clear in the chapter that follows. However, this does not mean that true, traditional Satanists have not existed (and continue to exist today), worshipping Satan as a spiritual being and performing rituals that praise their master and make a mockery of Christian symbols and traditions, as well as wholeheartedly believing in the possibility of invoking demons.

SEX, SATAN AND THE MIDDLE AGES

The melding of sex, Satanism and the black arts of witchcraft began during the Middle Ages, at a time when the Christian Church held most of the religious world in the grip of both devotion and fear. Christianity spread outward from Rome nearly 2,000 years ago, marching along with the Roman legions as they conquered the far-flung lands of the empire. In many places, like Britain, Christianity shared equal status with the gods of the Norse invaders who came to the isles after the departure of the Romans and with the ancient pagan rites that had been passed along for generations. England saw the arrival of St. Augustine and the building of the Canterbury Cathedral hundreds of years later but this did little, at first, to convert the British people to Christianity. Kings, Queens and the greater part of the nobility accepted the new religion and, in most cases, blackmailed by a fanatical and militant priesthood with threats of hellfire and damnation, they handed over much of their wealth for the building of churches, abbeys and priories.

By the height of the Middle Ages, the Church had succeeded in imposing the Christian faith on the upper classes and a large portion of those who came into close contact with them. This had little effect on the common people and they continued their pagan beliefs for many years to come, often being baptized as Christians, but continuing their worship of the old gods. They attended church because the lord of the manor ordered them to do so, but they continued to rely on the old gods when they needed rain, good harvests, protection from misfortune or other blessings.

This was not completely forbidden by the Church at that time. Many of the rules and laws that were created in the years to come had not been placed into effect. Perhaps the greatest of these would be when Rome decreed that all of its priests should remain celibate. When it expected the tens of thousands of priests who were then officiating throughout Europe, most of whom were young, virile men, all to lead a life of chastity, it was asking the impossible. Many of them doubtless suppressed their urges by fasting, self-flagellation and other methods. But, based on the literature of the time, it cannot be doubted that many gave in to temptation and managed to seduce their pretty, young parishioners. Before the decree, most priests had lived normal lives as married men and had not unduly condemned their flocks for their pagan festivals and celebrations. Some of them even joined in. They knew about the old religions and, as it did not menace their own, allowed it to continue.

But all of that began to change and as the power of the Church grew, its tolerance for the old gods began to disappear. Much of the increase in power of the Church was due to the Crusaders. This romantic adventure of going to the Holy Land on an armed pilgrimage, to capture Jerusalem from the infidels, affected thousands of ordinary soldiers, who had no choice but to accompany their feudal lords. The Crusades, where the soldiers were constantly reminded that if they put their faith in God they would return home safely, led to many of them being converted to Christianity. When they returned home, their families were converted to the faith, as well.

The Knights Templar were formed during the Crusades to protect pilgrims to the Holy Land

During the age of the Crusades, it was not only knights, squires, and soldiers that went to the Holy Land. Many of the thousands of people who made the arduous journey were devoted pilgrims, anxious to see the land where Christ walked. To protect them from thieves, killers and infidels, the Order of the Knights Templar were formed. The Knights were drawn from several countries and each man was sworn to celibacy and poverty – although this did not stop them from freely indulging in vice or from becoming immensely wealthy. They made their headquarters in Malta, and for many years, they dominated a large portion of the world.

The order was founded in Jerusalem in 1119 by Hughes de Payns and his comrade, Geoffrey de St. Omer. It was officially endorsed by the Church in Rome in 1129 and after that, became a favorite charity throughout Christendom, growing rapidly in membership and power. Templar knights, in their distinctive white mantles with a red cross, were among the most skilled fighting units of the Crusades. The Templars' success was tied closely to the Crusades and when the Holy Land was lost, support for the order faded, although most believed it would continue, thanks to the vast business and banking dealings that the Templars had created across Europe.

However, it was not long before their enemies began to

plot against them. Rumors quickly spread about the Templars and their true anti-Christian leanings. Reports claimed that the Order worshipped Baphomet, a pagan deity that had been envisaged by Arab mystics. The figure of Baphomet had the head and hooves of a goat with a black candle placed between its horns. It had human hands, one pointing up and one down. Each hand pointed to a crescent moon, one white and one black. The belly was green and had scales like a fish. It had female breasts and sexual organs of both a man and a woman. A pentagram, a symbol of magical power, was on its forehead. When initiated, a Templar allegedly had to renounce Christ and pledge his allegiance to this idol. Afterwards, it was rumored that he would be stripped naked and all of the Knights present would engage in a homosexual orgy.

These stories were soon acted upon by King Phillip IV of France, who was deeply in debt to the Templars after his war with England. The Templars disputed the charges but King Phillip managed to get assistance from the new Pope Clement V, who was based in France, to start an investigation into the Templar's activities. He then began to pressure the Church to take action against the order as a way of freeing himself from his debts.

On Friday, October 13, 1307, Phillip ordered the Templar Grand Master Jacques de Molay and scores of other French Templars to be simultaneously arrested. The Templars were charged with a number of heresies and were tortured to extract false confessions of blasphemy. The confessions, despite having been obtained under duress, caused a scandal in Paris. After more pressure from Phillip, Pope Clement issued an

The Templars became associated with the symbol of Baphomet, a deity that represented the dual nature of man and sexuality.

order that instructed all of the monarchs of Europe to arrest the Templars and seize their assets. He called for papal hearings to determine the guilt or innocence of the Templars and once freed from torture, the knights recanted their confessions. In spite of this, dozens of them were burned at the stake in Paris. Phillip then threatened military action unless the Pope disbanded the order and in 1312, the Templars officially ceased to exist and their assets were taken by the Church and by governments across Europe.

Grand Master of the Templars Jacque de Molay had confessed under torture to being a high priest of Satan, but he later retracted his statement. He was burned at the stake in 1314, but remained defiant until the end. According to legend, he called out from the flames that both Pope Clement and King Phillip would soon meet him before God. Pope Clement died just one month later, and King Phillip died in a hunting accident before the end of the year.

The Middle Ages advanced and while an increasing number of people began to put their faith in the Christian God, the Holy Virgin, and the saints, the Church was still not powerful enough to suppress the pagan feasts, so it began to simply replace them. In many cases, though, the old traditions remained. On the eve of May Day, the day of Beltane, young men still jumped over bonfires and carried young women off into the darkness. On May Day itself, young people kept up the custom of dancing around the phallus – now disguised under the new name of the Maypole. Christmas was substituted for the old Roman holiday of Saturnalia and, although attendance was required at church on Christmas day, the people had until Twelfth Night, on January 6, for merry-making. And during these feasts, the Church usually overlooked at least two of the deadly sins – drunkenness and lust.

But, for the most part, life continued to be grim during this era. Even the wealthiest rulers lived in cold, drafty castles and they wore rich garments that were rarely free from lice. Only the rich could afford to have their floors cleaned on a regular basis, only to have them fouled again by hunting dogs and by having residents and guests dirty them by relieving themselves in the nearest corner. Except for the lord and lady, in their withdrawing rooms, there was no privacy and bathrooms were unknown.

It was a canon of the Christian Church that dirtiness was next to godliness in those days. In Roman times, visiting the baths had been a daily event, but times had changed. In the Christian nations alone (Muslims had great concern for physical cleanliness), the people worshipped a god whose priesthood insisted upon the deliberate cultivation of dirt and misery. The rich and poor alike lived in stench and squalor. They stayed in inns infested with bed bugs, lived in homes coated in filth and even their bodies were dirt- and sweat-covered breeding places for every type of disease imaginable.

Their God, they were told, would reward them for their suffering, so penances were given that forced people to whip themselves, crawl through the streets on their knees and wear shirts made from hair. Whatever sin had been committed, there at least a dozen punishments by which they could atone.

And perhaps the greatest of these sins was sex. By the Middle Ages, sex had come to dominate the Church's thinking in a way that can only be seen today as pathological. The Christian sexual code was comprised of many regulations but its basic law was that sexual intercourse was to be performed as seldom as possible (and if you were a priest, not at all) and then only for the purpose of procreation. For the weak members of the Church, who fell to their natural impulses, a constant recitation of the need for abstinence was drummed into them, creating guilt and confusion. It was not actually the sex act itself that so dismayed the Church, but the pleasure that might be derived from it. Joyless sex for the sole purpose of procreation could be tolerated, but the warm-blooded enjoyment of sexual love was something that could damn a soul for eternity.

In addition, to desire a member of the opposite sex, even though no actual physical contact occurred, was also a sin. Marriage, as already noted, provided no sanctuary for physical love. To desire one's wife was just as sinful as desiring a buxom young woman in the marketplace. One theologian stated that if a man loved his wife too passionately, he had committed a sin that was worse than adultery.

The Church eventually put together a strict system of morality in a series of "penitential books," which explored the subject of sex in every possible detail. Every conceivable misdeed was discussed and analyzed and appropriate penalties were listed for each. The basic code of the Church stated that all were urged to accept the idea of complete celibacy, meaning that virginity was better than marriage. There was also a ban on all forms of sexual expression, other than relations between a married couple, which could occur only on a set number of dates per year. All other sex was forbidden.

The codes also created the mystical concept that all virgins were "brides of Christ," and that anyone who seduced a virgin not only committed the sin of fornication, but, at the same time, committed the more serious crime of adultery. God was cast in the role of the outraged husband and the Church, as his earthly representative, was empowered to exact a terrible vengeance on the perpetrator. The violated virgin, unless she had been forcibly raped, had also committed a mortal sin and she could be charged with adultery.

It was not only for the sexual act that the church prescribed punishments for sinners. Kissing, fondling, attempting to fornicate and even thinking about sex could have dire consequences. Dreams were held equally suspect, and if a young man should experience an involuntary nocturnal emission, he was instructed to get out of bed at once, sing seven psalms and then sing and additional thirty in the morning before breakfast.

Masturbation was another sin with which the Church was obsessed and it held the greatest number of penalties. In five brief codes, there were twenty-two paragraphs dealing with various types of sodomy and bestiality, but there were twenty-five paragraphs dealing with masturbation committed by laymen and several more that dealt separately with member of the clergy who indulged in it. St. Thomas Aquinas stated that masturbation was a greater sin than fornication – for not only was this enhancing the sin of lust, it was also considered murder because a man's spilled seed would never be used to impregnate a woman and create a child.

The sex act itself – when it was permitted to be performed – was strictly regulated and controlled. No position other than the "missionary position" of a man on top of the woman was permitted. Women were not allowed to be on top and a rear entry position was regarded with the greatest amount of horror because it was thought to offer the greatest amount of pleasure. Confessors were instructed to specifically ask married couples if they had dared perform in this position and if they admitted to it, they were made to do penance for seven years.

When the Church proclaimed that intercourse was illegal on Sundays, Wednesday and Fridays, it effectively removed the equivalent of five months of the year from the possible taint of sexual pleasure. The Church then decided to enforce abstinence for forty days before Easter and forty days before Christmas, removing the equivalent of eight months from the sexual calendar of the year. It also seemed sensible to the clergy to prohibit intercourse for three days prior to Holy Communion, at which regular attendance was required. From the remaining four months of possible sexual activity, another month had been removed. Then, of course, sex was forbidden during pregnancy and at any time during a penance that had been invoked by the clergy.

The frustrated populace was left with the equivalent of about two months during the year in which they might, for the purpose of procreation alone, have sex without any sensations of pleasure. If a child had been born to them and had been delivered at a particular time of the year that would fit into the wrong time of the Church calendar, their faith would prevent them from having sex for a year or more.

It has been said that the Church passed such stringent and ruthless codes of behavior in order to save the souls of the weaker brethren in its midst. Such an extreme ban on sex was certainly never preached by Christ and was not supported by anything in the Bible. The Middle Ages were simply a time of intolerable sexual frustration and obsession – making it possible for a sexual revolution to occur. The traditions of the old gods, which had lain dormant but had never died, were made all the more attractive thanks to sexual frustrations and the enforced sexual repression of the people by the Church. As people began to compare the old ways and new ways the beginnings of Satanism began to emerge in the troubled era of the Middle Ages.

One can easily see how appealing the tales of the old ways, the old customs and the old religion, with its emphasis on fertility and communal sex rituals, could be to the young as they listened to the older folks tell stories about the past. Wild stories described orgies in the woods when everyone present "mixed" their bodies and joined at the loins and tales told of the bodies of women past child bearing age serving as "living altars" for young and inexperienced bachelors.

The sexual repressions of the Church placed special emphasis on the woman as the source of all fleshly evil. In the past, women had been regarded as property but in the Middle Ages, they were held responsible for all sexual guilt. It was a woman who had caused the fall from grace when she had tempted man, who would have otherwise surely remained pure. The mere presence of a woman was liable to attract evil. St. Chrysostom of Constantinople, who was likely more tolerant that most of his contemporaries, declared that women were a "necessary evil, a natural temptation, a desirable calamity, a domestic peril, a deadly fascination, and a painted ill." In the infamous *Malleus Maleficarum,* the authors stated:

A woman is beautiful to look upon, contaminating to the touch, and deadly to keep. She is a foe to friendship, a necessary evil and a natural temptation. She is a domestic danger and an evil of nature, painted with fair colors. A liar by nature, she seethes with anger and impatience in her whole soul. Since women are feeble in both mind and body, it is not surprising that they should come under the spell of witchcraft more than men would succumb. A woman is more carnal than a man. All witchcraft comes from carnal lust, which in a woman in insatiable.

Witches satisfy their filthy lusts not only in themselves, but even in the mighty ones of the age, of whatever sort and condition, causing by all sorts of witchcraft the death of their souls through the excessive infatuation of carnal love.

And the witch-finder's manual was not referring just to witches – it meant "good" women too, which is how "woman" and "witch" became largely synonymous in the Middle Ages and even into the so-called enlightenment of the Renaissance era. St. Augustine declared that mankind had been sent to destruction by the actions of Eve, who was, of course, a woman. Women had been offered equal roles in the early days of Christianity. The early

Depictions of witches in the Middle Ages by Martin van Maele. The Church considered women to be the source of all evil, tempting men into sin with their carnal nature.

Church leaders permitted women to preach, heal, exorcize and baptize. By the Middle Ages, though, women had lost all vestige of legal rights. The Church leaders seemed to hate women – perhaps because they lusted after them so much.

The penitential books were suffused by an obsession with sex. The Church reformers expressed a horror and hatred of sex that seems to hide a fascination with the temptation and delights of the flesh. The works of the Christian writers of the time literally throb with the sensual agony of devout men who sought to banish desire from their bodies by prayer, scourging and fasting. And it was primarily these men who won positions of power in the Church.

Eventually, the Church's repressive ways provided the catalyst for the old religions to return and to lead to the loss of hundreds of thousands, perhaps millions, of innocent lives during the witch hunts and inquisitions of the Middle Ages. To the Church, the old religion was inhabited by devils that were personified as Satan, the enemy of the Church's work on earth. To the people, who didn't care about such things, the old gods offered a release from oppression and unrelenting punishment. The Church soon began to try and combat the "evil" influence of the resurrected Pan, the god of fertility, nature and freedom. The Church scholars began to consult ancient manuscripts to determine how best to deal with the formidable adversary who had returned to torment their parishioners. They saw it as the Devil's establishment of power and began to declare that the old religion was henceforth Satanic and the women who knew about the old traditions were witches. The traditional gatherings, festivals and feasts became witches' Sabbaths and the broom, a symbol of the sacred hearth, became an evil tool. The sexual rites of old, created to stimulate fertility in nature, were now manifestations of forbidden carnal lust.

The peasants felt quite differently about the old traditions that had been revived. Their lords had conditioned them not to feel jealousy if they or their knights should desire a village woman for the evening. The noblemen had long considered the villages as large, informal harems and no peasant's wife or daughter was immune if she was desired by a lord or one of his men. Now, the peasant protested, he was being threatened with torture and death as a witch if he freely shared his wife or daughter with one that he considered an equal during a fertility rite. But he did not let his fear of punishment forbid him from embracing the old ways. He could not experience pleasure without the interference of the Church, which sought to control and repress human emotions. The rebellion took hold and swept across Europe and the old religions once again found their place again among the common people. But eventually, even the natural instincts of the old ways began to darken and change into something else.

THE SABBATHS

It was obvious by the height of the Middle Ages that, despite the best efforts of the Church, the old horned god had not died, because the people still had need of him. They found no satisfaction in a religion that failed to provide an outlet for their carnal needs. Many of them had more faith in the old gods as providers of good harvests and healthy babies than in a sad figure that hung pitifully from a cross. After all, no amount of fasting, chanting of dirges and sexual abstinence had put a stop to the Black Death until the terrible plague had killed off millions of people.

As the old ways returned, the Sabbaths became a regular feature of country life throughout Western Europe and for many years, there was nothing wicked about them. In those days, there was little in the way of enjoyment in the lives of the common people. They were poor and they often worked from dawn to dusk. Very few of them could read or could afford candles to light indoor amusements during the winter months. Apart from fairs and the feasts of the Church, their only form of relaxation was the Sabbath of the old religion. Sabbaths were usually held during a full moon and four times each year, there were Grand Sabbaths at which several villages might join together to celebrate the feasts of the old gods. These were February 2 (Candlemas), April 30 (Walpurgisnacht), August 1 (Lammas), and October 31 (Halloween).

Those who attended these celebrations contributed poultry, game, fruit, cakes, honey and home-brewed drinks and they gathered in open fields or in forest clearings. The man who represented the horned god dressed for the part as a goat or stag, and received homage in the god's name. When homage had been paid, he and a village elder would give advice about problems that the villagers did not care to share with a priest and provide herbal remedies for those in need of them. He then assumed the role of a reveler and led the party in the celebration that followed. Those who brought instruments formed a band and everyone joined in to dance and play games. After the feast was over, and everyone had gotten plenty to eat and likely had too much to drink, the sexual rituals began in earnest. Fornication was a sin according to the Christian Church, but the old religion taught that sexual intercourse aided in the fertility of crops and cattle. When it was all over, the villagers returned, tired and happy, to their homes, facing another day of grueling work, but knowing that the night of another Sabbath was just around the corner.

A Sabbath of the Old Religion

But time changes all things and early in the sixteenth century, the nature of the Sabbaths began to take on a different character. Many believe that this was caused by the coming of the Reformation. Before this, the peasants had no love for the wealthy priests and abbots, but the vices of the clergy kept them from doing anything about the carnal escapades of their flocks. They knew all about the revels of the old religion, yet they never interfered. The only people tried and condemned for heresy in those days were those foolish enough to publicly deny Christ or to commit sacrilege in a church. The Reformation changed all of that. The movement began as an attempt to reform the Catholic Church. Many Catholics were troubled by what they saw as false doctrines and malpractices within the Church, particularly involving the buying and selling of church positions and what was seen as considerable corruption within the Church's hierarchy, even reaching the position of the Pope. The Reformation swept away many of the tolerant priests, or forced them to become zealots. A new type of clergy came along, earnest, vociferous, puritanical men, who took their religion very seriously and were determined to force their beliefs on everyone else. It was they who stigmatized the old god as the Devil, and threatened with eternal torment in hell any of their parishioners who attended a Sabbath.

This must have scared many worthy folks into ceasing their attendance at these pagan celebrations. Moreover, this new type of priest spoke with real conviction about the goodness of Christ and of how he had sacrificed himself to redeem mankind. Services were not always conducted in Latin, but in languages that everyone could understand. The printing press was invented and books began to circulate, allowing many peasants to learn how to read. Much of the literature of the period was religious, telling wonderful tales of saints and martyrs and offering horrifying accounts of how worshippers of the old gods were often carried away by demons.

In the course of just two generations, the bulk of the population had changed from being nominal Christians who also still worshipped in the old ways, to devout believers. This change in attitude was not solely accomplished by prayer and priests – it was largely accomplished by fear. Not only could those who followed the old ways find torment in hell, they could also find it on earth because the witch trials and Holy Inquisition had now arrived. Sheer terror was felt at the thought of being denounced as having attended a Sabbath. The mere idea of being burned alive at the stake caused the greater part of the people to abandon the old gods and after a time, they became devout Christians. They simply had no other choice.

Soon, only the worst elements of the population still followed the old ways. They were the outlaws and robbers who lived in the woods, those who felt the need to defy authority, and the greedy and unscrupulous who were prepared to risk discovery and punishment in order to obtain the secrets of casting spells and making potions and poisons that they could sell for money. There were also those who had a pure, burning hatred for the Church and all that it stood for and believed that only the powers of darkness could provide them with complete satisfaction.

It was these groups who changed the midnight gaiety of the Sabbath to a blasphemous parody of the Christian faith. Anyone who wanted to attend them had to first be initiated into the coven, and the chief of the coven ruled it by terror. The initiate had to deny Christ, spit on the cross and, in a token of submission to Satan, kiss the bared rump of the leader of the coven. They also had to sign a blood oath to Satan in which they surrendered their souls to him in return for a life of prosperity. Such signed pacts could also be used as blackmail if the initiate ever decided to leave the coven or pass along its secrets to someone outside of the group. It was also customary for worshippers to present their children to the coven and have them baptized in the name of Satan.

The new Black Sabbaths (or Black Mass, as they came to be called) were always held away from the villages or cities on areas of flat ground. Wherever the rituals were held, it was essential that they take place in wooded areas. The clearing would serve, according to tradition, as the imitation of the sanctuary of a church. At the far end, worshippers erected an altar of stones and placed an image of Satan on top of it. The idol's torso was that of a man, but its bottom half was like a goat. Its head was also goat-like and sometimes had a small torch between its horns. The central feature of it was a prominent penis of large and lusty proportions.

The tortures of the witchcraft trials brought forth all manner of obscene versions of the Black Sabbath, but scholars believe that each began with the ceremonial entrance of the naked worshippers, led by the leader of the coven. After the procession and the completion of an opening prayer, the female leader of the coven delivered a kiss to the hindquarters and the erect penis of the satanic image on the altar. Some reports state that after the ceremonial kiss, the priestess would then mount the oversized penis of the effigy and offer herself to the dark god. After that, a banquet would take place with all of the members of the coven. The only steadfast rule of the Black Sabbath was that there must be an equal number of both sexes. Every worshipper had to have a mate. Under torture, many told their confessors that Satan would conjure up demons to take the place of either sex if the human company was short. While many are skeptical of this, there is some evidence to suggest that freshly interred corpses were sometimes used as cold, uncomplaining partners for the some male worshippers.

Each member of the coven was required to bring food and drink for the banquet and attendees were encouraged to eat and drink their fill. In the opinion of many scholars, the food and drink were likely sprinkled with liberal does of trance-inducing herbs, which would break down the last inhibitions of the worshippers. It was important that everyone take part in the Sabbath dance or, as it was commonly known, the "witches' round." The round was performed with the dancers in a back-to-back position with their hands clasped and their heads turned so that they might see one another. The wild, circular dance resulted in an ecstatic condition where, as movement progressed, the group was united as if in one body. A mass sexual communion followed the dancing and it became the responsibility of the coven's leader to make sure that he had sex with each of the female participants using a large, oversized phallus during the orgy. Such a ritual likely caused the women a great amount of pain and may have been responsible for those who were tortured to believe that they had sex with Satan during the drug-addled Sabbath.

Acts of sodomy were also reported under duress but both the Church and the worshippers were in agreement that the semen of Satan was completely sterile. At a time before any birth control methods, other than withdrawal, were used, sexual intercourse without fear of becoming pregnant would have been an exciting and pleasurable aspect of the Sabbath.

The rituals of the Black Sabbath were flexible and most authorities believe that they changed and developed over time. In the sixteenth century, Florin de Raemond described the Black Mass:

The presiding deity is a black goat with two horns. A man dressed as a priest is attended by two women servers. A young initiate is presented to the goat who makes the sign of the cross with the left hand and commands those present to salute him with a kiss to the hind-quarters. Between his horns, the creature carries a black lighted candle from which the worshippers' tapers are lighted. As each adores the goat, money is dropped into a silver dish.

He added in his description that a new witch was initiated to the coven, she gave the goat figure, which personified Satan, a lock of her hair as a token of allegiance. She then went "apart with him into a wood," where she offered him her body. He also went on to write:

The Sabbat dance follows in the familiar back-to-

A scene of a Black Mass

back positions and the Mass proper begins. A black cape without any cross embroidered upon it is worn by the celebrant. A segment of turnip, dyed black, is used in place of the Host for the elevation. On seeing it above the priest's head, the congregation cry 'Master, save us!' Water replaces wine in the chalice. Offensive material is used a substitute for holy water in the black asperges. (An asperges or aspergil was the sprinkler filled with holy water used by priests during Mass.)

Other accounts of Black Mass from the sixteenth and seventeenth centuries vary only slightly in their descriptions. In other cases, the leader of the coven would read the litany of Satan out of a black book, followed by a report from every member of the evil that he or she had committed since the last meeting. Anyone who had not caused trouble or grief for someone was savagely whipped. The leader was always dressed as some sort of animal. When the feast was held, filthy brews were consumed, loaded with drugs and aphrodisiacs that could arouse the members into a sexual frenzy. Some accounts said that the revelers ate human waste and others went so far as to say that the flesh of a murdered child would sometimes be consumed. The orgies were not encounters of joyful lust, but were dark tangles of sweaty flesh that deteriorated into every type of depravity possible.

The Black Sabbaths that occurred during this time period established the pattern that would continue into the modern era and create what we commonly think of Satanism today. Author Dennis Wheatley, who made a name for himself in the 1960s writing about the occult and penning thrilling novels about battles between good and evil like *The Devil Rides Out* and *To The Devil, A Daughter*, published his own descriptions of contemporary Black Masses, based on first-hand research that he did at the time:

A Black Mass in Paris in 1926

At a Black Mass, everything possible is done the opposite way to the correct procedure. The cross on the altar is upside down, crooked or broken. The acolytes should be youths who readily give themselves to sodomy. In the censers that they swing, instead of incense, opium and other drugs are burnt. The celebrant wears a black cape embroidered with serpents and other satanic emblems. He is naked beneath it, and it is open down the front, exposing his genitals. The congregation should, preferably, be wearing animal costumes and masks. The litany and prayers are recited backwards. The congregation's responses are animal howls, snuffling and grunts. The ceremony is performed on the body of a naked woman, preferably a virgin, on her bottom and later on her belly. On the altar is a mattress covered with a black cloth. She lies on this with her head on a pillow below a broken crucifix; her arms spread out and in her hands she holds two black candles made from human fat. Her legs dangle down over the edge of the altar, and each time during the ritual that the priest should kiss the altar, instead he kisses the vagina of the woman. Sacramental wafers stolen from a church are scattered on the floor. The congregation tramples, then urinates, on them while repudiating Christ and vilifying the Virgin Mary. Some of the broken wafers are put into a chalice. The celebrant is handed an infant. He cuts its throat on the belly of the woman who is lying on the altar, and catches its blood in the chalice. Having drunk some of the blood, he sprinkles the rest of it on the congregation, who, by then, incited to a frenzy by the smoke from the drugs in the censers, are howling imprecations and blasphemies. Finally, the celebrant copulates with the woman, while the congregation, as though possessed by demons, frantically slakes their lust on one another in every way possible to perceive.

By the sixteenth cemetery, most scholars believe that the remaining practitioners of the old religion went completely underground, while the hardened few turned the Sabbaths into something more macabre and much darker than those who revived the belief in the old gods even intended. The Black Mass also gained the attention of many members of the decadent aristocracy of the day, who seized upon its sinister indulgences as sort of a hedonistic parlor game, expressing their sexual fantasies and cavorting about in the nude.

But no matter what the actual beliefs of those who began practicing these horrific rituals, the fact that they were occurring, and spreading across Europe, was proof that the power of darkness was coming into its own.

SATANISM, TORTURE AND THE GREAT WITCH HUNTS

It was not long after the revival of the old religion that the rival faiths – the old ways and the Church – began to clash. In 1303, the Bishop of Coventry was accused of paying homage to a deity in the form of an animal, but he managed to escape punishment. So did Dame Alice Kyteler, who in 1324 was accused of sacrificing animals to the Devil. Even the Carmelite friar Pierre Recordi, who was placed on trial in 1329, was only imprisoned for life, even though he admitted to having seduced three women by making wax images of them that were mixed with his own blood and spittle and burying them under the women's windows. When he achieved success, he celebrated by making a sacrifice to Satan.

It's possible that such statements and confessions were not taken seriously at the time, but all of that was about to change. In 1335, Catherine Delort and Anne-Marie de Georgel were tried in Toulouse, France, and confessed that, over a twenty-year period, they had attended satanic Sabbaths and had given themselves to the Devil. Catherine claimed that she had first been taken to a Sabbath by her lover, a shepherd, and had submitted sexually to a man dressed as a goat in front of the assembled company. She said that they drank horrid liquids and ate the flesh of infants, but were rewarded by being taught spells that would harm the people they disliked.

Anne-Marie testified that when she was washing the family laundry one day she had seen a huge dark-skinned   man with glowing eyes and dressed in animal skins coming toward her from across a river. He had blown into her mouth, thereby possessing her. On the following Saturday, she was carried to a Sabbath by the sheer force of his will. It was presided over by the man in the animal skins, who urged those present to do all of the harm they could to Christians and instructed them on magic incantations and how to make potions from poisonous plants.

In 1441, Roger Bolingbroke, an astronomer; Thomas Southwell, a Canon of St. Peter's Westminster; and a woman named Margery Goodmayne, were all charged with having conspired against the life of England's King Henry VI by sorcery, carried out under instructions by Dame Eleanor, daughter of Lord Cobham. Southwell died in the infamous Tower of London, Goodmayne was burned at the stake and Bolingbroke was dragged through the streets behind a horse before being hanged, drawn and quartered. Dame Eleanor was pardoned for her role in the "assassination attempt" after doing a public penance. Charges of black magic were now being seen as a much more serious offense.

During the reign of Edward IV, the Duchess of Bedford was accused of having employed a sorcerer named Thomas Wake to bewitch the king into marrying Elizabeth Woodville, by whom he had the two princes who were later murdered in the Tower. The charges against her were later dropped. After Edward's death, his one-time mistress, Jane Shore, was convicted of using witchcraft against his successor, Richard III. However, the common people, who loved her, refused to believe the charges. She was forced to walk the streets with a sign around her neck that declared that she was a harlot, but she was met with nothing but sympathy and affection by the crowds.

In 1477, a witch named Antoine Rose was brought to trial. She had told a neighbor that she badly needed money, so he took her to a Sabbath, where she was persuaded to give homage to the Devil. He took the form of a large, black dog and everyone present kissed his hindquarters. Then the men had sexual intercourse with all of the women in rear-entry style, as further satanic tribute. They were told to take the communion host, hold it in their mouths and then spit it out and trample it. They were given potions for making people and cattle ill and told to do as much harm to their fellow man as possible.

These accounts, and others, appeared over the course of almost a century before Pope Innocent VIII declared open war on Satanism on December 5, 1484. He published a decree that led to the formation of the Holy Office, as the Inquisition was officially called. It empowered inquisitors that were appointed by the Church to participate in trials for heresy, to override the decisions of local courts, to proceed against persons of any rank, and to punish all those who were found guilty of practicing witchcraft and black magic.

The object of the decree was to stamp out the lawlessness that was believed to be affecting society. Practitioners of what became known as the "Left-Hand Path" had become so numerous that, by casting spells, inciting rebellion and endorsing other nefarious activities, they had become a menace to the Church and to the Christian way of life. In 1487, a Dominican friar named Tomas de Torquemada was appointed as the Grand Inquisitor of Spain and under the patronage of the fanatical Queen Isabella, he began a reign of terror that is still remembered today as one of the darkest periods in the history of the world.

The Pope's decree had been initially aimed at Germany, where Satanism was particularly rife at the time, and it inspired Jacobus Sprenger, the Prior of the Convent of Cologne, and Prior Heinrich Kramer, to write the previously mentioned witch-finder's book *Malleus Maleficarum*. It was first published in 1486 and it ran for many editions. The book was written with great care as an examination of witchcraft and it offered a lengthy analysis on the best methods of dealing with the menace. The authors took extreme care to correct errors, to instruct against ignorance, and to carefully direct action. In spite of this, it remains one of the most appalling texts ever written and it led to the deaths of hundreds of thousands of people during the terrifying era of the Inquisition.

As was the standard with Church writings of the time, the authors were obsessed with sex. They made it clear that interference with sexual intercourse in marriage was one of the chief activities of witches, who used their unholy alliance with Satan to corrupt the generative powers of man. In addition, they noted, witches sought to depopulate Christendom by demanding the sacrifice of infants and children.

The inquisitors of the Church followed the writings in the book as they directed their tortures of accused witches to target the private areas of the body, mutilating female breasts and running red-hot pokers into their vaginas. Once an accused woman found herself in prison because of the testimony of those who had seen her alleged evil powers in action (which could include jealous neighbors, a rejected suitor or even a relative who wanted her money), she was as good as dead. At the height of the Inquisition, an accusation was the same as guilt in the eyes of the judges. And no lawyer would dare to come to the accused person's aid for fear that he might also be accused of heresy if he pled her case too well.

The Inquisition charged that no witch could be condemned to

The infamous Malleus Malefic arum (Witches' Hammer), an instructional manual for the depraved torture and execution of accused witches. Thousands went needlessly to their deaths because of this horrific book.

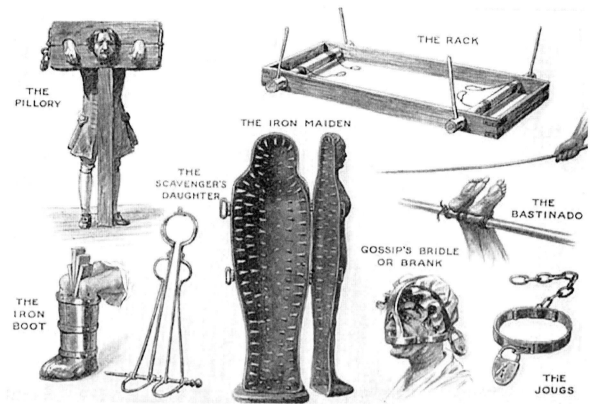

THE RACK

THE PILLORY

THE IRON MAIDEN

THE SCAVENGER'S DAUGHTER

THE BASTINADO

GOSSIP'S BRIDLE OR BRANK

THE IRON BOOT

THE JOUGS

An array of devices used to torture confessions from accused witches.

death unless they convicted themselves by their own confession. This left the judges with no choice but to torture the accused in ways that were so horrific that they would admit to anything to end the pain, even if it meant being put to death for what they confessed to. The judges turned the accused over to black-hooded torturers who hacked, burned, branded, stretched, starved and raped them in order to obtain confessions about their crimes.

The tortures began with a search of the witch's body for the alleged "Devil's Mark," a red blemish that Satan placed on all of those who swore allegiance to him. Often, the women had all of their hair shaved off to search for such a mark – which could be anything from a pimple to a scratch, a cut or even a birthmark. They were also stripped naked for the search, which made the abuses that followed even easier for the torturers. Long sharp pins were inserted into the victim's flesh as the sadistic questioners searched for insensitive spots of flesh that Satan left behind on his chosen ones. The pins were stabbed into breasts, cheeks, and private areas and if a woman did not scream in pain, then she was obviously a witch. The accused were often raped, were branded with hot irons, had their nipples torn away with iron pincers, were stretched and broken on the rack, had their feet crushed by the iron boot, had sulphur inserted in their anus and vagina, and were scalded with boiling oil, among other things. It's not surprising that many so-called "witches" confessed to anything their accusers suggested to them, preferring death over the continued agony of the torture chamber.

Once a confession was made, the admitted witch was made to stand before the judges and confess to them of her own free will. According to law, the judges were unable to hear confessions unless made freely, which is why the accused had to tortured into admitting that they practiced the black arts. Once they confessed, they were

eligible to be reconciled to the Church, absolved of sin, and burned at the stake. Even those who managed not to confess were burned anyway — for merely the accusation was enough to make a person guilty in the eyes of the Inquisition. The difference, as far as the Church was concerned, was whether a person died as guilty but penitent, or guilty and not sorry for the things they had done.

In addition to those who were dragged kicking and screaming in the courtroom, there was also those who came and proudly boasted of their intercourse with Satan and of the times that they roasted children alive and ate them. The confessions of these pathological people were eagerly recorded by the court's secretaries and were readily accepted by the Inquisition as an admission of guilt. But even these foolish wretches didn't escape the horrors of the torture chamber. Torture, in cases where a witch confessed readily, was considered to be good for thei soul and was prescribed as a way to get into heaven.

One of the most horrific —and hypocritical — stories that I have found about the Inquisition is the grisly account of Joan Bohorquia, a noblewoman and the wife of Lord of Higuera in Seville, who was brought to trial as a witch during her sixth month of pregnancy. Although she was confined in a cell, Lady Bohorquia was not mistreated or abused until after her baby had been born. Eight days later,

The cruel and sexually depraved methods of torture were carried out against young women by priests and hired torturers.

she was taken into the torture chamber. She was placed on the rack and stretched so tightly that the ropes that bound her cut into the bones of her arms, thighs and lower legs. Not satisfied that she would confess, the priests instructed the torturers to tighten the device and as they did, Lady Bohorquia's bowels burst, sending a torrent of blood from every orifice of her body. She died eight days later, never having confessed to being a witch. This proved embarrassing to the court and after her husband expressed outrage, it was declared that Lady Bohorquia had been found innocent of all charges of witchcraft. She was pronounced absolved from any further process and any damage done to her reputation was ordered restored. This was small relief to her grieving husband, whose wife had been murdered in one of the most cruel and hideous manners possible, but the inquisitioners believed that they could not be blamed for the travesty of justice that had occurred.

Persecution of "witches" soon became an industry. The attack on the forces of Satan depended on judges, jailers, torturers, exorcists, woodcutters, scribes and a legion of experts on the forces of darkness. The livelihoods of many depended on the continued rooting out of witches and minions of Satan. It was not long before the torturers discovered a foolproof method of continuing their profession: under torture, nearly any witch could be

After a witch "confessed" to being in a league with Satan, they were punished, which meant a public hanging or being burned at the stake.

forced to name a long string of her fellow Satanists, thereby causing one trial to turn into hundreds.

But not everyone in the Church approved of what was going on. The Jesuit scholar Friedrich von Spree became an opponent of the trials when the Duke of Brunswick brought him and a fellow priest into a torture chamber. As the Duke and the two Jesuits, who were believers in the Inquisition, stood beside a confessed witch who had been tortured further for the good of her soul, the Duke asked the Jesuits if they truly believed the Holy Tribunal was doing God's work. The priests replied that they did and so the Duke asked the poor woman who was tied to the rack to look closely at his two companions. He told them woman that he suspected the two priests of being witches. With this, he indicated to the torturer that the ropes that stretched the woman should be turned even tighter. At once, she began to scream that the two Jesuits were agents of Satan, that she had seen them having sex with demons and dining on the flesh of a roasted baby. After this, Father von Spree became a dedicated opponent of the Inquisition. He wrote: "Often I have thought that the only reason why we are not all wizards is due to the fact that we have not all been tortured. And there is truth is what an inquisitor dared to boast lately, that if he could reach the Pope, he would make him confess that he was a wizard."

In 1583, Reginald Scot wrote *The Discovery of Witchcraft*, which served as an answer to the earlier *Malleus Maleficarum*. In it, Scot wrote that the Inquisitors were sexually obsessed madmen, who took delight in inflicting sadistic tortures on their victims. He chastised the Holy Tribunal for spending so much time examining the naked bodies of young women for the secret marks of Satan, which they claimed could only be found in the most secret curves and hollows. When one catalogued the terrible agonies that were carried out, Scot asked, who would not confess to anything? Scot's voice was that of one of only a few sane men at the time, railing against the sexual mania that had provided one of the strongest reasons behind the horrible witchcraft persecutions.

The Inquisition eventually died away, but it was only one of the abominations that wreaked havoc during the sixteenth and seventeenth centuries, when religious figures took it upon themselves to try and uncover and destroy the followers of Satan in the world.

THE WITCH-FINDER GENERAL

In 1591, a Grand Sabbath was held by three covens in England, allegedly for the purpose of destroying King James IV of Scotland, late King James I of England. The king was about to travel to Demark to bring back his new bride, Princess Anne. The Grand Master at this Black Sabbath, John Fane, shared the duties with all of those who were present. Some of them arranged to bring a piece of the king's clothing, then made a wax image of him, wrapped in cloth and slowly burned. Others attempted to poison him and others tried to use magic to make storms that would destroy his ship at sea. A storm did succeed in delaying his departure for three weeks and it was later learned at trial that after he sailed, a witch name Agnes Simpson named a cat after him and drowned it in the ocean. This was said to have aroused another terrible storm, but King James, owing it to his great piety, managed to survive and return safely to Scotland. Not surprisingly, he initiated the first great witch hunt in the land, hoping to gain vengeance on those who had attempted to kill him.

Fane, Simpson, and many others were arrested, tortured, brought to trial and burned at the stake. The confessions that were extracted revealed numerous satanic practices in the country. Fane admitted that he had broken into a church one night by means of a "hand of glory." This was the hand of a murdered man that was cut from his corpse, then dipped in wax and used as a candle. All locks were supposed to open for this charm and everyone in the building would fall into a deep sleep under its power. Fane had then performed a Black Mass to Satan inside of the church, desecrating the holy place. Simpson claimed that she often foretold the future by devilish means and had caused sickness to fall upon more than one hundred people during her allegiance with Satan.

By the early seventeenth century, scores of witches had been put to death in Scotland. In Pendle Forest, a ruin that was known as Malkin Tower was a favorite place for holding Sabbaths. Two rival witches caused so much trouble in the region that the local magistrate had them arrested. On the night of Good Friday 1612, their two covens met at the tower to cast spells and try and free their leaders. Unfortunately for them, a child named Janet Device had been brought along and she betrayed all she saw and heard that night. Nearly the entire group of witches was seized and went to the stake a short time later.

In Scotland, and soon in England, professional witch-hunters began to be employed with each man receiving a good fee for every witch that he detected. There is no doubt that many of these unscrupulous fanatics sent many innocent victims to their deaths. Many of these men were known as "prickers" and they employed a method that involved stripping their prisoners, blindfolding them, and then feeling all over the bodies for some place where, perhaps after an accident, the skin had grown hard. A pin was then pushed into the skin at that spot. If the prisoner died not cry out, or did not bleed, they were told to find the pin and pull it out. If their hand went to some other part of the body, it was accepted as proof that the place where the pin had been stuck into them had been touched by the Devil – so the accused was most definitely a witch!

Perhaps the most infamous of the witch hunters was Matthew Hopkins, who with his assistant John Stearne, began a reign of terror during the time of the English Civil War. Hopkins held, or claimed to hold, the office of "Witch-Finder General," although this title was never bestowed upon him by Parliament. He conducted witch hunts in Suffolk, Essex, Norfolk and other eastern counties.

Hopkins was a Puritan and a religious fanatic who started a career as a shipping clerk, not as a lawyer, as some have suggested. According to his book *The Discovery of Witches*, he began his career as a witch-finder when he overheard various women discussing their meetings with the Devil in March 1644 in Manningtree, a town near Colchester, where he was living at the time. Hopkins brought this to the attention of the authorities and as a result of his accusations, nineteen alleged witches were hanged and four more died in prison.

Hopkins recognized this as a message from God and soon began traveling all over eastern England, claiming to be officially commissioned by Parliament to uncover and prosecute

An illustration of Matthew Hopkins, the so-called "Witch-Finder General", at work

witches. His witch-finding career spanned only from 1645 to 1647, but he claimed many victims during those two bloody years. Hopkins and Stearne were well paid for their work, earning £20 from one visit to Stowmarket, Suffolk, which was then more than a year's wages for most people.

While torture was technically illegal in England, Hopkins used various other methods to extract confessions from his victims. He often employed sleep deprivation and also used a "swimming test" to see if the accused would float or sink in the water. The theory behind this was that witches had renounced their Christian baptism, so water would supernaturally reject them. If a prisoner floated on the surface of a pond or river, then she was likely a witch. If she sank to the bottom and drowned, she was innocent. Of course, a finding of innocence served little purpose for the dead.

Matthew Hopkins' career was cut short by an illness, possibly tuberculosis, and he died in his home in August 1647 – perhaps saving a number of innocent lives.

Hopkins' career as a witch-finder was made possible by the events of the era, namely the English Civil War. The victory by the Parliamentarians in the Great Rebellion greatly intensified the witch hunts because Oliver

Cromwell's "Roundheads" were Puritans, who strongly believed in the rooting out of evil from the country. All of the fanatical sects that thrived in England at the time continued the witch trials and during the sixteen years that Britain was a republic, hundreds of men and women, mostly innocent, were drowned, whipped, and hanged as Satanists.

On May 8, 1660, the great civil war came to and end and thirty-year-old Charles II was proclaimed king. With his landing at Dover, the worst period of repression in England's history came to an end. History has regarded him as the "merry monarch" and a kind and forgiving man. He even called a halt to the hangings of the men who had carried out the murder of his father after only ten of them had been executed. "I am weary of hanging, let it rest," he said, and spared the lives of the rest of the conspirators.

The indiscriminate witch hunts were brought to an end, but random trials and burnings continued up until the nineteenth century. Witches continued to assert that they could not be induced to give up the Devil as their lover, even though his embrace was said to be as agonizing as childbirth. In 1662, a woman named Isobel Gowdie told her accusers that the Devil's scrotum was as heavy as a malt sack and his huge member was as cold as ice but he was "abler than any man can be." Another accused witch, Jeannette d'Abadie claimed that Satan's member was enormous and that it, and his semen, were as cold as ice. Although she said that she suffered severe pain whenever she joined with him, that pain was mingled with such exquisite delight that she was nearly driven mad by the ecstasy of it.

There can be no doubt that, during this period in history, many thousands of wretched people were accused of witchcraft and unjustly sent to the deaths at the end of a rope or were burned at the stake. But there were also a great number of people who died who were unquestionably guilty. It must be remembered that while many may have only angered a neighbor or indulged in sex practices that were not approved of by the Church, leading to their execution, there were also many burned at the stake who were murderers of children, poisoners, blackmailers, criminals, and worse. But were a few legitimate punishments enough to justify all of the innocent lives that were swept away, as well? No – because the crime of which the Church was most guilty was that, while claiming devotion to God, they could have inflicted such unspeakable cruelties on those who could not defend themselves.

THE SALEM WITCH TRIALS

The American colonies had their share of witch cults, although Satanism was much less prevalent across the Atlantic than it was in Europe during this era. However, as we have seen that the most relentless persecution of Witchcraft in Britain took place when the country was dominated by the Puritans, it's no surprise that most American witches were hunted down in Puritan New England. The courage and endurance displayed by the founding members of the colonies unquestionably came from their absolute faith in God, but this faith sometimes veered into fanaticism. Their religious beliefs forced a strict adherence to the word of God and they would not tolerate anyone who questioned even a single passage in the Bible – including the Old Testament verse about not "suffering a witch to live."

Starting in the early seventeenth century, a number of witch trials took place in Boston and in other parts of New England, but the most notorious affair at Salem did not occur until 1692, and it has become so infamous that it's still talked about regularly today.

The events began in the Massachusetts colony village of Salem, at the home of The Reverend Samuel Parris. He had a nine-year-old daughter, Betty, a quiet, nervous child. Also living in his household was an eleven-year-old niece, Abigail Williams, who was much bolder and who dominated her cousin. Of the reverend's wife, we know little, except that she was a devout woman who spent most of her time doing charitable works in the village. Parris had lived for a time in Barbados and had brought two black slaves to Salem with him: John Indian, who did outside work, and his wife, Tituba, who cooked and cleaned. The children were mostly cared for by Tituba, who loved them. Often, to entertain the girls, she told them stories about her island home, usually involving voodoo, and showed how to cast harmless spells. The girls were very proud of this secret knowledge and they boasted about it to some older friends - Mary Walcott, Elizabeth Booth, and Susanna Sheldon – and later, to several others, including Ann Putnam, the malicious daughter of a neurotic, gossipy mother. Ignorant rumors soon began to spread.

A short time later, both Betty and Abigail, and later other girls, were "possessed." They began to suffer from seizures that Reverend Parris claimed went far beyond anything caused by epilepsy. They were said to suffer from vacancy of mind, fits of dizziness and spells during which they crawled about on all fours and make horrible animal noises. Prayer proved to be of no avail and doctors could find nothing physically wrong with the girls. Accounts stated that the girls screamed as though touched with burning coals whenever sacred words were said over their bodies. Reverend Parris appealed for help and two ministers, Nicholas Noyes and John Hale, arrived in the village.

Many modern scholars, not surprisingly, do not believe that the girls were in any way "bewitched." Some believe the whole thing was a hoax, while others have suggested that perhaps the girls were poisoned, or accidentally drugged, by something that Tituba had brought with her from Barbados. It's believed that an herb that caused hallucinations, used during voodoo ceremonies, could have been the culprit in the case.

However, knowing nothing of magical drugs or accidental poisonings, the faithful Puritans of Salem quickly came to believe that the Devil was at work in their village. They reportedly asked all of the girls who their tormentors were but could not get a straight answer from any of them. Mary Walcott's aunt, who suspected Tituba, persuaded the slave to make a witch cake from an old country recipe, consisting of rye meal and the urine of the children. The idea was that if the family dog ate the cake made with the urine of the "possessed" girls, the dog would begin to act as if it were bewitched if the girls were truly under the influence of witchcraft. When Parris learned of this and accused his daughter of being involved with the making of the cake, she went into such terrible hysterics that he feared she would die. Betty and the other girls soon accused Tituba of witchcraft. Two other women, Sarah Good and Sarah Osbourne, were also charged.

Two magistrates, John Hathorne and Jonathan Corwin, were sent to examine the alleged witches. The law was primitive at that time and the concept that an accused was innocent until proven guilty did not yet exist. The prisoners were allowed no defense counsel and it was enough for a witness to declare that he had seen the "shape" of the accused riding through the air on a broomstick for his word to be believed. It didn't matter how much the poor soul on trial protested the testimony.

Tituba, who was considered Parris' property at the time since she was a slave, was thoroughly beaten by her master as he tried to obtain a confession from her about her evil acts. Eventually, hoping to avoid further punishment, gave him what he wanted – and confessed to anything that she could think of. Once started, she was nearly impossible to stop. She claimed that a "tall man" had come to her, told her that he was God, and ordered her to serve him for the next six years. He had brought her a book that contained nine names and

During the trials that were held in Salem, the accusers had seizures and spells in the courtroom, sealing the fates of those they claimed were witches.

among them were those of Sarah Good and Sarah Osbourne. She had flown to Sabbaths with the "tall man," accompanied by a hog, two red cats and the winged head of a cat that belonged to Sarah Osbourne. The "shapes" that belonged to the two witches had tried to force her to harm Betty and Abigail, but she had resisted.

The court readily accepted her testimony and it was evident to them that the uneducated slave had been deceived by the Devil and was an innocent victim of the witches. Evidence of this was given as Tituba also became "possessed," rolling her eyes, frothing at the mouth, and screaming that she was being attacked by a demon for having spoken out against the forces of darkness. Her husband also got involved in the ruse and he roared, blasphemed, and threw himself onto the floor of the courtroom, also apparently in agony. The court believed that he was also another victim of the horror that had come to Salem.

Hysteria soon gripped the village. A dozen people came forward, including some who may have honestly believed what they were saying, who claimed that they had seen the "shapes" of others sticking pins into dolls and taking a bloody sacrament of red bread and bloody wine. Rebecca Nurse, a respected old woman, was dragged from her sick bed to be charged as a witch. John Proctor, an honest farmer, had the courage to declare that the girls were liars and their "possession" self-induced merely to draw attention to themselves. The result of his brave speech was that he was arrested as a witch and his property was confiscated before he had even been tried.

During each of the trials, the girls were brought into the courtroom. Their behavior had an unsettling effect on the accused. If the prisoner lifted his eyes, the girls all lifted theirs; if he rubbed his face, the girls did the same; if he coughed, the girls all coughed; and so on. If the prisoner denied the charges brought against him, the girls went into a frenzy, howling and throwing themselves on the floor. Still worse, they became the jury and executioner of the accused. One by one, the girls were carried to the prisoner and he was forced to take each of their hands. If she continued to rave and thrash about, he was innocent; but if she became quiet, it was assumed that he had removed the demon that he had sent to torture her, and so was obviously guilty.

The girls had a terrifying effect on not only the trials, but on the people of the village, as well. They were constantly seeing "shapes" all over the place, and so unshakable had their belief in them become that, at the children's direction, they stabbed with swords and pitchforks at the empty air where the "shapes" were supposed to be.

A new governor arrived from England, Sir William Phips, who came to the village with Increase Mather, the father of Cotton Mather and later president of Harvard University. Mather had been prominent in the earlier witch trials in Boston, but Phips was only interested in getting together a military expedition against the French in Canada. After decreeing that all of those who had been accused of witchcraft be left chained in their cells, he left the business of trying them to the courts. A special court was formed with Deputy Governor William Stoughton as president, and six other judges.

People in Salem who feared being "cried out," as it was called, began to leave the village. Among them was John Willard, the deputy constable, who had arrested several of the accused witches. In a sudden fit of disgust, he turned on the girls, accused them of being fakes, and said that they should be hanged for what they had done. The girls retaliated against him by claiming that they had seen his "shape" strangling his own nephew, a young man who

The hanging of one of the Salem witches

had recently died. Willard tried to flee but was captured and chained up in prison, accused of having witched to death a number of other people.

Around this time, the "possessed" girls finally announced the identity of the man who had played the part of the Devil at the local Sabbaths. It was, they declared, The Reverend George Burroughs, who had been a minister in Salem a number of years before. Even though they were shocked at the idea that a minister would be involved, the magistrates quickly dispatched officers to the parish where Burroughs now lived. They stormed into his home in the middle of a meal and dragged him back to Salem. To Burroughs' amazement, he was accused of murdering a number of soldiers who had been killed near his

The grave of one of the Salem witch trial victims in the witches memorial section of the old Salem cemetery

parish while fighting Indians – not physically, of course, but as a sinister "shape," just like the other alleged witches. What possible defense could he offer to prove his innocence?

Rebecca Nurse was brought to trial. Her good reputation served her well – at first. Her numerous friends and family were brave enough to testify on her behalf and she was found to be not guilty of the crimes for which she was accused. Instantly, the courtroom was plunged into chaos. The girls howled, pulled their hair, and rolled around on the floor screaming that the woman was guilty. Unbelievably, she was brought back into court and the jury was ordered to think things over again. This time, they reversed their verdict and she was found guilty. On Tuesday, July 19, she was one of five women hanged as witches in Salem.

The terror continued to spread. Scores of people were "cried out" and the court continued its travesty of justice. Prisoners who confessed could hope for clemency, but those who denied their guilt were condemned. On September 22, eight more were hanged, including a woman named Mary Esty – which strangely, led to one of the most bizarre incidents to occur during these hysterical times. According to a servant girl named Mary Herrick, the ghost of Mary Esty appeared to her on the day that she was hanged. She said to her, "I am going upon the ladder to be hanged for a witch, but I am innocent and before a twelve-month be past you shall believe it." Shortly afterwards, Herrick claimed that the ghost told her to denounce the wife of minister John Hale as a witch. Reverend Hale knew the charge to be utterly false and he suddenly realized how many others of the accused might also be innocent.

This event – perhaps caused by the ghost of Mary Esty – marked the beginning of the end of the insanity. The governor returned from the Canadian border and was shocked to find that one hundred and fifty people were chained up in prison, waiting to be put on trial for witchcraft. He decreed that in the future, supernatural evidence would be inadmissible in his courts. This made trying the other defendants impossible. They were found to be not guilty, and the Salem witch hysteria came to an end.

"SATANIC PANIC"

The hysteria of the Salem Witch Trials marked a definitive point in American history but most believe that nothing of that nature could happen in modern times, an assumption that would turn out to be false. On the 1980s, the idea ran rampant that Satanists were everywhere. The hysteria was spread by fundamentalist Christians, radical religious groups, talk show hosts like Geraldo Rivera, and many otherwise well-intentioned people and organizations who lived in fear that a vast satanic underground was infiltrating the country. They claimed that satanic groups were spreading their message through rock and roll music, kidnapping and abusing children and could even be partially responsible for the thousands of people who went missing in America every year, never to be seen again. Those missing persons, they believed, had fallen victim to satanic cults who used them for blood sacrifices to the Devil. The evidence for such an underground was obvious, they claimed, and pointed to a handful of murders carried out by pseudo-Satanists in black t-shirts, child abuse cases that would turn out to be more than a little questionable and, of course, "recovered memories" of ritualistic sexual abuse.

But if there was one thing that can truly credited with what became known as "Satanic Panic" in the 1980s, it was the publication of a book called *Michelle Remembers*, co-written by a Canadian psychiatrist named Dr. Lawrence Pazder and his patient, Michelle Smith. I discovered this book when I was just starting my first year of high school and confess to being terrified by the contents. Not only did I believe that what I was reading was possible, I was convinced that it had all taken place. Like so many others at the time, I was fooled by the startling, horrific contents of the book, but my gullibility would not last for long. Within a few years, I began to realize, as many others also did, that the satanic hysteria of the 1980s had very little basis in truth. Unfortunately, though, the movement was only just beginning. It was just too colorful and too sensational for the talk show hosts and television evangelists to relinquish and they found that by ignoring the facts and spreading half-truths, they could keep their audiences glued to their seats – and utterly terrified that devil-worshipping boogiemen were around every corner waiting to get them.

Michelle Remembers was published in 1980 and became an almost instant bestseller. It was truly the first book of its kind and the first to deal with satanic ritual abuse, a phenomenon that would soon take the psychiatric community – and the tabloid world – by storm. The book chronicled Dr. Pazder's 1970s-era treatment of his patient, Michelle Smith. He had first started treating her in 1973 at his private practice in Victoria, British Columbia. In 1976, Smith began suffering from depression after a miscarriage, and confided in Pazder that she felt that she had something very important to tell him, but could not remember what it was. Shortly thereafter, Pazder and Smith had a session where Smith screamed hysterically for almost twenty-five minutes, then began speaking in a voice that sounded like that of a five-year-old child. Over the next fourteen months, Pazder spent over six hundred hours using hypnosis to help Smith recover alleged memories of Satanic ritual abuse that she suffered when she was a child. The abuse spanned the years 1954 and 1955 and it was carried out at the hands of her mother, Virginia Proby, and others. Smith claimed they were part of an underground "satanic cult" in the Victoria area.

The book is put together as a narrative, flashing back and forth between the past and present, and offers the version of events that Smith remembers during her therapy. It documents her mother's involvement with the cult, the many Satanic rituals that the young Michelle was forced to attend and participate in, and the many horrifying events that occurred during a time when she was literally held prisoner by the cult. During the rites, Smith was allegedly tortured, locked in cages, sexually assaulted, witnessed several murders and was covered in the blood of slain infants and adults. Pazder maintained that Smith was abused by the Church of Satan, which he stated was a worldwide organization that pre-dated the Christian church. The first ritual that Smith was forced to attend was in 1954 and the final event that was documented was an eighty-one-day ritual in 1955 that summoned the Devil himself and involved the intervention of Jesus, the Virgin Mary and the archangel Michael. The angel (conveniently) removed all of the scars that Smith received during her year of abuse and repressed all of her memories of the events "until the time was right."

Michelle Remembers was first publicized in the tabloids, including the *National Enquirer,* and in *People magazine*. It became a publishing success, earned Pazder and Smith a hefty hardcover advance, paperback rights, royalties, and a potential movie deal. Pazder was a credentialed psychiatrist in Canada and the book stated that the source material (the therapy tapes) was carefully scrutinized. Despite this, questions about the accuracy of the book's allegations were raised shortly after it was published. One of the first problems was raised by Church of Satan founder Anton LaVey, who threatened to sue for libel if references to abuse by the Church of Satan (which he founded in 1966) were not removed from subsequent editions. LaVey stated that his organization had not been, in any way, involved with any of the alleged events. This was the first issue raised about the book, but it was far from the last.

In an October 27, 1980, article in the Canadian weekly news magazine, *Macleans*, reporter Paul Glescoe interviewed Smith's father, Jack Proby, who denied all of the allegations that had been made against Smith's mother, Virginia, who had died in 1964. He stated that he could refute all of the claims that had been made in the book. Glencoe also interviewed the mother of a childhood friend of Smith, who described Virginia Proby as a kind, caring woman. He also noted that the book failed to make any mention of Smith's two sisters, Charyl and Tertia, and that Pazder and Smith had divorced their spouses and had married each other.

Unfortunately, the article did not garner much attention in Canada and was not seen in the United States at all. For this reason the allegations in the book were still considered to be true, which gained Pazder a reputation as an expert in the area of "Satanic Ritual Abuse." As more and more abuse cases began to be recovered through treatment of so-called "repressed memories," Pazder's expertise was frequently called on. He acted as a consultant for several high-profile cases and in 1985, he appeared on the first major news report on Satanism for the ABC news program 20/20. He became a part of the CCIN (Cult Crime Impact Network) and lectured to police agencies about satanic ritual abuse during the late 1980s, reporting that he spent nearly one-third of his time consulting on such cases. In September 1990, Pazder reported that he had acted as a consultant "in more than 1,000 'ritual abuse' cases." With people suddenly being prosecuted for satanic ritual abuse, district attorneys used *Michelle Remembers* as a guide when preparing cases against alleged Satanists.

It was not long, though, before the veracity of the book began to fall apart. In 1990, reporters were finally exposing further inconsistencies and problems with the book. Many who were involved with the events described in the book were interviewed and described *Michelle Remembers* as "the hysterical ravings of an uncontrolled imagination." Jack Proby was interviewed once again and maintained that the book was filled with lies. Although he indicated that he had decided not to sue, he did file a notice of intent to sue against the book's publisher if *Michelle Remembers* was ever made into a movie. Smith's childhood family doctor said that, "I believe it was ... an over-active imagination." A former neighbor of the Proby family said, "I dismissed the book as crazy. The mother was a nice, gracious lady. A little girl could not have been tortured without someone hearing." A former childhood friend of Smith told reporters, "Virginia was like a second mother to me. I certainly never had a bad feeling about her." Smith's ex-husband said that, "Not once during our marriage or the birth of our daughter did Michelle ever mention her experience."

As this new information began to surface, the local Catholic Church and Bishop Remi De Roo began to distance themselves from Pazder and Smith. Bishop De Roo now claimed that he had asked for details about the abuse years before, but the information that he requested was never supplied. It was also reported that the Royal Canadian Mounted Police stated there had never been a single prosecution in Victoria for satanic practices.

Even Dr. Pazder began to back-pedal. When asked what was more important – if the story was true, or if Michelle believed that it was true, he replied: "It is a real experience. If you talk to Michelle today, she will say, 'That's what I remember.' We still leave the question open. For her it was very real. Every case I hear I have skepticism. You have to complete a long course of therapy before you can come to conclusions. We are all eager to prove or disprove what happened, but in the end it doesn't matter."

The truth of the story may not have mattered to Pazder, but it certainly mattered to those who had believed in the book, and to those who lives had been ruined by others who suddenly began to recall instances of "satanic abuse" that may, or may not have, taken place.

In 1995, more inconsistencies in the story came out. In the book, a car accident is described but no record of the crash could be found, despite the fact that the local newspaper reported on all vehicle accidents at the time.

Former friends, neighbors and teachers were interviewed and yearbooks from Smith's elementary school were reviewed and no indication was found that Smith had been absent for any length of time, including during the alleged eighty-one-day ceremony. No one who knew Smith in the 1950s could corroborate any of the details in her allegations.

A 2002 article by Canadian occult author and Detective Constable Charles Ennis not only explored the inconsistencies in Smith's story, it also looked into the unlikely nature of her allegations. Among other things, he noted that it was improbable that a cult that had secretly existed for generations could be outwitted by a five-year- old; that the cult's rituals in Ross Bay Cemetery could go unnoticed since it was surrounded on three sides by a residential neighborhood; that an eighty-one-day, non-stop ritual that involved hundreds of participants in a massive round room could have gone unnoticed; that none of Smith's abusers (except for her mother) have ever been identified, especially since some of them had cut off their middle fingers during Black Mass. Ennis noted that Smith's "recovered memories" were nothing more than reflections of the popular culture of the time, notably the film *The Exorcist* and its many imitators. He also made notes about how Pazder's own religious beliefs and experiences living in Africa in the early 1960s seeped into the narrative. During that time, there had been widespread concern about secret, blood-drinking cannibal cults – which sounded a lot like Smith's so-called "Satanists."

To this day, the book's contents have remained unsubstantiated, other than by Smith's recollections. Even though there are still people out there who believe that the contents of *Michelle Remembers* are the truth and that there is a vast, underground conspiracy of devil worshippers who are abusing and murdering children and adults, most see the book for what it is – the colorful product of a overactive imagination and the manipulations of therapy involving "repressed memories."

Michelle Remembers was the first book of its kind, but its success would inspire dozens of copy-cat titles and it would become an important part of the controversies regarding satanic ritual abuse and repressed memory. "Satanic ritual abuse" first made headlines after the publication of the book and referred to reports of physical and sexual abuse that reportedly occurred during occult or satanic ceremonies. The phenomenon began in the early 1980s, mostly in the United States, but spread to other parts of the world, impacting how the legal, therapeutic and social work professions dealt with allegations of abuse.

The panic over satanic ritual abuse was very much like the witch hunts of the 16th and 17th centuries. In those days, allegations were made against various individuals that included cannibalism, child murder, torture and incestuous orgies, and authorities even used torture and imprisonment to coerce confessions from alleged "witches." In the modern era, the allegations had not changed much, although most of the accusations were "recovered" from the victims through hypnosis. In spite of this, the often outlandish stories were readily believed by the authorities, who still coerced the accused "Satanists" into giving confessions.

The book *Michelle Remembers* was the first to link the abuse of children to satanic rituals and it provided the model for the ritual abuse allegations that followed. The book not only influenced later allegations of ritual abuse, but many believe that such allegations only existed because of it. In the early 1980s, during the implementation of mandatory reporting laws, there was an increase in the number of child protection investigations in the United States and an increased public awareness about child abuse. The investigation of incest allegations in California was also changed, and many cases were submitted by social workers who could use leading and coercive interviewing techniques that could not be used by the police. The result was a greater number of confessions by abusers, offered in exchange for plea bargains. Shortly thereafter, some children in child protection cases began making allegations of physical and sexual abuse that took place during organized rituals that used satanic images. Such allegations were labeled "satanic ritual abuse" in the media and among professionals. Not long after, memories of similar abuse began to appear during psychotherapy sessions with adults, who often stated that the memories had been "repressed" until being recalled by stress or by hypnotic techniques.

In 1983, charges were filed in what became known as the McMartin Preschool Trial in California. The case received nationwide attention and contained allegations of satanic ritual abuse. The effect on people across the country was immediate and startling, and soon, more than one hundred preschools across the country were faced with similar sensationalistic allegations, all of which were eagerly reported by the press. Throughout the McMartin trial, the media coverage against the defendants was unrelentingly negative. Michelle Smith and Dr. Lawrence Pazder, co-authors of *Michelle Remembers,* along with other alleged abuse survivors met with the parents involved during the trial and it's believed their presence influenced the testimony that was heard in the courtroom.

The McMartin case began when Judy Johnson, mother of one of the Manhattan Beach, California, preschool's students, complained to the police that her son had been sodomized by her estranged husband and by McMartin teacher Ray Buckey, grandson of school founder Virginia McMartin and son of school administrator Peggy McMartin Buckey. Johnson's belief began when he son had some painful bowel movements, but what happened next is still in dispute. Some sources reported that he denied her suggestion that had had been molested, but another source stated that during a hospital exam, he confirmed that he was sodomized and accused a teacher at school of abusing him. Johnson soon made a number of other accusations, including that teachers at the daycare had sex with animals, that Peggy "drilled a child under the arms" and that "Ray flew in the air." Buckey was questioned but was released due to lack of any evidence. Unbelievably, though, the police sent an open letter to about two hundred parents of children at the McMartin school – stating that the children might have been abused and asking parents to question the students. In the letter, parents were supposed to check and see if their children had been involved in oral sex, fondling of the genitals, sodomy, and child pornography. Ray Buckey was named in the letter as a suspect.

The letter, not surprisingly, created an uproar and in the end, it should have never been sent at all. Judy Johnson was diagnosed and hospitalized for acute paranoid schizophrenia and in 1986, she was found dead in her home from complications of chronic alcoholism. Although the prosecution asserted that Johnson's mental illness was caused by the events in the case, Johnson admitted that she was mentally ill beforehand, which begs the question as to why her claims, including those that Ray Buckey could fly, were taken seriously by the authorities. Evidence of Johnson's mental state was withheld from the defense in the case for three years and when it was provided, was only available in the form of sanitized reports, edited by the prosecution. One of the original state's attorneys in the case, Glenn Stevens, left the case due to the way that the prosecution had withheld evidence – and over the fact that Johnson's son was unable to identify Ray Buckey in a series of photographs. He also accused the deputy district attorney in the case of lying and of withholding evidence from the court and from defense lawyers. But the trial's problems were still to come...

Long before this, in spite of the continued lack of any hard evidence, several hundred children had been interviewed by the Children's Institute International, a Los Angeles-based abuse therapy clinic. The interviewing techniques used during the investigations were highly suggestive and misleading and by the spring of 1984, claims were being made that as many as 360 children had been abused. The children were asked repetitive, leading questions that almost always yielded positive results, making it impossible to know what the alleged victims actually experienced. Some have stated that they believe that the suggestive questioning led the children to "remember" events that never took place. The interviews were later criticized as being improper, coercive, and directed in a way that forced the children to follow a rigid script that was run by the examiner. The interviews contained far more speech by the adult questioners than by the children and the situation created vivid and dramatic testimonies that likely had nothing to do with any actual abuse being suffered. Ultimately, only forty-one of the original three hundred and sixty children testified during the grand jury and pre-trial hearings and less than a dozen appeared at the actual trial.

Not surprisingly, the often "bizarre" accusations included elements of satanic ritual abuse, a panic that was just starting to emerge in the United States at the time of the McMartin case. It was alleged that, in addition to having been sexual abused, the children saw witches fly, traveled in a hot air balloon, and were taken through underground tunnels. When shown a series of photographs by Danny Davis, the McMartins' attorney, one child identified actor Chuck Norris as one of the abusers. Some of the abuse was said to have occurred in secret tunnels under the school. Several investigations turned up evidence of old buildings on the site and debris from before the school was built, but the mysterious tunnels were never found. There were also claims of orgies taking place at car washes and at airports, and of children being flushed down toilets to secret rooms where they would be abused, cleaned up and then given back to their unsuspecting parents.

On March 22, 1984, Virginia McMartin, Peggy McMartin Buckey, Ray Buckey, Ray's sister Peggy Ann Buckey and teachers Mary Ann Jackson, Bette Raidor, and Babette Spitler were charged with one hundred and fifteen incidents of child abuse, later expanded to three hundred and twenty-one incidents of child abuse involving forty-eight children. Over the course of twenty months of preliminary hearings, the prosecution presented its case, which included inconsistent statements by the alleged victims and meetings that involved the parents in the case with Michelle Smith and Dr. Lawrence Pazder, which prosecutor Glenn Stevens believed influenced the children's testimony. In 1986, a new district attorney called the evidence "incredibly weak," and dropped all charges against Virginia McMartin, Peggy Ann Buckey, Mary Ann Jackson, Bette Raidor and Babette Spitler. Peggy McMartin Buckey and Ray Buckey remained in custody awaiting trial.

In 1989, Peggy Anne Buckey appealed to have her teaching credentials re-instated and the judge in her hearing ruled that there had been no credible evidence to lead to the license being suspended in the first place. A review of the videotaped interviews with the McMartin children led the judge to issue a statement saying that they "reveal a pronounced absence of any evidence implicating [Peggy Ann] in any wrongdoing and…raise additional doubts of credibility with respect to the children interviewed or with respect to the value of CII interviewing techniques themselves." The board that issued credentials in Sacramento agreed with the judge's ruling and restored Buckey's license – adding further doubts about the entire case.

In 1990, after three years of testimony and nine weeks of deliberation by the jury, Peggy McMartin Buckey was acquitted on all counts. Ray Buckey was cleared on fifty-two of the sixty-five counts against him, and finally freed on bail after five years behind bars. During a press conference after the trial, eleven of the jurors voted to acquit Ray Buckey of all charges but the refusal of the remaining two to vote for a not guilty verdict resulted in a deadlock on the last charges. The media overwhelming focused on the two jurors who voted guilty. Buckey was retried later on six of the thirteen counts, which produced another hung jury. The prosecution then gave up trying to obtain a conviction, and the case was closed with all charges against Ray Buckey dismissed. He had been jailed for five years without ever being convicted of anything.

It was the media and social workers who helped to fan the flames of the "witch hunt" in the McMartin case and they continued to spread the word about so-called "satanic ritual abuse" in the months and years to come. Kee McFarlane of Children's Institute International, an unlicensed social worker, had recently developed a new way to interrogate children with anatomically correct dolls while in the process of writing a book on child sexual abuse. McFarlane tested their use when interviewing the McMartin children. Using the dolls, and with leading questions, she diagnosed sexual abuse in almost all of the children. She was accused of using coercion in lengthy interviews that rewarded the children for discussions about abuse and punished those who denied it. But McFarlane alone could not be blamed. She had assistance when it came to allegation of satanic abuse, both from the prosecution and by Smith and Pazder, who were called as "experts" into the case. Strangely, though, the initial charges in the case featured claims of satanic abuse, but those features were later dropped. Thanks to the media, however, they would soon surface again in other cases and claims of ritual abuse began to take on even greater proportions.

The "witch hunt" continued as the McMartin case was still going on. Psychiatrist Roland Summit spoke at conferences while the case was In progress that depicted satanic ritual abuse as part of a nationwide conspiracy. He stated that anyone who denied the existence of the abuse, as well as an underground satanic movement, was part of the conspiracy. In 1986, a social worker named Carol Darling argued in a grand jury hearing that the conspiracy reached into the highest levels of the government. Her husband, Brad Darling, gave conferences about the satanic conspiracy, which he alleged dated back for centuries.

By the late 1980s, the recognition that mental health workers had given to satanic ritual abuse led to the formation of Christian psychotherapy groups, exorcisms, multiple personality claims and the development of groups for "survivors'" of abuse. Thanks to all of the attention, federal funding was increased for research on child abuse, with large portions of the funds going towards sexual abuse. Funding was also provided for conferences supporting the idea of satanic ritual abuse, adding a bit of respectability to the idea, as well as offering an opportunity for prosecutors to exchange ideas on the best ways to secure convictions on cases that might be many years old. Many cases were prosecuted based on adult's "recovered memories" from alleged childhood assaults.

The media continued to add fuel to the fire. In 1987, Geraldo Rivera produced a national television special on the alleged satanic cults, claiming that "estimates are that there are over one million Satanists [in the United States] linked in a highly organized, secretive network." This show, along with others that began appearing at the time, were subsequently used by religious groups, psychotherapists, social workers and law enforcement agencies to promote the idea that a conspiracy of satanic cults existed and was actually involved in serious crimes across the country.

Perhaps the groups that benefited the most from the claims of satanic conspiracies were conservative Christian organizations, which were enthusiastic in promoting rumors of satanic ritual abuse. Just as the Church had been quick to condemn the accused during the witchcraft scares of hundreds of years before, religious fundamentalists in the late 1980s were using "Satanic Panic" to frighten believers and to bring new members into their churches. Christian psychotherapists began working with patients to "recover" lost and repressed memories and soon after, accounts similar to those in *Michelle Remembers* began to appear. Religious groups were instrumental in starting, spreading and maintaining rumors about satanic ritual abuse through sermons about its dangers, by way of lectures by purported experts, and by prayer sessions and showings of programs like Geraldo Rivera's 1987 "exposé."

Eventually, though, even the sensationalistic media couldn't ignore the fact that there was little in the way of hard evidence that would confirm the thousands of alleged accounts of satanic abuse, or that a vast underground conspiracy existed that was covering everything up. Media coverage began to turn negative toward the end of the 1980s and the "panic" finally came to an end between 1992 and 1995. By the end of the 1990s, allegations of ritual abuse were finally being met with great skepticism and belief in satanic ritual abuse finally stopped being given much credence in mainstream professional psychological circles.

But has "Satanic Panic" finally come to an end? Not entirely, for there are still a small number of believers out there who feel there is veracity to the idea of satanic ritual abuse and who continue to research the topic. They are the same people who still accept books like Michelle Smith's account of her own torture and abuse by a devil cult as fact. Despite the lack of evidence and inconsistencies surrounding the allegations made in *Michelle Remembers*, they believe that Smith's claims are the literal truth and that there really is a conspiracy of satanic worshipers abusing and murdering children and adults – just as many people believed that cultists were bewitching townspeople in Europe during the sixteenth and seventeenth centuries.

The philosopher George Santayana once said, "Those who cannot remember the past are condemned to repeat it." Such was the case when it came to the "Satanic Panic" of the 1980s. One needed only to look back to the era of the great witch hunts to see what was taking place in modern America, but the panic of the time was definitive proof that the rational mind can often be clouded by fear.

4. DEMON LOVERS
HISTORY AND HORROR OF DEMONIC RAPISTS

The terms "incubus" (a demon that has sexual intercourse with a woman) and "succubus" (a female demon that has sex with a man) first came into common usage during the infamous heresy and witchcraft trials from the fourteenth to the seventeenth centuries. The inquisitors believed that demons in male and female form actually copulated with the unfortunate accused in scores of cases. Although thousands of trials and condemnations produced no hard evidence of these creatures' existence, the idea that they did exist and could force themselves on the bodies of unsuspecting people became a common belief. A belief of this kind shines a glaring light on some of the darkest corners of the human mind and presents a tragic example of how easily our beliefs can be manipulated when they are twisted by those who are truly experts at it.

The rabid belief in incubi and succubi is a direct creation of the Christian Church. From its beginnings, Christianity has been beset with contentions and violence arising within and outside of the faith, although none of the problems arose quickly. The world at large was not stunned by the story of Jesus, or its shocking climax. Very few people outside of Jerusalem even heard about it. His disciples were simple men, with limited skills and intelligence, and they were not equipped to spread the message to the world. It was nearly twenty years after Jesus was killed before a powerful, eloquent man gave voice to the movement in the form of Paul of Tarsus. He was an intellectual, long familiar with Grecian theology and the ancient Jewish teachings. He had never met any of the early disciples and although skeptical at first, he created a theological system and a doctrine of belief on which the Church was founded.

It seems unlikely that the followers of the pagan gods were disturbed by the arrival of a strange new sect that had come from the old Hebrew legends. However, to the authorities, the new church had a revolutionary air about it. The real cause of the persecution of the early Christians was not their assurance in Christ's existence, but their simple faith and courage when they refused to acknowledge either the pagan gods or the divinity of Caesar. The emperor, his patience exhausted, issued an edict with an aim to have them exterminated. The Christian churches were to be razed, their holy writings destroyed, assembly for worship became punishable by death and the followers themselves lost all of their rights under the law. Tortures and executions followed, much to the approval of the general public.

But the policy didn't work. In fact, the persecution of the Christians unified them and their numbers began to grow. Two decades later, the Emperor Constantine turned the now disturbingly large movement into a national asset by granting the Christians complete religious freedom. It was from perhaps this moment that the spirit that

One of two separate paintings by Henry Fuseli illustrating the incubus, entitled "Nightmare"

marked the Christians' defiance of an outside enemy turned inward, becoming a series of fierce theological dissensions that often threatened to tear the Church apart.

Nevertheless, the Church survived and lived on while the Roman Empire crumbled under the Goths and the Vandals. When the "Holy Roman Empire" rose again, it faced a new enemy that had been created by Mohammed, stretching eastward along the entire North African shore to the Holy Land and beyond, where men prayed five times each day to the One and Only God of Islam. The Crusades against this new threat began with an enthusiasm that suggested that Christianity had regained its defiant soul, but after two centuries, the effort ended in failure and disillusionment. The Church was now lost in the moral vacancy of its leaders. However, it held its position of power, for within the kingdoms of Christendom, it had become a state within a state, maintaining its prisons, and with the Pope as the supreme law-giver of the Christian world.

Money was always needed and it as the duty of the lowly priests who were much closer to the parishioners, to find it. Any success that they had was probably due as much to their own devotion as to the brew of truth, garbled theology and superstition that was now being served by the Church. To poor response or any hint of disbelief, there was always the threat of an accusation of heresy, which could be punished by torture, or even death.

In the beginning, charges of heresy were only made against professed Christians who committed "religious error," but that began to change. Soon accusations were being made against groups like the Cathars, a highly ascetic sect that held great sway in southern France. They believed that the Earth was ruled by Satan as the God of Evil and Heaven was ruled by the God of Good. In 1199, Pope Innocent III called for a crusade to rid the Empire of the Cathar heresies. Soon after, at Beziers, the entire populace – men, women, children and infants – were slaughtered. The city was plundered and burned, becoming a vast funeral pyre. Nearly forty years later, the remnants of the Cathars, long hidden in a small fortress south of Toulouse, surrendered under a truce. The troops departed, leaving them to the mercy of the inquisitors. The Cathars were offered life in return for their submission to the Catholic authority. All of them refused – and all of them were burned as heretics.

The extermination of the Cathars was an extreme case – usually the Church found its victims much closer to home and much less ready to defend themselves. When a person was accused of being a heretic, he was first excommunicated and then handed over for execution. His worldly goods were confiscated by the Church, a rule that became an important source of revenue. By the fourteenth century, "religious error" was not the only thing that could earn a charge of heresy. By that time, witchcraft was deemed to be the work of heretics, as well.

The Church was now seeking its victims among the humble people whose magic worked through rites and charms intended to cajole the old nature spirits into actions that were either favorable to the supplicant or unfavorable to someone else. There were, of course, many signs to detect a witch, from a mere skin blemish to the sickness of a neighbor's cow, but one of the most popular accusations in those sex-obsessed times related to sexual intercourse with the Devil or one of his minions – the incubi or succubi. Such beings were part of the demonology of Christianity and were accepted without question by all but a few practical folks, who doubted whether devils, who had no actual substance, could achieve a sexual act with someone of flesh and blood.

Church officials worked quickly to ensure that having sex with a demon was truly a punishable act. To do this, they called upon the most learned theologians of the day. The most eminent of these, Thomas Aquinas, was quite specific on the matter, making it clear that human sexual intercourse with devils was not only possible but could result in pregnancy. The objection that devils had no seed was met with a convoluted explanation. A human male might copulate with a female demon, who, having received his seed, would change into a male so that it could also have sex with a woman. Aquinas also provided a simpler explanation stating, "Because the incubus demon is able to steal the semen of an innocent youth in nocturnal emissions and pour it into the womb of a woman, she is able to conceive an offspring whose father is not the demon incubus but the man whose semen impregnated her. Therefore, it seems that a man is able without a miracle to be at one and the same time both a virgin and a father." He also noted that a man, equally unknowingly but less innocently, could also provide a demon with semen through the act of masturbation.

A torrent of demonological literature appeared during the course of the next few centuries, but it was Thomas Aquinas' conception of man's sexual association with demons that laid the foundation for the witchcraft mania that followed – and provided a powerful influence on the thinking of the Church during the next five centuries.

But Aquinas did not invent the concept of a sex demon. Great thinkers from several faiths had been pondering their existence long before the creatures began conveniently ravishing the women that the Church accused of being witches. Even the mere concept of a sex demon was a perplexing problem for theologians. That God had created them directly was a unattractive idea, although it was one that was occasionally presented. However, it seemed more palatable to believe that while God might have created these monsters, they had become evil of their own free will.

Hebrew intellectuals had been dealing with the idea of demons for centuries. One of their theories was that demons were fallen angels and there was a widely accepted theology based on this idea. They believed that the angels, or Sons of God, looked upon the Daughters of Men (human women) and "lusted after them." The angels then descended to earth, had sex with women, and their children became the "giants in the earth" that were described in biblical writings. These angels, led by Azazel, were then punished by God for their transgressions – doomed to remain on earth for eternity. The lustful creatures became the incubi and succubi of legend, continuing their seduction of men and women through the ages.

Another ancient story allegedly made an impression on Christian theologians. The incident occurred after

Satan was banished from heaven. Looking for angels to add to his ranks, he tried to tempt them with descriptions of the daughters of men and the ecstasies of sex. When they failed to respond to his imagery, he made a hole in the wall of heaven, brought a woman to it and placed her outside. When the angels saw her, their lust was awakened and they swarmed out through the breach in the wall. Finally God, saw what was happening, and fearing that the entire population of heaven would be lost if he failed to act, sealed the wall and locked out all of those angels who had already departed. These became the followers of Satan.

Christians believed that the story showed how ravenous the sexual desires of men (even angels) could be and how irresistibly tempting the carnal wonder of women actually was. The angels could not withstand women's lustful allure, so how could mere mortals? In addition, the sexual contact with women was so contaminating that angels could actually be turned into demons. If that were the case, what could happen to a mortal man? Such stories helped to cement the belief that the Church was establishing about the evil power of sexual intercourse.

In the early years of the Christian Church, theologians combined the legends of ancient times and created their own theology from it concerning sex demons. Justin Martyr declared that angels copulated with women and hence, demons were born into the world. These demons then introduced evil into the minds of men, including lust, murder, war, and the entire gamut of man's vices. The early Christians also decided that the ranks of demons included all of the gods of antiquity, especially those of the Greeks and Romans. A few variations on this idea appeared, including that some of the offspring between the angels and human women became the "giants" mentioned in biblical writings. In this part of the story, however, the giants could not be admitted to heaven and were forced to wander the earth, eventually being worshipped as the gods of the pagans.

Early in the fifth century, Sulpicius Severus agreed that angels fell as the result of their erotic attraction to human women but distinguished himself by claiming that it was only to virgins that the angels were attracted. But even a virgin was capable, it seems by this way of thinking, of corrupting an angel and as a result, their offspring fell into evil.

During the Middle Ages, the old ideas about sex demons lingered on, but there continued to be modifications to the theories, as well as new ideas. Theophrastus Bombastus von Hohenheim, better known as Paracelsus, stated in the early sixteenth century that incubi and succubi were formed by the semen of those who "commit the unnatural sin of Onan," meaning masturbation. The lustful demons came to men and women at night and caused nightmares. Paracelsus believed that demons were basically the spawn of the lewd imagination of men and women, which causes them to masturbate. In other words, humans created the demons themselves by thinking them into existence. Still others believe that the smell of sexual intercourse created the demons or that dreams of sex, either by men or women, gave the demons life.

In the eighteenth and nineteenth centuries, writers and authorities on the supernatural began to subscribe other sources as the cause of demonic sexual attacks. However, even then, their explanations were various and conflicting. According to different experts, the phenomena derived from an abundance of semen in the testicles; disease in the semen; overactive imaginations; malfunctions of the uterus; and from hysteria. Incubi and succubi were described as amorous illusions, hallucinations, the result of religious or moral derangements, and one of many symptoms of insanity. In 1900, a German psychologist named Hoefler wrote that a belief in sex demons originated in nightmares and erotic dreams. Others agreed with the theory and noted that many nightmares are sexual anxiety dreams stemming from repressed incestuous conflicts.

The relationship between nightmares and witchcraft had been noted long before Hoefler. Many writers in the fifteenth and sixteenth centuries remarked that witchcraft seemed to be most prevalent in mountainous regions where nightmares are also most common. However, witchcraft authorities of the time were not likely to believe that incubi and succubi were nothing more than fantasies derived from horrific sex dreams. They claimed that the poverty and lack of education among the people of the mountain regions accounted for their interest in witchcraft, evil spirits and devil worship – which, of course, invited the sex demons to have their ways with them.

SLEEPING WITH THE ENEMY

Intercourse with an incubus was almost always described as a painful experience for the women involved,

A series from erotic drawings from the early 1800s by Achille Deveria -- *Diabolico Foutro Manie* -- illustrates the dangers and temptations of sex with demons.

although there were exceptions. Most of the women who confessed to having sex with demons compared it to childbirth and described the demon's member as being icy cold. Some men said the same thing about the vaginas of succubi they encountered. One woman, Francoise Secretain, said that while the penis of the demon was in inside of her, she felt like her whole belly was on fire.

Author Nicholas Remy in *Demonolatry* cited many witches who testified to the painfulness of demonic intercourse:

But all they who have spoken to us of their copulations with demons agree in saying that nothing is colder or more unpleasant could be imagined or described. At Dalheim, Petrone of Armentieres declared that as soon as he embraced his succubus all of his limbs at once went stiff. Hennezel at Vergaville, July 1586, said that it was as if he had entered an ice-bound cavity, and that he left his succubus with the matter unaccomplished. And all female witches maintain the so-called genital organs of their demons are so huge and excessively rigid that they cannot be admitted without the greatest pain. Alexie Drigie (at

Haraucourt, November 1586) reported that her demon's penis, even when only at half erection, was as long as kitchen utensils, which she pointed to as she spoke; and that neither testicles not scrotum attached to it. Claudia Fellet (at Mazieres, November 1584) said that she often felt it like a spindle swollen to an immense size to that it could not be contained by even the most capacious woman without pain. This agrees with the complaint of Nicole Morle (at Serre, January 1587) that, after such miserable copulation, she always had to go straight to bed as if she had been tired out by some long and violent agitation. Didatia of Miremont (at Preny, July 1588) also said that, although she had many years experience of men, her vulva was always so stretched by the member of her demon that the streets were drenched with blood. And nearly all witches protest that it is wholly against their will that they are embraced by demons, but that it is useless for them to resist.

Of course, not all complaints like these were universal – and all witches did not claim that the intercourse was carried out against their will. Most likely, they described their experiences in the terms of the expectations of their torturers and judges, in the same way that people today will produce dreams and "memories" that go along with the theories of their psychologists.

Church officials were quick to dismiss the virility of demons, lest, they argued, all women be seduced to witchcraft. It was mentioned earlier in the book that Scottish witch Isobel Gowdie stated that having sex with the devil was immensely satisfying. She stated that his member was "exceeding great and long" and that "he is abler for us that way than any man can be." This was not something that the judges and torturers wanted to hear, which made them more ready to publicize the accounts of blood, pain and enormous members that could not be contained by even the most experienced of women. They downplayed reports of women who claimed to copulate with demons as many as fifty times in one night, feeling an obligation to make the incubi less potent. They argued that only one or two of these numerous encounters were fact and that the others were illusions created by the demon to deceive the women and impress them with the incomparable stamina of the incubi. This was not, it should be noted, a good argument. After all, an illusory round of sex that provides real satisfaction is no less great than an actual one. However, it might have helped dissuade the inexperienced from inviting a demon in their beds – and it certainly made Church officials feel better.

Demons often seduced women by appearing to them in the forms of their husbands or lovers. Since they usually approached women in their beds, late at night and when they were half asleep, it was not difficult for them to accomplish this deception. Only after they had achieved their goal would they reveal their true natures. By that time, the women might be convinced that she had committed a mortal sin and believing that she was subject to torture and conviction under Church laws, had no choice but to put her trust in her only remaining ally – the Devil.

Succubi usually appeared to men in very attractive female forms in order to make them as appealing as possible. In many cases, though, in the middle of the sex act, the true nature of the creatures would become known, which could be terrifying to say the least. In some cases, men were obliged to perform cunnilingus on the succubus, forced to tongue at gaping and clammy clefts from which the smell of feces, urine and other awful stenches exuded. But this seems to be the exception more than the rule and, historically speaking; most who encountered the succubi did not tell stories of horror.

It was mostly the Christian hermits of the desert who feared encounters with the succubi. They were often tormented by these demons, which appeared to them as seductive females who sought to lead them into sin. St. Jerome and St. Hippolytus were both nightly harassed by nude succubi who tempted them with wide-spread legs and ample breasts. The holy men were, of course, staunch in their resistance and did not succumb. But exceptions were noted in the writings of the Middle Ages. One story was told of a hermit who began to take pride in his piety. He was approached by a demon in the form of a beautiful woman who said that she was lost in the desert and urgently needed a place to stay for the night. He took her in and in the dark of the night, he succumbed to her charms. But when he actually attempted to enter her, she vanished with a mocking laugh, leaving a crowd of demons in her wake, all who "assailed him for his lust." The hermit abandoned the religious life soon after and gave himself to a life of evil and depravity.

The Succubus by Henry Fuseli, 1781

Another story told of a hermit who was seduced by a succubus whose sexual demands were so intense that the hermit died from exhaustion within a month. But the succubi did not appear merely to Christian hermits. One account told of a demon that appeared in a beautiful form to a monastery blacksmith, who branded her on the face with an iron. After that, God rewarded him for his virtue by miraculously allowing him to handle hot iron without injury.

In the Middle Ages, Pope Sylvester II was allegedly a noted magician and occultist. Born Gerbert d'Aurillac, was also a prolific scholar and teacher. He introduced Arabic knowledge of arithmetic, mathematics, and astronomy to Europe, and was the first French pope, ruling briefly from 999 until his death in 1003. Due to his knowledge of science and the intellectualism of the Islamic world, rumors spreads that Sylvester was in a league with the Devil. He was also said to have had as his life-long mistress a sex demon named Meridiana, who gave him both wealth and carnal pleasure. Sylvester repented shortly before his death and was buried in the Basilica of St. John Lateran in Rome. Legend has it that his tomb will sweat just before some prominent person died. If a pope is about to die, the sweat becomes a stream that turns into a sizable puddle.

Eparchius, Bishop of Tuvergne, visited his church late one night and arrived to find a cluster of demons engaged in defiling the altar. Satan himself, who was dressed in women's clothing, presided over the celebration. Eparchius, outraged, made the mistake of calling Satan an "infamous whore" and Satan laughed at him. He then promised to give the Bishop all of the whores that he could want, seeing as he was so concerned with such behavior. The stories say, "poor Eparchius felt the torments of the fleshly appetites each night until his death."

It is remarkable, in the many stories of the relations of men and women with demons, how often men were able to resist the wiles of the creatures, in contrast to women, who seemed to find incubi irresistible. This did not, of course, imply that succubi were less attractive then incubi, and in fact the opposite seems to be the case. The stories rested on, and promoted, the idea that women, whorishly lustful and naturally inclined to vice, would always offer a more feeble defense against seduction than men would – or at least that's what the Church wanted everyone to believe.

But how was all of this possible? How were demons, supposedly ethereal beings, having physical sex with humans? The questions of whether or not incubi and succubi had material bodies, and if they didn't, how they managed to have sex was a much-debated one. The answers most often arrived at by religious thinkers were that they did have physical bodies that could be used and shaped however they liked; that they created temporary bodies for themselves from water and gases; that they animated corpses; that used the bodies of people who were drunk, drugged or possessed; and that they had no bodies but were able to create an illusion in which it seemed to the human partner that they were physically real.

Theologians and philosophers had a tough time agreeing on the ins and outs of the problem. St. Augustine declared that incubi and succubi possessed only "phantasmal" bodies, not real ones, but he later changed his mind on the matter. St. Thomas Aquinas claimed to have personal knowledge of many cases of demons having sex with humans and believed that while they were phantasmal spirits, the could sometimes borrow the bodies of living men and women. Nicolaus Jauer, a theologian from the late fourteenth and early fifteenth centuries, held that demons had no bodies at all. St. Basil and others argued that the bodies of demons were made from a solidifying of condensed vapors. English philosopher Henry More explained that the reason that the sex organs of demons were so cold was because they were formed of coagulated water, which made them like snow and ice.

However, the coldness of the incubus' penis and the icy feeling of the succubus' vaginas were taken by others as evidence of the fact that copulation had occurred with a cadaver, temporarily animated by the demon for the purpose of seduction. It was believed that fresh, uncorrupted bodies could be reanimated for these purposes. Although it seems a little silly to think that most people would be sexually tempted by a rotting corpse, there were many who insisted this was the answer to the dilemma. As proof, they pointed to the stench for which all witches were notorious, an odor that was directly caused by their intercourse with dead bodies.

It was also proposed that demons might use the bodies of living persons and force them to carry out their sexual missions. The theory was fleshed out by suggesting that possession might occur when someone was hypnotized or in a mediumistic trance. Respected occultist Montague Summers suggested that the bodies of demons might be made of ectoplasm, the same substance said to exude from the bodies of Spiritualist mediums while in contact with the spirit world. If the dead were able to materialize by using ectoplasm, he asked, then why not demons? He said that such a thing could most likely occur in situations where a medium succeeds in contacting a discarnate, evil intelligence.

How much truth is there to this theory? In the 1950s, a young woman went to see a female medium of questionable repute. This medium had taken great care to develop a reputation of association with voodoo practitioners, black magicians, drug addicts and criminals and in the days well before the "Goth" era, painted her face a ghostly white, colored her hair black and wore bright red lipstick. The young woman, mostly seeking a morbid thrill, attended several group séances with the medium and then arranged for a private sitting. The medium agreed, but stipulated that the client would have to adhere to all of the conditions that were placed on her. The first of these conditions was that both of them should be naked for the sitting. That sat down together in a gloomy parlor, facing one another in large upholstered chairs. The silence, both before and after the medium entered her trance, was unnerving and the young woman later reported that while she wished that she had not come, she was too frightened of the medium to leave.

After about a half hour, as she was becoming very drowsy, the client saw something starting to emerge between the medium's legs. Whatever it was, it was chalk white and stood out in sharp contrast to the large mass of wiry black public hair that surrounded the medium's vagina. The white vapor grew rapidly more solid, elongating and taking on a sinuous, snake-like form. Both fascinated and horrified, the young woman watched as this presumed ectoplasmic mass, clearly phallic, approached her. Then, against her will, she spread her thighs and allowed the mass to penetrate her, linking her vagina to that of the medium. It was, she said, very cold and it felt like an icicle entering her body. She recalled experiencing an overwhelming feeling of dread and yet a kind of "unholy pleasure" as it slid in and out of her. Finally, she fainted and when she awoke, the medium, still naked, was bending over her, attempting to force her nipple between the young woman's lips. Somehow, the client managed to fend her off, recover her clothing and take flight. Needless to say, she never went back for another sitting.

SATAN'S SPAWN

Demons, even if regarded as being physical, were generally conceded to have the power to be visible or invisible, whichever they preferred. Facius Cardan, an Italian lawyer and mathematician who was a contemporary and friend of Leonardo da Vinci, recounted a story suggesting that demons retained their natural form while copulating, but caused the humans to see them in some other, more attractive guise.

Cardan related that a beautiful young woman turned up pregnant and confessed to her parents that she had

Is it possible for demons to spawn children?

taken a handsome young man for her lover. He mysteriously appeared in her room at night, got into bed with her and then vanished. The girl's parents were alarmed by this and decided to spy on her. When they heard suspicious sounds in her room one night, they broke open the door and found her in the embrace of a hideous monster. They rebuked the demon, reading from the Gospel of St. John, and he quickly departed, crashing through the ceiling and setting fire to the furniture. The girl later gave birth to a monstrous infant, which was destroyed by burning it alive. The young woman never saw her demon lover in his true aspect, the way that her parents did, but only as a handsome man, presumably because he hypnotized her in some way.

This story, in addition to offering another theory about the physical or ethereal bodies of demons, also brings up another dilemma about demon lovers: was it possible that the sexual unions between demons and humans could produce offspring? Since the beginning of history, man has believed that there were creatures in the world that had been born from a union between demons (and other supernatural beings) and mortal women. According to tradition, the Great Flood had been sent by God to cleanse the earth of the fallen angels and the giants they had spawned during their intercourse with the daughters of men. In fact, demons were wantonly seducing even the sons and daughters of Noah, who felt obliged to caution his children to shun all contact with them. At this point, God sent the flood but even that did not solve the problem. Some of the demons survived and no sooner had the waters subsided than lascivious demons were once again coupling with the children of Noah.

All of the inhabitants of the island of Cyprus were once believed to be sired by demons, as were the Huns, the Eurasian tribes that later united under Attila. The demon bloodline of the Huns was said to result from Filmer, King of the Goths, becoming angry at the camp followers who had attached themselves to his army. He drove them into the woods where the insatiable women, lacking human lovers, mated with devils and their offspring were the Huns.

It has been seriously said of many famous men throughout history that their fathers had been demons. Among those thought to have been fathered by demons were Romulus and Remus, founders of Rome; Plato; Alexander the Great; Caesar Augustus; Merlin, whose father was a demon and his mother a nun; and of course, Martin Luther, leader of the great reformation against the Catholic Church. Another famous offspring of a demon and a human woman was said to be Belkis, the Queen of Sheba, who was additionally distinguished as the possessor of a luxuriant thatch of silky black pubic hair that ranged from her navel to her knees.

Some of the individuals named as being sired by demons were born, it was said, as part of the Devil's efforts to bring the Anti-Christ into the world. Merlin and Robert der Teufel (Robert, Duke of Normandy, who was also known as "Robert the Devil") were two such attempts, along with Nero, Mohammed, and Martin Luther. The Anti-Christ was thought to literally be the son of Satan, born into the world to oppose Christ. It is a Christian belief that the arrival of the Anti-Christ is a sign of the end of the world, as we know it.

An account (particularly popular with Catholics) attributed Martin Luther's origin to a time when the Devil took the form of a traveling merchant and seduced the daughter of Luther's grandfather, who had been generous enough to have provided the stranger with lodging for the night.

There are two versions of Merlin's demonic birth. In the first, the Devil came to the house of Merlin's grandmother, who was the widow of a rich man that she had murdered for his money. He then easily succeeded in seducing two of the daughters of the house, but the third daughter resisted his advances. Angry, Satan caused her to fall into an enchanted slumber and he raped the reluctant virgin while she slept. The girl became pregnant and would have given birth to the Anti-Christ, but Merlin was baptized when he was born, foiling the Devil's plan. In another version of the story, Merlin was not actually the spawn of an incubus, although Merlin's mother believed that he was. She was deceived by the demon that raped her and made her think she was pregnant because she was only bloated with gas. When the time for the birth arrived, she fell unconscious, the demon deflated her belly and then placed a stolen infant in her bed. When she awoke, she believed she had given birth to the boy.

Such false pregnancies – malignant gas filling the belly – were often visited upon women by demons who wished, for whatever reason, to deceive their human lovers. The authors of the *Malleus Maleficarum* wrote, "At times also women think they have been made pregnant by the incubus, and their bellies grow to an enormous size; but when the time of parturition comes, their swelling is relieved by no more than the expulsion of a great quantity of wind. For by taking ants' eggs in drink, or the seeds of spurge [a leafy plant used as a purgative or a herbal remedy] or of the black pine, an incredible amount of wind and flatulence is generated in the human stomach. And it is very easy for the Devil to cause these and even greater disorders in the stomach."

A story that was recounted from 1545 involved a young woman named Margaret, who experienced a distressing pregnancy after intercourse with her demon lover. It was said that her belly became so immense that those at her bedside were almost unable to find her face and her feet. From within her stomach, a disturbing racket of animal cries were heard: cocks crowing, hens cackling, cats meowing, dogs barking, the lowing of cattle, the cries of sheep, horses and more. In some versions of the tale, her pregnancy was authentic and she actually gave birth to all manner of strange, bestial creatures.

Angela de Lalbarethe, a noblewoman of Toulouse, stands out among alleged witches bearing the offspring of demons because she was the first woman to be executed for the offense by the Inquisition in 1275. The monstrous child that she bore was said to have had the head of a wolf and a tail like a serpent. She added to the list of her crimes by supposedly feeding the child the raw flesh of babies, which she kidnapped and slaughtered to appease the hunger of her own demon child.

There is little doubt that most of these so-called "monstrous offspring," believed to be demon spawn, were simply deformed infants, those born without brains or lacking limbs, for example. Many others were likely affected by dwarfism, mongolism, or other birth defects. In the days when such problems would not be as understood as they are today, such children, both those born alive and those that were stillborn, could be mistaken as creatures of the Devil.

Some children born of the union between women and demons might appear to be normal, at first, but many Church officials were wary of the devil lurking inside. Johann Wier, a sixteenth-century physician who once performed the heroic act of saving a virgin from being carried away by the Devil, declared that he had ways to detect devil children, no matter what they looked like on the surface. He stated that while such children might be small in appearance, it was a proven fact that they were heavier than normal children. They also died earlier than human children, usually not surviving beyond their seventh year. In their short life spans, they allegedly also manifested a number of disagreeable character traits, like laughing and mocking the misfortunes of others, keeping the entire household awake by crying at night, demanding more food than normal children, and abusing everyone in the house by lashing out at them physically.

They were also reported to sometimes grow at an unusual rate, as was the case of a baby born to a Herefordshire woman in 1249. At the age of six months, the child was as tall as a grown man and had a full set of teeth. It was also believed that a demonic child of extraordinary size was carried by a woman who died in 1337 after being tricked into sleeping with an incubus. She died before she gave birth to the child and it required eight men to remove her swollen body from her house for burial.

Those demon offspring who managed to survive early childhood were often believed to grow into hardy adults who were filled with pride and wickedness. They were also likely to be exceptionally tall, standing out in the medieval era, when grown men were much shorter on the average than they are today. Tall people were often met with suspicion in those days, leading many to wonder if they truly knew who both of their parents were.

BLOOD AND FIRE: THE CRUEL EMBRACE OF DEMONS

In the early days of Christian theology, demons were seen as rapists who ravished their unwilling victims. In time, though, that opinion began to change as the Church began looking for new crimes against those they were accusing of heresy and witchcraft. Women were accused of having been seduced, not raped, by these demonic intruders. Eventually, it was said, these shameless women turned to sin and lust as they continued their unnatural and unholy relationships with their demon lovers.

But even after demons stopped being regarded solely as rapists, there was no question about the fact that their attentions to human women were, to say the least, cruel and unusual. Their most prevalent cruelty was intercourse itself. As mentioned, it could be painful, if not downright agonizing. The penis of the demon might stab at the uterus like a knife or scrape the vaginal walls with rough scales. It might be freezing or burning hot and when a demon withdrew, he might bring flesh and blood along with him. The demon, with his penis erect, might penetrate both the vagina and anus all night long, switching back and forth between them, ignoring all pleas that he stop for even a moment. He also might present himself in terrifying form, forcing the woman to have sex with him amidst nauseating odors. And if he paused to give her anything to eat or drink, the food might turn to feces and the beverage to urine in her mouth.

Men were not treated nearly as cruelly during the sex act, although intercourse with a succubus might have serious or event fatal consequences sooner or later. Exhaustion was usually the greatest risk and there were many reported cases of men who were "drained dry" in a month or less. Another man who had repeated sex with a demon was made completely impotent as a result and could neither sit nor stand because of the incessant demands that were made on him by his insatiable demon lover. Eventual nervous collapse was likely to overtake the man who allowed himself to be used by a succubus for an extended length of time.

Those who were unwillingly embraced by demons sometimes became ill after their first sexual contact, or even died during the throes of an orgasm, thus sealing their damnation. It was said that witches, in the agreements that they arranged with Satan, were protected from this untimely demise, no matter how pleasurable the orgasm might be.

Theologians repeatedly claimed that once an accused witch was incarcerated, she was safe from the advances of her incubus. Yet a great many cases were cited of demons that ignored or defied this protection and visited the jailed witches in their cells. There, the incubus would have sex with the witch, threaten her, beat her and sometimes, break her neck in order to prevent her from testifying against other witches while being tortured. Demons broke the necks of their victims in a manner that would become characteristic for demonic assassins: when the body was found, the head would be completely turned around, facing backwards. Some writers have blamed suspects other than demons for these murders. The deaths, usually ascribed to suicide or demons, were probably assassinations committed by members of the witch's coven or persons hired by them, likely the jailers. The purpose was to silence

the witch before she could implicate others under torture. Considering how horrible the tortures were that most victims faced, the murders were probably merciful acts.

Witches were also often said to be abused by the incubi outside of their cells. Demons were allegedly firm believers in punctuality and if a witch arrived even a few minutes later for a Sabbath or some other engagement, they could be mercilessly beaten. An offense that was considered even graver was to cure someone without the demon's permission, or to fail to commit a crime as instructed. For such misconduct, a witch might have her womb torn out, or might be savagely beaten by a flaming hammer.

Other cruelties were less brutal and more humiliating. For example, demons enjoyed catching men and women having illicit sex and, when finding such a couple, they would cause them to become stuck together like dogs so that they would be caught in the act. Demons also thrived on making false accusations of sexual misbehavior against "righteous" men and women. One case in point told of a demon that caused a man to be persecuted by his neighbors after he was falsely accused of molesting a young girl. Demons also delighted in causing husbands and wives to believe that the other had been unfaithful, then convincing the supposedly aggrieved spouse to commit adultery in retaliation.

Demons often forced their cruelties on a person's spouse, forcing them to watch while they ravished a wife or husband in the marriage bed. Enchanted by the demon, they "became like immovable statues and were forced to watch their honor being violated before their eyes without being able to prevent it."

Husbands were at a great disadvantage in attempting to deal with their wives' demon lovers. The incubus might come to the wife in her dreams, or while the husband slept. And if the husband did not sleep soundly enough the demon might bewitch him in a way that made it impossible for him to awaken. In addition, demons were able to create lifelike effigies of women so that they could be placed in the marriage bed while the wife was in fact miles away, taking part in the orgies of the Sabbath.

How was an average person supposed to defend himself or herself against such supernatural cruelties? Answers to this question were pursued, but not with much intensity. When it was decided that women were offering themselves to demons willingly, the matter of defense against seductive and rapist devils no longer seemed urgent. There were some cases, mostly in convents, of assaults by impassioned incubi, but more often, nuns were possessed and then driven to erotic excesses with priests or with one another. In those cases, as we will see in the next chapter, the only remedy was exorcism.

In early Christian times, however, when demons were thought to be habitually attacking men and women, particularly the most pious, there were many methods for preventing and defending against such attacks. Crosses, holy water, prayers, horseshoes and garlic were often mentioned, as were the method of calling on God, the Virgin Mary, or any number of saints to directly intervene in the situation. In the sixteenth century, Martin Luther suggested baring one's buttocks in the direction of a demon and breaking wind – a risky business since it's been long established that demons are fanatical sodomists! However, Luther, who claimed to have often been visited by demons, employed the method successfully on numerous occasions.

Sometimes the preventive measures against demonic attacks happened by accident. An incubus might be incapacitated if a woman happened to be wearing a certain charm for instance, or had the grass of the St. John's wort plant around her. There were other herbs, as well as stones, symbols, relics, and more that possessed the same protective virtues. Those who were attacked could also recite prayers, sing songs, or perhaps even offer fierce resistance. In many cases, the demons would tire themselves out and retreat. A woman named Angela de Foligny reportedly withstood a demonic attack by repeatedly calling out the Lord's name. The incubus beat her severely and caused her body to ache with lust, but somehow she managed to resist.

Nuns, holy men and saints were always the main targets for attacks by incubi and succubi, likely with the idea that those who had been sworn to chastity would sin more grievously if they entered into sexual contact with demons than would ordinary people. Sex demons disguised as naked, lovely maidens were sent to tempt both St. Hilarion and St. Anthony the Great, both dedicated servants of God. Another saint that was approached was Margaret of Cortona, who was tormented in her room by a demon who made obscene advances toward her and sang lewd songs while she prayed and sang hymns. The demon demanded that she join him in his blasphemies, but she resisted and eventually was able to drive the creature out.

St. Caesarius told of a former prostitute who entered a convent as penitence for her sins. There, she was approached by a lustful incubus. She crossed herself and fended him off with holy water, but he returned a short time later to try and seduce her once more. Prayers drove him away temporarily but he continued to return for the rest of the woman's life. She could never banish him permanently, but she was able to keep him at a safe distance. St. Caesarius also told of a devout nun who was constantly approached in her bed by an incubus, even when she was at prayer. She took the advice of a priest, who told her to pronounce the word "Benedicite" (an exclamation that means something like "bless you!") when the demon returned. This time, the monster fled from her room.

For some reason, demons were apparently afraid of being beaten. In many cases, the mere sight of a club or a stick could protect a woman from attack. St. Bernard is said to have employed this method to help a woman who had been having sex with the same demon for six years. Her husband had finally left her after he learned of her supernatural adultery. St. Bernard gave the woman a stick to take into her bed with her and as long as the stick was there, the demon was too frightened to attack her. He flew into horrible rages, cursed at her and filled the air with loathsome odors, but he never tried to have intercourse with her again.

Thomas of Cantimpre was a great believer in thrashing demons with clubs, sticks or even fists, although only if religious methods failed. He told the story of a young monk who was visited in his bed at night by a succubus disguised as a voluptuous woman. The monk was about to try and defend himself by making the sign of the cross, but found that the succubus, anticipating this defense, caused both of his arms to become paralyzed. Undaunted, the monk kicked the demon, first in the face, then in her vagina, after which she abruptly disappeared.

LUST IN THE NIGHT

Albertus Magnus, the German theologian, wrote of demons, "There are places in which a man can scarcely sleep at night without a succubus accosting him."

There are few places in the world that do not have stories of incubi and succubi preying on innocent – and not so innocent – men and women. But not all of the stories date back to the Middle Ages. For instance, in 1966, a beautiful young woman in Zurich, Switzerland, named Bernadette Hasler reportedly claimed that she was having repeated sex with a demon. She said that she had experienced the creature more than 1,000 times and maintained her love for him until the end of her life. Was she really having sex with a demonic spirit, or was she merely mentally unbalanced? We will never know for sure because Bernadette died cruelly at the hands of six religious zealots who attempted to "beat the Devil out of her." It seems that the "witchcraft hysteria" of long ago is not as forgotten as we would like to pretend that it is.

Dr. Nandor Fodor

But are all phantom rapists who come in the night actually demons? Or could they be negative spirits of those who once lived? If that's the case, what could cause them to become invisible attackers after death? Could it be that they are simply continuing the same personality traits that they exhibited when they were alive? This seems possible, especially when we explore the idea that a traditional spirit is merely the disembodied energy, or the personality, of a dead person. If they were angry, violent or sex-crazed in life, doesn't it make sense that these character traits would remain as they become spirits?

There are a number of stories told of people who have been molested against their will by spirits, lustful attackers and even outright phantom rapists. Dr. Nandor Fodor, the late psychoanalyst and psychical investigator, told of a strange series of incidents involving a Long Island woman who contacted him in the 1960s. The lady, to whom he referred only as "Jean," contacted him after his appearance on a New York television show and told him that she was being plagued by nightly visits from a phantom attacker. The presence had also made advances toward the twenty-six-year-old woman's middle-aged mother.

Fodor met with Jean and her mother and learned that the spirit was someone whom Jean had known when he was alive. She was a writer and he had been a medical doctor. They had known one another casually and had never dated. Then the man died at only thirty-four, after a brief illness. Jean told Fodor that on the day the man had died, she felt his presence and heard a voice that whispered to her, "I'm not dead."

She was sitting on her bed the following day when she felt someone sit down next to her. She even saw an impression form on the mattress, although no one was there. Hands suddenly began caressing her and as time passed, the unseen presence became more intimate. It was only a matter of time before they were making love, which Jean described as "the most rapturous delight I've ever experienced."

Eventually, though, her obsession with sex with her supernatural lover began to control her life. She found herself looking forward to their nightly encounters and daydreaming about them to the point that she was unable to work. She tried to get on with her life and began dating, only to discover that her spirit lover angrily resented it. As the spirit began to demand more and more of her time, Jean started to make a conscious effort to get out from under his control.

After that, things became more ominous. She started to notice a disagreeable smell whenever the presence was nearby; what she referred to as a "male sex odor." She began to feel his hands all over her body, even in public places. Sometimes, he would cause her to have an orgasm while talking with people, which would prove to be embarrassing, to say the least. She even experienced his presence while riding on the subway. Jean's mother began sleeping in the same bed with her, hoping that her presence would keep the spirit away. Instead, he began making passes at the older woman, as well.

An exorcism was performed in Jean's house, but it had no effect on the presence. He returned that same night, jumping up and down on the bed to prove that he could not be forced to leave. She took a large crucifix and bent it in such a way that she could wear it as a chastity belt, which stopped the spirit for just one day. She took it off to get into the bathtub but when she got out, he began rubbing against her and entered her from behind. She put the crucifix back on in a hurry, but the spirit came after her every time she took it off.

Eventually, a séance was held in the hope of contacting the spirit and asking him to leave, but he refused to speak or materialize. However, his presence did begin to weaken after that and his visits became less and less frequent, before finally fading away.

Not every case of a phantom attacker is quite so dramatic, but they are normally very unnerving to those involved. Last year, I received a letter from a reader who told me of her own strange contact with an unseen attacker. The incident occurred about fifteen years before, when she was dating the man whom she later married. He lived in the upper flat of a duplex that one of his friends owned and nothing strange ever happened there until he and my correspondent started dating. Soon after, they started to hear odd noises, sounds like footsteps, and they began to experience the eerie feeling of being watched. Since her boyfriend often fell asleep on the couch while watching television, she had the bed to herself many nights. One time, she woke up in the early morning hours and felt someone next to her in the bed. She assumed that it was her boyfriend, but when she looked, she saw what appeared to be a dense shadow. Terrified, she jumped out of bed and ran into the living room, where she found her boyfriend asleep on the couch.

"I just kept telling myself that I was imagining it or dreaming," she later recalled.

About a week later, she stayed over at her boyfriend's place again and this time, he woke up with her knees pushed back against her chest, her legs open and the same dark shadow looming above her! She recalled that she could move her head and arms but her shoulders were pressed onto the bed and a weird weight was on top of her, preventing her from closing her legs and putting them down. She cried out for her boyfriend, who was next to her in bed, but he didn't wake up. The only thing that managed to get the presence to stop was when she looked straight up at it and screamed, "No! No! No, stop!" The shadow vanished and when it did, her boyfriend woke up and just assumed that she had been having a bad dream.

In the days that followed, she tried to tell her boyfriend about what was happening in the house, but he didn't want to hear about it. She later found out that it was because he was scared. His friends who lived on the floor below told him several times that they heard peculiar noises coming from the flat whenever no one was home, which had him spooked. Eventually, the friends spoke with the previous owner of the duplex and he recalled that a few years before he sold the place, a young man that was renting the upstairs apartment committed suicide by hanging himself in the garage. When my correspondent told her mother about this, she told her daughter to pray for the boy and she did. She went to the flat, sat down on the bed, talked out loud to the young man and then said a prayer. She later told me, "I don't know if he went away after that or if he just went into hiding but we didn't hear anything or experience anything anymore."

Perhaps the most famous incident involving a phantom rapist started in 1974, when the "Entity" case began. Researchers Dr. Barry Taff and Kerry Gaynor from the now-defunct Department of Parapsychology at UCLA, became involved in the bizarre case, which would go on to be the basis for a book and film, as well as for years of study and speculation.

On August 22, 1974, Taff and Gaynor began a ten-week investigation of the home of Doris Bither, who had overheard Kerry Gaynor's conversation with a friend as they were taking about haunted houses in a Los Angeles bookstore. Doris approached him and told him that her house was haunted. After a brief discussion, Gaynor took her contact information and told her that he would be in touch with her as soon as possible.

On their first visit to Doris' small, crowded home in Culver City, Taff and Gaynor spent the evening getting information about the phenomena that the family had been experiencing over the past few months. The family consisted of Doris, a petite woman in her late 30s, her six-year-old daughter and three sons, ages ten, thirteen and sixteen. They all told the same story about what had been going on, especially in regards to an apparition seen in the house. The described it as being semi-solid in form and standing well over six feet in height. Both Doris and her eldest son also claimed to have seen two dark, solid figures with Asian features in Doris' bedroom, where the figures seemed to be struggling with one another. This peculiar event occurred several times and once, Doris claimed that she physically bumped into one of them in the hallway. The family members were sure that they had not imagined the apparitions and refused to accept the possibility that they might have been intruders who entered the house.

Doris believed that the "Asian beings" were evil and was very distraught about the idea that they might injure her family. This belief came from the fact that she claimed to have been sexually assaulted by them. She told the investigators that the two smaller beings had held her down by her wrists and ankles, while the remaining towering form had raped her. According to Doris' account, this happened several times and each time, large black and blue bruises were left behind on her ankles, wrists, breasts, vagina and along her inner thighs. Doris also dramatically claimed that, during one attack, her eldest son had overheard the scuffle and entered her bedroom. According to Doris, he had witnessed her being tossed around the room by the entities and when he came to her aid, an invisible force slammed him against a wall. The son corroborated the story, stating that he was terrified by what had happened.

Unfortunately, Doris' claims of spectral rape could not be substantiated since they had occurred several weeks before Gaynor and Taff arrived at the house. This prevented them from seeing the bruises, although they admitted that everyone in the house seemed shaken and upset. Even so, they became concerned that Doris was either mentally disturbed or making things up, upsetting the rest of the family with her anxiety. They didn't plan to continue pursuing the case, believing that she could be better helped by someone in UCLA's psychology department.

However, before they could turn down the case, Doris called and informed them that five individuals outside of her family had now seen the apparitions. So Taff and Gaynor decided to return to the house with cameras and tape recorders. They immediately noticed something odd when they entered Doris' bedroom. Even though it was a hot, August night and the windows were closed, the temperature was unusually low when compared to the rest of the house. The cold spots faded in and out irregularly, sometimes completely disappearing. They could find no source for the cold areas, but they soon discovered that this was just the first of the many oddities about the house.

The first inexplicable happening occurred while Gaynor was talking to Doris' eldest son in the kitchen. He was standing a short distance from a lower kitchen cabinet when the cabinet door suddenly swung open and a pan jumped out, landing about three feet away.

After examining the cabinet, Taff and Gaynor went into the bedroom again with Doris and her friend, Candy, who had joined them for the evening and who claimed to be psychic. Taff took a photograph of the bedroom with a Polaroid SX-70 camera and it came out perfectly. After they were in the room for about fifteen minutes, Candy shouted that she sensed something in the corner. Taff ran back into the room with the camera and immediately aimed and fired it at the area Candy had indicated.

The photograph that resulted was bleached completely white, as if it had been exposed to some sort of intense energy or radiation. The same thing happened a few minutes later when Candy again directed their attention to the corner. This time, the photo was still bleached out, but not as badly as the first time. Puzzled, Taff took another photo, this time in the living room, thinking that something might be wrong with the camera. This photo came out fine, as did subsequent photos taken by Kerry Gaynor in the bedroom. The only difference was that these photos were not taken while Candy "sensed" a presence in the room with them.

A short time later, Taff took another photo, this time because of a cold breeze that came from the closed bedroom door. This photo turned out to be the strangest of the night, showing a ball of light that was about one foot in diameter. It hovered a few inches from the door in the photo, but no one had actually seen the light appear.

Moments later, while the investigators were poring over the photo, Taff happened to glance toward the bedroom's east window. In a flash, he spotted several rapidly moving, blue balls of light. He immediately raised the Polaroid camera and took a picture in the direction of the curtains. The resulting photo was blurred and badly bleached but the blue lights that Taff had seen were nowhere to be found.

A few minutes later, Candy again warned about the presence of an entity in the room, this time standing directly in front of her. Taff fired the Polaroid in her direction and he obtained an odd photo of Candy. Her face was completely bleached out, yet her dress and the room behind and around her was completely clear and distinct. Another photo, this time taken by Kerry Gaynor under the same conditions, again captured Candy with bleaching about her face while the rest of the photograph again very clear.

At this point, the investigators became convinced that something out of the ordinary was occurring in the house.

Over the course of the next ten weeks, a team from UCLA was almost always present in the house. They returned many times for investigations, bringing dozens of eyewitnesses, researchers and photographers with them. Initially, most of researchers were skeptical of the events reported by Taff and Gaynor but soon, more of them began to share their belief that something supernatural was happening after witnessing inexplicable things happen for themselves.

One night, what can only be described as a "light show" took place in the house in front of twenty startled onlookers. Most of the photos that were taken though, were disappointing. The lights were so bright that most of them came out overexposed. One photo,

One of the strange photographs taken during the investigation of the "Entity" case

though, did manage to show what the investigators saw that night. The frame was filled with reverse arcs of light. The reason this photo was so important is that the arc on the wall, if it were really on the wall, would be bent because the two walls are perpendicular to each other. In the photo however, the arc is not bent, which means that it was floating in space at the time and signifies that it was dimensional and not just a flashlight being aimed at the wall.

One of the witnesses present that night was Frank De Felitta, a filmmaker and author who would go on to write the book based on the case. De Felitta would later vividly recall the light as it moved into the center of the room and the shouts from those present. He said that Doris started screaming as the light moved toward her, cursing and daring the entity to show itself, instead of just producing a light. At that point, it started to appear and witnesses would later claim to see a part of an arm, a neck and what looked like a bald head. Everyone present saw the same thing at the same time, ruling out any individual's hallucinations.

Another interesting event of the evening involved an extremely sensitive Geiger counter that had been brought along to record any activity in the radiation field of the house. The instrument began behaving very oddly when the lights were most active, as the previously constant background radiation registering on the device dropped off to zero. When the light activity began to dwindle and then fade away, the Geiger counter's meter returned to its normal level of ambient background radiation. Barry Taff believed that it was possible that the strange activity either used the background radiation as an energy source or that the energy given off by the lights scattered the ambient energy field in such a way that it could no longer be registered.

On the evening after the fifth full-scale investigation of the house, they received a frantic telephone call from Doris informing them that black poster boards that had been taped up on the walls to assist with photographing the scene had been torn down. Literally "all hell" had broken loose in the house that afternoon, she said, ending with the destruction of the boards. Doris said that she had been in the bathroom, which was adjacent to the bedroom, and heard the boards being ripped down – pulled by unseen hands.

Taff and Gaynor returned to the house that night and saw that the tape and poster boards had been ripped away with such force that large portions of paint and plaster had been removed along with them. They also noted that the bedroom was sharply colder and than the rest of the house and that a foul smell that had been encountered in previous nights had again returned. Doris told of seeing more apparitions in the house and it took until nearly midnight before the investigators could calm her down enough for them to feel they could safely leave.

Five days later, they returned for another investigation and once again, all of them witnessed the apparition of a large, muscular man as it begin to form in Doris' bedroom. His shoulders, head and arms were clearly seen by the twenty people who were present. Suddenly, they heard two loud thuds and Taff turned to see two of the investigators on the team fall to the floor. Seeing the apparition proved to be too much for them and they both passed out. Needless to say, neither ever worked with them on a case again.

The seventh investigation of the house took place six nights later and it began with Doris recounting a series of incidents from the night before. Both Doris and her thirteen-year-old year old son stated that a pair of candelabra had left the kitchen sink and flew across the room to strike her on the arm. The boy corroborated Doris's story and added that the candelabra had barely missed him as they flew across the room to hit Doris. They also claimed that a large wooden board, firmly nailed to the wall under one of the bedroom windows, was literally torn loose and propelled about fifteen feet across the room. The board narrowly missed hitting Doris. This time, Taff and Gaynor were both able to examine the large red bruise on Doris' forearm, sustained from the flying candelabras, and saw the loose board.

The walls in the bedroom were bare again because all of the poster boards had again been ripped down. At several locations on the walls, pieces of tape were left hanging with large sections of dislodged paint and plaster beside them, while everything else within the bedroom, as on previous occasions, remained untouched. Again, Doris claimed to have heard the boards being torn down.

The team was accompanied that night by Dr. Thelma Moss, head of the laboratory in UCLA's Neuropsychiatric Institute, various assistants from the lab, several psychiatrists from the institute who professed an interest in such phenomena, and Frank De Felitta, who had brought along a professional cameraman in hopes of capturing the eerie lights that had been seen in the house on other occasions. The group decided to try a séance, which would hopefully make contact with the entities in the house. They replaced all of the poster boards on the walls and set up for the séance.

The strange lights did not return on that night, however, at one point, Gaynor suggested to the presence in the house that it should demonstrate its strength by again tearing the poster boards off the walls, but this time in their presence. As if in immediate reply, several of the poster boards directly above Doris' head were suddenly torn loose and one of them struck her sharply in the face. Everyone present watched the boards being torn loose from the tape on the walls, as if by invisible hands. After quieting an upset Doris, Gaynor again requested the presence to remove more poster boards from the walls. Once again, two more well-secured boards were ripped from their position from the back wall and thrown across the bed to the floor, although this time missing Doris completely, to her great relief.

Dr. Thelma Moss

The eighth and final visit to the house came on October 31, 1974. It turned out to be a great disappointment and Taff later realized that the previous investigation had marked the first decline in visual phenomena at the house. On Halloween night, there was only a weak odor and a slight sensation of cold, but no lights, no strange movements or anything else.

After this final visit, they temporarily lost contact with Doris as she finally moved out of house in Culver City. Three months later, in February 1975, they heard from her again. This time, she stated that the phenomena had followed her to her new home in Carson, although it was much less frightening than it had been. As time went on, Doris' rather tragic story continued. She claimed that the presence followed her first to Carson, then to San Bernardino, then all of the way to Texas, then back to San Bernardino again. In an even stranger twist to the story, while in San Bernardino, Doris claimed that she had been impregnated by the spirit that was raping her. However, medical results were more consistent with either an ectopic or a hysterical pregnancy. It was no surprise, given the circumstances, that Doris believed that the presence would eventually kill her.

Thanks largely to the fact that the phenomena seemed to follow Doris wherever she went, Barry Taff eventually came to believe that the strange events were the product of Doris's troubled mind. According to the case history, Doris was an alcoholic, had suffered a traumatic childhood, and had been involved in several abusive relationships as an adult. Some have even suggested that the "three entities" that held her down and raped her were merely fantasies created in her subconscious as representations of her three sons, with whom frequently fought. Even leaving out mental illness Taff felt that everything that had occurred could be explained as a poltergeist outbreak, created by the anxiety and tension of the human agent that was present, which was in this case, Doris.

But, overtime, even Taff has remained concerned about this possible answer to the mystery. "What if we are wrong," he later wrote. "What if there really are discarnate entities that prey on weak and emotionally troubled individuals? What if ancient mythology regarding the incubus and succubus are more than just legend, superstition and religious hysteria? Are we so cock-fired sure of ourselves and our neonatal paranormal science that such a definitive statement is possible?"

SEX DEMONS: REAL OR UNREAL?

What's really going on here? Have incubi and succubi really been sexually tormenting humans for thousands of years? Or is there another explanation for all of the tales of terror that have haunted us for centuries? There is no question that since the dawn of recorded history, people believe they have been teased, tortured, raped and intimidated in their sleep. But is this really the work of sex demons?

Most readers scoff and say that such stories should be relegated to the era of the Middle Ages, where they belong. But consider a report from just a few years ago from the Zanzibar islands, where every decade or so, a creature with talons and bat-like ears and wings reportedly terrorizes men in their beds at night. This demonic creature breaks into homes and sodomizes men as they sleep. One victim of the demon, Mjaka Hamad, was quoted as saying: "I could feel it, something pressing on me. You feel as if you are screaming with no voice . . . He had come to do something terrible to me, something sexual." After the men are raped, the demon insists that the victims spread the word of his visit. Otherwise, he warns them that he will return for another visit – and it will be much worse.

The attacks are so real to these men that they run through the streets, crying of the monster. Many of them rush to the emergency room, attributing broken hips and an assortment of cuts and bruises to the demon. The people are so terrified that families sleep arm-in-arm in front of their homes, guarding against the monster's intrusion. Even those who don't believe in the demon admit that it is real to the injured and terrified men.

The skeptics have no explanation for what is taking place but, based on history, the men appear to be the victims of a modern-day incubus attack. Such creatures normally prey on women, but as the men of Zanzibar have discovered, that's not always the case. The incubus frequently creates a feeling of pressure on the victim's chest, making the person feel as if he or she is suffocating. Others become temporarily paralyzed. And while the poor victim lies terrified, gasping for breath and physically unable to resist, the incubus carries out his savage rape.

Such stories have always been with us, as evidenced by the preceding chapter, and the incubi and succubi have appeared in countless, varied form, including shape-shifting monsters and vampires. Even so-called alien abductions are thought to be nothing more than modern versions of attacks by sex demons. Times change and so do our monsters, although the essence of the attacks has remained the same. Millions of people, centuries apart and across all geographical and cultural lines, have experienced essentially the same nighttime attack – but how?

Most accounts of nighttime attacks are the same. The victim awakens and a demon, or a sense of something evil, lurks nearby. They cannot move. They cannot speak or call out for help. Their eyes may be open, but they are utterly helpless and terrified. Often, a creature sits on the victim's chest, making them feel as if they are being smothered. As they become more and more terrified, the heartbeat quickens and they begin to sweat. These experiences have been well documented. Some of the attacks are sexually stimulating, but often the creature comes only to terrify the unsuspecting soul.

Today, most people scoff at the idea of nocturnal attacks being caused by demonic spirits. Sleep researchers have offered a scientific explanation and claim they are, in fact, a physiological condition known as sleep paralysis. It is a phenomenon that is also referred to as a "waking dream." In this twilight state, our dreams are so vivid and bizarre that they seem terrifyingly real.

Sleep paralysis strikes during the transition between REM sleep and becoming fully awake. While you are in REM sleep, your body temporarily paralyzes you, which safeguards you against acting out your dreams. But occasionally something short-circuits in the mechanism that controls the waking and sleeping states. We wake up, or feel as if we have awakened, but the body hasn't yet turned off the paralysis that protects us in our sleeping world. Often, our dreams haven't been totally switched off either. And since neither our essential organs nor our eyes are paralyzed while we sleep, the victim's eyes can be wide open. He can literally watch his nightmare unfold around him in the waking world. His heart will race and he'll be, understandably, terrified.

To make matters worse, sleep paralysis can often be accompanied by strange noises. Some people see eerie lights or feel a pressure on their chest, as if they are suffocating. Uncannily, most people report sensing an evil presence. This is a state that brings out your worst nightmares and many feel as if they are going insane. And though this state generally passes within a few minutes, and is almost never harmful, most victims report that at the time of the occurrence, they feel certain they are going to die. Although many people have never heard of this condition, it's not rare. A large percentage of people have experienced it to some degree at least once.

The logistics behind it are pretty easy to understand. If one wakes and finds herself paralyzed, naturally she will be terrified. Her heart rate will zoom, causing her to feel pressure on the chest. And the brain, which is still partially asleep in this state, will provide a reasonable accompanying nightmare. Naturally, when one is so petrified, her respiratory rate will go up. She will hyperventilate, which leads to carbon dioxide retention, which in turn leads to sexual arousal. So it seems quite plausible that all these physical manifestations could bring about horrible, and sometimes sexual, waking nightmares.

Countless legends have sprung from people's visions while experiencing sleep paralysis, which may explain why so many have experienced the same types of encounters. Perhaps a woman is disturbed by a story about an incubus, wakes in the night with sleep paralysis and her nightmare comes to life as a demon that is attacking her.

One of the most prevalent demons connected to sleep paralysis is the Old Hag, a legend that grew out of Newfoundland. In fact, another name for sleep paralysis is "Old Hag Syndrome." The Old Hag is generally toothless and hideous, with white hair and scales on her face. She sits on her victim's chest, sometimes trying to suffocate him. But the Old Hag is not alone. In the darkest corners of our mind, many strange creatures lurk, all waiting to be brought to life by one restless night of troubled sleep.

Or is that really all there is to the idea of sex demon attacks?

Perhaps we should not dismiss the elements of the supernatural in this phenomenon so quickly. Even some of the most eminent experts in the field have been unable to entirely explain the remarkably consistent "hallucinations" of victims of sleep paralysis. They are especially amazed at the similarities of those who have claimed to see the Old Hag. Such "hag attacks" have been documented in countries all over the world and many of the victims had no knowledge of the folklore surrounding these attacks.

Coincidence? Collective consciousness? Perhaps – but then again, perhaps not. Perhaps there really are monsters out there, lurking under our beds, just waiting until our guard is down, or our prayers unspoken, before they descend on us with cold, oversized members and vaginal clefts that feel like ice and reek of moldering flesh.

Makes you think twice about leaving the lights on at night, doesn't it?

5. BY LUST POSSESSED
SEX AND DEMONIC POSSESSION

When most people think of demons, and their dark works, the idea of "possession" is usually the first thing that comes to mind. It's been portrayed in books for centuries and has become commonplace in films and on television over the last several decades. Most people are aware of what happens when someone is demonically possessed: heads spin around, furniture and people levitate, pea soup is vomited all over the room, along with all sorts of other scary and nasty stuff. But is any of this real, or was it merely created years ago from the minds of Church officials, novelists and screenwriters? Do people really become possessed?

The state of "possession" had been defined as the presence of a spirit entity that occupies and controls the physical body of the subject. Belief in this phenomenon has long existed in most countries of the world and in the Christian religion it was once regarded as the exclusive domain of demons acting in the interest of Satan. This belief comes from a number of references in the Bible, including a passage from Mark that states: "In my name shall they cast out devils;" from Luke that reads: "Then he called his twelve disciples together and gave them power and authority over all devils," and also from Luke: "And the seventy returned again with joy, saying Lord, even the devils are subject unto us through Thy name." There is also the story of when Jesus confronts a man who is possessed by so many demons that they call themselves "Legion." He exorcizes the spirits and banishes them into a herd of pigs, which commit mass suicide by throwing themselves off a cliff. Thanks to references such as these, demonic possession remains a tenet of the Catholic Church, as well as fundamentalist sects in the modern day.

But possession, as such, has many faces. The symptoms can include agonized convulsions, often with writhing and posturing of sexual desire, the mouthing of obscenities, vomiting, reports of poltergeist-like happenings, terrible violence and even a state of unnatural calm. No unanimous opinion exists today as to the causes, or causes, of possession and the subject has involved such varied disciplines as religion, medicine, psychiatry, spiritualism and demonology. As in most cases of possible supernatural behavior, the possibility of fraud cannot be overlooked and many cases that were once thought to be genuine have later been questioned or disproved. However, it is clear that in many cases, the symptoms, sometimes of deep distress, mental or even physical torment, are genuine, no matter how controversial

Jesus casts out demons in this biblical scene

the cause. This does not dismiss the possibility that the symptoms of the possession may be the result of suggestion, either external or self-induced, and that victims may be better served by the care of a psychiatrist rather than an exorcist.

As far as most doctors and mental health specialists are concerned, the diagnosis of demonic possession is one that reeks of medieval superstition and ignorance. The symptoms, they believe, are subject to either a wide range of medical and psychiatric interpretations or can be dismissed as misperceptions and hallucinations. They feel that the cases of possession in the past were nothing more than conditions like epilepsy, hysteria or what has been referred to as multiple personality disorder, which is rare in itself.

During a convulsive seizure, a person with epilepsy can experience extreme muscular rigidity, foaming at the mouth and rapid back and forth head movements. His face may be distorted and he may produce strange, guttural noises that are caused by a spasm of the throat muscles. During the period just before a seizure, the patient may experience hallucinations, seeing things and hearing weird sounds and voices.

These are all things that are sometimes attributed to people who are thought to be possessed but there are also distinguishing characteristics of the "real thing." The first of these is that a demonic attack may last for hours at a time, as opposed to the five minutes or so that an epileptic seizure usually lasts. Extreme movements, rather than rigidity, are more characteristic to a possessed person and muscular reflexes tend to be strong. According to church records, other signs of a possession include "the ability to speak with some familiarity in a strange tongue or to understand it when spoken by another; the faculty of divulging future and hidden events; and the display of powers which are beyond the subject's age and natural condition."

A condition called hysteria also produces many of the symptoms of someone who is possessed. The following description of a female hysteric was recorded in the early 1900s by Professor Paul Richter, a French doctor at La Salpetriere, a famous mental hospital in Paris:

Suddenly, we heard loud cries and shouting. Her body, which went through a series of elaborate motions, was either in the throes of wild gyrations or catatonically motionless. Her legs became entangled, then disentangled, her arms twisted and disjointed, her wrists bent. Some of her fingers were stretched out straight, while others were twisted. Her body was either bent in a semi-circle or loose-limbed. Her head was at times thrown to the right or left or, when thrown backward with vehemence, seemed to emerge from a bloated neck. The face alternately mirrored horror, anger and sometimes fury; it was bloated and showed shades of violet in its coloration...

Two of the most striking details in Richter's description are that of the woman's entangling and disentangling legs and that of her body "bent in a semi-circle." The description of what is referred to as the "hysterical arch," or the bending of the body in a semi-circle, appears in some texts describing characteristics frequently seen in cases of possession. All of the other symptoms described above have also been observed by exorcists over the years. In addition, the appearance of livid marks on the skin ---- sometimes resembling bites, symbols or even letters ---- is also known to be produced by hysterics.

Given this partial duplication of symptoms, how does the Church distinguish between hysteria and genuine cases of possession? The determining factor is the context in which they occur. If the symptoms come about at the same time as an aversion to religious objects and if they are accompanied by paranormal phenomena (the ability to detect religious items that have been hidden, understand languages never learned, levitations, and so on), the Church is much more likely to consider the symptoms to be manifestations of possession.

As mysterious as hysteria, and as likely to be confused with possession, is multiple personality disorder, in which a person can manifest several different personalities. Each personality may have its own likes, dislikes and speech patterns, and may be opposed to the others or indifferent of them. If one, or more, of them seems diabolical in nature, it's possible that the disorder could be mistaken for possession. It should be noted, however, that true cases of multiple personality disorder are extremely rare. They are usually connected to repressed memories of traumatic events, such as sexual molestation, and often emerge to protect the victim from facing what happened. For this reason, labeling cases of possible possession as multiple personality disorder can be

Two depictions of exorcisms of the possessed -- from Medieval times and in the modern day.

problematic at best.

Even so, doctors are usually violently opposed to even considering the idea of demonic possession when medical or psychiatric disorder might explain the symptoms being exhibited by a patient. With only a hatred of religious objects and instances of paranormal phenomena (which most of them do not believe in anyway) standing as the criteria for a case to be considered to be one of possession rather than hysteria, most doctors and psychiatrists are likely to reject these incidents as misperceptions and hallucinations on the part of the witness. A few, less skeptical medical professionals might concede that something strange can be going on, but they will probably steer toward parapsychology rather than possession.

In cases where objects are reported to move about without anyone touching them, many will point toward poltergeist phenomena rather than the work of demonic spirits. The word "poltergeist" actually means "noisy ghost" in German and for many years, researchers believed that boisterous ghosts were causing the phenomena reported in haunted house cases of a violent and destructive nature. The variety of activity connected with such cases can include knocking and pounding sounds, disturbance of stationary objects, doors slamming and violent, physical actions by sometimes heavy objects. Despite what some believe, many cases like this have nothing to do with ghosts --- or with demons either.

The most widely accepted theory in many "poltergeist-like" cases is that the activity is not caused by a ghost, but by a person in the household. This person is usually (but not always) an adolescent girl, and normally one who is troubled emotionally. It is thought that she is unconsciously manipulating the items in the house by "psychokinesis," the power to move things using energy generated in the mind. It is unknown why this rare ability seems to appear in some females around the age of puberty but it has been documented to occur. Most of these disturbances are short-lived because the conditions that cause them to occur often pass quickly. The living person or "agent" subconsciously vents her repressed anger or frustration in ways that science has yet to explain. An unhappy or emotionally disturbed young person might exhibit symptoms of this type, which match some of the criteria of a possession but again, is something else entirely.

As the reader has undoubtedly discovered by now, modern science is quick to try and explain away the idea of spiritual or demonic possession. There are many possible explanations as to why a person cannot be possessed and yet, the explanations fail to account for all of the symptoms that a possessed person is alleged to exhibit. Does this mean that possession can be real --- or is simply that science has not yet found a reason as to why some so-called "possessions" defy explanation?

One thing is certain, whether possession exists or not, there are people all over the world who believe that it does --- and they have whole-heartedly believed this for centuries. The belief in possession dates back to the years of the early Catholic Church but it gained prominence due to a number of famous cases during the Middle Ages. Instances of nuns possessed by satanic influences affected convents in France, Italy, Spain, Germany and elsewhere. Commonly beginning with a single nun, the possession proved to be highly contagious and whole groups became involved. Coinciding with the relentless years of the Spanish Inquisition, the cases often had tragic consequences for anyone who might be accused of causing a person to become possessed. Usually the victims themselves were not considered to be responsible for what had occurred to them and their treatment was confined to the expulsion of the demons by exorcism. The exorcists, who formed one of the minor orders of the Church, were priests who specialized in the work using methods that had been drawn out in the *Rituale Romanum*.

The *Rituale Romanum*, which is still used in the Catholic Church today, was issued in 1614 at the behest of Pope Paul V. It was designed to formalize practices that had developed during the early days of the Christian Church and it placed special emphasis on identifying diabolical possession, selection of the exorcist and defining the setting and texts to be used during an exorcism ritual. The ritual has retained its central features over the past centuries, although recent revisions were made in 1952 and 1999. Today, the text is initially designed to establish the actual presence of demonic possession. For this, it specifies:

First of all, one should not easily assume that someone is possessed by a demon unless he shows signs that distinguish the possessed person from those who suffer from melancholy [mental Illnois] or some [physical] disease. The signs indicating the presence of a possessed person are as follows: speaking in an unknown tongue or understanding someone who speaks in a language unknown to the person; revelation of distant and unknown matters; manifestation of powers beyond one's natural age and condition; as well as other such matters, all of which, when taken together, compound such indications.

However, as noted earlier here and by Monsignor Carlo Balducci in 1959, parapsychology has widened the possibility of natural phenomena (such as psychokinesis and precognition) being interpreted as demonic in origin. Combine that with mental illness and some types of medical conditions and it becomes much harder to determine what is a real possession and what is not. For this reason, the exorcist's first task was to confirm that the victim was indeed possessed by a Christian devil, who existed only by the permission of God. In that way, the demon was subject to the authority of the Christian priest. Numerous manuals covered not only the discovery and expulsion of demons from humans and animals but many techniques for countering demonic offenses, both small and large. There was, it was believed in the past, scarcely any evil that a demon was not capable of, from the drying up of milk cows to the more serious grievance of inhibiting the sexual intercourse of married couples.

Once a satanic origin was established, the exorcist's next problem was to find the manner of the demon's entry into the possessed, which might be due to the demon's own initiative, invitation by the possessed person or, as believed in past centuries, by the incantations of a witch. The latter was usually preferred because it meant an easier expulsion and when the witch was discovered, she could be tried, hanged or burned. The most difficult process of discovery involved situations when there seemed to be no clear reason for the victim to become possessed. In many historic cases, pious and religious people were often reportedly possessed by demons. In these cases, it was often believed that the possessions occurred as a test of the victim's faith or that of the exorcist himself.

From the records, it is clear that an exorcism had the nature of a contest between the exorcist, armed with the authority of God and the Church, and the demonic intruder. An exorcist could fail, he could even be destroyed if the battle went against him and the fact that several exorcists died prematurely ---- and several went insane --- seems to lend credence to the horror of the exorcism itself. The prayers, adjurations and commands of the exorcist, along with the ritual acts prescribed, were in themselves dramatic and when they provoked, as they were intended to do, a dialogue between the exorcist and the demon, they could be overwhelming and fantastic. For it was here that the drama of the confrontation reached its height as the demon's bestial voice belched out its obscenities while the priest answered with commands and prayers.

While we think of an exorcism as "driving out" the demon, it is really more of a case of forcing the demon to make a binding agreement. In some instances, there may be more than one demon possessing a person. The word "exorcism" is derived from the Greek "ek" with the verb "horkizo", which means "I cause [someone] to swear" and refers to "putting the spirit or demon on oath." To put it simply, it means invoking a higher authority to bind the entity in order to control it and command it to act contrary to its own will. In the Christian sense, this higher authority is Jesus Christ, based on the belief that demons and evil spirits fear Christ. This belief hearkens back to the story mentioned earlier when Jesus cast out a legion of devils from an afflicted man. And not only did Christ exorcize demons and unclean spirits but he gave the power to his disciples as well. "….He gave the power against unclean spirits, to cast them out, and to heal all manners of sickness, and all manner of disease." (Book of Matthew)

Thanks to passages in the Bible that mention the expulsion of demons, Catholics and Protestants alike believe they have the power to cast out devils and to heal the sick. The Catholic Church uses the *Rituale Romanum* as an outline for exorcisms but the ritual may vary as determined by the exorcist performing the expulsion. The code of Canon Law allows authorized ministers (exorcists) to perform solemn exorcisms over not only the faithful but also over non-Catholics and those who have been excommunicated from the church.

The greatest danger to the exorcist during the ritual is becoming possessed by the demon himself. This is the reason why the exorcist must feel as free from sin as possible and to feel no secret need for punishment. Many priests will fast and pray for some time before taking part in the ritual and during a prolonged exorcism, while they continue to fast, some will report extreme weight loss. Only a priest who is convinced that he is right with God can be safe during an exorcism. Otherwise, the demon can easily entrap him.

The *Rituale Romanum* has its own special qualifications for the priest who served as an exorcist. He had to lead a genuinely religious and virtuous life; must adhere to the rules and regulations governing exorcism, as defined by the Bishop of his diocese; must have a profound knowledge of the theory and practice of exorcism; and had to make sure that the location and manner of exorcism was selected in accordance with faith and human dignity. In other words, there could be no undignified behavior during the exorcism, no idle talk with the entity, and no questioning of the demon about occult or future events.

The solemn "Great Exorcism Rite" in the *Rituale Romanum* covers twenty-three printed pages. During the ritual, a number of items are usually present, including salt, which represents purity, and wine, representing the blood of Christ. The victim will be asked to hold a crucifix during the rite and the exorcist may also use holy water, religious medals, rosaries and relics, which may be physical items that were once a part of a saint (like a splinter of bone) or objects touched or blessed by saints. The reading of the ritual begins with a series of prayers, psalm readings and an initial command for the unclean spirit. Next, biblical passages concerning possession are read. The priest's stole and his right hand are placed on the possessed person and the specific words of exorcism are spoken. Interspersed by the sign of the cross, made on the possessed person's forehead and chest, the two exorcism passages are as follows:

A possessed woman sees the face of a demon in the mirror.

I exorcise thee, most evil spirit, direct embodiment of our enemy, the entire entity and its whole legion, in the name of Jesus Christ, to go hence and escape from this creature of God. He, himself, commands thee, who is master from the heights of heaven to the depth of the earth. He who commands the sea, the winds and the tempests, now commands thee.

Listen, then, be filled with fear. O Satan, enemy of the Faith, enemy of the human race, who creates death and steals life, who destroys justice and is at the root of evil, who stimulates vice, tempts men, betrays nations, originated envy and greed, causes discord and brings suffering. Why dost thou remain and resist, when thou knowest that Christ the Lord will destroy thy strength? Fear him who was sacrificed in Isaac, sold in Joseph, and slaughtered in the Lamb, crucified in man, and yet is triumphant over Hell.

Depart, therefore, in the name of the Father and the Son and the Holy Ghost. Make way for the Holy Ghost, but the sign of the cross of Jesus Christ, our Lord, who with the Father and the Holy Ghost lives and reigns, one God, for ever and ever, world without end.

The second exorcism is as follows:

I adjure thee, thou old serpent, by the judge of the quick and the dead, by thy maker and the maker of the world, by him who has power to send thee to Hell, that thou depart quickly from this servant of God [name of the possessed individual], who returns to the bosom of the Church, with fear and the affliction of thy terror. I adjure thee again, not in my own infirmity, but by the virtue of the Holy Ghost, that thou depart from this servant of God [name again], whom Almighty God hath made in his own image.

Yield, therefore; yield not to me but to the Ministry of Christ. For his power compels thee, he who subjugated thee to his cross. Tremble at his arms, he who led the souls to light after the lamentations of Hell had been subdued. May the body of man be a terror to thee, let the image of God be terrible to thee. Resist not, neither delay to flee this man [woman], since it has pleased Christ to dwell in his [her] body. And although thou knowest me to be a sinner, do not think me contemptible.

For it is God who commands thee.

The majesty of Christ commands thee.

God the Feather commands thee.

God the Son commands thee.

God the Holy Ghost commands thee.

The sacred cross commands thee.

The faith of the holy apostles Peter and Paul, and of all other saints, commands thee.

The exorcism cannot be expected to be achieved as the result of one rite, outlined in the *Rituale Romanum*, or without delays, frustrations and problems. When such a struggle occurs, the exorcist is advised to add a variety of prayers and readings from the Psalms. A "Prayer Following Liberation" may be said when complete success has been achieved. As mentioned earlier, the use of holy water, the laying on of hands and the placing of the priest's stole on the possessed person may also become part of the ceremony.

Exorcisms were always considered dangerous, dating back to the days of the early Church. According to the story, from the Book of Acts, several "itinerant Jewish exorcists" began trying to expel demons from the afflicted and their ritual included a phrase that cast out the demons "in the name of Jesus, whom Paul preaches, I command you to come out." During one such attempt, the evil spirit turned on the men and demanded of them, "Jesus, I know, and I know about Paul, but who are you?" The possessed man then turned and attacked them like a wild animal. He beat the men mercilessly and stripped them of their clothing, before throwing them into the street, naked and bleeding.

Exorcisms were never to be entered into lightly, but for several centuries during the Middle Ages, they became commonplace for, as mentioned already, Satan seemed to be everywhere in those days.

EXORCISM IN THE MIDDLE AGES

Possessions and exorcisms were a part of Church theology from the very beginning. However, it would not be until the Middle Ages that demons began randomly possessing people on a grand scale, or so it was believed at the time. Exorcists who gained a reputation for success were in steady demand. Their first task in every case was to make sure that the possessed person was, in fact, a victim of a Christian devil and a minion of Satan. In that way, they were subject to the conjurations of a Christian priest since a pagan demon could scarcely be expected to obey. Once satanic origin was established, the exorcist's next problem was to determine the manner of the demon's entry into the possessed, which might be due to its own initiative or the incantations of a witch. The latter was preferred because it was usually much simpler to drive the demon out and a witch to be identified, tried and burned.

Since in Christian demonology the names of individual demons (there were about 6,000 of them listed!) were known, they could sometimes be identified by the ravings of the afflicted and could be addressed by name. Questions that could only be answered by the demon – like how many demons were present and how long they planned to stay – were asked. As mentioned, an exorcism was a contest between the exorcist and the demon and if the priest failed, it could mean insanity or perhaps even death. The official prayers, adjurations and commands of the exorcist were dramatic and when they provoked, as they were meant to do, a dialogue between the exorcist and the demon, they could be sensational. Stories, tales and legends surrounded the many exorcisms that were occurring and never before the epidemic of possessions in the sixteenth and seventeenth centuries were the demons of the Church so well exposed to the public. Their names and individual characters, crimes and vices became familiar to the most common and uneducated of people.

In many cases, victims of possession were known to seduce, or even attempt to rape, other people and these incidents were always blamed on the devil that possessed the person. If something like this occurred, a traditional exorcism could be performed to try and rid the person of the offensive creature. Sometimes, however, exorcisms were used as a weapon against visiting incubi. A priest would wait with the woman in her room until the expected demon arrived, and then perform the exorcism before the incubus could carry out his assault. It was well known that exorcists in these situations were putting themselves in great peril since the demon could make use of the woman's body to try and disarm and seduce the priest.

In the early days of the Church, exorcisms often consisted of nothing more than punching a possession victim in the nose, thus dispelling the demon. Unfortunately, though, possessing demons became much harder to handle by the Middle Ages and their victims became much more tragic – and much more public.

THE DEVIL IN THE CONVENT

During the Middle Ages, sex demons seemed drawn to convents and monasteries across Europe. Nuns and monks were not only raped by demons but began to be possessed by them also, causing them to act in ways that were completely the opposite of their normal behavior. The holy sisters began to discover strange and unusual fires burned in their bellies while seductive voices whispered in their heads, exhorting them to uninhibited erotic acts. During the seventeenth century, epidemics of possession swept through the convents of France with dramatic outbreaks that have become the stuff of legend today.

In 1609, the first signs of a demonic infestation came to light at the Ursuline convent of Aix-en-Provence and involved a young woman, Sister Madeleine de Demandolx de la Palud. Only one other girl was actually claimed to be possessed but the contagion spread to other convents later and the consequences of Madeleine's possession were as tragic as any other of the day.

Madeleine was born into a wealthy family and was always said to have religious inclinations. Perhaps for this reason, at the age of twelve, she was sent to live in a small convent of six nuns at Aix, which was a sister establishment to one of the Ursuline order in Marseilles. Life there was apparently uncomfortable for a girl from a fine household and after two years, she returned to her family in Marseilles. She was bored and depressed when she returned home but her personality began to change after she met Father Louis Gaufridi, a local parish priest. He began visiting her parents' home and Madeleine was immediately taken with the young, handsome and virile man. And Madeleine was not alone. His lively personality had made him very popular with all of the women in the parish and he led an active social life.

There is little doubt that many of the local women were in love with him and not surprisingly, Madeleine followed suit. Before long, rumors began to spread concerning the frequency and the length of the priest's visits to her home, especially when her parents were absent. The rumors came to the attention of the Reverend Mother of the convent in Marseilles, who dropped a hint to Madeleine's mother about the situation and warned Father Gaufridi about his conduct. The priest took heed of the warning and stopped coming to the house. And although Madeleine told her mother that he "had stolen her most beautiful rose", no lasting damage seemed to have been done.

The following year, Madeleine entered the Marseilles convent as a novice and confessed to the Reverend Mother that certain intimacies had occurred with Father Gaufridi. There were no drastic actions taken, although the girl was transferred to the convent at Aix. Just before Christmas 1609, Madeleine began acting very strangely. She started suffering from cramps, convulsive tremors and fits, having visions of devils and one day, during confession, she smashed a crucifix. She was believed to be possessed and Father Jean-Baptiste Romillon, who had founded the convents at Aix and Marseilles, attempted an exorcism. Unfortunately, the ritual failed and three other nuns began to suffer from the same cramps that troubled Madeleine.

Anxious about what could have occurred to cause the girl to become possessed, Father Gaufridi was questioned about his contact with her. Although he denied having any sexual contact with the girl, Madeleine stated that she had, in fact, engaged in intercourse with him, starting at the age of twelve, and that as a precaution to divert suspicion away from him, he had given her a potion so that any baby she might have would not resemble him.

Father Romillon continued the exorcism and five other nuns became infected by Madeleine's symptoms, although only one of them, Sister Louise Capeau, showed signs of also being possessed. In desperation, Father Romillon took both of the young women to the Grand Inquisitor in Avignon, Father Sebastian Michaelis, an aged and experienced priest who had burned eighteen witches at Avignon in the preceding months. His attempts at an exorcism were as fruitless as those of Romillon had been. Only a Dominican priest named Francois Domptius was able to make any progress toward saving the girls, but his attempt at exorcism was not without its share of drama.

During one ritual, Louise began to speak in a "deep bass voice" that named the various demons that possessed her. Her body was being tormented by three of the vile creatures, but Madeleine, she claimed, was inhabited by a legion of monsters. Madeleine began to blaspheme, "howling and crying with a loud mouth" and at one point, one of the possessing demons revealed that Father Gaufridi was the cause of her possession.

With the possession of the two young women beyond doubt, the Grand Inquisitor summoned the man accused of having caused it, ordering him to attempt an exorcism that would undo the damage. When the nervous priest arrived, he attempted to carry out the order. Unfortunately, he had no experience with exorcisms and his attempts provoked cries of jeering laughter from the two nuns. His angry response made him appear all the more guilty to Church officials and he was locked in a cell to await trial.

Not only had Madeleine laughed at him, but she also charged him with a list of obscene acts that only devils could possibly accomplish. However, a search of his home in Marseilles produced no evidence of the kind of depravity of which he had been accused. On the contrary, the investigators found only indications of his good character and fine standing among his parishioners. Perhaps reluctantly, he was released and allowed to return to Marseilles. But this was not the end for him – Father Gaufridi wanted vindication. With the help of other clerics, he appealed to the Bishop and the Pope to suppress both of the convents and to have the two nuns placed in prison. In the end, he should have left the situation alone. His appeals led to further investigation and he was once again arrested.

While this was taking place, Madeleine began to develop a new assortment of symptoms. She behaved wildly, danced, sang lewd songs and experienced bizarre erotic and often violent visions. She reportedly "neighed like a horse" and raved of Sabbaths involving sodomy and the eating of small children. She vomited strange objects and would stop anywhere she was standing and deposit unnaturally huge piles of steaming feces on the floor. After these torments, she would lapse into a deep, coma-like sleep.

Father Gaufridi's case was moved forward and the matter went before the civil courts of the parliament of Aix in February 1611. The head judge, Guillame de Vair, was a superstitious man and was quite ready to accept purely "spiritual evidence" as the basis of the trial. The events at the exorcisms were re-told and during the recital, the two girls experienced seizures and convulsions. Their behavior alternated between anger and penitence, but they were always insolent toward the clerical witnesses. On February 21, Madeleine confessed that her allegations toward Father Gaufridi were false – "all imaginings, illusions and not a word of truth to them." Later in the trial, she spoke raptly of her love for the priest, and then suddenly began to convulse into motions "representing the sexual act with violent movements of the lower part of her belly." While on the witness stand over the course of several days, she contradicted herself repeatedly. It was said that she twice attempted suicide while the trial was going on.

Father Gaufridi was not allowed to testify until March. He was sick and haggard by then, worn down by nearly a year of dealing with the Inquisition. His second arrest had landed him in a damp underground cell, where he was kept heavily chained. After months of torture and abuse, his health was broken and after his entire body was shaved, and three "devil's marks" were revealed, he was ready to confess and sign anything that was placed before him. His confession was a lurid one, claiming that he had signed a pact in his own blood and that he had gotten promises from the Devil that he could have any woman that he wanted, among other things. He was charged with fifty-two offenses, all of which he admitted – until his health improved. After that he denied everything, stating that his confession had been extorted through torture.

His retraction was, of course, ignored and in April he was found guilty by his own confession and on all charges, which included fornication since a medical examination had revealed that Madeleine was not a virgin. Her claim that he had stolen "her most beautiful rose" may have been one of the only truths that she spoke about the matter.

An illustration of a possessed nun by Felicien Rops

Father Gaufridi was sentenced to be burned alive in the most terrible way possible, with a pyre made from bushes, rather than wood. This had already proven to burn much slower and caused more torment to the condemned. Meanwhile, he continued to be interrogated and tortured as the officials tried to learn the names of any accomplices that he might have had. He confessed to taking part in Sabbaths (although his "confession" showed a genuine ignorance of what occurred during these rituals) but no matter what the torture inflicted upon him, he swore that he could name no names. The last five hours of his life were spent with him asking forgiveness from God and being taken by cart to the stake. Because of his final confession before God, the Bishop of Marseilles allowed him to be strangled before the pyre at his feet was lit.

On the day after Father Gaufridi was burned, Sister Madeleine was miraculously cured.

Nevertheless, a short time later, she was also accused of witchcraft and a few years later, a second charge was made. This time, she was condemned to life in prison, although family influence eventually allowed her to be released into the custody of relatives. She died at the age of seventy-seven.

Sister Louise Capeau was never cured. Within a year of Gaufridi's death, she accused a blind girl of witchcraft and helped to have her burned at the stake. After that, she vanished into history.

From about 1628 to 1647, nuns in Louviers alleged themselves to be possessed by demons that were in league with the father confessors of the convent. During that time, the nuns claimed to have fornicated with black cats, which had penises like those of large men. They attended Black Sabbaths and participated in orgies with devils, clerics and the ghost of the dead priest who had been their initial seducer. Every crucifix in the convent was supposedly turned upside-down.

According to reports from a trial that gained more than its share of public interest, the priests involved instructed the women on lesbian intercourse and then watched as they carried out the directions. Nuns wandered about the convent, proudly confessing their sins, were baptized in urine and took communion in the nude. During these ceremonies, the priests would place the communion host on their upright penis and encourage the nuns to place it in their mouths.

Most instances of possession in the convents of the seventeenth century arose from sexual yearnings aroused by a man who was brought by duty or routine into the confines of the cloister. A case that worried Church officials between 1658 and 1663 was different only because of the fact that the accusations of sexual bewitchment were not against some attractive or revered priest but against the mother superior of the Ursuline convent of Auxonne. Barbara Buvee, known as Sister St. Colombe, was the one who aroused, or

This painting from 1581 shows a lustful monk preying on a nun under his control. An epidemic of sex-crazed Church officials often to led to reports of "possession" as an excuse for what was going on behind convent walls.

attempted to arouse, the desires in question. This caused great concern because lesbian tendencies, although less common than heterosexual temptation, could never be ignored. The Church was well aware of how quickly outbreaks of sexual possession could spread and the matter called for an immediate careful and quiet investigation. It was, in fact, so quiet that it took nearly two years for the scandal to become public, when Barbara Buvee was accused of having bewitched eight nuns.

All of the women testified that they were sexually excited by one of their confessors, the young but unattractive Father Nouvelet. One of the nuns, Marie Borthon, claimed that she had suffered great temptations of the flesh for him, others had erotic fantasies during menstruation, and all were convinced that only witchcraft could be the cause of their desires. The earnest young priest must have been relieved when he was not named as having contrived the possessions of the nuns, but as a safeguard, found it wise to suggest that he had also been bewitched. Two local women were accused of having cast spells on the priest, although in the absence of any evidence, they were merely sentenced to be banished from the region. Tragically, as they were ushered out of the court they were lynched by a mob that was waiting outside.

Father Nouvelet suggested that an exorcism be attempted on the nuns, and that he should be the one to carry it out. The idea was well received by all, including the nuns, who were documented to display some unusual happenings during the rituals that followed. Records say that, "Sister Denise, with only two fingers, lifted a heavy vase which two strong men could scarcely move, other nuns adored the sacrament by lying on their bellies, heads and arms raised off the ground and their legs bent backward to form an arc." Father Nouvelet initiated his own highly specialized form of exorcism, which involved either lying in bed naked with the women or conducting services during which they struck erotic poses before the altar.

There seemed to be little evidence to incriminate Barbara Buvee in any of this, but more was to come, which would suggest an immoral, but highly complicated, motive. It was said that Buvee had quarreled with Father Nouvelet's predecessor, Father Borthon, whose three sisters were members of the convent. She had been punished for her insubordination toward the priest with floggings and an enforced fast. After Father Nouvelet began his rather unique attempts at exorcism, Sister St. Colombe protested his methods – only to be met with anger by the nuns, who blamed her for their possessions and began making vile accusations against her. On October 26, 1660, Barbara Buvee, as Sister St. Colombe, was formally accused of witchcraft and held in solitary confinement until her trial began on January 5, 1661.

The nuns, including the three Borthon sisters, who had all been possessed of lustful desires for the young confessor priest, gave detailed testimony of Sister St. Colombe's sexual advances toward them. A Sister Henriette stated that Buvee had kissed her passionately and placed her hand on her breast and when Henriette protested, her superior replied that she thought she was kissing a holy statue. Sister Humberte had visions of hell, in which the Mother Superior had embraced her and "lay down on her like a man on a woman." Sister Charlotte Joly testified that she had witnessed interaction between Buvee and Sister Gabrielle de Malo, including tongue kissing and reciprocal touching beneath their skirts. Sister Francoise Borthon had been made to sit across the lap of Buvee, she said, and the woman had "put her finger into her private parts just like a man would have done." Another sister said that she had a vision of the Mother Superior holding a sacred host in one hand and an artificial phallus in another, "with which she committed on herself impure acts." She was also said to have introduced the nuns to the pleasure of cunnilingus and masturbated them with her artificial penis. All of this, it was charged, was done with the aid of the Devil, who possessed the nuns, afflicting then with hot and aching vaginas and making them helpless to resist Sister St. Colombe when she wanted to have her way with them.

One of the most curious developments in the case was the way that it was handled by the court. On March 18, 1661, further investigation was ordered into the situation and in August 1662, all charges were dismissed against Sister St. Colombe. During the months between, further medical and other reports had been obtained. They varied and included fraud, sickness in a few cases, genuine demonic possession in others, but there was a sort of "not proven" verdict in regards to whether or not Sister St. Colombe had anything to do with the situation.

Another famous possession was that of Angela de Foligny, who became a raging sex addict as a result of being influenced by demons. Later, she claimed to have copulated with Christ, a not uncommon craving for holy women of the time.

But France was not the only country to suffer from convent infestations. Another place that was overwhelmed with sex demons was the Diocese of Cologne in Germany. There, investigators searching for forbidden works on black magic found a packet of love letters in the belongings of a nun that had been written to her incubus. Her bizarre appetites spread to the other nuns of the convent and they began reporting having sex with demons that were disguised as handsome young men and being knocked to the ground by a large black dog that pounced on them and licked their vaginas. When this occurred, the Devil rendered them powerless and unable to stop it.

The nuns of Cologne were not alone. The holy sisters of Nimeguen were victimized by a black dog that raped them in their beds. Similar erotic manias, which included hallucinations of rapes by huge-membered demons, were rampant in the convents of Kentorp and St. Bridget.

It has been rumored that convents were still plagued by waves of erotic mania even in the nineteenth and twentieth centuries, though the epidemics may have taken a different form, and the Church was able to keep the embarrassing incidents quiet.

One of the most recent instances of convent infestation by demons was reported to have occurred in the late nineteenth century. It involved a young woman named Cantianille who had been placed in a convent of Mont Saint-Surplice at Auxerre. At the age of fifteen, the girl was alleged to have been violated by a local priest, who dedicated her to the Devil. The story added that the priest himself had been corrupted in early childhood by a nun who had belonged to a sect of possessed sisters that had been created on the very day Louis XVI was guillotined. Cantianille's possession caused a frenzy of other possessions in the convent, followed by reports of orgies, lewd behavior and lesbian encounters. Cantianille was sent away from the convent, where she was exorcized by a priest of the district, Father Thorey, who was apparently "contaminated" by the girl he was trying to assist. As the hysteria at the convent grew worse, the Bishop was forced to intervene. Cantianille was driven out of the country, Father Thorey was disciplined and the entire affair had to be settled in Rome. The most curious after note to the case was that the Bishop, terrified by what he had seen at the convent, requested to be dismissed from his position soon after. He retired to Fontainebleau, where he died two years later – reportedly still disturbed by the incident behind the convent walls.

The strange affair at Auxerre was perhaps the most recent case of alleged possession involving nuns, a convent and the sexual obsessions of an isolated group of desperate women – but it not would be the most famous to emerge from the annals of the supernatural.

THE DEVILS OF LOUDON

One of the strangest, most notorious and most terrifying cases of mass possession was the episode that involved Urbain Grandier and the nuns of Loudon in 1634. Few such cases have been more thoroughly documented, both in official records and in contemporary writings, and few have offered such a bizarre look into the minds of the people involved.

The Loudon case centered around one man, a priest named Urbain Grandier. He was born in 1590 and as a young man, entered the priesthood. In 1617, he was appointed to the position of parish priest of St. Pierre de Marche in Loudon, France. Grandier was a handsome, cultivated man who, despite his avocation, had an eye for attractive young women.

Father Urbain Grandier

He was a worldly type of priest, which was not uncommon in seventeenth century France. Unfortunately, he lacked discretion in the conduct of his numerous affairs and his arrogance made him many enemies. As it would later turn out, many of those enemies eventually found themselves in positions from which they could engineer Grandier's downfall.

In times, Grandier's sexual affairs became so notorious that they attracted attention in high places. Perhaps most shocking was the news that came in 1630 that the priest was not only carrying on a relationship with Madeleine de Brou, one of his young penitents, but was also accused of being the father of an illegitimate child born to Philippa Trincant, daughter of the public prosecutor at Loudon. Grandier was arrested, charged with immorality and found guilty. Somehow, though, he managed to persuade Archbishop Sourdis of Bordeaux to allow him to go free and to resume his clerical duties.

Grandier returned to Loudon to find that his enemies had joined forces with a Father Mignon, a priest who filled the post of confessor at a small Ursuline convent in Loudon and notably, hated Grandier with a passion. Between Mignon and an assortment of Grandier's enemies, a scheme had been hatched to discredit Grandier further by persuading some of the nuns at the convent that there were possessed. They were to confess during their exorcism that Grandier had bewitched them. The mother superior, Sister Jeanne des Anges, was involved in the conspiracy and she was the first to exhibit signs of demonic possession. Soon, other nuns began to mimic her symptoms and it was not long before a full-scale infestation was under way. The mother superior, along with several of the other sisters, began going into convulsions, acting out in lewd and erotic ways, holding their breath, and distorting their faces and voices. One of the nuns, at the height of the attack, whispered Grandier's name and soon several others began to claim that Grandier was to blame for their possession – they claimed that the demons that tormented them hissed his name into their ears. Sister Jeanne confirmed his guilt and gradually the story grew more and more elaborate. The motive that was given for Grandier's evil bewitchment was his thwarted ambitions and a desire to exact revenge on the nuns because Jeanne des Anges was known to oppose his advancement.

Alarmed at the growing scandal, Archbishop Sourdis stepped in and came to Grandier's rescue again. He sent his personal physician to Loudon and after examining the nuns the doctor pronounced that they were not possessed. The archbishop forbade Father Mignon to continue with any further exorcisms and these sensible measures put a stop – as if by magic – to the nuns' strange behavior.

Although calm was restored at the convent, the conspiracy against Grandier continued to fester. Thanks to the priest's past behavior and penchant for making enemies, his opponents soon found other ways with which to continue their attack against him. A relative of Sister Jeanne des Anges named Jean de Laubardemont, who was an agent of the crown and a close supporter of Cardinal Richelieu, was sent to Loudon on business. When he arrived, he was apprised of the situation with Grandier, whom he knew had once written a satire that infuriated the Cardinal, by his relative, the nun in the notorious convent. He realized that Grandier's demise could be worked to the advantage of everyone involved. He contacted Richelieu, who planned, for purely political motives, to revive the institution of the Inquisition. He wanted to stage great public exorcisms, which would bring fear to the Protestants and clear the way for the revoking of the freedom of religion act that had recently passed. With Grandier's case, he would instigate a trial at Loudon and at the same time pay off a personal score against Grandier, which dated back to the priest's embarrassing satire. He gave orders to de Laubardemont to form a hand-picked commission to arrest – and convict – Grandier.

To gain witnesses to support the original case against Grandier, Laubardemont appointed three priests to begin a public exorcism of the allegedly still-possessed nuns. Under the thrall of Father Surin, a Jesuit; Father Lactance, a Franciscan; and the Capuchin Father Tranquille, the women repeated their demonic accusations of possession, displaying new symptoms of even greater intensity than in the previous attack – the one that had been halted by a medical doctor and common sense. They shouted, screamed, contorted their bodies in hideous positions, masturbated publicly and entered convulsive trances as the exorcisms wore on. Various methods were attempted by the priests, including the use of a large brass enema

The "real" proof against Grandier was provided in the form of an actual written pact that the priest had allegedly made with the Devil. The document, hand-signed by Satan, Beelzebub, Leviathan and Astaroth, was seriously presented by the prosecution as having been stolen by the demon Asmodeus from the Devil's own files.

syringe, which was supposed to flush the more stubborn demons out of the nuns' anuses. Grandier himself was coerced into taking part in the exorcism, since it was alleged that he was the one responsible for the nuns' condition.

Meanwhile, the charges against Grandier continued to pile up. Not only was he charged with causing the nuns to become possessed, but he was also accused of incest, sacrilege and a number of other crimes. Richelieu's agent was able to gather sixty witnesses who would attest to these crimes. But even at this stage, Grandier continued to underestimate the power of those who were working against him. He believed that he had little to fear since the charges that had been brought against him were imaginary. Much to his surprise, he was arrested on November 20, 1633 and thrown into prison in the castle of Angers. Proof of guilt was soon found in the form of a four "devil's marks" on his body, spots that were insensitive to pain.

Grandier went on trial in 1634, but the hearing was fixed against him right from the start. Richelieu had made a calculated choice to have an investigating committee handle the case, instead of a normal secular court. The committee denied Grandier's legal right to appeal to the courts in Paris, leading to a complete travesty of justice. When the bailiff of Loudon led a public protest (Grandier did still have some friends left), the movement was quashed by Laubardemont, who portrayed the protest as being critical of the King, and hence an act of treason. All evidence in support of Grandier's innocence was disregarded and pressure was applied on a number of his defense witnesses to keep silent – or face an accusation of witchcraft. Several of the nuns had a change of heart and attempted to recant their previous accusations, but the court would not allow them to be heard. Jeanne des Anges herself was denied a hearing when it became evident that she wished to refute her earlier statements and claims.

The "real" proof against Grandier was provided in the form of an actual written pact that the priest had allegedly made with the Devil. The document, hand-signed by Satan, Beelzebub, Leviathan and Astaroth, was seriously

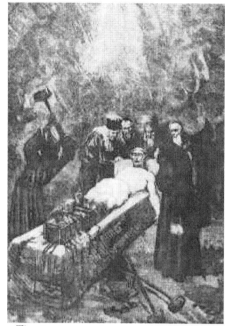

The torture and execution of Father Grandier is depicted in these illustrations.

presented by the prosecution as having been stolen by the demon Asmodeus from the Devil's own files. When it was displayed in court, the words were shown to be written from right to left, in "mirror writing," following the widely held belief that devils performed most of their actions in reverse to show their hostility towards Christianity.

Judgment was found against Grandier on August 18 and, not surprisingly, he was found to be guilty of magic, *malefica* (attempting to do harm by witchcraft), and causing the nuns to be possessed by demons. Sentence was passed and the priest was to be tortured according to "first and last degrees," which was designed to force him to incriminate others. Then, on the day of his execution, he would be allowed to ask for God's pardon and then would be taken to the public square of St. Croix and burned alive.

Grandier showed great courage and dignity under torture. A writer of the time wrote that his torture was so extreme that marrow actually oozed out of his broken bones. His strength served to infuriate his torturers but he refused to obtain mercy by naming imaginary accomplices. In the end, although he was assured that he would be strangled before being burned, the knot was purposely tied in such a way that it could not be drawn tight enough to put an end to his suffering. Urbain Grandier was burned alive for a crime that he most certainly did not commit.

Even after the scandal has passed, the convent continued to be a tourist attraction of sorts for the town of Loudon. People traveled from all over the country to see the nuns, who continued to claim they were possessed. It seemed that fits of erotic abandonment might come on them at any time – especially when large crowds were at hand.

One young nun, Sister Claire, would regularly fall onto her back in front of the spectators, lift her habit to expose her genitals, masturbate frantically with both hands and implore the men in the audience to have sex with her. Other nuns did the same, revealing knowledge of sex and depravity that seemed beyond their experience – although, of course, it was claimed that that it was a demon that was speaking, not the demure nuns.

The story of Loudon eventually faded into the pages of history, only to be revived again during the twentieth century as the subject of a fascinating book by Aldous Huxley and a strange, but compelling, film by Ken Russell starring Vanessa Redgrave as Sister Jeanne and Oliver Reed as Father Grandier. It's a story that does not seem to want to let us go, even centuries later, and provides a shocking look at the mystery of sex, Satan and possession in the seventeenth century.

THE DEVIL MADE ME DO IT...

There are many who say that evil thoughts and actions cannot overpower the healthy brain of a normal person. The mind cannot be overtaken, except by physical impairment or mental disease. There are no spirits, no devils and demons that are waiting to claim the bodies and minds of individuals, causing them to behave in ways that they would not ordinarily, either conscious or subconsciously.

But there are many intelligent men and women who feel otherwise. They are convinced that devils and demons are real and that they can, and do, possess the living. Serious individuals claim to have witnessed and experienced fearsome ordeals in which ordinary people became the targets of vile entities that wanted nothing more than actual possession of a living body – so that they might enjoy the sensations of demonically aroused mortals who yield to unholy temptations.

But is possession real? Skeptics will dismiss such stories as examples of psychological disorders and wild imaginations. But is a logical explanation for possession always the answer? Many don't believe so. There are dozens of what seem to be authentic cases of possession in the annals of the supernatural, cases that were witnessed by reliable people who were unable to provide an explanation for what they saw, heard and experienced, except to say that the Devil was at work. Many of these cases reeked of sex and lust, which should be no surprise if the possessions were really the work of demons.

Almost every documented case of possession seems to have a sexual element. It seems that by mentioning sex, especially in graphic and lurid detail, demons (or perhaps the inner workings of the human mind – if demons don't really exist) know that this will be the most shocking way to frighten those who attempt to subdue them during an exorcism. Almost every possession victim also seems to act out sexually. In the famous 1949 St. Louis Exorcism case (see my book *The Devil Came to St. Louis*, 2006), the allegedly possessed boy reportedly masturbated in front of the priests, made sexual remarks about the exorcists and the Virgin Mary, and often mimicked the sex act to confuse and intimidate them.

And this was not the only case in which sex played a role of some sort, either as the cause of the possession, an alleged sex pact with the Devil, or worse.

A PACT WITH SATAN

At the age of sixteen, Clara Germana Cele told her confessor, Father Erasmus Horner, she had made a pact with Satan. Not only was her soul promised to him, but her body, as well. She claimed that she had sex with him on a nightly basis and that he ravished her in her room when no one else was around. This confession occurred at the Marianhill Order mission school in Umzinto, South Africa, where Clara had been living since the age of four. In the weeks that followed the girl's chilling words, Clara began to behave wildly and on August 20, 1906, she terrified the nuns in charge of the school by tearing off her clothes, breaking one of the posts on her bed, growling and grunting like an animal and appearing to fornicate with an invisible being. In more lucid moments, she begged the sisters to call for Father Horner --- or Satan was going to kill her.

Before this strange confession, and the outbursts that followed, Clara had been considered a normal, healthy, although somewhat erratic young woman. As her condition worsened, she began to manifest signs of what the Church considered a case of authentic demonic possession. Holy water burned her when she was sprinkled with it but when she was sprinkled with ordinary water from the tap, she simply laughed. She complained loudly whenever a crucifix was brought into her presence and she could detect a religious object, like a rosary or holy medal, even when it was heavily wrapped or otherwise concealed.

One of the outstanding features of the possession was the great physical strength that the girl manifested whenever she was under demonic control. She battered those who tried to control her and in the early days of the possession, she avenged herself brutally against two nuns who accused her of faking her condition. The two nuns were accompanied by three large assistants when they came to watch over Clara one evening. At first, Clara was quiet and subdued but soon, she began to ask "tricky questions," apparently of a theological nature, of the sisters and an argument began. Father Horner later wrote that before anyone could realize what was going on, Clara "stood before the sisters in blazing anger and upbraided them in a manner that would always remember for its lack of devotion and grace."

When the nuns tried to strike the girl, Clara ran for the door, locked it and put the key in her pocket. Then she grabbed the two nuns by their habits, shook them furiously and then, with incredible strength, slammed one into a corner and threw the other to the far side of the room. Clara severely beat one of the sisters, tore the veil from her head and then pushed her under the bed. With great speed, she jumped on top of the other nun, who was crouching in the corner in fear, and choked and beat her. The three brawny assistants cowered in terror during the assault, too afraid to come near the girl.

Mysterious fires also sprang up in Clara's presence. Once, when she entered a kitchen where a small coal fire was burning, a huge flame suddenly shot into the air. While others who were present screamed and ran away, Clara only laughed and seemed to bask in the heat. The room then seemed to fill with flames, even though only a few half-glowing pieces of coal had remained in the ashes. On another occasion, another fire broke out as the girls were going to bed and when Clara was surrounded by twenty other girls. The girls had just entered their dormitory room and the room supervisor, Sister Juliana, was resting in a nearby chair. A few moments after Clara climbed into bed, the bed frame started to make a loud creaking sound and then flames rushed out from underneath it. They subsided when Sister Juliana sprinkled holy water on the bed. When the bed was later examined, the bed and bedposts were found to be charred but the girl's bed clothes and blankets were completely untouched.

Strange sounds and explained noises were also frequently heard around Clara. Often during the night, loud noises could be heard at the door of the dormitory where the girls slept. Father Horner and another priest armed themselves and began to guard the house, thinking that an outsider who was hostile to the mission school might be at work, trying to frighten the young women and the nuns. The two priests occupied an empty room close to the women's sleeping quarters and as they began their vigil, found everything to be quiet. Things did not stay quiet for long....

Father Horner wrote:

Suddenly, at ten o'clock, there was a sound like a thunderclap at the door. Inside, everyone cried out in fear and horror. We hurried outside to find out what was going on. Then, once again, one, two, five tremendous blows. We went out once more, and again there was nothing in sight. Banging and pounding could be heard on several doors inside the house. We went to investigate and found nothing. The noise and pounding continued in the rooms of the brothers, in the smithy, in the storage section, and even in the shed where the animals had become restless, but nowhere was there anything to be seen. The noise stopped by eleven-fifteen.

The idea that Clara was engaged in some sort of hoax began to fade as the strange events continued, particularly when everyone saw how much she suffered during the times when she was allegedly under demonic control. Father Horner repeatedly reported to his superiors about the incredible speed with which Clara moved when she was visibly possessed. Another curious capacity that astonished the priests and nuns was her ability to transform into a snake-like creature. Her whole body seemed to become as flexible as rubber and she would writhe and slither, her neck seeming to elongate like a serpent. Father Horner wrote that she "sometimes moved on her back, at other times on her belly, with snake-like motions" and "when she moved backwards, her head settled on the ground as if it were a foot and her whole body moved downward, snake fashion." On one occasion, while a nun was kneeling before her in prayer, Clara darted at her in "typical snake manner" and bit the woman on her arm. Where the girl's teeth had left their mark, a reddish point showed at the center and a small wound resembling a snake bite appeared.

In addition to being credited with the ability to run up a wall, two yards high, with such speed that "it seemed she was moving on solid ground," Clara was also said to be able to defy gravity while under demonic control. Although rarely seen outside of the realm of stage magicians and questionable accounts of spirit mediums, Clara was said to levitate during times of possession. Father Horner wrote:

She floated often three, four and up to five feet in the air, sometimes vertically, with her feet downward, and at other times horizontally, with her whole body floating above her bed. She was in a rigid position. Even her clothing did not fall downward, as would have been normal; instead, her dresses remained tightly attached to her body and legs. If she was sprinkled with holy water, she moved down immediately, and her clothing fell loosely onto her bed. This type of phenomenon took place in the presence of witnesses, including outsiders. Even in church, where she could be seen by everyone, she floated above her seat. Some people tried to pull her down forcibly, holding on to her feet, but it proved to be impossible.

Father Horner's account should not leave the impression that Clara was in a state of relaxation as she levitated above her bed. On the contrary, levitation occurred during periods of such physical and verbal violence that she often had to be restrained and tied up to keep her from destroying property or hurting those who were nearby. He wrote about one of these incidents:

Everyone sought to help, but it still took another three hours before we were finally able to get handcuffs on the girl as she was in a state of violent anger. Both her arms were stiff and immovable. At the same time, and amid horrible noise and disturbance, she was, over and over again, levitated off the ground while sitting in her chair.

Permission to perform an exorcism on Clara, to rid her of diabolical possession, was issued by the local Bishop on September 10, 1906, slightly less than a month after the incidents began. Father Erasmus Horner was assisted in the rite by the house father of the mission, Father Mansuet. As is standard during exorcisms, the diabolical entity inside of the girl was asked to identify itself. Using a voice much different from that of Clara, it identified itself and gave several names, such as "Yiminia" and either "Balek" or "Malek." When pressed for accuracy, the voice replied, "We do not all have names. Only the important ones have names, not those that are small and insignificant. I am small and insignificant."

The rites of exorcism began the following morning, ended at noon and then began again at 3:00 p.m. that afternoon. The rituals lasted late into the night and then started once more the following morning. As with the days leading up to the exorcism, Clara had moments of clarity and peace during the process. Alternating between states of diabolical possession and her normal personality, she was able to take part in confession and communion. This however, involved great spiritual risks, of which Father Horner quickly became aware. She often asked him to hear her confession, just to have a few moments of respite from the possession. He said that hearing her confession was a difficult task because he could not be sure if it was Clara or the demon who spoke to him. In some cases, a self-dialogue seemed to be going on. It was as if two beings were speaking through Clara's mouth.

Father Horner also noted that he had to very careful during Holy Communion, as "Satan tempted her constantly." Clara seemed to be tempted to spit out the communion wine or to withdraw the wafer from her mouth and degrade it in some manner. At other times, she was unable to swallow at all. She gagged and strained but the back of her mouth remained rigid. When Father Horner placed two fingers on her neck, though, this difficulty disappeared instantly. She often trembled and shook during the communion, spilling the wine, even when she had assistance. In many cases, though, she quieted down and listened to prayer and on these evenings, after a peaceful communion, the service was followed by the times of the most vicious attacks. As Father Horner wrote, "Those were the times of Satan's revenge."

In addition to the spiritual risks of Clara's exorcism, there were the physical risks to the girl --- and to the exorcists too. While in the midst of a severe possession crisis, while raving and acting destructively, Father Mansuet began the exorcism ritual. With his stole draped around his neck and across his shoulders, he began reading from the *Rituale Romanum*. He was soon interrupted by a voice speaking through Clara. When the priest commanded the voice to be silent, Clara began to react violently, straining at the bonds that held her to her bed. The voice raged at him, offering the body of the young girl to the priest for sex. Enraged, and momentarily losing control, the priest slapped the girl across the face. Instantly speaking in Clara's voice again, the young woman cried and asked why he was beating her ---- unaware of what she had been doing and saying just moments before.

Regretful, the priest leaned down to comfort the girl and as he did so, the demon returned. Snapping out of her restraints, Clara knocked the prayer book from his hands and in a quick movement, tore the stole from his neck and ripped it to shreds. As Father Mansuet tried to scramble away, Clara seized hold of him by the neck, choking him and throwing him to the ground. The priest tried to fight back but was no match for Clara's brutal strength. She hammered him against the bedpost and then shoved him under the bed. Moments later, the demonic rage vanished and Clara began to weep. She cowered into the corner as the priest gingerly crawled out from under the bed. His fingers were badly bruised and his body was covered with scratches and abrasions. When Clara saw what she had apparently done, she began to weep. She was still sitting in the corner, apparently shattered with grief, when others came into the room to see what the commotion was about.

The exorcism rites continued with several hopeful days and a number of setbacks, like the one that occurred after Father Horner announced that he had to make a trip to Europe. Clara asked him not to go, or at least to postpone the trip, but he was unable to do so. While he was away, the girl experienced a relapse, announcing that she had made a new pact with the Devil. Horner was stunned and heartsick by this latest development, but encouraged by the fact that Clara wanted the exorcism to continue.

In April 1907, the rituals began again and were only interrupted by a visit from the Apostolic Vicar, Dr. Henri Delalle, Bishop of Natal, who came to the mission to see if Clara's possession was indeed genuine. Accompanied by others, Bishop Delalle checked the girl's condition and verified that she was authentically possessed. The new exorcism began on April 24.

Although Father Horner and the others continued to be discouraged by some of the problems they faced, Clara herself insisted that the exorcism continue. It lasted for only two more days and at last the demon departed, leaving behind a stench that "could not be compared with anything else."

The horrible events were now over and Clara began a normal life, unhampered by the threat of possession. She stayed on at the mission for the next seven years, living an ordinary and peaceful life. Sadly, though, she died on March 14, 1912 during a tuberculosis outbreak. She was only twenty-three years old.

THE POSSESSION OF EMMA SCHMIDT

The case of Emma Schmidt has become known as one of the most chilling and horrific cases of possession in American history and is one that was well documented by those who were present. It was a case of possession that was said to be caused directly by a young girl's refusal to give into the sexual demands of her father, a ruthless, maniacal man who literally offered the girl to the Devil – to have in any way that he wanted.

The events in the case began a number of years before their culmination in an Iowa convent. At that time, Emma was a young woman, living in Wisconsin. Following the death of her father, she began to develop a strangeness that no one recalled about her before. In later years, Emma would say that her father had cursed her upon his death because she had refused to give in to the incestuous demands that he placed on her after her mother had died. She was only a young girl when her mother had passed away, but her father didn't care. He constantly followed her about as she worked at her chores on the family's farm, stroking her legs and her breasts and trying to get her to put her hands on his stiffened penis. On more than one occasion, he had tried to force himself on her in the barn on the property and she always locked her door tightly at night to keep him away.

Just before his death, he had cursed at her, telling her that he hoped that all of the devils in hell crawled into her body and raped her in just the way that she always feared. The Devil himself could have her, he said, and he hoped that she would not have a moment's peace until the day she died.

Emma should have been freed from his hatred and lust when he died, but instead, she began to act very strangely. The once sensitive, quiet and religious young woman became increasingly angry, hurling obscenities and laughing inappropriately during church services and in public places. She became flirtatious and even downright brazen and lewd with young men in town, behaving in ways that she would have never dreamed about in the past. Many of the local people who had known the girl her entire life remarked on the bizarre changes in her personality. Doctors who examined her first believed that she was either hysterical or prone to nervous spells and hallucinations, but then could find absolutely nothing wrong with her. She was a medical mystery, they thought, and ran test after test. All of them proved to be negative -- but there was obviously something wrong.

After exhausting the doctors, Emma appealed to the Church for help. Several of the priests that she spoke with agreed with the findings of the physicians, that Emma was clearly hysterical and in need of psychiatric help. Others disagreed --- the woman understood languages that she had neither heard nor read. When a priest blessed her in Latin, she foamed at the mouth with rage. If she handled an object that was sprinkled with holy water, she would scream curses and blasphemies and throw it against the wall. Slowly, very slowly, it began to be realized that there was something going on with her that could not easily be dismissed. The Church did not take the rite of exorcism lightly and only after intense study and observation, and the passing of a number of years, did the priests agree that Emma was actually possessed by evil spirits.

Father Theophilus Riesinger, a Capuchin monk and a man with past experience with exorcisms, agreed to take on the case. He knew Emma well, as she was a member of his parish in Marathon, Wisconsin, but he wanted to protect her privacy as much as possible. He made arrangements for her to travel to the small town of Earling, Iowa, where the ritual was to take place at the convent of the Franciscan Sisters. Joseph Steiger, the parish priest at Earling, was a long-time friend of Father Theophilus, but he was not eager for the exorcism to take place in his parish. It was only after urging from his friend and the mother superior of the convent that he agreed.

Emma traveled to Earling by train, passing the time alone and filled with desperate worry over what was about to take place and also overwhelmed with anger and rage, brought on by the evil spirits that plagued her. When she stepped off the train, she waved her arms wildly at the nuns who came to collect her. She screamed at them and called them foul names before inexplicably going limp. The startled sisters gathered Emma and her belongings and helped her into their car. The group rode in silence to the convent.

Father Theophilus arrived later that evening, but the first signs of trouble had already begun. A well-meaning sister in the kitchen had sprinkled Emma's food with holy water and the enraged woman threw it on the floor, screaming that the food smelled horrible. When unblessed food was substituted for the first tray, she devoured it, almost without chewing. There was no way that Emma could have known that either tray, containing the same items ---- save for the holy water ---- was different from the other.

The exorcism began early the next morning. Emma was placed on the mattress of an iron bed. The sleeves and the skirt of her dress were tightly bound and Father Theophilus instructed several of the nuns to hold her firmly to the bed. The exorcist, with Father Steiger standing beside him, began to pray. Then, as she would on every day that followed, Emma sank into unconsciousness.

Moments later, she tore loose from the sisters who were holding her and by some mysterious energy, reportedly flung her body from the bed, into the air, and against the closest wall. She was pinned there by a force so strong that neither priest could pull her free. The nuns, now trembling with fright, tugged at her until they finally were able to pull her loose and return her to the bed. Moments later, the exorcism continued and Emma began to howl. But according to the statements of those present, her mouth never opened. Mewling, inhuman sounds and guttural growls issued forth from her throat but her lips never moved.

News of the exorcism spread through the nearby community and people came from all directions to find out what was happening at the convent. Crowds soon assembled beneath the windows of the room where Emma was kept but many of them left, reportedly unable to stand the excruciating sounds that issued from inside.

Over the course of the next few days, those inside the room endured the ordeal alongside of Emma. Twelve nuns took turns attending to her, afterwards leaving the building to get some fresh air, and often to weep. Only Father Theophilus remained composed. Emma, seemingly helpless to prevent what was happening to her, continually frothed at the mouth and then spewed out torrents of stinking vomit that filled both pitchers and pails. She had scarcely eaten for days and yet was said to have thrown up as many as 30 times in one day. On several occasions, when the exorcist brought the Blessed Sacrament near Emma, he saw her flesh twist and contort, as though something was moving beneath her skin.

The exorcism continued until late at night, every day, hour after hour. The bellowing voices and cries continued to come from the stricken woman and the howling, like that of an animal, broke the usual stillness of the convent. At times, the voices became so frightening that Father Steiger and the nuns fled from the room. The exorcist persisted in his task, though, praying and screaming for the devils to leave Emma. His work was so strenuous that he often had to change his sweat-soaked clothing three times or more each day.

During the sessions, a number of voices allegedly came though Emma. They claimed to be various demons and evil spirits from her past, including her father, who had tried to force her to have sex with him, and even her father's mistress, who according to the priest's report, had murdered her own children. During this manifestation, Emma was said to have vomited with such violence that Father Theophilus and Father Steiger had to use towels to clean the fluid from their clothing.

Whatever was expressing itself in these voices, it demonstrated an uncanny knowledge of things that could not have been known to Emma. On one occasion, as a test, a piece of paper with a Latin inscription was placed on Emma's head. The nuns, thinking the words were a prayer, were surprised to see that the demons tolerated its presence. In truth, though, the words had no religious content at all. However, when a second piece of paper, which had been secretly blessed, was placed on Emma's head, it was immediately ripped to pieces.

The exorcism continued day after horrible day. Emma was unable to eat and the nuns were only able to get liquid down her throat. In a short time, it would usually come right back up again. Her now-emaciated body was said to no longer resemble anything human. Her head swelled and caused her features to distort. Her eyes bulged out and her lips bloated to twice their normal size. Her face was flushed with heat as her skin stretched and took on an unnatural shine. The nuns feared that her limbs might actually burst as they were so badly swollen. They also claimed that her body seemed to take on such weight that the iron bedstead bent and curved down to where it almost touched the floor.

As the exhausting days passed, a change came over Father Steiger. He developed a strong dislike for the entire procedure and began to dislike Father Theophilus, his old friend. In one bout of anger, he raged at the exorcist but Father Theophilus took it in stride, explaining that the demons were using the priest to confuse things. As the voices that came from Emma began berating Father Steiger, his friend commanded that they leave the priest alone. But the voices only laughed and continued to threaten Father Steiger. "Just wait until Friday...", they said..

Sick of the constant howling, Father Steiger learned to ignore the voices but then on Friday, as promised, he nearly lost his life. It happened as he was returning from performing the last rites for the mother of a local farmer. On his return to Earling, he crossed a bridge over a ravine and would later claim that a large, black cloud suddenly descended on the car. Unable to see, he yanked the vehicle into low gear but it was too late to stop. The automobile veered to the side and collided with the steel railings of the bridge. Metal smashed and glass shattered and the car tore through the rails until it was left hanging, teetering on the edge of the ravine. A farmer who was plowing a field a short distance away heard the crash and came running. He managed to pull Father Steiger from the wreckage. The priest was stunned and numb with shock, but unhurt.

The farmer was kind enough to drive him to the convent and when he arrived, he went straight to Emma's room. As he walked in, she began laughing uproariously. A guttural voice from inside of her laughed at the priest and celebrated the destruction of his car. Father Theophilus and the nuns were shocked and asked if this was true. Father Steiger agreed that it was but added that the demon did not have the strength to hurt him personally. The voice cursed and stated that only the priest's patron saint had saved his life.

On several occasions after this, Father Steiger continued to be bedeviled by the spirits. He was often awakened at night by knocking coming from inside his walls, scratching noises and weird banging sounds that would often last throughout the night.

But none of this could match the suffering endured by Emma Schmidt. She continued to lose consciousness each day as the exorcism began and would only awaken late at night when it was over. She remembered nothing of what transpired during the day, the violent sickness that she suffered from or the horrible curses that came from her mouth. As she became more and more frail from her daily ordeal, she was soon no longer able to walk. She had to be carried back and forth between her private quarters and the exorcism room. The nuns feared that she might die before the exorcism could end.

The records say that the events continued for more than two weeks before there was any indication that the spirits might be forced out of Emma's body. At that point, Father Theophilus doubled his efforts and for three days and nights, he continued the exorcism without sleep and with very little rest. In addition to what must have been nerves of steel, the priest also seemed to have incredible powers of endurance, as well. But even so, toward the end of the third night, he became so weak that he nearly collapsed. He prayed to God to spare his life and finally, the marathon session was finished.

The end seemed to be near and later, the nuns would testify that a miraculous figure appeared to Emma one day and urged her not to give up hope. The nuns claimed that they saw a cluster of white roses appear on the ceiling of the room but it disappeared before Father Steiger could be brought in. Regardless, the sign gave hope to the priest and he and Father Theophilus both knew that the horror was finally reaching its climax.

More days of pain and exhaustion followed but on the evening of September 23, 1928, Emma Schmidt jerked free from the hands of the nuns who held her and she stood upon the bed with only her heels still touching the mattress. Fearful that she might be hurled against the wall again ---- or perhaps this time the ceiling ---- Father Steiger urged the sisters to pull her back down. As they reached for her, Father Theophilus blessed her and demanded once more that the demons depart from her. At that moment, Emma reportedly collapsed and the sounds of screams and piercing voices filled the room.

Everyone present froze as Emma contorted one last time and then opened her eyes and smiled. As she looked from one face to another, she began to weep. Her torment was over ---- the exorcism was finished at last. So happy were they about what had occurred that the witnesses did not at first notice the stomach-churning smell of human waste that filled the room. It was the final indignity left behind by the departing spirits, it was said. The nuns opened all of the windows and a fresh cool breeze blew across the sills, soon driving out the foul odors.

There was little to say in the aftermath of the Earling case. Had Emma Schmidt truly been plagued by demons? The exorcism caused a heated debate among members of the Catholic Church, as many of them continued to believe that she was a troubled woman who had been in the grips of hysteria. This may have been the case, but even if it was, Emma lived a quiet and peaceful life after the exorcism and was never bothered by her troubles again. For the rest of his life, Father Theophilus maintained that she had been possessed and Father Steiger and the Franciscan sisters agreed. They only saw a young woman who had finally been freed from the lustful demands of a demented old man – and the legion of devils that he managed to conjure up.

6. BLOOD, SEX AND VAMPIRES

There is perhaps no supernatural creature more closely connected to sex than the vampire. Although long considered to be nothing more than a myth, the vampire is a still a strangely attractive and enticing being to the modern reader. We think of them as being nothing more than the fanciful creation of folklore and literature, but what if we are wrong? What is some vampires were real? What if they once stalked the fields, forests and towns of history – and what if some of them still do?

Few can really say what the traditional vampire is. Some believe that he is an evil spirit that wears the body of the newly dead, while others believe that he is a corpse, re-animated by his original soul. What everyone can agree on is what this creature must have to survive -- blood. This vital bodily ingredient must be taken from the veins of a living person so that the vampire can survive.

In nearly every case, a vampire that is exhumed from his grave, or resting place, is always found to be ruddy of complexion, well-nourished and apparently in good health. This is in spite of the fact that he had been dead for some time. His appearance is often marked by long, curving fingernails (having grown long in the grave) and blood smeared about the mouth. According to European legends, the only way to destroy one of these living corpses is to drive a stake through its heart. After that, the body should be burned. The American legends suggest a different method of disposal. According to old reports, the heart of the vampire must be cut out of the chest and then burned. Often, a potion must be mixed from the ashes given to the vampire's victims. This is to prevent them from dying and becoming a vampire themselves.

The legends of vampires have their roots in traditional fears. In days past, it was not uncommon for people to be fearful about the dead returning from their grave, especially in cases of suicides or of unfortunates being buried without the last rites. Occasional deviants who practiced necrophilia or corpse-stealing often provided apparent "proof" that some of the dead could leave the graveyard. An empty coffin was not seen as evidence of theft, but evidence of vampirism instead.

Terrible and what seemed to be mysterious outbreaks of disease and plagues were sometimes thought to be caused by supernatural means. In America, an outbreak of the "white death" or tuberculosis was believed to actually be a string of vampire-related deaths. Another ailment thought to have created the vampire legend was a rare disorder called *porphyria*. This is a skin pigment disorder in which the body produces an excess of red blood cells. The result is an unbearable itching, redness and bleeding cracks in the skin that appear after a brief exposure to sunlight. Sufferers naturally avoided coming out in the daylight and appeared only at night. The disease was not diagnosed until the nineteenth century and many afflicted individuals were regarded with superstitious fear.

Probably the most common source of vampire legends came from premature burials. People suffering from catalepsy and other ailments sometimes found themselves buried alive and when later exhumed, the distorted state of the corpses led many to believe the dead had been coming and going from their coffins for some time. In the eighteenth century, it was not uncommon for bodies to be dug up to see if they had become vampires, especially when it involved the death of a suicide, a murder victim or someone who had died during a spate of

The vampire is perhaps the most sexual of all
supernatural creatures

unexplained deaths. If a body was discovered to be in any way out of the ordinary, it was burned to prevent it leaving the grave again.

Vampire-like creatures have existed in the folklore of the world since almost the beginning of recorded history, but a true, traditional vampire was originally a Slavonic monster, bringing fear to the superstitious in Eastern Europe – Hungary, Czechoslovakia, Rumania, the Balkan countries, and their neighbors. Even the word "vampire" is an adaptation of the Magyar word *vampir*, which also had close ties to Bulgarian and Russian words that meant the same thing. It is believed that the vampire legend began to grow in notoriety around the sixteenth century. Within the next few decades, a considerable spate of vampire activity began to be reported, creating eerie tales and haunting rumors throughout the region.

Soon after, the legend began to spread. A Greek writer, Leone Allacci, produced a small book about vampire belief and other travelers began to pick up stories as they passed through Eastern Europe. Learned clergymen alluded to stories of vampires that were reported to them by parishioners, but in 1746, a Benedictine monk named Don Augustin Calmet published a full-length treatise on ghosts and vampires that firmly planted the legend within the lore of the western world.

The arrival of the vampire in Western Europe was achieved in part by the dissemination of Balkan folk tales, but the process was completed by another important thread in the construction of the legend – pure fiction. The German romantics of the late eighteenth century found useful images in the horrors of folklore and the use of the vampire motif in poems by Goethe spread the tales ever further. A vampire appeared in a poem by Lord Byron, and in another by Southey, fairly early in the nineteenth century's English romantic tradition. Oddly, though, none of the earlier writers of "Gothic" horror fiction, like Horace Walpole, Ann Radcliffe or Matthew Lewis, ever brought in vampires as one of their eerie effects.

What has been regarded as the first true vampire story was written in 1819 by Dr. John Polidori and it was titled simply "The Vampyre." This short tale was written during the same fateful summer that the twenty-year-old Polidori spent with his friend and patient, Lord Byron, along with Percy Shelley and Mary Shelley on the shores of Lake Geneva. A writing contest that summer spawned not only the first vampire story, but Mary Shelley's *Frankenstein*, as well. The short piece appeared in the *New Monthly Magazine*, a British literary journal, and delighted readers with its gloomy atmosphere and its depraved aristocratic vampire, Lord Ruthven, which had been modeled on Lord Byron. It was not one of the finest stories ever written, but it had the advantage of being the first about vampires and, thanks to this, Polidori has earned a place of honor in the annals of horror.

Decades passed and the public gained a taste for blood – at least in a literary sense. In Paris, a play about vampires was one of the most popular theater attractions of the 1820s. Alexandre Dumas wrote a play about vampires in the 1850s, joining other productions that were all the rage across Europe. The French poet, Gautier, used the vampire theme in one of his poems, as did Baudelaire. Then, in 1847, one of the first major written works appeared on the subject in the form of a "penny dreadful" novel by Thomas Preskett Prest called *Varney, the Vampire.* Although it was more than 800 pages long – it appeared in a series of cheap, penny booklets – this simple, fast-moving horror story became a sensation with the masses. Vampires, clearly, had come to stay.

One of the most exciting – and definitely most sensual -- literary vampires of the nineteenth century appeared in a small 1872 novella by Joseph Sheridan Le Fanu called *Carmilla.* The book tells the story of a young woman named Laura who lives with her father, an English widower, in a solitary castle in Austria. A carefully arranged accident brings a young woman named Carmilla into the care of the family. Carmilla and Laura grow to be very close friends, but occasionally Carmilla's moods change and she makes unsettling romantic advances toward Laura. She sleeps much of the day and seems to sleepwalk at night. Oddly, a family heirloom is found in the castle and Laura finds a portrait of an ancestor, "Mircalla, Countess Karnstein," which eerily resembles Carmilla. Laura soon begins to have nightmares that a creature has entered her room at night, biting her on the breasts. As her health declines, she is examined by a doctor who privately tells her father that Laura must never be left unattended.

A short time later, Laura and her father go to a nearby ruined village, Karnstein. En route, they meet General Spielsdorf, who tells of how he and his niece met a young woman named Mircalla, who befriended his niece and then came to stay with the family. The General's niece became ill and suffered the same symptoms as Laura. After consulting with a doctor who dabbled in the occult, it was realized that the niece was being visited by a vampire. The General hid in his niece's closet one night and when the vampire returned, he attacked and then realized the vampire was Mircalla. She fled out the window and got away unharmed. His niece died immediately afterward.

When they arrive at Karnstein, the General asks a woodsman where he can find the tomb of Mircalla Karnstein but the woodsman explains that it was relocated long ago by a hero who destroyed the vampires in the region. While the General and Laura are alone in a ruined church, Carmilla appears. The General and Carmilla both fly into a rage when they see each other and the General attacks her with an ax. Carmilla flees and the General is forced to explain to Laura that her friend is really Mircalla, the vampire that killed his niece. The group is then joined by Baron Vordenburg, a descendant of the original vampire killer in the region. He manages to track down the lair of Carmilla and dispatches the vampire before she can do any more damage.

Audiences thrilled to *Carmilla* in the 1870s and the story is considered a classic today. The title character became the prototype for a legion of female and lesbian vampires. Though Le Fanu portrays his vampire's sexuality with the cautiousness that one would expect for his time, it is evident that lesbian attraction is the main dynamic between Carmilla and Laura, the narrator of the story. Carmilla selected exclusively female victims, though only became emotionally involved with a few of them. She was a little different than the accepted form of a vampire in that she had nocturnal habits, but was not confined to the darkness. She had unearthly beauty and slept in a coffin, as many of the vampires that followed her would also do.

But there would be no other book that would so affect the literary vampire like the one that came along at the end of the nineteenth century, written by an Irish author named Bram Stoker – *Dracula.* Stoker's *Dracula* became a virtual synonym for the vampire; if the ordinary person knows anything about

An illustration from *Carmilla*

(Left) Bela Lugosi as Bram Stoker's creation, Dracula, in the 1931 Universal film.

(Above) The real Dracula, Vlad the Impaler, a Romanian hero who saved the country from the invading Turks by bloodthirsty methods.

the vampire legend, he probably learned it from the bits and pieces of authentic lore that Stoker included in the book. Stoker actually studied Balkan folklore while working on his book and included a number of references to regional history. His title character took the name of a historical figure, Transylvanian-born Vlad III Dracula of Wallachia. During the main years of his reign, between 1456 and 1462, "Vlad the Impaler" was said to have killed from 20,000 to 40,000 European civilians (political rivals, criminals, and anyone else he considered "useless to humanity"). His favorite method of death was impaling his victims on a sharp pole. Historically, the name "Dracul" is derived from a secret fraternal order of knights called the Order of the Dragon, founded by Sigismund of Luxembourg to uphold Christianity and defend the Empire against the Ottoman Turks. Vlad II Dracul was admitted to the order around 1431 because of his bravery in fighting the Turks. From 1431 onward, he wore the emblem of the order and later, as ruler of Wallachia, his coinage bore the dragon symbol. The name Dracula means "Son of Dracul," a title that his son, Vlad III, took as his own.

Stoker came across the name "Dracula" in his reading on Romanian history and chose it to replace the name "Count Wampyr," which he originally intended to use for his villain. However, the name may have been the only connection between the fictional and real-life Draculas. Stoker likely knew little about the historic figure, aside from his nickname, although there are sections in the novel where Dracula refers to his own background, and these speeches show that Stoker had some knowledge of Romanian history. However, Stoker includes no details about Vlad's reign and does not mention his penchant for impalement. Given Stoker's use of historical background to make his novel more horrific, it seems unlikely he would have failed to mention that his villain had impaled thousands of people. Some scholars have suggested that he did not intend his character Dracula to be the same person as Vlad III.

Historical connections or not, there seems to be no question that *Dracula* set the standard for every piece of literary fiction about vampires that followed. The novel also had the unique position of actually changing the folklore about what vampires could and could not do. Stoker managed to mix in real Balkan folklore with his own imaginative elements, jumbling up the popular conception about what a vampire should be. In this way, folklore lent itself to fiction, which in turn, altered folklore.

THE VAMPIRE IN LEGEND

Everything about the vampire clearly indicated his nature of being "undead." Often described as lean and cadaverous, he was sometimes leathery and skeletal like a long-dead corpse, or more often described as gaunt, sinewy and thin. The well-fed vampire was said to be horribly bloated or swollen with blood, but in most cases, the nature of his diet was indicated only by the stark redness of his lips and his extended canine teeth. His skin was white, almost transparent, and his flesh was always cold – raised only to warmth after a particularly hearty meal. His eyes gleamed, sometimes flashing red, and his eyebrows were said to meet above his nose. His fingernails were curved like claws, his ears might be pointed, and his breath had the fetid, coppery smell of blood. He was also supernaturally strong, said to have the strength of a dozen or more men.

The vampire, as a living corpse, was permanently attached to its burial place, or at least to the soil in which he had been buried. One of the many rules that seemed to govern a vampire's behavior was his need to return to his coffin, grave or tomb before daylight each morning and sleep in it during the day. Although Hollywood suggested that sunlight could destroy a vampire, folklore said nothing of the kind, only relegated most of the vampire's activities to the nocturnal hours. Since they only prowled at night, Bram Stoker created the idea that a vampire must spend his days in his own coffin, very much at the mercy of the living vampire hunters.

Luckily, the vampires weaknesses were overshadowed by its variety of magical powers – not the least of which was his ability, in many tales, to get in and out of a grave through six feet of soil. This was an example of an old unwillingness to bother with the distinctions between a corpse and a ghost. A vampire was a material corpse with some of the powers of an immaterial spirit, but no one in the old days saw any contradiction. Hungarian tales got around this problem by giving the vampire the supernatural ability to change into a cloud or mist. Stoker also used this trick in *Dracula* and he also used the Balkan belief that vampires can control a variety of fearsome animals like wolves or bats.

Occasionally, a few tales would give the vampire himself the ability to change into an animal, which was probably a bit of lore left over from ancient witch and shape-shifter stories. Occasionally, a vampire would become a wolf, a cat or an owl, but only in a few Rumanian stories was it even vaguely mentioned that he could turn himself into a bat. Bats, of course, are nocturnal animals, often associated with dark and evil deeds, so it's not a surprise that it was worked into the vampire legend. But mention of this remained rare until the nineteenth century. It was at this time that European travelers first began to regularly visit South America – and returned with tales about a bat that nourished itself solely and exclusively on blood. It was promptly named after its human counterpart from folklore, and was just as promptly incorporated into the vampire stories.

Finally, one of the more useful of the vampire's talents was his hypnotic ability, which enabled him to mesmerize his victims and send them to sleep, so that he could feed on them without a struggle. A victim might wake up feeling tired and drained, but would remember nothing of the previous night's visitor – perhaps until she saw the two small punctures on the side of her neck.

Perhaps it is another magical power, or perhaps

The Vampire by Edward Munch

just another rule in vampire lore, but the vampire seemed to have many ways to recruit new bloodsuckers to the ranks. In the most traditional sense, a person could become a vampire after being fed upon and then drinking some of the vampire's own blood. This exchange of fluids seemed to be the most reliable method, although some stories claimed that a person who was drained of his blood would rise from the grave after three days as a vampire himself.

But according to the lore, this was, by no means, the only way that you might end up as one of the undead. The old tales stressed most frequently that anyone who died in a state of sin, without the blessings of the Church, risked becoming a vampire. So did those who were exceedingly wicked, or who dabbled in black magic. Balkan legends added that people might return as vampires if they died after perjuring themselves, or were cursed by their parents, committed suicide, or – most prominently – after being excommunicated from the Church. In all of these cases, the fearful horror of becoming one of the undead was seen as a punishment for evildoers.

But a man could turn into a vampire through no fault of his own. If his corpse did not receive full funeral rites of the Church, if he died without being baptized, or was murdered and his death was never avenged, he might become a vampire. Some were cursed, it was said, by something as simple as a cat jumping over a coffin that had not been buried. If anyone saw the cat perform this act, the transformation of a corpse into a vampire could be prevented with a little homemade magic. They simply had to place a piece of iron in the corpse's hand, put a piece of hawthorn in the coffin or hang a wreath of garlic around the cadaver's neck.

Such remedies were expected to protect a person from a vampire, as well. But folk magic was not the only thing that was believed to keep vampires away. In the past, vampire legends briefly overlapped with Christian demonology, so that many Church officials ascribed Balkan tales of vampires to actions of various devils, who had entered and reanimated corpses for demonic purposes. And while later tales refuted this idea, claiming that vampires were not demons but the original person re-inhabiting his own body, some Christian elements were not entirely absent from vampire traditions. The most common Christian element was the protective nature of the crucifix, which was believed to repel a vampire. Other Christian items could also be used, including holy water, relics and communion wafers, but given the creature's evil nature, the best defense was reportedly the crucifix, which was regarded as the most powerful symbol of good. Wearing a cross around one's neck was always a good insurance policy, as was clutching a piece of silver, which was universally feared by every kind of evil spirit.

If anyone suspected that a recently buried body might rise again as a vampire, and it was too late to place hawthorn or garlic in the coffin, Slavonic legend suggested thrusting iron skewers straight down into the grave. The vampire would be pinned into his coffin by these sharp points. It also might be possible to bury a person in question, such as a suicide, under running water to prevent his return as a vampire. Running water had always been considered a barrier to evil creatures and in some cases, could even kill vampires if they fell into it.

If vampire activity broke out in some region and no one knew where to find the monster, a few traditional tests could be applied in the local graveyard. Vampire hunters examined the graves for scatterings of small holes, through which a vampire could emerge as a mist. Or, Hungarian tradition had it that a white stallion that had never been to stud could be taken to the cemetery and he would refuse to cross over any grave that contained a vampire. If all of the tests failed to reveal the villain, and the vampire's attacks continued unchecked, stories stated that the graves had to be opened and the corpses examined to find the one that had not decomposed. Such activity had to take place in the daylight, when the vampire was dormant and could do no harm.

If a vampire was found at night, he could only be killed by a silver bullet that had been blessed by a priest. However, most vampire hunters considered it safer to hunt for their prey during the daylight hours. Once the body was disinterred a wooden stake – preferably of hawthorn, aspen or another sacred wood – was driven through the creature's heart. Usually, this was the end of the ritual, but some traditions called for the vampire's head to be cut off, the body burned, or the heart torn from its body. Some versions claimed that only a consecrated dagger, in the shape of a crucifix, could destroy the vampire.

SEX AND THE VAMPIRE

Unlike ghosts, which haunt the world for a variety of purposes like revenge, unfinished business, messages to the living and dozens of others, vampires seem to remain among the living for one purpose only – because they are hungry for blood. But behind this blood thirst, which the most compelling and dominant element in the nature of vampires, there lurks a darker truth of a sort that the nineteenth century could only hint at. The vampire legend is not simply an assortment of gory horror tales spawned by primitive superstitions about the dead. It is a blatantly sexual motif that is riddled with eroticism.

At one time, the sexual side of vampires was explicit in the old Balkan tales. Vampires were said to return to bestow their terrible attentions on their marriage partners, although unmarried vampires visited any attractive young person of the opposite sex. And in those tales, it was not just a thirst for blood that the vampire satisfied. But presumably, the censors of the Victorian era made it clear that murder

and brutality were all right, but sex was not, and chose to remove the explicit sex angle from the tales of vampires. All the same, enough remained in a symbolic and repressed way to make the vampire myth a gold mine for Freudian psychologists.

Some of the sexual elements can be found from any part of the legend, censored or otherwise. The vampire bites his victim and no one needs to be an expert on sex to know that a bite is a kind of a kiss – sadism mixed with eroticism. Even the vampire's appearance – full, red lips, pale skin, and thin frame – corresponds to the long-held belief in what sex-oriented people look like. It is not accidental then, that male vampires tend to choose young, full-blooded women for their victims. And to fulfill just about every red-blooded man's fantasies, a female vampire chooses the same kind of ripe young girls for her victims.

Blood itself is not only the stuff of life, but it's profoundly tied up with man's sexual emotions. There were dozens of ancient taboos involving menstruating women, some of which still exist today, and scores of rituals all revolving around the same thing. Modern psychologists write of how often blood, and bloodletting, appears in the erotic fantasies of mental patients. Some have even suggested that the primary motive in sex murders may be to shed blood, not necessarily to end life.

This may make unpleasant reading for some and may even make us feel a little dubious about our enjoyment of tales like *Dracula* or *Carmilla*, but even more unpleasant are the many case histories of *real* vampires. In years past, many brutal and horrific crimes were blamed on monsters and vampires. Many had a hard time believing that a human being could be capable of bloody and terrifying crimes, so it was explained away as the work of a supernatural creature. In such cases, the vampires in question were not resurrected corpses, but living psychopaths with a mania for the taste of blood. These types bear resemblances to certain others – like cannibals and necrophiliacs – who have also made indirect contributions to the vampire legend over the centuries. The existence of such people, their perversions, and the stories that must have spread about them when they were discovered in the superstitious past, provide a foundation of truth on which all of the folklore and fictional elements were constructed to create the concept of the vampire.

A Romanian "Vampire Hunter's Kit" from the 1910s -- believed to be authentic

Vampires are simply the creation of horror writers and superstitious people who believed in monsters. Or are they?

Could real, supernatural creatures that feed on the blood of the living actually exist? Before you scoff at this idea, the open-minded reader is advised to look over the case histories that follow, as well as the strange incidents that have yet to be explained. As you will soon discover, there were many men, perhaps much wiser than we are, who wholeheartedly believed in the existence of vampires. Were they mistaken or possibly insane? In the late nineteenth century, it was possible to purchase "vampire hunting kits" from a variety of reputable sources.

Perhaps such kits were sold for a very good reason!

VAMPIRES AMONG US
TRUE TALES OF VAMPIRES THROUGHOUT HISTORY

While vampires have been a part of history since nearly the beginning of recorded time, vampire hunters truly came into their own in the nineteenth century, when vampires apparently left the shadowy world of folklore and stepped into the real world. At a time of scientific enlightenment, when superstitions should have died off, a belief in the supernatural seized the public. Not only did vampires come to the forefront but so did ghosts and a variety of other occult phenomena. This was the era of the Spiritualist movement and a strong belief in séances and communication with the dead. It's no surprise that vampires, another form of the resurrected dead, also captured the imagination of the public.

Perhaps the greatest of all vampire hunters was Dr. Franz Hartmann. His life was as curious as his belief in the living dead. Hartmann was a noted occultist and writer born in Bavaria, Germany, in 1838. He claimed to be descended on his mother's side from the old Irish kings of Ulster. He became a physician and immigrated to the United States in 1865, traveling as a doctor to various cities and also living among the Native Americans to study their religious beliefs. He later became a Theosophist and became involved with Helene Blavatsky, staying with her as her constant companion until her death. Before that, Hartmann was an ardent Spiritualist, studied paranormal manifestations, and wrote extensive accounts of séances that were held in his home. He died at Kempten, Bavaria, in 1912.

In addition to being a scholar of black magic and the occult, Hartmann was also fascinated with vampires. He was an active researcher and studied both the folklore of vampires, and contemporary case studies that he believed proved that vampires were not merely the stuff of the imagination. In 1891, he wrote a biography of the famous medieval alchemist Paracelsus, who had believed that vampire attacks were caused by various supernatural entities. In the book, Hartmann agreed with many of the alchemist's theories and continued the idea of the Church, which claimed that it was possible for suicides to turn into the undead. Unlike Paracelsus, though,

Hartmann was more than simply a scholar. He searched out actual instances of vampirism and investigated them first hand. He wrote a number of articles for occult journals on vampire attacks and was a true believer in the phenomenon.

Two cohorts of Hartmann, themselves no amateurs when it came to the occult, were Ralph Shirley and Bram Stoker. Shirley was a pioneer in British publishing and for more than three decades was the head of William Rider & Son, the foremost publisher of literature dealing with the occult, black magic and psychical research. He was a legend in the field, especially after the start of his magazine, the *Occult Review*, which ran for twenty-one years. Shirley was serious about his studies of the paranormal and stated in 1924, "It may be doubted indeed, in spite of the lack of records, whether vampirism in one form or another, is quite as absent from the conditions of modern civilization as is commonly supposed."

While we mostly associated Bram Stoker with his novel *Dracula*, he was, in fact, keenly interested in the vampire legend outside of its literary possibilities and actually traveled to Hungary to do research before he started his book. When *Dracula* appeared in 1897, it was re-published by Ralph Shirley at William Rider & Son, which brings together the interesting parallel of publisher Shirley, investigator Hartmann and author Stoker. Hartmann would often conduct séances to try and make contact with vampire spirits. Toward the end of *Dracula*, Mina Harker becomes a trance medium and provides the whereabouts of the

Dr. Franz Hartmann

vampire so that his pursuers can track him to his homeland and destroy him. This is the same method that Hartmann claimed to use with professional mediums when he was also trying to track down evidence of vampires. In fact, the vampire expert in the book, Dr. Van Helsing, is an obvious caricature of Dr. Franz Hartmann, with even the names being similar.

During the early years of the twentieth century, belief in bloodsucking vampires was mostly relegated to works of fiction, but random reports still appeared – including some of the most terrifying accounts in the pages ahead. Strangely, the only authority that was not quite ready to give up on the supernatural aspects of the vampire seemed to be the Catholic Church. By 1930, two books had recently appeared that re-evaluated and supported the Church's views on vampirism: *The Vampire: His Kith and Kin* and *The Vampire in Europe*. Both books were written by witchcraft scholar Montague Summers, who, like many of his colleagues, led a curious and mysterious life. Although he was an ordained minister of the Church of England, he converted to Roman Catholicism shortly after his ordination and thereafter devoted his life to the study of witchcraft. For long periods of time, he actually disappeared, only to emerge again with volumes of notes and strange writings. The only person that he remained in touch with during his absences was his secretary, who ominously died shortly before Summers.

In both of Summers' books about vampires, he addressed the subject from a personal viewpoint as a Catholic. He was intrigued by the blood-drinking aspects of vampirism, rather than the contemporary ideas of vampires being living people who absorb the vitality of others. He also believed the vampire to be inherently evil and a servant of Satan. Summers stated that the actual mechanics of vampires are unknown, but that they were not self-animated. Like zombies, he believed they were brought to life by some sort of evil spirit – a spirit that was a direct emissary of the Devil. He also disagreed with the popular custom of people warding off vampires with amulets (even Christian ones) but offered no alternate methods. Despite Summers' possibly out-of-date ideas, he was a very intelligent man who was not at all prone to seeing monsters beneath the bed.

This is, perhaps, what makes the idea of true vampires all the more unsettling. The believers in the phenomenon are not always frustrated readers of romance novels or wannabe gothic kids who think it's cool to drink a little of each other's blood on weekends – they are authors, doctors, scientists, scholars, occultists and otherwise logical people. Do vampires really exist? Or are they simply madmen with a taste for human blood? Can there be real supernatural creatures that feed on other humans?

Leave the lights on when you read the rest of this chapter – you may just be surprised.

The Vampire of Croglin Grange

One of the most famous accounts of vampires in the late nineteenth century was included in the book *Story of Life* by Augustine Hare, published in 1892. It was passed along to Hare by a "Captain Fisher", who told the story to the author. The incident in question reportedly occurred in 1875 (although for reasons soon to be explained, it may have been much earlier) at a house called Croglin Grange in Cumberland (modern-day Cumbria), England.

The account of the vampire read:

"Fisher," said the Captain, "may sound a very plebeian name, but this family is of a very ancient lineage, and for many hundreds of years they have possessed a very curious old place in Cumberland, which bears the weird name of Croglin Grange. The great characteristic of the house is that never at any period of its very long existence has it been more than one story high, but it has a terrace from which large grounds sweep away towards the church in the hollow, and a fine distant view.

When, in lapse of years, the Fishers outgrew Croglin Grange in family and fortune, they were wise enough not to destroy the long-standing characteristic of the place by adding another story to the house, but they went away to the south, to reside at Thorncombe near Guildford, and they let Croglin Grange

They were extremely fortunate in their tenants, two brothers and a sister. They heard their praises from all quarters. To their poorer neighbours they were all that is most kind and beneficent, and their neighbours of a higher class spoke of them as a most welcome addition to the little society of the neighbourhood. On their part, the tenants were greatly delighted with their new residence. The arrangement of the house, which would have been a trial to many, was not so to them. In every respect Croglin Grange was exactly suited to them.

The winter was spent most happily by the new inmates of Croglin Grange, who shared in all the little social pleasures of the district, and made themselves very popular. In the following summer there was one day which was dreadfully, annihilatingly hot. The brothers lay under the trees with their books, for it was too hot for any active occupation. The sister sat in the veranda and worked, or tried to work, for in the intense sultriness of that summer day, work was next to impossible. They dined early, and after dinner they still sat out on the veranda, enjoying the cool air which came with the evening, and they watched the sun set, and the moon rise over the belt of trees which separated the grounds from the churchyard, seeing it mount the heavens till the whole lawn was bathed in silver light, across which the long shadows from the shrubbery fell as if embossed, so vivid and distinct were they.

When they separated for the night, all retiring to their rooms on the ground floor (for, as I said, there was no upstairs in that house), the sister felt that the heat was still so great that she could not sleep, and having fastened her window, she did not close the shutters--in that very quiet place it was not necessary--and, propped against the pillows, she still watched the wonderful, the marvelous beauty of that summer night. Gradually she became aware of two lights, two lights which flickered in and out in the belt of trees which separated the lawn from the churchyard, and, as her gaze became fixed upon them, she saw them emerge, fixed in a dark substance, a definite ghastly something, which seemed every moment to become nearer, increasing in size and substance as it approached. Every now and then it was lost for a moment in the long shadows which stretched across the lawn from the trees, and then it emerged larger than ever, and still coming on. As she watched it, the most uncontrollable horror seized her. She longed to get away, but the door was close to the window, and the door was locked on the inside, and while she was unlocking it she must be for an instant nearer to it. She longed to scream, but her voice seemed paralysed, her tongue glued to the roof of her mouth.

Suddenly--she could never explain why afterwards--the terrible object seemed to turn to one side, seemed to be going round the house, not to be coming to her at all, and immediately she jumped out of bed and rushed to the door, but as she was unlocking it she heard scratch, scratch, scratch upon the window, and saw a hideous brown face with flaming eyes glaring in at her. She rushed back to the bed, but the creature continued to scratch, scratch, scratch upon the window. She felt a sort of mental comfort in the knowledge that the window was securely fastened on the inside. Suddenly the scratching sound ceased, and a kind of pecking sound took its place. Then, in her agony, she became aware that the creature was unpicking the lead! The noise continued, and a diamond pane of glass fell into the room. Then a long bony finger of the creature came in and turned the handle of the window, and the window opened, and the creature came in; and it came across the room, and her terror was so great that she could not scream, and it came up to the bed, and it twisted its long, bony fingers into her hair, and it dragged her head over the side of the bed, and--it bit her violently in the throat.

As it bit her, her voice was released, and she screamed with all her might and main. Her brothers rushed out of their rooms, but the door was locked on the inside. A moment was lost while they got a poker and broke it open. Then the creature had already escaped through the window, and the sister, bleeding violently from a wound in the throat, was lying unconscious over the side of the bed. One brother pursued the creature, which fled before him through the moonlight with gigantic strides, and eventually seemed to disappear over the wall into the churchyard. Then he rejoined his brother by the sister's bedside. She was dreadfully hurt, and her wound was a very definite one, but she was of strong disposition, not even given to romance or superstition, and when she came to herself she said, 'What has happened is most extraordinary and I am very much hurt. It seems inexplicable, but of course there is an explanation, and we must wait for it. It will turn out that a lunatic has escaped from some asylum and found his way here.' The wound healed, and she appeared to get well, but the doctor who was sent for to her would not believe that she could bear so terrible a shock so easily, and insisted that she must have change, mental and physical; so her brothers took her to Switzerland.

Being a sensible girl, when she went abroad she threw herself at once into the interests of the country she was in. She dried plants, she made sketches, she went up mountains, and as autumn came on, she was the person who urged that they should return to Croglin Grange. 'We have taken it,' she said, 'for seven years, and we have only been there one; and we shall always find it difficult to let a house which is only one story high, so we had better return there; lunatics do not escape every day.' As she urged it, her brothers wished nothing better, and the family returned to Cumberland. From there being no upstairs in the house it was impossible to make any great change in their arrangements. The sister occupied the same room, but it is unnecessary to say she always closed the shutters, which, however, as in many old houses, always left one top pane of the window uncovered. The brothers moved, and occupied a room together, exactly opposite that of their sister, and they always kept loaded pistols in their room.

The winter passed most peacefully and happily. In the following March, the sister was suddenly awakened by a sound she remembered only too well--scratch, scratch, scratch upon the window, and, looking up, she saw, climbed up to the topmost pane of the window, the same hideous brown shrivelled face, with glaring eyes, looking in at her. This time she screamed as loud as she could. Her brothers rushed out of their room with pistols, and out of the front door. The creature was already scudding away across the lawn. One of the brothers fired and hit it in the leg, but still with the other leg it continued to make way, scrambled over the wall into the churchyard, and seemed to disappear into a vault which belonged to a family long extinct.

"The next day the brothers summoned all the tenants of Croglin Grange, and in their presence the vault was opened. A horrible scene revealed itself. The vault was full of coffins; they had been broken open, and their contents, horribly mangled and distorted, were scattered over the floor. One coffin alone remained intact. Of that the lid had been lifted, but still lay loose upon the coffin. They raised it, and there, brown, withered, shrivelled, mummified, but quite entire, was the same hideous figure which had looked in at the windows of Croglin Grange, with the marks of a recent pistol-shot in the leg; and they did the only thing that can lay a vampire--they burnt it."

Ever since its first appearance, many have questioned the authenticity of the Croglin Grange vampire story. Early problems emerged when it was discovered that there was no house called "Croglin Grange" in the area. Other homes with similar names differed in style from the account and most damning, were two stories, rather than the one-story house described in the account.

Others agreed that the story was a complete fabrication. They complained that the story closely resembles elements of Thomas Preskett Prest's "penny dreadful" novel, Varney the Vampyre. One excerpt from the book reads:

It is its fingernails upon the glass that produces sounds so like the hail.. a small pane of glass is broken and the form introduces a long gaunt hand. The fastening is removed and one half of the window, which opens like folding doors, is swung wide open upon its hinges – and yet now she could not scream... The terrible object seemed to turn to one side... It approached the bed... The figure seized the long tresses of hair and twining them around his bony hands, he held her to the bed. He drags her head to the bed's edge – he seized her neck in his fang-like teeth..."

It was suggested that Captain Fisher might have concocted the story in order to produce another tourist attraction with the appeal of many British haunted houses. But, if this were the case, why would he change the name of the place and make it harder to find? Some believe that it was Captain Fisher's desire to try and protect the privacy of the real home, which is why he used another name.

In 1968, writer F. Clive-Ross became determined to get to the bottom of the mystery. He personally journeyed to Cumbria, where the incident allegedly occurred, and visited the local church. Many believed that "Croglin Grange" was actually another house called Croglin Low Hall, but no one could explain the part of the story that mentioned the nearby churchyard. The church was more than a mile away from the house. But while visiting the church, Clive-Ross found a printed history of the church, including the information, "Croglin Low Hall is the ancient Manor House of Little Croglin... There was a second church in Croglin here, probably serving as a private chapel for the house. Nothing of this church now exists." The implications of this were clear. If a church once existed near Croglin Low Hall, it would certainly explain the placement of the churchyard in the account.

Further investigation brought Clive-Ross into the very room where the vampire was said to have bitten the girl. The windows of the house were of a more recent vintage, altered considerably from the original leaded plane design. It also turned out that the house had actually been raised one story in 1720, which explained why it was now two stories instead of just one, as it was described in the account. Clive-Ross believed that this meant the incident may have taken place much earlier than was thought by Captain Fisher, pre-dating Varney the Vampyre by more than a century.

This idea was confirmed by an interview with a local woman, Mrs. Parkins, who gave Clive-Ross more information about the authenticity of the account. According to Mrs. Parkins, the ruined foundation of the original church could be seen as late as 1933 and evidence of the cemetery could still be found by those who knew where to look. The vampire story, she said, actually dated between 1680 and 1690 and she knew this because she was acquainted with a member of the Fisher family who was born in the 1860s. He had heard the story from his grandparents. In conclusion, she stated that, according to the deeds of Croglin Low Hall, the name commonly used for the house before 1720 was Croglin Grange.

The history of the story had certainly been corroborated, but what of the horror behind it? The truth of the vampire remains a mystery to this day.

MERCY BROWN

Although vampires seemed to be most deeply rooted in Europe, the American colonists were well aware of such creatures. The vampire, they believed, was a death-bringer and something to be feared. An unsuspecting community that fell under the spell of one of these monsters could very well be destroyed. One such American vampire was Mercy Brown and her story remains today as one of the most mysterious in American history.

Mercy Brown's story came to an end in 1892, but it began several years before that in 1883, when an epidemic of tuberculosis swept through the Exeter, Rhode Island, area. It's not hard to imagine how consumption may have given birth to the legends of vampires in New England. Consumption, or what we now call tuberculosis, was the plague of the 1800s. Death tolls from the illness were staggering as it was highly contagious and would pass easily through entire families. It was generally fatal and often referred to as the "White Death." The name came from the fact that the affected person's skin became very pale, thin and almost ghost-like. There was also a reddening of the face, fainting spells and a general weakening of the body. It was easy to see, in more superstitious times, how this could have been mistaken for the draining of the lifeblood by a vampire. It was thought that when someone died from consumption, he or she might come back from the dead and try to feed off their living relatives, who by this time, had probably come down with the disease themselves. In order to stop them from returning, family members would go to the grave and try to "kill" the deceased again.

The grave of Mercy Brown
(Derek Bartlett)

One might believe that one look at the decaying corpse would dispel any rumors of vampires, but this was not the case. In fact, when the coffin was opened, the recently dead consumptive would be found to be bloated in death, even though the disease had made them wasted and thin when alive. Their fingernails and hair would have grown and worst of all, their mouths would be filled with naturally regurgitated blood. The evidence of vampirism seemed blatantly obvious and tales of vampires spread through Rhode Island, Connecticut, Massachusetts, and beyond.

George Brown was a hard-working farmer who prospered in the Exeter area of southern Rhode Island, not far from Providence. He and his wife, Mary, had raised six children and lived a comfortable, but simple life. In late 1883, the first in a series of terrible events occurred on the Brown farm when Mary Brown began to show signs of consumption. The sturdy, once healthy woman began to suffer from fainting spells and periods of weakness. Most of all, she was gripped with a harsh cough that kept her awake through the night. The disease began to ravage her body and on December 8, she slipped into unconsciousness and did not awaken.

The following spring, Mary Olive, George's oldest daughter, also came down with the dreaded illness. She began to complain of terrible dreams and of a great pressure that was crushing her chest at night, making it impossible for her to breathe. Mary Olive grew paler and weaker with each passing day and on June 6, 1884; she

The crypt, or "keep", where Mercy's body was placed during the cold winter months -- and where her body was found by those who believed she was a vampire. (Derek Bartlett)

followed her mother to the grave.

Several years of peace followed the death of Mary Olive and during this time, Edwin Brown, George and Mary's only son, got married and bought his own farm in nearby West Wickford. Here, he hoped to make a life for himself and his new bride while he worked in a store to support his family and save money for the future. All was going well until about 1891, when Edwin began to notice the symptoms of the disease that had killed his sister and mother. He resigned from his job and following advice from friends, moved west to Colorado Springs. Here, he hoped that mineral waters and a drier climate might restore his health.

While Edwin was out West, things got worse for the family in Exeter. In January 1892, he received word that his sister Mercy had become sick and had died. He also began to realize that his health was not improving. He came to the decision that he should return home and spend the remainder of his days with his family, friends and loved ones.

By the time he reached Rhode Island, he found his father in a dreadful and worried state. He had become convinced that the family was being preyed upon by a vampire. After much debate, it was decided that they should exhume the bodies of the other family members and see which one of them it was. How they convinced Edwin to go along with this is unknown, but a group of men went out to the cemetery during the early morning hours of March 18, 1892.

It is likely that this exhumation would have remained a secret, if not for the fact that the men sought official sanction for it from the local doctor. They approached the district medical examiner, Dr. Harold Metcalf, and asked him to come to the graveyard to examine the bodies. He discouraged them, but eventually agreed to go along; realizing that he could not persuade them from what they believed was their duty. By the time he arrived at the cemetery, the bodies of Mary Brown and her daughter, Mary Olive, had already been unearthed. Dr. Metcalf took a look at them and found them in a state of advanced decay. They were, he said with certainty, "just what might be expected from a similar examination of almost any person after the same length of time."

Mercy's body had not yet been buried. As she had died in the winter, the ground was too hard for a burial. Her body had rested for the past two months inside a small crypt on the cemetery grounds. The coffin was placed on a small cart inside the tomb. Once the casket was opened, Dr. Metcalf looked inside and began a quick autopsy of the corpse. He noted some signs of decay and the marks left by consumption on her lungs. This did not convince him that she was a vampire, so he finished his examination and left.

The other men remained behind in the cemetery. To them, Mercy seemed relatively intact, or at least more so than she should be after two months in the grave. In addition, they were also sure that her body had moved. She had been laid to rest on her back and somehow the corpse was now resting on its side. Could she have left the casket? Dr. Metcalf, they believed, was simply trying to protect his reputation as a man of science and wanted no part of vampires.

The men were convinced that something was wrong with Mercy Brown and what happened next convinced them entirely. One of the men opened up her heart with his knife and was startled to see fresh blood come pouring out of the organ. It was quickly removed from her chest and burned in the cemetery. As it was engulfed in the flames, ashes were gathered with which to make a tonic that would hopefully cure Edwin of the disease.

Edwin consumed the macabre mixture, but it did no good and he died soon afterwards. On May 2, he too was buried in the cemetery. While tragic, all was not lost. He became the last of the Brown family to die from the mysterious "White Death." Tuberculosis had lost its grip on the region, but the family believed that it had been the exhumation that had ended the vampire's control over them once and for all.

Vampire Killers

As mentioned earlier, there have been scores of attacks on people throughout history that have been attributed to monsters and vampires. People simply could not conceive of the idea that a human being could be responsible for the kind of atrocities that occurred. It was easier to believe that a supernatural force was at work, but this was not always the case. Occasionally, these vicious blood-obsessed killers believed that they were in some way supernatural – or at least were involved in supernatural rituals – but in most cases, they were simply depraved.

In 1886, German neurologist Richard von Krafft-Ebing noted the compulsive and sexual presentation of the attacks and wrote about them in his landmark book *Psychopathia Sexualis*. Many of his two hundred and thirty-eight case histories concerned a violent eroticism triggered by blood. One man described was a twenty-four-year-old vineyard worker who murdered a twelve-year-old girl, drank her blood, mutilated her genitals, and ate part of her heart. When caught, he confessed with indifference. Another man would cut his arm for his wife to suck on because it aroused her so strongly. There have been dozens of so-called "vampire killers" over the years, including:

☠ Martin Dumollard, who killed several girls in France in 1861 and drank their blood.

☠ Joseph Vacher, who drank the blood from his murder victims in France in 1897.

☠ Eusebius Piedagnelle, who killed six women in Milan in 1878. He said that the smell of blood in a butcher's shop made him so excited that he began prowling for victims at night.

☠ Florencio Roque was an Argentinean man who was identified by fifteen women as the man who broke into their bedrooms at night, attacked them, and drank their blood.

☠ Magdalena Solis was part of a blood-drinking sex cult in Mexico in 1963. She helped to convince villagers in Yerba Buena that she was a goddess and presided over blood rituals that involved numerous murders. When the remains from the human sacrifices were discovered outside the village, authorities raided the cult and shut it down.

☠ Juan Koltrun, a Polish man, was dubbed the "Podaski Vampire" in 1982 after killing two of his seven rape victims and drinking their blood.

☠ John Crutchley was arrested in 1985 after holding a woman prisoner and drinking her blood. During questioning, he confessed to drinking blood from other women for years.

☠ Andrei Chikatlio, the Soviet "Forest Strip Vampire," was arrested for the murders of over fifty people between 1978 and 1990. He admitted to eating their body parts and drinking their blood.

☠ Marcello de Andrade killed fourteen boys in Rio de Janiero in 1991, sodomizing them and drinking their blood as a method of "becoming as beautiful as they were."

☠ Deborah Finch murdered Brandon McMichaels in Santa Cruz, California in 1992 in what he called a "suicide pact". She stabbed him twenty-seven times and drank his blood.

More than one killer has been nicknamed after "Dracula," the infamous character of history, literature, stage and screen. One such deviant was Richard Trenton Chase. He drank other people's blood, he claimed, because he was afraid of disintegrating. He was institutionalized several times and was obsessed with any sign that something was physically wrong with him. He once entered an emergency room because he was sure that his pulmonary artery had been stolen and complained that his bones were coming out through the back of his head, his stomach was backwards, and his heart often stopped beating. After being committed to a mental hospital, he earned the nickname of "Dracula" when nurses discovered him one day with blood around his mouth. Two dead birds, their necks broken, lay outside his window. Eventually he was released and deemed no longer a danger. Chase moved into another apartment and began to catch and torture cats, dogs, and rabbits. He killed them to drink their blood.

In 1978, Chase shot a man just to see what it would feel like and then entered the home of Teresa Wallin, who was three months pregnant. He shot her twice and then dragged her body to the bedroom. With a knife, he carved off her left nipple, cut open her torso, and stabbed her repeatedly. He also cut out her kidneys and severed her pancreas. With a yogurt container that he got from the trash, he drank her blood.

On January 27, 1978 Chase killed Evelyn Miroth, a male friend who was visiting her, and her six-year-old son, Jason. He also grabbed her infant son from his cradle, smashed the boy's head, and took the body with him when he left. Back at home, he removed the baby's head and consumed several of the organs.

He was arrested a short time later as he was leaving his apartment. In prison, he told another inmate that he needed the blood of his victims because of blood poisoning, and he'd grown tired of hunting for animals. He was convicted of six counts of first-degree murder and sentenced to death. Before his execution could be carried out, he died in his cell from a drug overdose.

In March 2005, a woman from Ukraine, Diana Semenuha, was arrested after police discovered that she had lured street children to her home to drink their blood. She admitted to the accusations, apparently believing that by drinking blood, she could cure a muscle-wasting condition that she had. However, newspaper reports claimed that she had even darker motives, if possible.

The Odessa press, which dubbed her the "vampire witch," claimed that she invited the children to her home with promises of food and a bed, gave them alcohol to make them agreeable, and then bled them. Whatever blood she did not use for herself, she sold to Satanists in the black magic circles with which she was involved in the region. Once a blood source weakened, she moved the child back out to the streets and found a replacement.

The police were tipped off to what was going on and raided her Odessa home. The place was entirely painted in black, the windows covered with black curtains, and the only lighting was provided by black candles. Seven children were found strapped in beds in the house, all of them drugged. The raid also turned up a large knife and a silver, bloodstained goblet. During the subsequent investigation, Semenuha admitted that she took blood from the children and said that she taught witchcraft to others and allowed her students to drink blood from her. She did not view what she was doing as a crime, since there was a fair exchange and no force or violence. Since she had fed the children and given them shelter, she believed she had paid for their blood. The seven children who were rescued from her home disappeared into the streets again, making the case against the "vampire witch" difficult to prosecute.

COUNTESS OF BLOOD

Countess Elizabeth Bathory of Hungary was born into the renowned Bathory family, which achieved fame for defending the country against the Ottoman Turks – and for their legendary depravity. She was possibly the most prolific female serial killer in history and her nickname of the "Blood Countess" also spoke volumes about her infamy as one of the world's most famous vampires. After her husband's death, she and four collaborators were accused of torturing and killing hundreds of young women, with one witness attributing them to over six hundred victims, though she was only convicted on eighty counts. In 1610, she was imprisoned in Cachtice Castle, where she remained bricked into a set of rooms until her death four years later.

Elizabeth was born on a family estate in Nyírbátor, at that time part of Hungary, around 1560. According to legend, her brother was an accused rapist, her uncle was charged with worshipping the Devil and her aunt was a notorious lesbian. Young Elizabeth reportedly learned a great deal from her family, including the practice of witchcraft, which she was accused of dabbling in later in life.

At the age of fifteen, Elizabeth was engaged to Ferenc Nádasdy and moved to Nádasdy Castle in Sárvár. The two of them were married in 1575 and Nádasdy presented Cachtice Castle to his new wife as a wedding gift. The castle was situated in the Little Carpathian Mountains, near Trenčín, and the estate included a country house and seventeen adjacent villages.

In 1578, Nádasdy became the chief commander of Hungarian troops, leading them to war against the Ottomans. With her husband away at war, Elizabeth managed business affairs and the estates. Over the

Elizabeth Bathory, the so-called "Countess of Blood"

years of the Long War, which began in 1593 and lasted for thirteen years, she was forced to defend her husband's estates, which lay on the route to Vienna. The region was in great danger, having been sacked by the Ottomans on previous occasions. She handled herself well and made a name for herself as an educated woman who could read and write in four languages and knew much about science and astronomy. When her husband died in battle in 1604, Elizabeth was already managing his wealth and vast holdings. It was a simple matter for her to continue as the ruler of his domain. She had come to believe that her family connections and vast fortune could protect from anything, but rumors were already starting to spread about strange things taking place behind the walls of Cachtice Castle.

Elizabeth Bathory's bizarre practices began around the time she turned forty. She was still a beautiful and ravishing woman, but she feared the approach of her declining years. According to the legend, an accident occurred one day that instilled a terrible idea in Elizabeth's mind. A maid was brushing her long hair and accidentally pulled it. Elizabeth reached out and slapped the girl so hard that blood from her split lip splashed onto Elizabeth's hand. She looked at the crimson gore smeared across her hand and she later claimed that she could feel it seeping into her pores – causing her skin to take on the youth of the servant girl. Elizabeth suddenly had the method by which she could maintain her own youth and beauty – she would bathe her entire body in the blood of young virgins.

While the terrified maid cowered in one corner of the chamber, Elizabeth sent for her most trusted servants. Under her orders, they stripped the maid naked, cut her and then drained her blood into a bathtub. As it filled, Elizabeth undressed and slipped ecstatically into the warm blood. When she emerged, she claimed that she could feel the energy and vitality coursing through her gore-covered body.

This event allegedly began Elizabeth Bathory's reign of terror in Transylvania. She needed a constant supply of young maidens and her servants prowled the area, luring girls to the castle by offering them jobs. As girls started to disappear, it became harder and harder to convince new young women to cooperate and so they turned to kidnapping to obtain additional victims. Elizabeth's need for blood continued over the course of nearly a decade. The people of the region lived in a state of terror and the authorities feared crossing a member of the country's ruling class. But the rumors spread and eventually, they became impossible to ignore.

The first rumblings began in 1604, but were ignored for years. By 1610, a Lutheran minister finally dared to complain about the missing girls to the Hungarian court in Vienna. This prompted a response from King Matthias, who assigned Juraj Thurzo to investigate his cousin, Elizabeth. Thurzo began collecting evidence from villagers and survivors but even before this was completed, he met with Elizabeth's son, Paul, and two of her son-in-laws to discuss the situation – and how to cover it up. A trial and execution would have caused a public scandal and disgraced a noble and influential family, and Elizabeth's considerable property would have been seized by the crown. Thurzo, along with Elizabeth's family, made plans to have her secretly hidden away in a convent, but as accounts of murders of daughters of lesser nobility began to spread, it was agreed that Elizabeth should be kept under strict house arrest.

On December 30, 1610, Thurzo and his soldiers raided Cachtice Castle and arrested Elizabeth and four of her servants, who were accused of being her accomplices. Thurzo and his men reportedly found one dead girl in Elizabeth's chambers and another who was dying. A number of other women were confined to a torture chamber in the basement.

Elizabeth was placed under house arrest and her angry cousin, King Matthias, requested that she be put to death. However, Thurzo successfully convinced the king that such an act would negatively affect the nobility and the trial was postponed indefinitely. The countess' associates, however, were brought to court in January 1611 and they included Dorottya Szentes, Ilona, Katarína Benická, and János Újváry (Ficko). Dorottya, Ilona and Ficko were found guilty and were immediately put to death. Dorottya and Ilona had their fingernails ripped out before they were thrown into a fire, while Ficko, who was deemed less guilty, was beheaded before being consigned to the flames. A public scaffold was erected near the castle to show the public that justice had been done. Katarína Benická was sentenced to life imprisonment, as she only acted under the domination and bullying of the other women.

The sentences suffered by Elizabeth's accomplices were arrived upon after months of collected testimonies from more than three hundred witness accounts. Trial records included testimonies of the four defendants, as well as thirteen other witnesses. Priests, noblemen and commoners were questioned, intimidated and tortured. The witnesses stated that Elizabeth's original victims had been local peasant girls, many of whom were lured to Cachtice by offers of well-paid work as maidservants in the castle. Later, she began to kill daughters of lower gentry, who had been sent to the castle to learn courtly etiquette. Girls were also kidnapped, and allegedly forced to take part in Elizabeth's rituals and witchcraft practices.

And if killing the young women and draining their blood was not horrific enough, the accounts claimed that Elizabeth put them

The ruins of Bathory's castle at Cachtice, where she was walled up alive in her room and later died.

through other degradations before she took their lives. Stories claimed the girls were severely beaten; were burned and mutilated on their faces and genitals; suffered terrible bites on their faces, arms and other body parts; were cut and operated on with surgical devices; tortured with hot needles; and more. In all, it is believed that at least six hundred young women were killed by Elizabeth and her accomplices over a ten-year period.

Unfortunately for these scores of victims, Elizabeth was never truly punished for her crimes. Unlike her accomplices, she was placed under extended house arrest and walled up into a set of rooms inside her castle. On August 21, 1614, she was found dead in her rooms. Since there were several plates of food left untouched, her actual date of death remains unknown.

According to one of the guards who peered through the slit in the brick wall where food was passed, the once beautiful countess had died as a withered old hag.

THE "VAMPIRE OF HANOVER"

One of the most notorious killers of the early twentieth century was a German man named Fritz Haarmann, the fiend who would become known as the "Hanover Vampire" after it was discovered that he had killed dozens of young men and drained their bodies of blood.

Haarmann was born in October 1879 and was a troubled boy. He feared and hated his father, a taciturn railroad worker, and was unsuccessful in school. He eventually joined the military and did well as a soldier. His life seemed to be turning around until his release from duty and his return to his hometown of Hanover. Soon after he arrived, he was accused of molesting several children. Haarmann was arrested and was placed in a mental institution in Hildesheim, from which he soon escaped and fled to Switzerland. When charges were dismissed against him, he returned to Hanover and moved back into his father's home. The two of them argued incessantly and Haarmann entered the military again. This time, his service did not go as well and Haarmann was released on a medical discharge. He tried to live with his father again, but this time their fighting turned physical and the police were summoned. Haarmann was examined by a police psychiatrist and while the doctor believed that he was an amoral sociopath, he could find no legal cause to send him back to the asylum.

Haarmann began living on the street, surviving by theft, fraud and petty crime, for which he regularly spent time in jail. In 1918, he finally began to satisfy his sexual desires for blood. He was working at a delicatessen at the time, butchering and selling illegal meat during a time of great hunger in Germany, following World War I. Haarmann began strolling down to the Hanover railway station in the pre-dawn hours, looking for sleeping young boys. When he found one, he would awaken him and demand to see his ticket. When the boy was unable to produce one, Haarmann would inevitably hear a sad story from the youth and then offer him a place to stay for the night. Friedel Rothe, a seventeen-year-old runaway, became the first to satisfy Haarmann's lusts. The boy vanished from the railway station one morning and was never seen again. The police investigated, and even questioned Haarmann, but produce no clues. Years later, Haarmann would confess to the fact that when the detectives came to his house, Rothe's head was hidden under a newspaper behind his oven.

Haarmann began experimenting with – and killing – other young men. Most of his encounters with them ended in an unusual way. As he climaxed, he would bite into his victim's

Fritz Haarmann, the "Hanover Vampire"

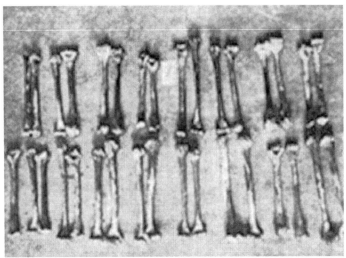
Some of the recovered bones of Haarmann's victims

throat, satisfying himself with the taste of their blood.

In 1919, Haarmann met a young man named Hans Grans, a blackmailer, male prostitute, thief and murderer. The two men developed an ongoing relationship and assumed the job of organizing many of Haarmann's murders, including those of two young men whom Grans convinced Haarmann to kill because he wanted their clothing. Grans soon became the driving force behind his grisly desires – pushing Haarmann into murder after murder.

In 1924, events occurred that brought an end to Haarmann's vampire career. Human skulls and bones were found in the Leine River on May 17 and then more were found on May 29. Two more skulls were uncovered from a mud bank on June 13 and then, on June 24, a sack that contained more remains was found, causing the police to consider the idea that some sort of monster was stalking the city.

On June 22, Haarmann had been arrested on an indecency charge. While he was in custody, the police searched his home and found numerous bloodstains. His practice of butchering and selling illegal meat was well known (although overlooked in those difficult times) but the discovery of twenty-two corpses, all belonging to young men and boys, made the "illegal meat" the subject of grotesque and ominous rumors. The public began screaming for vengeance against the human monster, although there was no actual evidence against Haarmann himself until the mother of one of the boys found a piece of clothing that could be traced to the butcher. Haarmann quickly broke down during an interrogation and confessed to everything, implicating his lover Hans Grans at the same time.

Haarmann gave detailed descriptions of kidnapping and killing his victims, then cutting them up and selling them as meat to his unsuspecting customers. He also described how he inflicted fatal bites on their throats before he drank their blood, and then ate portions of their flesh. Hans Grans was initially charged with participating in the murders, but prosecutors altered the charges to inciting murder and receiving stolen property. In court, Haarmann claimed that Grans usually selected his victims for him and more than once beat him for failing to kill the "game" that he brought in. The victim's clothing that Grans did not want was sold in the butcher shop. The bodies of the slaughtered young men were kept in a closet in the house until they could be completely dismembered. Since the back of the place was adjacent to the river, Haarmann usually placed the skulls and bones in a bag and tossed them into the water.

When asked how many murders he had committed, Haarmann replied, "Thirty or forty, I don't remember exactly."

The "Vampire of Hanover" was convicted of twenty-seven murders and sentenced to death. Hans Grans was initially found guilty of provoking the murder of twenty-four of the victims and also sentenced to death. However, the discovery of a letter from Haarmann that declared Grans innocent later led to a second trial and a twelve-year prison sentence for him. After serving his time, Grans continued to live in Hannover until his death in 1980.

Haarmann was beheaded and after the execution, scientists preserved his head in a jar to examine the structure of his brain. Haarmann's head is can still be found today at the Göttingen Medical School in Germany.

THE DUSSELDORF VAMPIRE

In 1931, the brilliant German film director Fritz Lang made a motion picture that not only became a cinema classic, but which launched the international career of an obscure young actor named Peter Lorre. The title of the picture was simply *M*. It was about a murderer, but not an ordinary murderer – it was a fictionalized version of a man named Peter Kurten, the so-called "Dusseldorf Vampire."

Peter Kurten, the depraved "Dusseldorf Vampire"

Like so many other monsters of the modern era, there is little point in speculating too extensively on what Kurten's fate might have been if he had lived during the Middle Ages. History has given us many bloody descriptions of punishments meted out to those who were believed to be witches, vampires and werewolves. What is fascinating about this particular vampire is the incredible personality that he developed over the years, but what is difficult to understand is how he managed to evade detection for as long as he did. But then, as we see his story of horror take shape, we begin to realize that Kurten was a fiend whose depravity was truly without parallel.

Peter Kurten was born in 1883 in the town of Mulheim, Germany, on the Rhine river. He was one of ten children and early in life, learned to fear and hate his father, an alcoholic who regularly beat his wife and children. Later in life, Kurten recalled that his family lived in the same house as the local dog-catcher. Any animals that were not claimed by their owners were killed and eaten. He remembered the strange pleasure that he experienced at watching the animals being slaughtered – a pleasure that he later experienced on his own by killing squirrels, cats and other small animals in the neighborhood.

At the age of nine, he committed his first murders. It happened while he played with two others on a raft along the banks of the Rhine. He pushed one of the boys into the water and under the raft, refusing to let him out until he drowned. When the other boy went in to try and help the first, Kurten forced him under the water and allowed him to drown, too.

Kurten later blamed many of his problems on the "martyrdom" of his youth. He father frequently beat him and he was forced to witness the man's mistreatment of his mother, who Kurten described as being "pure and good." As his father's brutality increased, he began to dream of revenge, an attitude that was provoked when Kurten's father was arrested for raping his own thirteen-year-old daughter.

By the time Kurten was sixteen, he began to experiment with sex. One afternoon, he took a willing former schoolmate into the woods and began to make love to her. Unfortunately for the girl, Kurten's ideas about sex were a little unusual and he began strangling the girl as he neared orgasm. Realizing that her life was in danger, she fought, kicked, scratched and bit until she finally managed to escape. Gathering her clothing around her, she ran home as quickly as she could. But this was not the end of the incident because, for whatever reason, Kurten became obsessed with her. The following day, he threw an ax through her kitchen window. The day after that, he threw a rock through her bedroom window. Before the week was over, he had gotten his hands on a pistol and shot at her father. Kurten pleaded with her to see him again, but the girl, understandably terrified, refused. Finally, he wrote a vicious letter, threatening her life and the lives of her family. They reported the matter to the police, Kurten was arrested and sentenced to prison for four years.

After Kurten's release, he became a full-fledged criminal. Although he received a number of sentences for theft and burglary, the authorities were completely unaware that he was also a killer and a dangerous arsonist.

During one year of freedom, between stretches in jail, he managed to commit four undetected acts of arson, in addition to other crimes. He also boasted that, while in prison, he managed to poison two fellow inmates without getting caught.

In 1912, after being freed from prison again, he returned to his career of petty crime, burglary and fraud. He developed a specialty that consisted of burglarizing small family taverns on weekend nights, when the owners were too busy with customers to worry about what was happening in their living quarters upstairs.

One night in Dusseldorf, while on one of his nocturnal forays, he crept into a tavern called the Losche-Ecke and found several children sleeping in their beds. He estimated that one of the girls was about seventeen years old. Unable to control himself, he claimed years later, he became voraciously aroused, jumped on the girl and tried to rape and strangle her. He failed to kill the girl that night because something alarmed him and made him flee, but he was so exhilarated by the experience that he tried it again later on that same month – and this time, he took a hatchet with him. As he crept into the house that he chose, he made his way to the darkened sleeping quarters on the second floor. In the first bedroom that he entered, he found a young woman asleep. As he stood next to the bed, hatchet in hand, planning to split open her skull, the door to the bedroom suddenly opened and a man walked in. Kurten silently tossed the hatchet onto the bed and slipped from the room. He miraculously escaped without being seen.

In the summer of 1913, Kurten committed his first vampire killing. He left Dusseldorf on a Saturday evening and went to the Cologne suburb of Mulheim, where he had been born. A fair was in progress and the streets were crowded with festive townspeople. Kurten melted into the throng and prowled about until he found a house that suited him. He broke inside and wandered the place, finding little worth taking. However, in one of the upstairs bedrooms, he found a girl of about ten years old asleep in a large, white bed. He began strangling the girl and then, just before she died, he cut her throat with a small knife that he carried with him. He felt the warm blood splash over his hand and spurt out onto the bed, dripping down onto the floor. He later said that the sound of dripping blood was the "most powerful aphrodisiac imaginable." After the girl stopped bleeding, Kurten silently locked the door of the house and returned to Dusseldorf. The following day, he returned to Mulheim and went into a café that was located just across the street from the house where he had killed the girl. As he sat there, drinking a glass of beer, he read the papers and listened to people talk about the murder. He later said, "All of this indignation and horror did me good."

Kurten was convicted of fraud and theft that same year and remained in prison until 1921. Two years later, he married a damaged woman who never learned of his double life. A tailor's daughter, she had served four years in prison for shooting a former fiancée who had, in her words, "betrayed her." Overcome with guilt, she was convinced that she would never lead a normal life and when she met Kurten, she was impressed with his neat appearance, charming manners and surface respectability. She did not love him, but believing that she would never find anyone better, she married him. Kurten had no love for his wife either, except for the fact that she reminded him of his mother. Perhaps for this reason, he always kept his secret life hidden away from her.

For years, Kurten had managed to keep his bizarre sexual needs under wraps. By the time his bloody career ended in 1930, his incredible list of felonies included the murders that he was eventually convicted for, twenty-three attempted strangulations of various women, twenty-two instances of arson, numerous stabbings and bludgeonings with hammers, axes and other tools. The savagery of his assaults certainly verifies the existence of a monster beneath his bland exterior. Many of his victims were so horribly mutilated that until his identity was known, he was frequently compared to Jack the Ripper. When he was finally arrested and indicted, he was charged with nine murders and seven attempted murders. The authorities were stunned by his various methods of murder, including strangulation, stabbing, drowning, beating and throat cutting, but Kurten insisted that a knife was his favorite tool. He became so aroused when using a blade that, even after his victim was dead, he continued to stab the body until he experienced an orgasm.

In 1929, Kurten began to spiral out of control. On February 3, He attacked a young woman named Kuhn and after warning her to be silent, stabbed her twenty-four times and left her to die. Although still alive when the police arrived, she was unable to give any description of her attacker.

Within five days, the mutilated corpse of a eight-year-old girl named Rose Ohliger was discovered. She had been stabbed thirteen times and then her body was drenched with kerosene and burned. On February 13, the body of a forty-five-year-old man named Rudolph Scheer was found. He had also been stabbed repeatedly and mutilated, leading the police and the people of Dusseldorf to believe that a homicidal maniac was loose in their city.

On April 2, 1929, Kurten changed the method of his kills. A sixteen-year-old girl named Erna Pinner was caught from behind when a rope was looped around her neck. She was violently pulled backward off her feet. She managed to fight her way free from her attacker and run away, again without seeing the man's face. The following day, a similar attempt was made on another woman, but it was disrupted by two men who were passing by. Once again, no one could describe the attacker.

As the city panicked, the police were under great pressure to find the killer. A suspect was found in the person of a feeble-minded epileptic named Rudolph Strausberg. He confessed to all of the crimes and was incarcerated in a mental institution. Meanwhile, the real killer – Peter Kurten – was still at large.

The murders resumed on July 30. The mutilated body of a prostitute named Emma Goss was found in a dilapidated hotel. The next day, three girls were slashed nearly to death. With these attacks so closely resembling the earlier ones, it was obvious that Rudolph Strausberg, no matter how disturbed he might be, was clearly not the killer. By the end of August, Kurten had brutally slaughtered nine victims in one month.

Delighting in the fear and indignation that he was arousing, Kurten took to flaunting his freedom to the authorities. In November 1929, he wrote a letter to the Communist newspaper, *Freiheit*. It included a map and specific instructions as to where the body of five-year-old Gertrude Albermann, who had been missing for two days, could be found. Even though the police managed to find the body shortly before the letter was given to them, they had no doubt that the missive had been written by the killer. Gertrude had been strangled, and then stabbed thirty-six times.

After this, Kurten was dormant for a time. It was not until May 1930 that he sought out another victim – the one that would become his last. On the evening of May 14, a young woman named Maria Budlick arrived at the Dusseldorf train station. She was approached by Kurten and perhaps because of his appearance and good manners, the girl trusted him and agreed to let him find a hotel for her. He was so convincing that Maria stopped at his apartment with him for dinner. After eating, Kurten eventually took the girl in to the Grafenburg woods. Maria was willing to engage in sex with Kurten, but became terrified when he started to strangle her. Then, strangely, he changed his mind and decided not to kill her. Stepping back, he asked Maria if she remembered where he lived. Lying, she said that she was a stranger in town and did not remember. For some strange reason – perhaps because he wanted to be caught – Kurten let her go. In less than twenty-four hours, the police were at his door. Maria identified him and then fled from the building. Kurten was taken into custody and once he began to confess, the stories that he told the police both sickened and shocked the hardened officers.

Utterly calm, Kurten detailed the attacks and murders that he had committed, going all of the way back to his childhood. He explained that he needed to shed blood to release the sexual tension that he felt. And while he apologized to the victims that had survived his attacks, he admitted that if he was released, he would go right back to killing again.

During the course of the trial that followed, Kurten's appearance never failed to perplex the press and the onlookers. He looked like anything but the "Dusseldorf Vampire". His suits were always clean and well pressed, his voice was soft and sedate, his hair was carefully combed into place and he was always clean shaven, except for a thin mustache. Peter Kurten was so ordinary-looking that it would be difficult to remember him or pick him out of a crowd. But if one looked closely, an examiner would see his cold, penetrating eyes and his pinched, cruel mouth. He was a man capable of enormous cruelty, no matter how well he managed to hide it.

When the trial ended, Kurten was sentenced to death. While he waited in jail for his punishment to be carried out, Kurten received fan mail from all over Europe. Scores of women proposed marriage to him and admirers flocked to the prison gates, in spite of – or because of – the horrific acts he had committed. Kurten, meanwhile, sent letters of apology to the families of his victims and told the court that he was pleased at being given a fair trial. He expressed no regrets, only the hope that when he was beheaded, he would live long enough to hear his own blood gushing forth from his body.

Whether he did or not, we will never know.

At 6:00 a.m. on July 2, 1931, Peter Kurten calmly walked out into the prison bell as the traditional "sinner's bell" rang out in the early morning hair. Without hesitation, he surrendered himself to the executioner and his strange and terrible life came to an end.

THE KENSINGTON VAMPIRE

In the years immediately following the devastation of World War II, the people of England were shocked by the revelations that a vampire had been killing in their midst. The bloody career of John George Haigh was one of the most successful vampire sprees in history, largely due to the fact that until his claimed his ninth victim, the police never even knew that he existed.

Haigh was born in 1910 and was raised by strict, religious parents who belonged to a fundamentalist sect called the Pilgrim Brethren. Haigh lived in an environment of repressive religious fanaticism, which banned all worldly pleasures including gambling, alcohol, dancing, the theater and even the daily newspapers. He was not allowed to play with other children and Haigh's only goal was supposed to be his own salvation. He became obsessed with the idea, knowing that the only way to attain happiness after death was through the blood of Jesus Christ. His superstitious mother planted the idea in his head that his dreams prophesized the future, which was especially disturbing to a boy whose only recurring dream was of Jesus, nailed to a cross, and slowly bleeding to death.

In time, Haigh no longer found significance in his family's religion and joined the Church of England, becoming a choir boy and later, the assistant organist. One day, Haigh claimed to be the recipient of a divine message that told him to drink his own urine. Actually, this was a bizarre misinterpretation of two biblical passages: "Drink water out of thine own cistern and running waters out of thine own well" from Proverbs, and "He that believeth on me, as the scriptures hath said, out of his belly shall flow rivers of living water" from John.

Haigh's dreams, which he still believed had a religious significance, were what eventually drove him to become a vampire. The dreams that he once had of a dying Christ eventually became that of a forest of crosses that changed into the shapes of trees dripping blood. As an unknown man collected the blood from a tree in a bowl, the tree became pale. In the dream, Haigh felt his own body drained of life, but as the man offered him the bowl from which to drink, he knew this was a way to restore his vitality. Each time that Haigh reached for the bowl, the man faded away. He awoke, unfulfilled, and knew that the only hope that he had to restore his essence was to drink the blood from living persons.

John George Haigh

Haigh began his gruesome task, managing to claim eight victims before the authorities realized that a fiend was preying on women in the city of London. His ninth victim was a sixty-nine-year-old widow named Mrs. Olivia Helen Henrietta Olive Roberts Durand-Deacon. He met her while they were both living at the Onslow Court Hotel in the South Kensington section of London. Haigh was working for a small firm at the time and made a steady income as the company director. This position gave him access to the firm's storehouse, a small shed in a builder's yard on Leopold Road in Cawley.

One evening at dinner, Haigh told Mrs. Durand-Deacon that he had invented a new process for manufacturing artificial fingernails. She expressed an interest in this ad he offered to take her to his "laboratory," where she might see the experiments for herself. He drove her to Cawley on the night of February 18, 1949 and led her into the darkened shed. While she patiently waited to see what he had promised, Haigh calmly shot her in the back of the head with a

.38 caliber Enfield revolver. As her body fell, Haigh quickly grabbed a drinking glass, made a slit in the side of her neck, collected the blood and drank it. After that, Haigh removed all of her clothing and jewelry and placed her body into a large tank to which he added thirty gallons of sulfuric acid. He locked up the shed, went to a nearby restaurant for tea and then returned to add more acid to the tank. Having worked up an appetite, he went to the George Hotel in Crawley, had dinner, and then returned to his lodgings in South Kensington.

The following day, he made the first mistake of his career when he decided to pawn Mrs. Durand-Deacon's watch and jewelry and take her fur coat into the dry cleaners.

On February 21, a friend of the murdered woman became alarmed that she was missing. Knowing that she was acquainted with Haigh, she asked him to accompany her to the police station to file a missing person's report. Haigh agreed, but stalled the trip long enough to return to Crawley and see if the woman's body had completely dissolved in the acid tank – it had not. He added more acid, cleared off some of the sludge and then hurried back to South Kensington to visit the authorities. He appeared to be quite concerned about Mrs. Durand-Deacon's disappearance, but the police were not convinced by his story. The detectives sensed that something was "off" about Haigh and so they decided to check up on him. They quickly learned that he had pawned the missing woman's jewelry and on February 26, Haigh was taken into custody. After much questioning, he admitted to the crime and then added that he had committed murders that the police were not even aware of. But he confidently told them that he could not be convicted, since there were no bodies that could be used as evidence against him.

The baffled inspectors were not sure what to do with Haigh, mostly convinced that he was a random nutcase who enjoyed confessing to murders that were all in his imagination. So, they finally convinced him to write down a detailed account of his crimes. A group of Scotland Yard investigators went to Crawley and gathered samples of earth and sludge remains from the acid tank. According to police commissioner Sir Harold Scott, they found, "... the handle of a red, plastic handbag, some false teeth, three gallstones, some fragments of human bone, and a mass of yellowish substance resembling body fat. Examination of the gallstones showed them to be of human type, the bones, too, were human and probably those of an elderly woman... the teeth were identified by the dentist who had supplied them to Mrs. Durand-Deacon."

There was a great deal more damning evidence, all of which pointed directly at Haigh. He was consequently placed under arrest and charged with murder. The authorities tried to keep the matter quiet and the press was prevented from running any sensational stories about the vampire murderer by British laws against pre-trial publicity. Nevertheless, a number of stories were printed anyway and one publisher was actually sentenced to three months in prison for violating the law. The stories and rumors that surrounded Haigh brought thousands of curious spectators to the trial when it opened at the Sussex Assizes in July. People were both excited and terrified by the idea of getting a glimpse of a real-life vampire.

Haigh remained calm and composed throughout the trial. There were thirty witnesses for the prosecution, but only one for the defense, a psychiatrist named Dr. Harvey Yellowlees, who attempted to show that Haigh was insane. The prosecution strenuously objected to this because according to British law, a person is not insane if he "knows the nature and quality" of his act. Haigh was perfectly aware of what he was doing, even though he believed that by drinking blood, he could somehow achieve eternal life. He had been commanded to claim his victims by God, he stated, because the consumption of blood was necessary for his salvation.

The courts judged him to be both sane and guilty and after his conviction, he was sentenced to death. The life of John George Haigh ended – not when a wooden stake was driven through his heart – but at the end of a hangman's rope.

VAMPIRES THAT DON'T DRINK BLOOD

Church of Satan founder Anton LaVey may have coined the name "psychic vampire" when he wrote about such people in his entertaining and thought-provoking *Satanic Bible*, but the idea was not a new, or wholly original one. Psychic vampires have been with us since the beginning of recorded history and in fact, there is a very good chance that every reader of this book knows, or has known, at least one of them in his or her lifetime.

To many occultists, a psychic vampire is exactly what the name implies – a person who can supernaturally or psychically drain the life force and vitality of someone through magical attack. In such cases, the victim will experience mysterious fatigue and exhaustion, troubling dreams, horrible nightmares and even sexual assaults. These are not physical attacks, but they might as well be because they do physical – and psychological – damage to the victim and can result in unexplained behavior, confusion, dizziness, illness, mental collapse, and even death. The attacking "vampire" seems to need the energy of other people to sustain his own life.

And while people like this may actually exist, there is a much more common type of "psychic vampire" that many more of us have encountered during our lives. Psychic vampires are simply individuals who drain others of their vital energy by practicing the fine art of making others feel responsible and even indebted to them, without cause. This type of person can be found in every walk of life and while they seem to fill no real, useful purpose in our lives, we feel responsible to them without really knowing why.

There are a few simple ways to know if you have been – or still are – the victim of such a person. Is there a person that you often call or visit, even though you don't have a pressing need to do so, but do it because you know you'll feel guilty if you don't? Or, do you find yourself constantly doing favors for someone who really doesn't ask you to, but hints at them? Often they will say, "Oh, I couldn't ask you to do that..." and you, in turn insist on doing it. Such a person never actually demands anything, they simply make their wishes known in ways that will prevent them from seeming like they want something. It's always what they *don't* say, not what they *do* say, that makes you feel that you should do things for them. They never make demands, knowing that you might resent that, and instead allow you to do favors for them.

A large percentage of these vampires have special "attributes," which makes their dependence on you more effective. Some of them are invalids (or pretend to be) or are "emotionally disturbed". Others offer sexual favors, seemingly because they really want to, just long enough to get your make sure you'll do them favors in hope of getting more. Others might feign ignorance or incompetence so you will, out of pity, do things for them.

Most people accept these individuals at face value because their true nature has never been revealed to the victim. The victim accepts them as being less fortunate than himself and feels he should help them in whatever way they can. It is this misdirected sense of responsibility that provides the nourishment that these parasites feed on. Psychic vampires exist because they cleverly choose conscientious, responsible people for their victims.

Their victims are carefully chosen. They know that it is difficult for a person who has been very giving throughout their life to suddenly start saying "no" when favors are asked of them. If allowed to do so, psychic vampires will gradually infiltrate a person's life until they have no privacy left and the constant feeling of concern for the vampire will deplete the victim of all ambition. They will find a person who is relatively content and happy with his life to feed upon. The very fact that the psychic vampire chooses to take advantage of a happy person shows that they are lacking all of the things that the victim has and will do everything possible to stir up trouble and disharmony between the victim and the people they care most about.

Many psychic vampires will give material things to their victims or, as mentioned, will have sex with them. This is done with the express purpose of making the victim feel as if they owe something in return, thereby binding the victim to them. They want their victims to feel obligated to them and would be disappointed, even resentful, if material objects were offered in repayment. In essence, the victim has "sold their soul" to them and the vampire will constantly remind them of their duty to them, by *not* reminding them.

But not everyone who falls prey to a psychic vampire remains a permanent victim. Eventually, many will discover the one-sided nature of the relationship, or realize their own affairs are being neglected as they try and help their "friend" deal with theirs. When the victim manages to extricate himself or herself from the situation, the psychic vampire will first act despondent and upset, hoping the victim's old feelings of duty and sympathy will return. However, if this doesn't happen, their true nature will emerge and they will become angry and vindictive. They are likely to do anything they can to torment their former prey, neglecting all else to plan the revenge to which they feel they are entitled.

So, take this bit of advice with you...

For the reasons just mentioned, it's best to try and avoid a relationship with this kind of person in the first place. Their dependence on your may, at first, be flattering, and their gifts and attention very attractive, but you will eventually find yourself paying for them many times over. This is a person who will ultimately destroy you, if you let them and it's best to instead concentrate on those people who appreciate your responsibility to them, and in turn, feel responsible to you. Your life is bound to be a whole lot happier by heeding these words of warning.

And how would I know?

As I stated in the opening to this section, we have probably all known at least one psychic vampire during our lifetime. Believe it or not, I've known a few. However, the most destructive one was (luckily) not one that I had to deal with first-hand. I watched a friend of mine deal with his own vampire and it nearly destroyed his career, his family and, in some ways, his sanity.

"Joe" first met his vampire, who we'll call "Zelda," at a writers' convention several years ago. Both of them were published authors and on the surface, had a lot in common. They had a mutual attraction for another, despite the fact that Zelda was married at the time, and they almost immediately became sexually involved. The two of them lived about three hours away from each other and Joe spent thousands of hours – and thousands of dollars – making telephone calls and traveling back and forth to see Zelda, who, she explained, was simply unable to get away from her business to come and visit him. Joe, meanwhile, was already neglecting his own business during the time he was paying all of his attention to Zelda. He had also stopped writing because he simply didn't have the time and energy to devote to it.

Within a couple of months, Zelda began to tell him of all of the problems she was having with her business and her staff. Her husband's behavior had become very erratic (he would eventually enter into an alcohol rehab program, which gave Joe hope that she would finally leave him) and Zelda told Joe that she had no idea what she was doing with her staff and records. Her husband had always handled all of that and with him gone, she didn't know what to do. Not surprisingly, Joe offered to help. Not only did he make numerous trips to run her business in person, he also began spending countless hours on it at home, further neglecting his own responsibilities. Zelda offered to pay him for his time, but Joe refused. He was helping out because he wanted to, he said, not because he was obligated to do so or because he wanted money.

Time passed and every couple of weeks, there would be some new drama in Zelda's life that would require Joe's complete attention. She broke off their relationship every month, determined that she needed to stay with her husband – only to invite Joe to her city again and have sex with him at his hotel. She wanted to be with him, she said, and was going to leave her husband. Next, it was a pregnancy scare, followed by an alleged beating by her husband, then a miscarriage – all of which required Joe to attend to her every need.

Things continued on like this for the next few months. He wasn't listening to any of his friends about the situation and all of us realized that he would just have to find out for himself that he was in a bad spot – and it would hopefully be before it was too late. By this time, Joe had sold off part of his business, but none of it was for profit, it was simply to keep paying the bills. His work was now so badly neglected that it didn't look like any part of it would survive. Zelda's business, naturally, was doing just fine.

But then an event took place that finally started to wake Joe up as to what was going on. A book that he had written for a major publisher the previous year had just been released and he was very excited about it. The publisher had set up a number of book signings for him and he was scheduled to be in Zelda's city for an entire week. He began making plans with her to attend some of the signings and events that had been set up in bookstores all over the city. Zelda feigned happiness for him, at the same time that she bemoaned the fact that she had not been able to write a new book in several years. She was simply too "overwhelmed" with the problems of everyday life, from her busy company to her husband's many issues. (Note: She and her husband were still together, despite his alleged abuses and her extramarital affairs – which would later to be revealed to be literally in the hundreds!)

Joe didn't let her lack of enthusiasm bother him. It's possible that he didn't even see it yet. Instead, he happily arrived for the many book signings that had been arranged for him. Each night, Zelda would claim that she was coming to support him, but each night, she didn't show. She was always too busy, or something came up. This left Joe feeling pretty sorry for himself. He was missing out on the excitement of the new book release, the interviews and the signings. He was also missing the fact that Zelda was punishing him because he was seeing a bit of success that was not all about her. It was jealously, plain and simple, and she was determined to find a way to make him pay.

On the night of the last book signing in Zelda's city, she was finally able to "clear her schedule" and arrange to come and show her support. She suggested that they have dinner first and then she would drive him to the bookstore for the event. At dinner, she ordered them drink after drink and at some point, became so incredibly "attracted" to him that she insisted that they go back to his hotel and have sex. They would have plenty of time before the signing, she assured him. Needless to say, they didn't. Joe managed to make it to the signing almost forty-five minutes late, only able to offer the feeble excuse to the store manager that he had been caught in traffic.

Soon after, Joe began calling less and had less time to help with Zelda's business. At one point, she suggested that he start seeing someone else because her life was just too chaotic to make any long-term plans. She had made such offers in the past, but Joe had always ignored them, explaining that he only wanted to be with her. This time, though, he agreed and made a date with a woman that he knew in his own town. He told Zelda that he was going to be unavailable that night and she wished him well. However, during the four hours that he was out on his date, she called his cell phone over and over again, leaving more frantic messages each time, claiming that she was unable to handle him being out with another woman. This time, thankfully, Joe wasn't fooled.

Over the next few weeks, things cooled down more and more between them. As Zelda realized that Joe was onto her game, she made several attempts to garner his sympathy and ask for his help, but he finally stopped working with her company altogether. What followed were her attempts at further revenge – bad-mouthing him to customers and bookstores, spreading rumors and lies about him and even going as far as to date one of his close friends. Joe tried to warn the friend about her, but in the end, the friend had to find out for himself – which is another case study on "psychic vampirism" in itself.

When all was said and done, Joe managed to get himself free from Zelda's clutches. He has absolutely no contact with her today, despite the several attempts that she made to try and patch things up. Joe is now happily married, working again and feels that he learned a valuable lesson on the ways of psychic vampires.

Thanks to Joe's nearly disastrous mistakes, several of his friends also learned from his mistakes and now writing about psychic vampires is something that I feel that I can do with some authority. Hopefully, what I have written here will be of assistance to you, the reader. Vampires don't always drink blood. Sometimes the "other kind" of vampire can be just as dangerous.

7. SEX AND POLTERGEISTS

Knocking and tapping sounds, doors opening and closing, objects flying around the house, glass shattering, furniture moving, lights turning on and off... Sounds like a haunted house, doesn't it? Psychical researchers believed this to be the case for almost a century and in fact, blamed all of the activity at a reportedly haunted location on the spirits at work. They even had a name for such destructive spirits. They called them "poltergeists" a German word that meant "noisy ghosts."

But was the damage being done in some of these haunted houses really caused by ghosts? Today, most investigators don't think so. While spirits may be the culprits in some cases, many such hauntings have a force behind they may be even more mysterious – and more controversial – than that of a disembodied presence.

The theory behind most poltergeist hauntings is that the activity is caused by a person in the household, known as the "human agent." The agent is usually an adolescent girl or boy and normally one who is troubled emotionally. It is believed that they unconsciously manipulate physical objects in the house by psychokinesis (PK), the power to move things by energy generated in the brain. This kinetic type of energy remains unexplained, but even some mainstream scientists are starting to explore the idea that it does exist.

It is unknown why this energy seems to appear in young people around the age of puberty, but documentation of its existence is starting to appear as more and more case studies have become public. In the vast majority of cases, the "agent" in the situation is female, but not in every case. What is very common, however, is that the person involved be in the midst of some sexual or emotional turmoil. There is no denying that puberty is a difficult, stressful and emotional time and somehow, the stress of it seems to react in some people in a very peculiar way. The presence of the energy is almost always an unconscious one and it is rare when any of the agents actually realize that they are the source of the destruction around them. They do not realize that they are the reason that objects in the home have become displaced and are usually of the impression that a ghost (or some sort of other supernatural entity) is present instead. The bursts of PK come and go and most poltergeist-like cases will peak early and then slowly fade away.

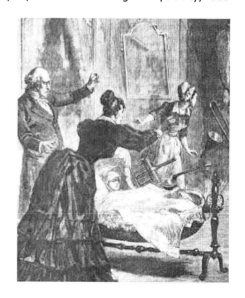

There have been scores of poltergeist cases over the years, some of them more dangerous than others. One of the most famous cases is one that I have researched for quite some time. It involved a disturbed young woman named Wanet McNeill. In 1948, she went to live with her father on a farm near Macomb, Illinois.

Despondent and depressed about her parents' recent divorce, and in the midst of puberty, she began to unconsciously cause fires to start on the farm. Over a period of a few weeks, literally hundreds of mysterious fires sprang up, causing thousands of dollars in damage and destroying two houses and several outbuildings. Startled witnesses saw fires suddenly appear on furniture, curtains and even on bare walls and ceilings. Investigations were launched by the Macomb Fire Department, the state fire marshal, the U.S. Air Force, Underwriters Laboratory and others, but the cause of the fires remained undetermined. Only the removal of Wanet from the farm, when she went to live with a relative, brought an end to the problem. Prior to that, the girl had been accused of starting the fires with kitchen matches, a feat that would have been impossible given the number of witnesses who were present at the farm. Only the work of researchers and reporters who were present, and a better understanding of paranormal events, has brought about a possible solution to the case in the person of Wanet McNeill. Those who accused her had the right suspect, but certainly the wrong method for starting the fires.

My own personal experiences with trying to research poltergeist cases have been varied and often frustrating. I have received many calls over the years from people who thought their houses were haunted. It's quite possible that many of those may have been, although even though I believed the witnesses were telling the truth about what they had seen or heard, I experienced nothing at the location for myself. Many of the cases sounded like poltergeist outbreaks, but this was hard to confirm and pretty frustrating, as well. My frustration with these cases is mostly because I almost always seemed to hear about them after the fact. Or, in a couple of cases, I arrived just as the outbreak was coming to an end.

In 1999, I was contacted about an apartment that was shared by four female students at a small Illinois university. They explained to me that weird events had been occurring for several months but by the time I arrived, they had become less frequent. After interviewing the young women, we deduced that the height of the outbreak had occurred during the most stressful time of the year, semester exams, and had actually started at the same time that one of them was going through a bad breakup with a boyfriend. By the time we were finished talking, even the young women were theorizing that it had been their own stress that was responsible for the activity. This did not make the phenomena any less unnerving, though, as they told of breaking glasses, slamming doors and cabinets and shower items that were constantly flying around the bathroom.

I have looked into other such cases over the years but out of all of them, I was only present during one case where the activity was actually taking place when I was there.

In 1997, I got involved in the case of a young woman whom I have since referred to as "Christine M." The house where she and her mother lived was the site of the first, and possibly most active, human agent poltergeist case that I have ever been involved with. In the case of "Christine M.," I believe that the outbreak was not only genuine, but I believe I really did experience phenomena that cannot be explained by natural means.

Christine originally contacted me because she believed her house was haunted. She told me of a wide variety of weird phenomena that was taking place like knocking sounds, lights turning on and off, doors slamming, cabinets opening and closing, windows breaking and other destructive happenings. Because she was under eighteen at the time, I contacted her mother, who assured me that the events described were actually taking place. She also agreed that an investigation might be in order.

During this initial interview, I asked her about the history of the location and if she had any thoughts on why the phenomenon was occurring. I also asked how long it had been going on. Her answer surprised me. She explained the phenomena had started just two years before, when Christine had gotten pregnant at the age of fifteen. She was very upset at the time and became depressed and anxious enough that her mother had taken her to see a therapist. She stopped going to see the counselor, however, and the weird activity began a short time later. While Christine believed that the house was haunted, her mother believed that her daughter was somehow causing these things to happen.

With the homeowner's permission, I began a series of five in-depth investigations of the house. My interviews with Christine and her family collected numerous accounts of the activity that was taking place. The event had begun one night when Christine was lying on the living room floor watching television. The living room was the largest room on the first floor and when I visited the house, it contained a couch, some chairs, a table and a large piano. There were three doors leading into the room, which led to a spare room, a screened porch and to the kitchen. As Christine and her mother were watching television, the piano began to loudly play by itself. Not long after that, things began to escalate. Soon, doors began to open and close by themselves, windows broke inside empty rooms and the sounds of knocking and footsteps began to be heard, usually on the empty upper floor of the house. Lights and radios turned on and off, and the volume of the television would often raise and lower without assistance. The footsteps and noises from upstairs became so bad that Christine insisted that her mother put a padlock on the door leading upstairs. She remained convinced, even after my initial visit and after her mother's insistence otherwise, that ghosts were haunting the house.

The other events in the house did not convince her of anything other than ghosts. The strangest event that reportedly occurred (and I did not witness this for myself) was when Christine's sister ended up with a horrible bite mark on the back of her upper arm. There were no pets in the house and no way that the girl could have managed to bite herself in that area of her body. I don't think that it was any coincidence that the bite mark appeared just shortly after Christine and her sister had a verbal (but non-physical) argument.

As you can imagine, I was having some reservations about the house being infested by spirits at this point, especially since her mother again told me that she was convinced that the activity centered around Christine. However, the young woman insisted that the house was infested with ghosts and would only agree to the investigations that I had planned if we would proceed as if the house were actually haunted. I reluctantly agreed and the five investigations began. Most of the time, things were fairly quiet, including the two uneventful investigations that were conducted with Christine removed from the house. Not a single trace of any sort of activity was detected when she was not present. However, on two occasions, I was present when violent phenomena occurred.

One evening, Christine, her mother and four investigators (myself included) clearly heard what seemed to be someone banging loudly on the walls of the second floor of the house. There was no one up there at the time but the sounds really seemed to be made by a person upstairs who was walking down the hallway and hitting the walls with his fists. Christine's mother told me that these were exactly the sorts of sounds that they had become used to over the past months. Unsure of what else to do, I ran up the stairs to see if anyone else was there. The downstairs door, as mentioned, had been padlocked, so Mrs. M. had to open it for me and I hurried up the staircase with another one of the investigators in tow. The pounding noises had stopped by the time we reached the upper floor, but if anyone had been there, we would have found them. Instead, we discovered the hallway and the rooms to be dark, quiet and empty.

During another investigation, on a separate night, I saw two cabinet doors actually slam shut under their own power. The incident occurred while I was in the living room with Christine, her mother and one other investigator. As we were sitting and talking, we began to hear a repeated rapping sound coming from the kitchen. It began to increase in volume until it started to sound like someone rapidly hammering on a wooden surface. The first sound was joined by a second and then a third. Each of the sounds were identical and my first thought was that it sounded just like someone slamming a cabinet door closed. Just as I had done when we heard mysterious sounds upstairs, I ran for the kitchen as quickly as possible. Hurrying from the carpeted floor and onto the linoleum floor of the kitchen, I slipped just as I was running in. I stumbled but was able to look up quickly enough to see two of the cabinet doors waving back and forth and cracking against the wooden frame. The movement ceased almost immediately, but I knew what I had seen.

Over the next several weeks, the activity in the house continued but it did begin to decrease after two months. Thanks to the relentless and in-depth interviews that I conducted with Christine and the fact that we made the two completely uneventful investigations with the girl removed from the house, I felt that we could determine that the cause of the haunting was indeed Christine. Eventually, her mother and I were able to get her to agree with these findings and she returned to the therapist. Not surprisingly, the phenomena ceased completely soon after and to this date, nothing else has occurred at her home. She is now happily married and no longer bothered by any strange activity.

Poltergeist cases can be pretty frightening and disturbing and there is no question that the families involved experience a complete disruption of their ordinary lives as the outbreaks are occurring. Thanks to the theory that the energy in the house is literally created by the expulsion of stress from the physical body of an adolescent, it's no surprise that poltergeists have been closely tied with sex over the years. There is no time of life that is more sexually stressful than puberty and for this reason, even some of the most famous poltergeist cases in history contain a sexual element that cannot be denied.

THE BELL WITCH: SEX OR SPIRITS?

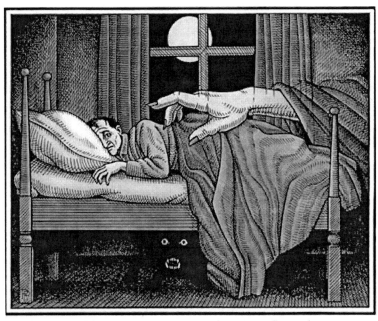

The Bell Witch -- illustration by Robert M. Place for the
Encyclopedia of Ghosts & Spirits
(Courtesy of Rosemary Ellen Guiley)

One of the most famous ghost stories in America history is that of the infamous Bell Witch of Tennessee, a case that came about during that shadowy time when Americans had stopped believing in witchcraft and had not yet discovered Spiritualism. This may be, despite the amount of documentation that later appeared, one of the reasons that this case remains so mysterious. It may also be because it is one of the only accounts of ghosts in human history in which a spirit actually took credit for killing one of the principles in the case!

But was it truly a poltergeist case? Were the events that occurred really created by a human agent who lived in the household? The jury is still out on this – and will likely always be out – and while I have always believed that there was an actual spirit behind the haunting, (see my book *Season of the Witch* for the full story) many renowned experts do not agree with me. Regardless of that, the story of the Bell Witch remains one of the strangest tales ever recounted.

The Bell Witch haunting began in 1817 in Robertson County, Tennessee. The events occurred on the farm of John Bell, a prosperous man who lived with his wife, Lucy, and his numerous children. One of those children was a daughter, Elizabeth, who was commonly called Betsy. The mysterious "family troubles" of the Bells seemed to revolve directly around this young woman.

As the years passed, John Bell became a well-liked and much respected man of the community. His neighbors and friends admired him and the men of the area often sought out his opinions. In addition, nothing but kind words were ever expressed about Lucy Bell, who was loved by everyone. Her home was always open to travelers and the house was a frequent location for social gatherings.

One of those who attended nearly every event at the Bell home was Richard Powell, a handsome schoolteacher who was also well liked in the community. He was the master of the local school and had tutored several of the Bell children, including Betsy. She was now starting to grow into womanhood and it was no secret that Powell was enamored of the girl. However, as she was still too young for courtship, Powell would often invent excuses to visit the Bell farm in order to see her.

Powell was not alone in his admiration for Betsy. A local young man named Joshua Gardner, who was much closer to Betsy's age, was also in love with her. It was well known that Betsy returned his affections, although it was an affair that would end tragically in the years to come.

The strange events in the Bell house started with a series of knockings that began to sound on the front door of the house. When a family member would go to let the caller in, no one would be there. The knockings and rappings were soon followed by hideous scratching sounds. It sounded as though the wood was being peeled from the outside walls, although no cause could be discovered for the noises.

Before long, the frightening sounds moved inside. They began as gnawing, scratching and scraping sounds that seemed to emanate from the bedroom belonging to the Bell sons. They would jump out of bed and light a candle, trying to find the source of the noise, but it would then stop. As soon as the candle was put out, they would start again. Soon, the sound of the rat-like scratching was joined by what sounded like a large dog, pawing at the wooden floor. Other noises were described as sounding like two large animals dragging chains through the house.

The crashing and scratching sounds were frightening, but not as terrifying as the noises that followed. It was not uncommon for the Bells to be awakened in the darkness by a noise like the smacking of lips, gulping sounds and eerie gurgling and choking -- sounds seemingly made by a human throat, although no living person was present. The nerves of the Bell family were beginning to unravel, as the sounds became a nightly occurrence.

The inhuman sounds were followed by the unseen hands that began to plague the household and they troubled Betsy more than anyone else. Items were broken around the house and blankets were yanked from the beds. Hair was pulled and the children were slapped and poked, causing them to cry in pain. Betsy was once slapped so hard that her cheeks remained bright red for hours.

Whatever the cause of this unseen force, the violence of it seemed to be especially directed at Betsy Bell. She would often run screaming from her room in terror as the unseen hands prodded, pinched and poked her. Strangely, it would be noticed later that the force became even crueler to Betsy after she entertained her young suitor, Joshua Gardner, at the house. For some reason, the spirit seemed to want to punish her whenever Joshua would call.

By this time, John Bell was out of ideas and explanations for the mysterious occurrences. To make matters worse, he had also begun to develop a nervous condition that affected his tongue and jaw muscles. This affliction caused him great difficulty when trying to eat and chew. When his doctor's cures failed to help him, he started to believe that the illness was caused by the force that had invaded his home. Desperately seeking answers, he realized that he needed to appeal to someone outside the household for assistance. At this point, Bell decided to enlist help from his friend and neighbor, James Johnson.

At Bell's request, Johnson and his wife came to spend the night at the Bell farm, determined to conduct an investigation that would lead them to the bottom of the events. That night, as everyone prepared to go to bed, Johnson, who was a devout Christian, read a chapter from the Bible and prayed fervently for the family to be delivered from the frightful disturbances, or at least for their origins to be revealed.

Almost as soon as the candles were extinguished, the strange sounds began, although this time they were even more violent, as though to show Johnson just what the force was capable of. The gnawing, knocking and scratching sounds began immediately and the disturbances continued to escalate as chairs overturned, blankets flew from the beds, and objects flew from one side of the room to the other.

James Johnson listened attentively to all of the sounds and closely observed the other incidents that were taking place. He realized, from the sounds of teeth grinding and the smacking of lips that an intelligent force seemed to be at work. He was determined to try and communicate with it and finally called out. "In the name of the Lord, what or who are you? What do you want and why are you here?"

As though shocked, the disturbances suddenly halted and the house remained quiet for some time. Unfortunately, it didn't last and the violence began again with the ripping of the covers from one of the beds. The disturbances moved from room to room, settling in for an attack against Betsy Bell. The young girl was slapped and pummeled mercilessly.

When the events of the evening finally came to a halt, Bell's wife and children, along with Johnson's wife, retired to bed, hoping to find at least some restless sleep. John Bell and James Johnson sat up late into the early morning hours, huddled around a candle in the front room. They whispered back and forth as Johnson tried to make some sense of what he had witnessed that night. He had arrived at the conclusion that the phenomenon was definitely "beyond his comprehension." He did believe, however, that it possessed an uncanny intelligence, based on the fact that it had ceased action when spoken to. By this, Johnson deduced that it could understand language.

He advised Bell to invite his other friends into the investigation and Bell took his advice. They formed a committee to investigate whatever was going on in the house. John Bell had chosen these men with care and had apparently chosen well, as each one of them stayed at his side until the very end.

Regardless of the diligence of the committee, the household was soon in chaos. Word began to spread of the strange events and friends, and even strangers, came to the farm to see what was happening. Dozens of people heard the clear banging and rapping sounds, inexplicable lights were reported in the yard and chunks of rock and wood were thrown at the curious guests. From all over Kentucky and Tennessee came exorcists and witch-finders, all of them claiming they could expel the evil force from the Bell house. Their efforts were all in vain as the disturbances soon had them fleeing from the premises.

The committee formed by Bell, Johnson and their friends continued to search for answers. They set up experiments, trying to communicate with the force, and they kept a close eye on all of the events that took place. They set up watches that lasted throughout the night, but it did no good and, if anything, the attacks increased in violence. Betsy was treated brutally and she began to have fainting spells and sensations of the breath being sucked out of her body. She was scratched and her flesh would bleed as though she was being pierced with invisible pins and needles.

Meanwhile, James Johnson continued with his investigations and theories of the force being controlled by an intelligent being of some sort. He, along with other members of the committee began speaking to the "witch" (as they had begun calling the force), asking it to speak and tell them what it wanted. Questions were asked which required either "yes" or "no" answers, or which could be answered with numbers, and the replies would come in knocks or raps, as if an invisible fist were tapping on the wall. This went on for some time but the committee members continued to harass the witch with questions, daring the presence to speak. First it whispered, as if it could not catch its breath, then faint words began to be formed but they could not be understood, at least at first.

But the voice of the witch began to be clearly heard and soon, the disembodied voice was coming from right out of thin air. When the questioners demanded to know who the witch was, the voice stated that it was a spirit whose rest had been disturbed, an ancient ghost, a murdered traveler, and much more. It lied, laughed and made eerie predictions of future events.

Excitement in the community grew as word spread of the witch's increasing number of communications. People came from around the area and from the far-flung regions to hear the unexplained voice. The stories attracted the believers in the unknown who credited the spirit as being the ghost of an Indian; an evil spirit; and even the result of genuine witchcraft.

The accounts also brought the skeptics, who came to the Bell farm intent on exposing the haunting as a hoax. Most of them ended up leaving in a state of puzzlement, while others expressed their opinions about the witch. Some charged that the voice was a sort of trickery being worked by the Bell family in order to draw crowds to the farm and make money off of them. However, this was not the case. The crowds who came to the farm paid no admission and the Bells allowed them to stay as long as they wished. Most were fed, along with their horses, and many stayed the night in a warm bed. No one ever left the farm hungry and while many offered to pay for their meals, Bell refused to accept their money. Even his friends tried to convince him to accept the donations, insisting that he could not afford to keep entertaining the large crowds. But Bell refused to take the money. He never considered the witch a wonder or an object of delight. He thought of the creature as "an affliction" and her presence in the house as "a calamity" of a most dire nature. His sense of honor did not allow him to accept money so that visitors could witness something so terrible.

The violent events continued in the house. Objects still moved about at will and most disturbing, of course, were the continued attacks on Betsy Bell and the physical ailments that plagued John Bell.

Strangely, the witch would sometimes regard Betsy with tenderness, only to attack her with terrible force later that same day. The attacks were especially severe after a visit by young Joshua Gardner. These incidents would leave her utterly exhausted and lifeless and she would black out for up to forty minutes at time.

The attacks on Betsy were serious, but were nothing compared to the problems suffered by John Bell. During the first year of the haunting, Bell began to complain of a curious numbness in his mouth that caused his tongue to become stiff and to swell. In fact, his tongue and throat became so swollen that he would be unable to eat for days at a time. He even had difficulty swallowing and drinking water, which added to his discomfort. As the haunting progressed, he began to come down with other unexplainable symptoms, as well. Most notable were the bizarre tics and twitches that would seize his face and make it impossible for him to eat or talk. These odd seizures would last anywhere from a few hours to as long as a week. However, once they passed, he would be in good health until the next attack came along. The spells gradually increased, both in length and in severity, and undoubtedly carried the man to his grave. The opposite was the case for Betsy Bell. It seemed that as her father's troubles increased, her afflictions began to go away.

But why was John Bell targeted?

This remains a mystery, but from the very beginning of the haunting, the witch had made it clear that she was going to get "Old Jack Bell" and would torment him until the end of his life. In addition to his illness, Bell was also physically abused by the witch and many witnesses would recall him being slapped by unseen hands or crying out in pain as he was prodded and stabbed with invisible pins. Whenever Bell's name was mentioned in the presence of the spirit, she would begin screaming and would call Bell every vile and offensive name she could muster up. It was obvious that she violently hated him and his torment would only end with his death. Bell's doctor was helpless when it came to finding a cure for the seizures and ailments. The witch laughed at his efforts and declared that she was the cause of John Bell's problems and no medicine existed which could cure him. The witch seemed determined to get John Bell any way that she could, but refused to say why she hated him. At one time, she claimed that she had been a sort of "curse" that had been sent to plague Bell by a woman named Kate Batts, a local eccentric with whom Bell had bad business dealings over some slaves. Batts may have hated Bell but there is no evidence to say that she ever tried to harm him by sending the witch to bedevil him. In fact, when she heard that she was being slandered in such a manner, she demanded that charges be pressed against John Bell, as she was sure that this was his way of trying to discredit her in the community.

After nearly four years of the haunting, John Bell continued to suffer from severe afflictions of the body. By late 1820, his physical condition had grown even worse. The jerking and twitching of his face still continued, as did the swelling of his tongue and the seizures that left him nearly paralyzed for hours and days at a time. The spells became even more violent and toward the end of his days, one of his sons, Richard Williams Bell, accompanied him everywhere he went. The family feared that a seizure would come upon him while working and if no one was with him, he might fall and be injured.

Around the middle of October, Bell once again became ill. This time, the spell lasted for eight days and he was confined to his bed the entire time. During his convalescence, the spirit stayed by his side. She raved and cursed in the sick room like a maniac, bothering him so that he could not rest and wishing loudly that he would simply die and leave the world a better place. But once again, John Bell managed to prevail and he came out of the sickness – but not for long. A week later, he was physically attacked by the witch and his paralysis returned. This time when we took to his bed, he never left it again. Bell slipped into a deep, pain-wracked sleep, only occasionally broken by convulsions caused by his seizures and by brief moments of clarity when he was able to eat and speak with his family. The spirit remained nearby the entire time, laughing and cursing at the dying man.

On December 20, 1820, John Bell breathed his last.

On the morning of the 19th, Bell failed to rise as he had every other morning. Even as sick as he was, he never failed to stir and take some sort of sustenance, even if it was only water and bread. On this morning, however, he did not awaken. Lucy went to check on him and it appeared that he was sleeping very soundly. She decided to let him rest for a bit longer while she made him some breakfast. She returned an hour later and gently touched her husband on the shoulder, but he did not wake up. Bell had lapsed into a coma.

Lucy called for the family and her oldest son, John, Jr., ran into the bedroom. He went to the cabinet where Bell's medicine was kept. His father had gone through similar periods before and usually a dose of his medicine would revive him. When John opened the cabinet, he discovered that all of the medicines that had been prescribed to his father had vanished. In their place was a small, "smoky-looking vial" that was about one-third full of a dark- colored liquid. He asked at once if anyone in the house had moved the medicine but all denying touching it, or even knowing what medicine had been there. No one had any idea what may have been in the vial. Bell's doctor was sent for, but neither he nor any of the Bells' friends could identify the vial.

The group gathered around the sickbed and continued to try and raise Bell from his stupor. Just then, the spirit's voice split the air of the room and she told them that Bell would not be awakened. She admitted that she had placed the dark vial in his medicine cupboard and had given him a large dose of it while he was sleeping. This was all the information that she would give in regard to the liquid and no one had any idea where it may have come from, or how John Bell had managed to ingest it. Even if she had not brought it into the house, it was possible that Bell, awake in the middle of the night and looking for his medicine, may have swallowed it by mistake. Even so, where the bottle had come from was still unexplained.

It was then suggested that the mysterious liquid be tested on something. One of the men disappeared outside and quickly returned with one of the barn cats that could be found on the property. John Jr. dipped a straw into the vial and then drew it through the cat's mouth, wiping the dark liquid on its tongue. The cat jumped out of his arms as if it had been prodded with a hot poker. It whirled about a few times and then fell to the floor with its legs kicking in the air. The animal was dead in less than a minute. Whatever was in the bottle appeared to be deadly.

Bell lay all day and through the night in a coma and could not be roused to swallow any medicine that might counteract the effects of the drug. The doctor was sure that he had taken, or had been given, the contents of the bottle, as Bell's breath smelled the same as the liquid in the vial. In the throes of despair, the vial and its contents were cast into the fire. A blue blaze shot up into the chimney "like a flash of powder."

John Bell never regained consciousness and early on the morning of December 20, he took one last shuddering breath and died.

His final moments were met by great joy from the witch. She laughed heartily and expressed the hope that Bell would burn in hell. With those chilling words, she departed and was not heard from again until after the funeral.

The burial was held a few days later and it has been said that the funeral was the largest ever held in Robertson County, before or since. Bell was laid to rest in a small cemetery, a short distance from the Bell house. After the grave was filled, the mourners began to walk away. As they left the scene, the voice of Kate returned, echoing loudly in the cold morning air. She was singing at the top of her spectral lungs, celebrating the death of John Bell as the last of the family and their friends entered the house.

This ended the most terrifying chapter of the haunting and marked the case of the Bell Witch in the annals of supernatural history forever. It became one of the only cases ever recorded in which a spirit was responsible for the death of one of the principles in the case.

After the death of John Bell, the witch largely seemed to lose interest in everyone in the family, except for

Betsy Bell. During the entire haunting, it was made clear that Betsy would be punished as long as she continued to allow herself to be courted by Joshua Gardner. After the death of John Bell, however, Betsy and Gardner began to believe that perhaps the witch might allow them to be together in peace.

As it had been with John Bell himself, the witch had never made it clear just why she disliked Joshua Gardner so much. She simply hated him and never explained why. Kate spent a great amount of time pleading with Betsy to end her relationship with him and also made it clear that she would beat the girl until she did so -- as if she were punishing the girl for her own good.

Once the violence of the haunting had subsided somewhat, Betsy and Joshua began to renew their relationship, which had previously cooled thanks to the witch. On Easter Sunday of 1821, the two of them celebrated the holiday by becoming engaged, much to the delight of their families and friends. The following day, the young couple, along with a group of friends, decided to go fishing and to have a picnic along the Red River.

The couples had settled down along the riverbank when Richard Powell appeared. Powell was in the midst of campaigning to represent Robertson County in the Tennessee legislature and had heard about the picnic. As all of those attending were former students of his, he had an excuse to join them. Obviously, Powell had joined them because he had heard of Betsy's engagement to Joshua Gardner. He was still in love with the young woman and only felt that their age difference was keeping them apart. He asked her if he could speak to her alone for a moment and then confessed his attraction to her. Betsy's only reply to this was that she promised him an invitation to the wedding. A short time later, the teacher left.

After lunch, the couples all decided to do a little fishing and Joshua and Betsy sat down on a large rock and cast a line into the water. A few minutes later, the line was seized and the line and pole were jerked into the river. At that same moment, the familiar voice of the witch rang out and pleaded with Betsy not to marry Joshua Gardner. The plea was repeated two more times and then the voice faded away.

This must have been the breaking point for Betsy. She must have finally realized that the witch was never going to leave her alone as long as she continued to stay with Gardner. She had seen what the creature had done to her father and she simply cared about Joshua too much to see the same thing happen to him. Kate had already shown what she was capable of and to marry Gardner would mean risking his life as well. That ended the engagement of Elizabeth Bell and Joshua Gardner. The two of them parted that afternoon and as far as history states, they never saw one another again.

After arranging his affairs, Joshua Gardner departed from Robertson County and went to live in western Tennessee at a place called Gardner's Station. He lived a long and successful life, married twice and died in 1887 at the age of eighty-four. Whether or not he ever thought of Betsy Bell again is unknown.

Shortly after Gardner's departure from the region, Richard Powell came calling at Betsy's door. The young girl was depressed for some time, but eventually succumbed to Powell's attentions and agreed to marry him. The former teacher was much older than Betsy, but no one frowned on the marriage, including the spirit, who showed her approval by keeping silent. The couple eventually married in 1824.

Powell later made it into public office, serving as a sheriff and as a member of the Tennessee legislature. In 1837, he suffered a massive stroke and his care left the family nearly destitute. He died in 1848 and Betsy remained a widow for the rest of her years.

As time passed, the mystery of the Bell Witch would continue to be discussed and rumors claimed that Betsy may have somehow been responsible for the strange occurrences on the farm. As one generation passed into the next and eyewitnesses passed away (who could have refuted such claims), the case achieved the status of legend. In 1849, the Saturday Evening Post published a lengthy sketch about the case that was written by a reporter who slanted to story to make it appear that Betsy had been the culprit behind the haunting. Betsy sued the paper and the story was retracted.

In 1875, Betsy moved to Panola County, Mississippi, where one of her children and other relatives lived. She died there in 1890 at the age of eighty-six. She never heard from the Bell Witch again.

The Bell Witch remained active in the region until 1821. She had little interaction with the family after Bell's death, aside from brief appearances. The spirit apparently refused to help John Bell, Jr. communicate with his deceased father, declaring that the dead could not be brought back. However, on one occasion, she told John to go to the window and look out onto a snowy field. As he did, he saw footprints appear in the snow, which the spirit claimed were identical to those made by his father's boots. John did not bother to test this claim.

One evening while the family was sitting at supper, there was a tremendous noise in the chimney, as if a cannon ball had rolled down it and out into the room. It burst into a ball of smoke. The witch's voice rang out and told the Bells that she was leaving – but would come back in seven years. With that, the haunting came to an end.

In 1828, only Lucy Bell and two of her sons remained in the homestead, although John Jr. lived nearby and would receive the majority of the witch's new manifestations. Things started again as they originally had, with scratching, items moved around and covers pulled from the bed. However, since Betsy had long since moved away and John Bell was dead, the witch seemed to have no one to torment. Lucy and her sons ignored the new happenings and within two weeks, the manifestations stopped. John Jr. claimed that the witch visited him several times in his home, allegedly making prophecies of future events, from the Civil War to the end of the world. She also promised to return in one hundred and seven years and plague one of his descendants; but 1935 came and went without any appearance of the Bell Witch.

Over the years, there have been many theories as to who, or what, the Bell Witch actually was. The theories have ranged from an elaborate hoax to practical jokes and a haunting by an actual spirit. Beginning in the 1930s, many renowned writers and psychologists theorized that the Bell Witch was not the ghost that so many believed it to be but that the haunting experienced at the Bell farm was merely caused by the unconscious effects of Betsy Bell's mind. They believed that all of the activity was caused by Betsy, who was definitely the right age for poltergeist manifestations of power. They also surmised that her religious and moral upbringing could have caused her suppressed sexual energies to act out in a manner that would allay her guilty feelings, especially where Joshua Gardner was concerned. The "spirit" punished Betsy for her impure thoughts about Gardner, even going as far as to cause their relationship to end for "supernatural" reasons.

The idea of this is certainly plausible. The connections between sexual impulses and repressed energy have long been discussed and frankly are quite believable in some cases. But it is a credible idea in the Bell Witch haunting? It doesn't seem likely. Even if we ignore the fact that so much of the activity occurred while Betsy Bell was not even present, we are still left with only her age bracket as the only solid evidence that her mind was at work.

Of course, that has not stopped people from speculating, including some of the most acclaimed authorities on paranormal phenomena and the human mind. Dr. Nandor Fodor, the esteemed expert on poltergeists and human agents, formulated a theory in the 1930s that also suggested that Betsy Bell was responsible for the haunting. Fodor was not only a researcher of the supernatural but also a Freudian psychiatrist, who took the view that the haunting was definitely sexual in nature.

His theory was that Betsy had developed a secondary personality, but this second personality was a mental force, which was gifted with both ESP and the ability to move solid objects by thought. The personality could exert physical force, but was not physical in nature. He believed that a deep-seated hatred, even an unconscious one, could create such a personality and that it could be mistaken for an avenging ghost.

Fodor believed that the secondary personality (which he called "Betsy-X") was created after the girl began to be sexually molested by her father, John Bell. The personality then took over her physical form in an effort to exact the revenge that Betsy wanted. Fodor pointed out correctly that Betsy's fainting spells closely mirrored the symptoms exhibited by Spiritualist mediums when they went into trances. He believed that Betsy, like naturally gifted mediums, was able to channel her budding sexual energies into a mysterious force that wreaked havoc in the household.

John Bell's illness started at the time of the first disturbances. He suffered at first from a mere facial tic, which grew to the proportions, Fodor stated, of a hysterical attack. The seizures served two purposes: they stopped him from eating and from talking. But the latter was the most important. Eating seldom gets anyone into trouble, but speaking does – especially if they have a guilty secret. If such a secret needed to be kept silent, a seizure of the type suffered by John Bell would serve the purpose. Fodor did not believe that it was a coincidence that Bell's attacks occurred at the same time as Betsy's spells.

Fodor also suggested that Bell's attacks were not due to the "spirit", but represented a brutal self-aggression, evidence of which he found in some of the interviews that were given to author M.V. Ingram when he wrote a book on the case in 1894. During an interview with Ingram, Mrs. Martha Dearden recalled that Bell behaved strangely on an occasion when her father invited him to dinner. He shook his head without saying anything, and seemed to be depressed, confused and unhappy. The following day, he rode over to the house and apologized for his behavior, saying that he felt his tongue swell up in his mouth so that he was unable to eat or talk. At the time of this incident, the haunting had not yet begun. Fodor inferred that Bell's unconscious was already stirring when the poltergeist made its first appearance.

The incestuous union had disastrous results. John Bell suffered the torments of his own conscience, creating the physical ailments that plagued, and eventually killed him. Betsy, tortured by shock, betrayal and guilt, created the secondary personality, which became the witch. Unfortunately, Fodor's speculations about the case sounded far more convincing in the 1930s than they do today, when Freud is no longer regarded as being infallible. Thanks to this, among other things, Fodor's theory hardly holds up to examination.

First, it should be noted that absolutely no evidence exists which says that incest between John Bell and his daughter ever occurred. In devising his theory, Fodor was drawing on his own years of clinical experience and simply took numerous pieces of evidence and placed them into a pattern that he had seen many times before. He believed that Betsy's hatred expressed itself as a psychokinetic energy, but this could not explain all of the events in the case. The presence not only moved objects about, but she talked as well. It also had a definite character and personality and one that sharply differed from Betsy's. It also failed to explain why Betsy was treated so badly in the beginning of the hauntings, how incidents managed to occur when she was not present in the house, and how the witch managed to return after Betsy had married and left home.

There is no denying that a "sexual poltergeist" is certainly an intriguing idea, but whether or not it fits in the case of the Bell Witch is open to conjecture and opinion, even after all of these years.

THE COCK LANE GHOST

The strange tale of the so-called "Cock Lane Ghost" remains one of the most mysterious in the annals of the supernatural. This bewildering account from London in the 1750s is one that is filled with mystery, sex, murder, poison, fraud and death – and is made all the more strange by the fact that the "ghost" in question was not actually a ghost at all!

The most notorious poltergeist case of the eighteenth century began with knocking noises in the home of Richard Parsons, the clerk of St. Sepulchre's Church in Smithfield, London, in November 1759. One night, a woman named Fanny Lynes, who was lodging in the house, asked ten-year-old Elizabeth Parsons, Richard Parson's eldest daughter, to sleep with her while her common-law husband was away on business. All went well for a few nights, but then the two of them began to be kept awake by scratching and rapping noises that were coming from inside the walls. When they told Parsons about it, he dismissed the sounds as coming from the cobbler who lived next door.

A short time later, Fanny became sick with smallpox. She was six months pregnant at the time and her husband, William Kent, was understandably upset. He and Fanny were unmarried only because she was his dead wife's sister. Kent had married Elizabeth Lynes two years earlier, but she had died in childbirth. Now it looked as though her sister, with whom Kent had also fallen in love, was following her to the grave. He moved Fanny out of the Parsons' house and into a nearby cottage where, on February 2, 1760, she died from smallpox.

Meanwhile, the knockings in the Parsons' house were continuing. Parsons finally called in a carpenter to come in and take down the wooden panels on the walls to see if rats were living behind them, but nothing was found. After that, the knocking just got louder and the story that the house was "haunted" began to spread through the neighborhood. The strange sounds seemed to be connected to Elizabeth Parson. They came from behind her bed and it was said that when they were about to begin, she would begin to tremble and shake. Later that same year,

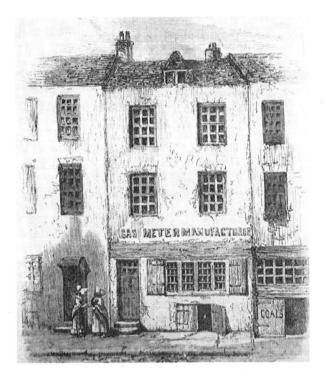

(Left) An illustration of Cock Lane in the
middle 1700s. The small street attracted
hundreds of visitors on a daily basis.

(Above) Cock Lane today

Elizabeth began to suffer from convulsions.

Parsons was perplexed about the weird sounds and decided to call a friend, The Reverend John Moore, to his home to investigate. Moore was the assistant pastor at St. Sepulchre's Church, where Parsons worked, and was a devout, Christian man. He proceeded to try and communicate with the "spirit," asking it to answer in a manner where one rap meant yes, two meant no. Moore soon added a scratching noise that would indicate if the presence was displeased.

By using this method, the spirit told a strange and upsetting story. The ghost claimed that it was the spirit of Fanny Lynes, returned from the dead to denounce her husband William Kent for killing her with poison. He had, it said, administered red arsenic into her "purl" (a mixture of herbs and beer) and this was what had killed her, not smallpox.

Richard Parsons was not entirely displeased to hear this story, for he bore a strong grudge against his former tenant. William Kent was a fairly wealthy man, having been a successful innkeeper in Norfolk, and he had loaned Parsons a good sum of money with the understanding that it would be repaid on a monthly basis. Parsons, who was apparently a heavy drinker, had failed to repay any of the debt, possibly because he discovered that Kent and Fanny were not married, and hoped to blackmail Kent into forgetting about the loan. Kent had placed the matter into the hands of his attorney.

If Parsons had not been so anxious to believe the worst about his former tenant, he might have suspected that the "ghost" was not telling the truth. To start with, the knocking in the house had begun when Fanny was still alive. In fact, she had been the first to report the strange sounds, along with Parsons' daughter, Elizabeth. However, Parsons quickly concocted an explanation for this: the spirit was actually that of Kent's first wife, Elizabeth, who was also trying to denounce him for murder!

Throughout 1761, the house in Cock Lane acquired a wide reputation for its ghost and the rumors of Kent's alleged murders were spread far and wide. Kent himself heard nothing about any of this until January 1762, when he saw an item in the *Public Ledger* newspaper about a man who had brought a young woman from Norfolk and poisoned her in London. A few days later, another item appeared about the "Cock Lane Ghost" and its revelations about Kent, which led him to The Reverend John Moore, the original investigator of the case. Moore, a respectable and well-liked man, could only suggest that Kent attend a séance in Elizabeth Parsons' bedroom and see what was happening for himself. Kent agreed and took along both the doctor and apothecary who had attended Fanny in her last illness.

The men crowded into the small bedroom, where Elizabeth and her younger sister lay side-by-side on the bed. At first, the spirit failed to manifest itself, but after the room was emptied, Moore succeeded in persuading it to come, and they all came back inside. Kent listened with something like panic as he heard Moore asking if the spirit was Kent's wife – one knock – and if anyone else was involved in the murder plot – two knocks. Kent was outraged and loudly declared that the spirit was lying as he stormed out of the house.

The ghost soon became famous all over London. Cock Lane was crowded with carriages and curiosity-seekers on a nightly basis. In February, a clergyman named Aldrich persuaded Parsons to allow his daughter to come to his home in Clerkenwell to be tested. An investigative committee, including the famous Dr. Samuel Johnson, was formed, but the ghost failed to manifest. It also refused to rap on the coffin of Fanny Lynes in the vault of the church when that was attempted. Johnson concluded that the "Ghost of Cock Lane" was a fraud and most of London agreed.

But was something paranormal going on, in spite of these opinions? On the day after the disastrous investigation, Elizabeth was staying in the home of a comb-maker in Cow Lane when the bell of Newgate Prison began to toll, which meant that someone was going to be hanged. The comb-maker asked the ghost whether or not a hanging was taking place and if the person to be executed was a man or a woman. The "ghost" answered both questions correctly. Later on that same day, a loose curtain began to spin on its rod – the only physical manifestation that ever occurred in the case.

The following day, while Elizabeth was sleeping, her father claimed to hear whispering noises. He carried a candle over to the bed, but the girl seemed to be asleep. The whispering continued, even though Elizabeth's lips were plainly closed. Two night later, the noises were so violent that the owner of the house where they were staying, trying to avoid the crowds in Cock Lane, asked them to leave. Elizabeth and her father went to the home of a family named Missiter, near Covent Garden, and the manifestations continued, even when a maid lay in bed next to Elizabeth and held onto her hands and feet.

By this time, William Kent was determined to prove his innocence through the law and the burden of proof lay on Parsons and his daughter. Elizabeth was told that unless the ghost made itself heard that night, her father and mother would be thrown into prison. Not surprisingly, the "spirit" made an appearance, but not under its own power. The servants peered through a crack in the door and saw Elizabeth take a piece of board and hide it in the bed. Later, when there were people in the room, the knocking noises sounded suspiciously like they were coming from the bed itself, not, as usual, from all around the room. The bed was searched and the board was found. The next day, the newspapers published the story of the fraud.

On February 25, 1762, a small booklet was published called *The Mystery Revealed: Containing a Series of Transactions and Authentic Testimonials respecting the supposed Cock Lane Ghost, which have been concealed from the Public* – the author was likely Johnson's friend Oliver Goldsmith. A satirical play called *The Drummer or the Haunted House* was presented at Covent Garden and William Kent began legal proceedings against Richard Parsons. In July, Mr. and Mrs. Parsons and a woman named Mary Frazer, who often acted as the "questioner" to the ghost, appeared before the magistrates at Guildhall. Parsons was charged with trying to ruin the life of William Kent by accusing him of murder. The judges heard evidence in his defense, but were unconvinced by the testimony of neighbors who heard raps all over the room, and who were certain that Elizabeth could not have made them. Parsons was eventually sentenced to two years in prison and to stand three times in the pillory, a wooden device that was like the stocks and which was used in punishment by public humiliation. Parsons' wife was sentenced to one year in prison, and Mary Frazer to six months. Moore and his associates were ordered to pay out a large sum in damages to Kent. There was sympathy for Parsons, and when he stood in the pillory, the mob took up a collection for him – an unusual gesture for a period when lawbreakers were often badly injured during this form of punishment.

For more than two centuries, the Cock Lane Ghost was considered a hoax. It was easy for researchers and students of the supernatural to believe that, because some amount of fraud was discovered in the case, the entire episode must have been fraudulent. However, researchers of poltergeist phenomena today will be the first to admit that during the waning stages of an authentic case, it is not uncommon for agents to resort to fraud in order to keep interest in the case alive. Most poltergeist outbreaks are short-lived events and the human agents, who are normally unhappy and starved for attention, don't want to let that attention go when the activity starts to fade. They will often resort to trickery to keep the attention focused on them or, in the case of Elizabeth Parsons, out of desperation. Her final flimsy attempts to fake the phenomenon were easily discovered. Wouldn't such attempts have also been discovered earlier if she had been faking it all along?

Unfortunately, too much time has passed for much explanation to be given about the nature of the Cock Lane Ghost – which was likely a young woman named Elizabeth Parsons. Elizabeth was slightly younger than most poltergeist agents, although the phenomenon continued as she grew older. There have been some suggestions made about her sexual maturity, as well as her unnatural closeness with her father, although there is no hard evidence of anything appropriate. We do know that her father was a drunkard and foolish with his money – the record is clear on that – which would indicate that the Parsons household was not a happy one. It's also conceivable that Elizabeth felt strong emotions toward William Kent, the upstanding tenant in the house, who had all of the good qualities that her father did not possess. If this were the case, sleeping in his bed while he was away might have aroused some unfamiliar emotions, especially if she was aware that he and Fanny were "living in sin." The convulsions that began about a year after the first disturbances suggest that she was passing through a period of emotional turmoil, but since so few records of Elizabeth exist all of these things must remain a matter for speculation.

One thing that seems fairly certain is that the "spirit" itself was neither Elizabeth Kent nor Fanny Lynes. The disturbances began while Fanny was still alive and besides that, there was no evidence at all to say that Kent murdered either one of his wives. He simply became a convenient scapegoat for Richard Parsons, a man who wanted to blame someone else for his own shortcomings.

THE STRATFORD POLTERGEIST

On a late winter morning in March 1850, strangeness came to the peaceful New England town of Stratford, Connecticut. It came quietly and without fanfare but its arrival would shake the community to its core and would create a mystery that remains unsolved more than a century and a half later.

The Reverend Eliakim Phelps came to Stratford in February 1848. He had been born in Belchertown, Massachusetts, to an old and respected New England family. He was a graduate of the Union and Andover seminaries and had been in charge of congregations in both Geneva and Huntington, New York. He had been widowed in his late fifties, but his children were all grown and had moved from home by then. He was well known in religious circles and was seen as somewhat unusual in his thinking, often expressing an interest in mysticism, mesmerism and later, in the growing Spiritualist movement in America. He devoted most of his time to reading and exploring his unique interests. Phelps was certainly not the average Presbyterian clergyman.

Phelps had decided to make some changes in his life at the age of fifty-nine. He married again to a much younger woman who had three children: Anna, sixteen, Henry, eleven, and another girl, who was six. The couple had another son together, who was three when Phelps decided to relocate his family from Philadelphia to the quiet town of Stratford. Despite what seemed to be a blissful life, most accounts state that the family was not entirely happy. Apparently, Mrs. Phelps did not care for Stratford and did not like her neighbors. She was constantly tired and upset and it was said that her daughter, Anna, suffered from a nervous disposition. As poltergeist outbreaks rarely occur in a home that is entirely happy, it's no surprise that the household was filled with stress.

The strange events began on Sunday, March 10, 1850. The entire Phelps family returned from church services that morning to find the door of their house standing wide open. Dr. Phelps was shocked by this because their maid was away, so he had been sure to secure the entire house, locking not only the exterior doors and windows, but the interior ones, as well. The only keys were in his pocket. But now, they discovered that all of the doors had been flung open, both inside and out.

Dr. Phelps cautiously entered the house, unsure of what he might find, but not expecting the chaos that awaited him. Someone had ransacked the place, knocking over furniture, smashing dishes, scattering books, papers and clothing. Yet strangely, they had not been robbed. Phelps found his gold watch, the family silver and his loose cash were in plain

The Phelps Mansion in the 1970s

sight, but had been left alone. He wondered if perhaps an unlocked window had provided the thieves means to escape when the family returned from church and caught them by surprise.

Phelps summoned his family and they went upstairs to inspect the bedrooms. They found no burglars hidden away, but instead, they discovered something even more unnerving. In one of the bedrooms, someone had spread a sheet over the bed and had placed one of Mrs. Phelps' nightgowns on top of it. Stockings had then been placed at the bottom of it to suggest feet and the arms of the gown had been folded over the chest. What sort of message had the thieves, or more likely vandals, been trying to send?

The family attempted to restore some order to the house before returning to the church for the afternoon services. When the clock struck noon, Mrs. Phelps and the children departed, but Dr. Phelps remained at the house, hoping to catch the burglars when they returned. He hid in his study, armed with a pistol, and waited in silence. A few hours passed and he heard no sounds but that of the house creaking in the wind. No doors opened or closed, no footsteps fell in the rooms or the corridors.

Eventually, he left his hiding place and wandered about the lower floor. He opened the door to the dining room and got a shocking discovery: the previously empty room was now filled with a crowd of women! They had entered the house without sound and now stood silent and still, standing and kneeling in positions of religious devotion. Several of them held bibles, others bowed so low that their foreheads nearly brushed the floor, and all of them seemed to be in a rough circle in the center of the room.

It was several moments before Dr. Phelps realized that the women in the room were incredibly lifelike effigies that had been fashioned from the family's clothing. The dresses had been filled with rags, muffs and other materials from around the house. The dummies had somehow been created and positioned during the time that Mrs. Phelps and the children had been away from the house -- and while Dr. Phelps had been so vigilantly standing guard. He had no idea how something like this had been accomplished, or what it could possibly mean.

Interestingly, this would not be the last time that the effigies would appear without explanation in the house. Over the months to come, these eleven "women" would be joined by nearly twenty more. They would appear without warning and with no clue as to how they were constructed so quickly or so secretly.

The events on March 10 were just the beginning. Activity became more frantic the following day as objects began to move about the house. An umbrella jumped into the air and traveled nearly twenty-five feet; forks, spoons, knives, books, pens and assorted small objects launched from places where no one had been standing; and pillows, sheets and blankets were pulled from beds and fluttered into the air. This continued all day long and finally, by evening, the activity seemed to have exhausted itself and the house fell silent.

But the next morning, it started all over again. Mrs. Phelps pleaded with her husband to call someone for help. So Phelps contacted The Reverend John Mitchell, a friend and a retired minister. Mitchell listened to the story and quickly suggested the most obvious solution: that the maid or the older children were playing tricks. He took the suspects away from the house and sequestered them nearby, but the activity continued. At first, he refused to give up on the idea that there was some logical explanation for the events that were occurring but once he saw some of the objects move for himself, he became convinced that the supernatural was at work.

On March 14, the strangeness took another turn. During the morning meal, a potato literally dropped from nowhere and landed on the breakfast table. This was the first such item, but not the last. Throughout the rest of the day, Dr. and Mrs. Phelps, along with Reverend Mitchell, witnessed forty-six objects appear and drop out of the air in the locked parlor. Most of the items were articles of clothing that had been somehow transported from the upstairs closets.

In the weeks to come, observers, friends and the curious witnessed objects appearing and flying through the air at the Phelps home. Most of these items would move at abnormally slow speeds and they would touch down on the floor as if carefully placed there. Phelps and others also claimed to see the objects change course while in flight.

There were many accusations of trickery toward the Phelps family but with each, Phelps invited the skeptics to see the house for themselves. He was hospitable to reporters, investigators, and even mere curiosity-seekers, and he permitted them to come to the house and to stay as long as they liked. Many of them witnessed the disturbances first hand.

Finally, after reading accounts of the haunting in newspapers, Phelps' son, Austin, journeyed to Stratford to get to the bottom of the matter. His uncle, Abner Phelps, a well-known Boston doctor and Massachusetts legislator, accompanied him. Austin himself was a professor at Andover Theological Seminary. Neither of the men was pleased with the family's growing notoriety and neither of them had approved of Dr. Phelps' marriage to his young wife. They were sure that they would discover a trickster among her children.

During their first night, they heard a loud pounding noise that they surmised was coming from the knocker on the front door. They took turns opening and guarding the door, but each time they expected to pounce on the prankster, they found the doorstep to be deserted. Finally, they stood on both sides of the door, Austin on the outside and his uncle inside. The loud knocking continued, but they could find no explanation for it. The men were also disturbed by rapping noises upstairs. On the second night, they determined the noise was coming from Anna's room, the daughter with the nervous condition. The hammering seemed to be coming from the inside panel of the door. They burst into the room, thinking to catch her in the act, but she was far from the door when they entered. Austin later wrote: "The young lady was in bed, covered up and out of reach of the door. We examined the panel and found dents where it had been struck." The two men would depart from the house believing that whatever phenomenon was being experienced there, it was genuine.

The outbreak continued, becoming both a physical and psychological attack on the entire family. The nighttime hours were filled with rapping, knockings, voices, screams and bizarre sounds, while the daylight hours saw objects sailing about through the rooms. Silverware bent and twisted, windows broke, papers scattered and tables and chairs danced across the floor as if they had come to life. And of course, the strange effigies continued to appear. It was reported in the *New Haven Journal*, "In a short space of time so many figures were constructed that it would not have been possible for a half a dozen women, working steadily for several hours, to have completed their design, and arrange the picturesque tableau. Yet these things happened in short space of time, with the whole house on the watch. In all, about thirty figures were constructed during this period." One of the knelling figures, wearing a dress that belonged to Mrs. Phelps, was so realistic that when the youngest child walked into a room with his sister and saw the effigy, he whispered to her, "Be still, Ma is saying prayers."

In addition to the destruction of the house, the eldest daughter, Anna, became a target of the poltergeist's wrath, as did her brother, Henry. A reporter from the *New York Sun* wrote that he visited the house at the end of April 1850 and was present in a room with Anna and Mrs. Phelps and was able to observe them at all times. At one point, he saw Anna's arm jerk and twitch and she announced that she had just been pinched. The reporter rolled back her sleeve and stated that her arm bore several savage-looking red marks. At other times, Anna was slapped by unseen hands. Those present sometimes only saw the girl shake or jerk her head, but reported hearing the sound of a slap. They often saw red marks and welts appear on her skin. Once, while she was asleep, a pillow was reportedly pressed over her head and then tied around her neck. According to the editor of the *Bridgeport Standard*, she nearly died.

Henry was also brutally tortured. He was beaten, pinched, struck and occasionally rendered unconscious. Once, in the presence of Dr. Phelps, he was hit with a flurry of small stones. A newspaper reporter claimed that he once saw the boy carried from this bed by an invisible force and dumped on the floor. In front of a number of witnesses, he was once lifted into the air so high that his hair brushed the ceiling of the room. One day, he vanished and would later be found outside, tied up and suspended from a tree. He had no idea how he had gotten there. The young boy was also burned, thrown into a cistern of water and his clothing torn apart in front of visiting clergymen. He was discovered missing one afternoon and he was later discovered shoved onto a closet shelf with a rope around his neck.

Numerous theories were put forth as to just what was going on in the Phelps house. Many believed that the house had been invaded by spirits that were determined to wreak havoc on the family. Some locals believed that the haunting was caused by the ghost of a Goody Bassett, who was hanged near the house for witchcraft in 1651. However, there was no evidence to support this piece of fanciful lore.

While the charges of the skeptics about trickery seemed to be mostly answered by more displays of incredible happenings, the most viable solution to the mystery was that a poltergeist was at work. The events could have been the unknowing manipulations of Anna (she of the "nervous condition") or even perhaps Mrs. Phelps, who was bitter and unhappy in her new home. All of the phenomena could be explained by this, even the bizarre human effigies that so frightened everyone and caused Dr. Phelps and others to believe the presence in the house was a demonic one. The Reverend John Mitchell, who spent the most time in the house as an investigator, managed to engage the "spirits" in conversation using an alphabet code of raps and replies. The foul and insulting replies to his questions had him agreeing that the force was an evil one.

And the communication continued beyond mere knocks and raps. On one occasion, Phelps was in his study alone, writing at his desk. He turned away for a moment and when he turned back he found that his sheet of paper, which had been blank, was now covered with strange-looking writing. The ink on the paper was still wet. In the days that followed, other family members and friends would experience the same thing and would find papers with writing on them. The letters sometimes appeared from thin air, floating down over the dinner table or appearing in a sealed box. None of the messages were very revealing and unfortunately, they were all disposed of as Phelps felt they were missives from an evil source.

Now, desperate for information that the spirits had been unwilling to provide, Phelps agreed reluctantly to perform a séance in the house. Communication was easily obtained and the spirit claimed to be a soul in hell, enduring torment for the sins he had committed in life. Phelps asked the spirit what he could do to help and using the knocking code, the ghost asked that Phelps bring him a piece of pumpkin pie. Thinking that he had been misunderstood, he asked again and this time the spirit asked for a glass of gin. Finally, Phelps asked why the spirit was causing such a disturbance in the house and the spirit replied, "For fun." He soon came to believe that such communications were worthless.

After months of madness in the house, the Phelps family decided to abandon the place and move back to Philadelphia. They would at least winter there and see how things looked in the spring. Following this decision, Phelps was in his office one night when a paper suddenly came from nowhere and fluttered down onto his desk. The message asked how soon the family would be leaving the house? On a nearby paper, Dr. Phelps scratched the words "October 1." Phelps sent his wife and family ahead of him to Philadelphia and he remained briefly in Stratford to put his affairs in order. During this period, the house was quiet and still. The "spirits" had apparently departed with the Phelps family. However, they did not accompany them to Philadelphia.

The family spent the winter and spring in the city and they returned to Stratford in the early summer days of 1851. The house was calm and still and over the course of the next eight years, nothing out of the ordinary occurred there. The supernatural forces, whether spiritual or man-made, seemed to have resolved themselves.

So, what did occur in the Phelps home? Was it actually a spirit who, for some reason, was wreaking havoc in the home? Or could the phenomena, even the most frightening and bizarre events, have been the unconscious work of the family themselves? Could this be why Anna and her brother, Henry, were the main targets of the outbreak? Could Anna, as some have suggested, have been subconsciously punishing herself (and her brother) for activity that was unknown to the other members of the household?

Well-known psychic Andrew Jackson Davis came to the Phelps home and asserted his belief in the genuineness of the activity. He stated that the outbreak was caused by "vital radiations" from Henry and Anna and that when the "magnetism" was at its strongest, objects were attracted to the two of them. He also believed that they could radiate a sort of "electricity," which would propel objects away from them – as concise an explanation for poltergeist activity than any other that was around in the middle nineteenth century.

THE GREAT AMHERST MYSTERY

One of the most troubling poltergeist cases in history occurred in Amherst, Nova Scotia, in 1878. The story of Esther Cox was so troubling that dozens of theories have been formed to try and explain just what took place with this young woman, from split personalities to demonic possession, but in the end, most researchers believe that she manifested some amazing abilities with her unconscious mind – abilities likely generated by a repressed desire for sex.

The small town of Amherst was home to a shoe factory worker named Daniel Teed in 1878. He lived in a very crowded two-story house on Princess Street with his wife, Olive Cox Teed; their two sons; his wife's brother, William Cox; his own brother, John, and his wife's two, unmarried sisters, Jane and Esther Cox. They were a religious, ordinary, working class family who, by all accounts, got long quite well, even in such close quarters. Jane Cox, the elder unmarried sister, was quite pretty and well liked, while Esther, nineteen, was short, stout and had what was politely called a "nervous disposition." Nevertheless, she did have a boyfriend, an employee at a local shoe factory like her brother-in-law, named Bob MacNeal.

In late August, Daniel Teed noticed that someone had been over-milking the family's cow in secret, depleting the amount that the animal could offer during the usual morning milking. Esther was accused because she had a fondness for fresh milk, but her denials bordered on hysterical. Her nervous issues began to intensify and she started complaining about unusually vivid dreams in which hundreds of black bulls with bright blue eyes and blood dripping from their mouths tried to break into the house, while Esther frantically tried to push the door closed. There was little doubt that she was dreaming about sex – both a strong desire and a violent aversion to it.

The following evening, Esther and Bob MacNeal went out for a drive. Bob, who apparently had a bad reputation in the area, drove her to a secluded area, where they engaged in some petting and necking. Finally, full aroused, Bob tried to persuade Esther to climb out of the carriage and go out into the woods with him, but she refused. According to Esther, he then tried to rape her at gunpoint, but the sounds of an approaching wagon startled him and he put the pistol away. He drove back to Amherst at a dangerous speed, let Esther off at home, and then left town for good. Esther cried herself to sleep that night and continued to weep on and off for the next several days.

On the damp, misty evening of September 4, Jane heard Esther crying in bed. Moments later, Esther began to scream that a mouse was in bed with her. They searched for it, but there was no mouse to be found. The next night, both young women heard a strange rustling sound and made another search. It seemed to be coming from a cardboard box that contained patchwork pieces for a quilt, so Jane moved it out into the middle of the room, expecting a mouse to run out of it. Instead, the box jumped into the air and tipped over. She stood it back up and the box jumped into the air again. The startled cries of the girls got the attention of Daniel Teed, who came into the bedroom to see what all of the noise was about. Unimpressed, he pushed the box under the bed and told them to go to bed.

The next night, Esther went to bed early and soon after the light was put out, she jumped out of bed and screamed at her sister that she was dying. Jane lit the lamp again and saw that Esther's face was bright red and that her hair was standing on end. Daniel Teed came in with John and William, his brother and brother-in-law, and they managed to get Esther back into bed. She began to scream, as her body appeared to swell up like a balloon. There was reportedly a loud sound, like thunder, and the men searched the house, but found nothing. When they came back, Esther was asleep.

Two nights later, as Esther was getting into bed, she began to feel sick again. Suddenly, all of the covers flew off the bed and landed in the far corner of the room. Jane was so startled by this that she fainted. Esther seemed to swell up again. The men hurried back into the room and tried to calm things down. The covers were replaced on the bed, but they were once again pulled off, apparently by unseen hands. A pillow flew up and slammed into the side of John Teed's head. He was so frightened by what he saw that he left the house the next morning and never returned. After another loud, booming sound, Esther stopped swelling and fell asleep.

A doctor was brought to examine Esther the next morning. As she lay in bed, the pillow under her head inflated as if someone had filled it with air, then collapsed, and then re-inflated itself. Rapping and banging noises were heard all over the room. The bed covers flew off and a lump of plaster detached itself from the wall and landed across the room at the doctor's feet. There was a scratching noise above the bed and as everyone watched, writing mysteriously appeared on the wall. In letters nearly one foot high, it read, "ESTHER COX YOU ARE MINE TO KILL." The rapping and banging continued for the next two hours while Esther lay, terrified and shaking, on her bed.

The following day, Esther complained of an "electric feeling" that was running through her body. The doctor gave her morphine and seconds later, a series of bangs and crashes sounded across the roof of the house.

The haunting followed Esther outside the house. Knocking and rapping noises interrupted the service at the Baptist Church were Esther was worshipping. Although Esther was seated near the rear or the church, the sounds seemed to come from the front pew, making it impossible to hear the minister's words. Humiliated, Esther fled the building. The sounds stopped immediately.

The disturbances continued for the next three weeks. Then, one night, Esther fell into a trance, her body became rigid, and she told the story of her attempted rape by Bob MacNeal. When she recovered and was asked about what she had said, she admitted that it was true. When Jane suggested that MacNeal might be responsible for Esther's problems, loud knocks sounded, implying that the "spirits" were in agreement. Jane devised a way to communicate with the presence, using the alphabet code of knocks, but when the doctor tried to communicate, there was no response.

Word spread of the strange manifestations and Esther became a local phenomenon. The house always seemed to be filled with people and onlookers packed into the yard, hoping for a glimpse of something exciting. The sounds continued to be heard, rapping and tapping on the walls and one day, when a minister came to visit, a bucket of cold water that was sitting on the kitchen table reportedly began to bubble, as if it were boiling.

Spiritualists advised Esther to try automatic writing in order to find the source of the phenomena. Messages produced proclaimed to be from a girl named Maggie Fisher, who had attended the same school as Esther and who had died in 1867. The two girls didn't know each other, but Esther was aware they'd gone to school together.

Other "ghosts" who produced messages in automatic writing claimed to be a sixty-year-old shoemaker named Bob Nickel; Mary Fisher, a sister of Maggie Fisher; Peter Teed; John Nickle and Eliza MacNeal.

In December, Esther developed a sore throat, which turned out to be diphtheria. During the time that she was sick, and during the time she was away convalescing, the manifestations ceased. However, when she returned, they started up again almost immediately. Esther claimed that she heard a voice telling her that the house was going to be set on fire – and moments later, a lit match allegedly appeared out of the air and fell onto the bed, setting the sheets on fire. Jane quickly put it out. More burning matches fell around the room, most of them going out immediately. Smoke appeared from under the bed and a burning dress that belonged to Esther was found there. The dress had somehow been transported from out of the closet, where Jane had seen it just a short time before.

Three days later, Mrs. Teed smelled smoke coming from the cellar. A burning barrel of wood shavings was found and the Teeds had some trouble putting out the blaze. The rest of the village was alarmed by this new development; the Teeds' house caught on fire, the entire village might burn. It was suggested that Esther be sent away and a neighbor named John White offered to take her in, as long as she would be willing to do some housework. For two weeks, all went well in the White home and then a scrubbing brush flew out of Esther's hand, rose up to the ceiling, and then came down and hit her on the head.

White owned a restaurant and he put Esther to work there, although things worked out no better. An oven door refused to stay closed and jumped off its hinges. Metal objects flew at Esther as if she were a magnet and some of them became too hot to touch when they were near her, including some iron spikes that landed in her lap. Esther was only injured once, by a boy's clasp knife that flew across the room and stabbed her in the back. People came to believe that Esther was somehow "electrified" and a special pair of shoes was made for her that had glass soles. When she tried to wear them, though, she got headaches and her nose would bleed.

When furniture began moving around the restaurant on its own, White decided that it was time for Esther to go home. She left town for a few months, first to stay with a man and his wife in New Brunswick, then to a farm that was located about three miles from Amherst. She told people that she often heard "voices" – voices that claimed to be those of the spirits that were causing her mischief.

In June 1879, an actor and stage magician named Walter Hubbell moved into the Teeds' house as a paying guest. He had heard about what was going on and thought that it would make the subject of a good book. Although he arrived a skeptic, he soon became convinced that was what going on was not a hoax. His umbrella sailed into the air, a carving knife landed at his feet, his bag was thrown across the room, and then a chair shot across the room and hit him so hard that he was nearly knocked to the floor. From then on, the chairs in every room that he entered performed a dance. Hubbell questioned the "spirits" and received correct replies about the words engraved on his watch and the number of coins in his pockets. Once, while lying on a settee and pretending to sleep, he secretly watched Esther enter the room. He thought that she might give herself away as a cheat if she thought he wasn't looking, but instead, he saw a large glass paperweight float across the room and bounce off the arm of the settee on which he was resting.

During the next few days, the manifestations put on a show for Hubbell. Objects floated around, strange noises were heard like sawing woods and scratching on a washboard, and Esther claimed to be stabbed by dozens of tiny pins. Small fires broke out; one day there were forty-five of them – and the sound of a trumpet was heard repeatedly in the house. When Esther went to see the local minister and pray, she said that she was attacked by a spirit, which cut her head open and stabbed her in the face with a fork.

Due to the local interest in what was happening, Hubbell believed there was money to be made from the phenomenon. He rented a theater and persuaded Esther to "put on a show" for the people of Amherst. Inevitably, the "spirits' declined to cooperate and the angry patrons demanded their money back.

Finally tired of the never-ending disturbances, Daniel Teed sent Esther off to stay with some agreeable friends, which were becoming harder and harder to find. Hubbell, who now had enough material to write his book, departed to write it. When it was released, after Esther's death, *The Great Amherst Mystery: A True Narrative of the Supernatural* was well received and went through several editions.

While Esther was staying with friends, the manifestations stopped. Soon after, she took a job one a farm owned by Arthur Davidson. When her friends discovered that several items were missing from their home, and found them in Davidson's barn, Esther was suspected of theft. Before the case could be investigated, the barn caught fire and burned to the ground. Esther was charged with arson and was sentenced to four months in jail but public support for her plight led to her release after one month. The manifestations did not return and, in fact, never occurred again.

There is little doubt that the unconscious mind of Esther Cox, rather than the work of the spirits, was responsible for the strange happenings in this case. Based on her dreams and actions, Esther was sexually frustrated. If Bob MacNeal had tried a more gentlemanly way of seducing her, there likely would have been no "Great Amherst Mystery." Esther was a classic case of the "divided self" – a part of her longed for a lover, while the inhibitions created by her background made this impossible. So when she rejected MacNeal's advances, and he left town, her unconscious mind blamed herself and set out to punish her for what she had done.

As to how the effects in the house actually occurred, it's possible that Esther served as some sort of energy conduit. She was nervous and high-strung to begin with, but something happened in her chemical makeup that allowed her to channel the energy, or magnetism, from the earth. When Esther wore the shoes with the glass soles, the manifestations stopped, but she developed headaches and nosebleeds. She also reported feeling an "electric" current coursing through her body, which could easily have been responsible for the movement of objects; the fires and even the brief moments of psychic abilities when she was about to "guess" the number of coins in Walter Hubbell's pockets.

There have been dozens of authentic cases of "human electric batteries" and nearly all of them were young women and men around the age of puberty and slightly later. Caroline Clare developed such powerful electric currents in 1877 that anyone who touched her received a strong shock. Piece of metal stuck to her as if she was a magnet. Jennie Morgan of Sedalia, Missouri, became an electric battery at age fourteen and when she touched metal objects, sparks flew. Frank McKinistry, also of Missouri, developed an electric charge each night and then lost it slowly during the day. When he was highly charged, his feet would stick to the ground in such a way that he had difficulty walking. The Reverend Edwin Clay, a minister in Amherst, was convinced that electricity was the secret of Esther's manifestations and he even delivered a lecture on the subject.

Esther's mind seemed to have created the phenomenon and the natural electric current of her body apparently gave it the power that it needed to act. Regardless, many people refused to give up on the idea that the whole thing was a hoax. If Hubbell's book were the only piece of evidence, then it would be correct to be suspicious, especially since he went to Amherst with the plan of writing it. But there are accounts in the local newspaper that confirmed everything that Hubbell wrote. In 1907, more than a quarter century after the events occurred, researcher Hereward Carrington went to Amherst and interviewed dozens of people who had witnessed the manifestations. By this time, Esther was an unhappily married, sullen woman who only agreed to talk with Carrington if he gave her $100. Carrington considered such testimony worthless, but he did speak with many people who considered the events to be genuine, including Davidson, the farmer whose barn had been destroyed. He said that he had often watched Esther as she came downstairs and had noticed that she seemed to fly, or float. In 1919, Walter Franklin Prince, another eminent investigator of the paranormal, wrote his own account of the Amherst case and criticized Hubbell for his vagueness and inaccuracies – but had to end by agreeing that there was no evidence of fraud.

Esther married a second time before dying in 1912, at the age of fifty-three.

So, what did happen in the Amherst case? Was it a situation created by a psychological explosion of energy from Esther Cox? Part of Esther wanted to be seduced by Bob MacNeal, but the personality structure induced by her upbringing made her resist his advances. If he had been more subtle, and succeeded in persuading her to become his lover, then the "old" Esther would have slipped into the background and the new, sexually experienced Esther would have taken her place. We spend our lives trying to get rid of our "old" selves and develop new, less constricting personalities. We all crave experience – but so many times, we spend our lives reacting automatically to familiar circumstances, unable to reach out and grab that new thing that comes along. Even the most dynamic people find it difficult to escape the "old self," which is largely just a set of habits. In the case of rather dull people, like Esther Cox, they become trapped to the point of suffocation in their old, habit-bound personality structure and in some cases, the unconscious mind rebels. Combine this rebellion with a physical body that is open to a natural, albeit mysterious energy and you have a volatile situation that occurs under just the right circumstances.

THE MENA POLTERGEIST

Most paranormal researchers place the blame for poltergeists in the hands of young women who are disturbed, repressed and otherwise dysfunctional. But many forget that young boys can also be responsible

The Shinn farmhouse in Mena, Arkansas

for mysterious activity too – with results that are just as weird and frightening. For a short time in December 1961, a strange outbreak occurred in rural Arkansas that had all of the signs of an authentic haunting. Suddenly, though, a local farm boy confessed that he had engineered the outbreak himself. But had he? Many of his friends, neighbors and the local authorities didn't think so.

The strange events were first reported on December 2, 1961 on the C.E. (Ed) Shinn farm near Mena, Arkansas, but they had actually begun almost a year before. The Shinns didn't report the strange activity for quite some time because, as Ed Shinn stated it, they were "afraid that people would think we were crazy."

At the time of the alleged outbreak, Shinn was a sturdy seventy-two-year-old farmer who still worked his own land about three miles east of Mena on Ransom Road. He and his wife, Birdie, and their grandson, Charles Elbert Shaeffer, lived in a five-room farmhouse on the property. The Shinns had been living in the house for fifteen years and had lived in the area for more than four decades before that. The older couple was well known and liked by almost everyone in the community and for this reason, the events that were later reported became even more disturbing to people who lived in the vicinity of Mena.

Alvin Dilbeck, the local butcher, told reporters, "I guess I must have started it all. When Ed told me about those things floating around, I got worried and sent a neighbor out to check on them."

The result was that word began to spread throughout the community about the strange things going on at the Shinn farm. People came from all over the area and after a year of dealing with what they believed was the paranormal, the Shinns now had to deal with curiosity-seekers and trespassers, as well. Hundreds of people began milling about on the farm, entering the outbuildings and the house without invitation.

"The other night, ten people barged into our house and went through it without saying a word," Mr. Shinn told newspapers in December. "You can see why we would be upset."

As word began to spread, the Shinns explained what they had been dealing with for so long. The unusual activities had started with windows rattling and knocking on the doors and walls, as if someone wanted to get inside. Sometimes the rapping on the windows was so hard that it seemed as if the glass would fall out of the frames. The knocking was sometimes accompanied by another sound, which Shinn described as "like a man working a hand saw." This noise usually came from between the walls, above the Shinns' bed.

The Shinns, and later witnesses, reported furniture, kitchen utensils, books and other objects floating about in the air; firewood, dining room chairs, marbles and kitchen utensils were thrown about; light bulbs were shattered in their sockets; pillows were pulled out from under the heads of the Shinns while they slept and bedcovers were pulled from the beds by force; the coffee table in the living room was turned upside down; upholstered chairs were overturned; venetian blinds were pulled off the windows; lamps were broken; and dining table chairs scooted across the floor and danced as though they were alive.

Elbert Shaeffer and his Grandfather in 1962

Following Mr. Shinn's talk with the butcher and the subsequent visit by a neighbor, Sheriff Bruce Scoggin of Polk County and two of his deputies, a state trooper and four reporters spent the night in the house. Nothing out of the ordinary took place, but it should be noted that the Shinns left the house and spent that night with relatives.

And while nothing occurred when the police officers and the reporters were present, there were plenty of other witnesses to the weird events. Mrs. W.E. Shinn, a daughter-in-law, said that she saw a coal bucket and some ears of corn come sailing toward her one afternoon. Gene Whittenberg, a brother of Mrs. Shinn, reported a can of dog food and a pencil hovering in midair. And not all of the reports came from family members. A neighbor named J.L. Ply was at the house on one occasion and saw a box of matches literally float into the air and dart across the room. He claimed to have spoken to a university professor about what he saw and the man allegedly suggested that the weird events might be caused by "uranium brought in through their well."

The activity continued even after the outbreak was made public. The Shinns reported that biscuits left the kitchen table and went hurtling into the living room and a figurine that flew from a shelf smacked Mr. Shinn in the head. After marbles were found scattered all over the floor, Mr. Shinn gathered them up and took them out to the barn, where they were placed between two bales of hay. They didn't bother him any longer after that.

Soon, the case took another, far stranger, turn. Not long after the newspapers began to report the events on the farm (and the place was deluged with unwanted visitors), grandson Charles Elbert Shaeffer confessed to creating the "haunting." He told authorities that it had been he who had overturned the chairs, knocked over the lamps and books and had made mysterious noises. "I didn't mean to hurt no one," he sobbed to Sheriff Bruce Scoggin. "I'm sorry for all the trouble I caused." According to the police, he started the noises as a prank because his grandfather was picking on him. He added, "I didn't mean for it to get out of hand, but I didn't know how to stop."

The boy apparently gave a detailed report of how he had manipulated the pranks, by tapping on his bed frame with steel pliers and tossing things from one room to the next in the dark. He also said that he pulled the bed covers off his grandparents as night, too, although he somehow managed to do all of this without being seen and completely outside the detection of his grandparents, their friends, neighbors and dozens of onlookers.

With the boy's confession, the Mena Poltergeist case was solved -- or was it? It certainly should have been, but the fact remained that no one believed Elbert's story! Neighbors and local residents stated that the confession could not explain the daytime happenings or the reports from friends and relatives. Even if Elbert had managed to do all of the things that he said he did under the cover of darkness, how did he manage to move objects about that were in plain sight?

Charles Albright, a columnist for the Little Rock *Arkansas Gazette*, was just one of the journalists who were openly skeptical of Elbert's confession. "Anyone who takes comfort in the 'confession' of the grandson, that he was the one who whipped up all of the weird doings in the farmhouse near Mena," he wrote, "either didn't read far enough or can't face the facts.... Personally, we are having no part of the confession. Elbert can't make biscuits float through the air any more than we can! Our theory is that he took the rap so that everybody could get some peace. If not, what about all the eyewitnesses to the ghostly goings-on - people who didn't even live in the house. Where does this leave them?"

And Albright's theory was certainly a compelling one. Could Ed Shinn have convinced his grandson to take the blame for the events so that the reporters, gawkers and trespassers would leave them alone? Possibly, for the "confession" did bring an end to both the local and the national coverage of the case. Perhaps the old farmer figured that if he gave the crowd something -- even something as implausible as Elbert's confession -- they would go away.

Some of those who didn't believe Elbert's confession suggested that perhaps the house was actually haunted. But if this were the case, then why had nothing occurred in the past? The Shinns had been living on the farm for many years prior to the events, which did not begin until the unhappy Elbert came to live with them. Elbert was just entering puberty at that time, which is a common age for poltergeist events to occur around human agents. In a number of similar cases, the young people at the center of the case are experiencing turmoil and emotional upheaval, such as occurs during puberty. Newspaper writers described Elbert as a "superior student" but photos from the time show an awkward, overweight young man with thick glasses and a backward demeanor. It isn't hard to imagine that he might have been shy and nervous around people and emotionally immature.

Would his awkwardness have been enough to create the aggressive suppression of energy that is needed to cause events to erupt in a poltergeist case? After all this time, that's impossible to say, but there seems to be no question that "something" took place on the Shinn farm in 1962.

THE BALTIMORE POLTERGEIST

On January 14, 1960, the peace of the Edgar Jones family home in Baltimore, Ohio, was shattered by the destruction of a miniature pottery pitcher. The ceramic knick-knack inexplicably blew into dozens of tiny pieces and with this strange event, a series of bizarre happenings began that would leave an ordinary American family shaken and never quite the same again.

The family had just seated themselves to dinner when the pitcher suddenly exploded, showering Jones with small fragments of pottery. Startled, he stood up from the table and puzzled over what could have happened. His wife had also jumped to her feet, just as their married daughter, Mrs. Theodore Pauls, let out a loud exclamation of her own as she walked in from the kitchen, carrying a steaming bowl of vegetables. Her surprise quickly changed to sympathy when she noted to her mother that the broken pitcher had been one of her mother's favorites. Visibly upset over the loss of a piece of her collection, and over the odd way that she had lost it, Mrs. Jones went into the kitchen for a broom and a dustpan.

Before she could leave the room, though, another of the miniature pitchers shattered! It was followed by another and then another, each of them literally blowing apart in turn along the length of the shelf. In moments, all fifteen of the prized ornaments had been broken. The Jones' and their daughter backed away from the table in confusion, fear, and perhaps even a touch of panic.

The bizarre incident of the exploding pitchers was the first in a succession of strange and otherworldly events at the Jones home between January 14 and February 8, 1960. On one occasion, with the entire family watching, a ceramic flowerpot rose from a shelf and crashed through a closed window. During another meal, a sugar bowl floated up to the ceiling light and dumped its contents all over the table. Pictures fell from their hooks and skittered across the floor, chairs moved about and overturned, books tumbled over and a brass incense holder was seen flying six feet across a room. One evening when Mrs. Jones and Mrs. Pauls were preparing a meal, several iced-tea glasses danced off a kitchen shelf and a case of soda bottles exploded their tops, washing down the walls with foam and sticky liquid.

A number of pottery pieces that had been left on a bed were smashed, as if struck by an unseen but heavy object. A small table that rested at a landing on the stairway suddenly "came to life" and did what witnesses referred to as a "dance." As it did so, it rocked and tipped down the staircase and splintered into pieces when it reached the bottom. A stack of firewood in the basement somehow shot out of its holder and flew in all directions. Pieces of wood and bark launched outward with such force that splinters were embedded in the walls. The dining room light swung violently back and forth during most of meals and soon the Jones' began eating in other rooms. Of course, this did not stop knives, spoons and forks from vanishing from beside their plates.

Despite what must have seemed like genuine violence, the only injury that occurred during the outbreak was suffered by Edgar Jones, a retired fireman. One afternoon, he bent down to pick up a can of corn that had jumped from a shelf and as he did so, a can of sauerkraut smacked him on the back of the head.

Not long after the bizarre events began, the Joneses did what so many people in similar circumstances did -- they called the police. The officers who came to investigate the scene were stunned by the weird events and searched for a cause. The crime lab came to examine the house for explanations and trickery and reported that they could find no trace of explosives being used to make items jump into the air and explode. City street workers were brought in to test for tremors with a seismograph, but they found nothing out of the ordinary. A radio repairman blamed the trouble on high frequency radio waves, but his test equipment couldn't detect any of them. A local plumber tested the pipes, looked for unusual water pressure and even checked the furnace, but he could find nothing to explain what was going on.

In what seems to be a natural progression in such cases, the media got involved in the events. Soon, reporters descended on the house and their accounts brought onlookers and curiosity-seekers flocking to the scene. Many of them stood around on the street outside, hoping for a glimpse of the weird activity. The Joneses were flooded with requests to investigate the house by paranormal investigators and psychics and they rarely turned anyone away. Each visitor seemed to have his or her own theory about the best method of "laying" the ghost, but nothing seemed to work. The majority of those who came to investigate were crackpots and kooks but even most of the seasoned investigators were as puzzled as the Jones family.

Then, the phenomena ceased as suddenly as it had started, leaving the family just as baffled as they had been when it all began. Not everyone involved in the case was surprised, though. The late psychoanalyst and psychic investigator Nandor Fodor personally interviewed the Jones family and was of the theory that a poltergeist was to blame for the wild and destructive goings-on in their home. The majority of all poltergeist cases only lasted for a few weeks at most. Fodor stated that poltergeists were not "ghosts" but were bundles of "projected repressions" and because of this, quickly wore themselves out.

Fodor noted that poltergeist activity was usually associated with a teenaged member of the family, usually a girl. When Fodor investigated the Jones case, he concentrated on the presence of the Jones' seventeen-year-old grandson, Ted Pauls, who was rarely mentioned in the newspaper coverage of the case, but was essential to Fodor's theory. Fodor found Ted to be a shy, brooding young man who had left school at the legal age because, according to his family, he was so brilliant that his classes bored him. According to Fodor, Ted had likely been the cause of the outbreaks, as his desperate need for attention for his mental abilities had created a "psychic disassociation." Despite Ted's mental agility, Fodor found him to be a repressed, desperate young man who had never had a girlfriend and was in the throes of puberty. As he reached his sexual peak, his unconscious looked for a way to expend the energy that was building up in his body. Fodor wrote, "The human body is capable of releasing energy in a matter similar to atomic bombardments as this force was apparently able to enter soda bottles that had not been uncapped and to burst them from within."

Fodor believed that Ted's sexual energy was the answer to the strange phenomenon, but why the activity suddenly ceased is unknown. Ted Pauls was barely mentioned during the press coverage of the case, so it's hard to say what happened to him next. We only know that the outbreaks soon came to an end and the case of the exploding pitchers became a minor footnote in the history of the American poltergeist.

THE OAKLAND POLTERGEIST

It is not uncommon to find accounts of poltergeists in homes, where the tapestry of human life is usually lived out and where all of the stress of our everyday existence is most often experienced. But what about in a busy office building? While this may seem odd at first, consider that many of us spend more of our waking time at work than we do relaxing at the end of the day in our own home. The office is, for many people, a place of drama, pain, and ridicule, where romance and heartbreak often go hand-in-hand, and where bottled-up emotions sometimes erupt in both good and bad ways. It was perhaps for just this reason that a poltergeist outbreak began at the office of court reporter George Wheeler in Oakland, California, in June 1964. Over the course of several days, dozens of strange events occurred in the office -- seemingly without explanation. The normally quiet space was soon filled with police officers, reporters, photographers, television crews and poltergeist investigators, both real and phony. For a time, Wheeler's work, which consisted of taking down the testimony of the Alameda County courts, came to an absolute standstill.

One of the main investigators of the strange events was Jim Hazelwood, a writer from northern California, who got involved in the case on June 15. Roy Grimm, the city editor of the *Oakland Tribune*, called Hazelwood and gave him the address of Wheeler's office on Franklin Street. He told Hazelwood that he had gotten a police call saying that, "things were jumping around over there." When Hazelwood asked him what he was talking about, Grimm replied that it was a "poltergeist," barely able to contain his laughter over the telephone.

Hazelwood took a cab over to the office building and took the elevator up to the third floor. There, he joined several other people who were milling around outside Wheeler's office -- who all got a start when they heard a loud crash from an empty room adjoining Wheeler's suite of three offices. The door was open and Hazelwood peered inside to see a metal filing cabinet lying on its back on the floor.

Feeling a little unnerved, Hazelwood went into the office and introduced himself. He found that the usual workers were Wheeler, his wife Zolo (who was also a court reporter), court reporters Robert Caya and Calvert

Bowles and two transcribers, Helen Rosenberg and John Orfanides. Wheeler was not present when the writer arrived, but Oakland police officer Charles Nye was there, having been called to the scene about fifteen minutes before.

Free for a moment, Hazelwood looked around the office suite and described it like this: "Wheeler's office is a suite of three rooms, side by side and connected by doors that usually stand open. Wheeler occupies the far right, which also contains a small cupboard in which the staff keeps coffee-making equipment, wax for polishing desks and floors and other miscellanea. ... The center room is the main entrance to the offices and is usually occupied by the transcribers, Mrs. Rosenberg and John Orfanides. The room on the left contains several telephones, Dictaphone equipment, a water cooler, wall cabinets for storing papers and equipment and a movable counter filled with office supplies."

As is readily obvious from Hazelwood's description, this was a standard and quite ordinary office from the 1960s. There was little (or nothing) there to suggest that something out of the ordinary would be occurring -- and yet it was.

Mrs. Wheeler took Hazelwood into the main office first. Her husband's room was admittedly, "a mess." An ashtray lay on floor, broken into pieces. Outside the coffee cupboard (as Hazelwood called it, but it was really a small closet), a pile of smashed crockery was lying in a pool of water. Officer Nye explained that he had inspected the premises as soon as he had arrived and had seen a empty blue flower vase and a glass water pitcher sitting on a shelf of the cabinet. He noted that they seemed to be right on the edge of the shelf and so, concerned that any vibrations in the building might dislodge them, he pushed both items back farther onto the shelf. A few minutes later, while in another room and with Wheeler's office vacant, the pitcher and the vase apparently flew through the air, made a right turn and shattered on the floor, a few steps from Wheeler's desk.

As Nye was recounting these events to Hazelwood, there was a banging sound that came from the room to the left. One of the telephones had managed to remove itself from the table and had fallen to the floor. The office was empty at the time so Hazelwood hastily called the newspaper and asked for a photographer to be sent.

Jim Edelen, a veteran of the *Tribune* staff, showed up a few minutes later and began snapping photos of the damage that had been done. He asked John Orfanides to pose with the shattered objects inside the coffee room and he snapped the photos. Moments later, as they turned to leave the room, there was a crash behind them. They turned to find that the broken shards on the floor were now covered with white powder. A large jar of non-dairy coffee creamer had flown out of the coffee room and it, too, had shattered on the floor.

Helen Rosenberg, who did most of her work in the office, was present during more of the strange events than anyone else. She told Hazelwood that the first burst of activity had occurred about two weeks before. At that time, the telephones had been behaving erratically with the rows of lights on each phone lighting up in quick succession, although no one was ever on the line. The telephone company could find nothing wrong with the units and the trouble continued even after they replaced the phones.

The electric typewriters began to act strangely next. In those days, the keys of the typewriters all had small coil springs beneath them so that they would return to position after being released. It was necessary for the top to be removed from the machine in order for anyone to reach the springs. Somehow, all of the typewriters began to act in a bizarre manner. All of the key springs went limp, twisted together and curled up. Repairman came and took them away, leaving loaner machines in their place. The springs on the borrowed machines did the exactly same thing, becoming completely inoperable. When the original machines were returned, their springs began acting up again. According to the company that made the typewriters, the springs were designed to last the entire life the machines.

When Hazelwood was in Wheeler's office on June 15, all eight of the telephones slid off the desks and fell to the floor over and over again. The metal top of a typewriter also flew across the room and struck the wall, leaving a dent, while a metal postal scale also jumped into the air without assistance. A porcelain cup that was sitting on Mrs. Wheeler's desk vaulted almost ten feet into the air and shattered against the ceiling, leaving a brown stain behind. Then, abruptly, at about 4:00 p.m., all of the phenomena stopped.

During the night, Wheeler returned to the office and moved a desk out of the left room. He moved it to an empty office downstairs in an attempt to escape from the phenomena. When he moved the desk out, he placed the telephones on the floor.

When Hazelwood returned to the scene the following morning, he found Bob Cava in the now-empty room, talking on the telephone and looking out the window. Hazelwood heard a loud thud and entered the room. Caya's back was to the door and he was still talking, but on the floor was a Dictaphone pedal that had apparently flown out of a cabinet and struck the counter, leaving a mark behind.

Hazelwood began to keep a log of the activity and soon noted that incidents seemed to occur about five minutes apart. One of the first things that he noticed was a metal box of papers that was on the floor in Wheeler's office. It had apparently fallen there soon after the office had opened for the day. He picked it up, examined it and placed it on top of a filing cabinet. Later, while standing in the doorway of the room with his back to the filing cabinet, the box flew about eight feet and hit the floor with a loud and frightening crash. Hazelwood whirled around but there was no one beside himself in the room.

By this time, the strange happenings had been widely publicized and all manner of curiosity-seekers began showing up to check things out for themselves. These included the usual tourists, occultists burning incense and Dr. Arthur Hastings from Stanford University. Although a teacher of speech and drama, Hastings was also fascinated with the unknown and had worked with the famed parapsychology foundation at Duke University. After speaking with Hazelwood and ruling out natural phenomena and the use of stage magic or a hoax, Hastings contacted Duke and asked to continue the investigations on their behalf. He told Hazelwood that the activity seemed to be connected to a "genuine poltergeist phenomenon."

The poltergeist continued to be busy throughout Hazelwood's second day at the office. A typewriter was tossed from a table in an empty room. A large electric coffee pot fell to the floor, cups exploded, telephones crashed and a filing cabinet fell over. The wooden file cabinet was one of the few things that those assembled actually saw in motion. Bob Goosey, the typewriter repairman, was standing in a doorway and saw the cabinet suddenly turn sideways and topple over, right before his eyes.

On Wednesday morning, June 17, the events reached a climax. Early that morning, Cal Bowles and John Orfanides opened the office and in the following minutes, the water cooler fell over, soaking the left office and covering the floor with broken glass, a eight-foot-tall wooden cabinet containing office supplies came down in the center of the room, scattering papers in every direction, and the movable counter flipped over onto its back.

Hazelwood arrived shortly after this had taken place and discovered that the police had taken John Orfanides down to headquarters for questioning. The poltergeist activity, meanwhile, had quieted down. Orfanides was later released and went home and the Wheeler office, now in shambles, was silent. This lasted for several days and Hazelwood began to realize that the outbreak had apparently come to an end. Hastings told him that this was frequently the case: the phenomenon would reach a breaking point and then apparently burn itself out.

Then, on June 29, there was a startling new development. Hazelwood was contacted and was told that John Orfanides had again been taken in by the police for questioning. He confessed to throwing the objects around, hiding them behind his back until no one was looking, and also to bending all of the typewriter springs. Hazelwood was stunned, knowing that the "confession" hardly explained all of the other things that had occurred, but the police were satisfied. They encouraged Orfanides to speak to the press and although the young man asked to speak only to Hazelwood, the police set up a full-scale press conference instead. Dozens of newspaper and television reporters attended but Hazelwood was out of town and another representative from the paper had to go in his place.

At the conference, a spokesman from the police department outline the young man's admissions and Orfanides glumly agreed with everything they said. The story went out that he had confessed to everything and the case was now considered closed. It was picked up by the wire services and the news went out all over the country that the much-publicized "Oakland poltergeist" was merely a prankster. But Hazelwood did not believe a word of the confession. This was not because he had become particularly friendly with the young man, but because Orfanides had been at Hazelwood's side on many occasions when events occurred in other rooms. In many cases, the writer had been the first on the scene when objects flew and seconds later had found the rooms empty.

He did not believe that he could have been fooled so completely. So a short time after the press conference, he went over to Orfanides' apartment to see him. He took with him Leo Cohen, a photographer from the paper. When Hazelwood asked him why he had confessed, he said that he did it because he knew the police would consider the case to be closed if he did. He also admitted that he had not thrown the objects, and that he could not have done so without being detected. Needless to say, this left Hazelwood and Cohen wondering again why he would have confessed. He certainly would not have done it for the publicity and in fact, could probably expect to be fired by Wheeler for wrecking the office.

He said that he had been extremely upset when the police questioned him and wanted to get the interrogation over with as quickly as he could. He told Hazelwood that the police kept suggesting ways he could have made the objects move, reminding him at the same time that he would probably not be prosecuted. Finally, he agreed to the methods they suggested and told them that he threw everything because that was the only way that he thought it could be done. "But these things are as much a mystery to me as to everybody else," he added.

And they remained that way, forever officially unsolved. What really happened in the Oakland Poltergeist case is anyone's guess, although Hastings continued to investigate the case and to work with Orfanides to determine if he could unconsciously have been the cause of the activity. In the end, Hastings surmised that he could have done so. Anyway, all poltergeist activity ceased in the office when Orfanides left the company.

Apparently, the young man, who was just twenty years old at the time and newly married, was often teased by the other men in the office for what they considered to be his effeminate behavior. However, there is no indication that he actually was gay.

Some researchers have suggested that for those who are hiding homosexual tendencies, the pressures of self-deception and the complications resulting from what can amount to living a double life could cause stress to build up to the point that in rare cases, it releases itself in poltergeist activity.

THE COLUMBUS POLTERGEIST
THE STRANGE CASE OF TINA RESCH

The tragic story of Tina Resch is one of the most intriguing and controversial cases in the modern annals of the paranormal. In 1984, a young girl in Columbus, Ohio, began apparently manifesting psychokinetic activity in her parents' home. The case captured the attention of the American public, believers and skeptics alike, and it went on to become one of the most famous paranormal happenings of the late twentieth century – and a horrific portrait of a young woman's shattered life.

In March 1984, the John and Joan Resch family living in the house on Blue Ash Road included their son, Craig, their adopted daughter, Tina, and four foster children. That month, 14-year-old Tina became the focus for a strange and very frightening series of events. On a Saturday morning, all of the lights in the Resch home suddenly went on at once, even though no one had touched any of the switches. John and Joan assumed the incident had been triggered by a power surge and they telephoned the local utility company. It was suggested that they call an electrician, which they did. An electrical contractor named Bruce Claggett came to the house and he assumed, as did John and Joan, that it was simply a problem with the circuit breaker. However, he soon learned differently. He was unable to make the lights stay off and even went as far as taping the switches in the off position. As fast as he could tape them, however, the lights would turn back on again. Closet lights that operated with a pull string would be turned out, but seconds later the bulbs would be glowing again. Claggett finally gave up, unable to explain what was going on.

By that evening, stranger things were being reported like lamps, brass candlesticks and clocks flying through the air; wine glasses shattering; the shower running on its own; eggs rising out of the carton by themselves and then smashing against the ceiling; knives flying from drawers; and more. A rattling wall picture was placed behind the couch, only to slide back out again three different times.

As the weekend wore on, a pattern began to develop. The intensity and focus of the activity seemed to be Tina, who was even struck by a number of the objects. A chair was seen tumbling across the floor in Tina's direction and it was only stopped from hitting her because it became wedged in a doorway. Family members, neighbors and unrelated witnesses actually saw Tina being hit by flying objects, which came from opposite sides of the room from where she was standing.

Near midnight on Saturday, the Columbus police were summoned to the house, but there was nothing they could do. The only respite from the strange events came on Sunday, when Tina left the house for church and then again in the afternoon when she went out to visit a friend.

By Monday morning, the house was a wreck and literally dozens of reliable witnesses, including reporters, police officers, church officials and neighbors, had reported unexplained phenomena in the Resch home. Desperate for help, the family turned to the news media for an explanation. When reporters for the *Columbus Dispatch* arrived, they also witnessed the strange happenings but one of the reporters, Mike Harden, knew of Dr. William G. Roll's work on similar cases and suggested to Joan Resch that she contact him immediately.

Roll arrived in Columbus on March 11. As the project director of the Psychical Research Foundation in Chapel Hill, North Carolina, he had long been considered the country's leading expert on poltergeist phenomena. Roll was born in Bremen, Germany, in 1926, where his father was the American vice-counsel. He graduated from University of California Berkeley in 1949, where he studied philosophy and psychology, the closest fields he could find to psychical research. In 1950, he went to England to study at Oxford and with the support of the Society for Psychical Research and famous psychic Eileen Garrett, he set up a small research laboratory, where he worked from 1952 to 1957.

Dr. William Roll

While at Oxford, Roll got in touch with J.B. Rhine at Duke University in North Carolina. In 1957, Rhine invited Roll to come to Duke and a year later, he was sent, along with fellow parapsychologist J.G. Pratt to investigate a poltergeist at Seaford, Long Island. Their report concluded that the disturbances were most likely the result of unconscious manipulations by a young boy in the family. Roll and Pratt coined the term "recurrent spontaneous psychokinesis" (RSPK) to explain these types of cases. It is in general use today as another name for poltergeist activity.

Since that time, Roll had investigated well over one hundred cases of poltergeists, both modern and historical. From his reports and personal observations, Roll determined that there were patterns of RSPK effects in the reportedly "haunted" locations. These inexplicable, spontaneous physical effects repeatedly occurred when a particular person was present. He believed that the activities were expressions of unconscious PK carried out by the individual acting as the agent.

His past research certainly made him qualified to study the events in Columbus but even so, he had little idea of what to expect from the case. He had come at the direct invitation of Joan Resch, after seeing the case widely reported in the newspapers. He and an assistant ended up spending a week in the house and while the poltergeist activity seemed to calm just after the pair arrived, it made a noisy return by the end of the week.

The most impressive events occurred on March 15, when Roll observed a brief flurry of activity first hand. The incidents that he witnessed took place when he and Tina were alone on the second floor of the house. As things began to happen, Roll stayed very close to her and left his tape recorder running so that he would have an accurate account of the events. A slamming sound came from the bathroom when what Roll believed to be a bar of soap was thrown from a dish on the sink. He and Tina walked into the bathroom and then emerged again. As they did so, a picture on the wall to their left suddenly fell to the floor. Roll had the girl under observation the entire time and saw no movement on her part. However, Tina did become upset because the picture was one of her mother's favorites. Fortunately, it was not broken, but the nail had been ripped out of the wall. Roll offered to nail it back up again and began to do so when the poltergeist once again began to react.

"I was keeping Tina under close watch throughout this period," Roll later reported. "So when I hammered in the nail, she was standing right next to me and I was very aware of her exact position and what she was doing. Before I proceeded, I placed my tape recorder on the dresser, which was behind us and to our left. As I was hammering in the nail, we heard a sound like something falling to the floor. We turned around and my tape recorder was on the ground." The recorder had somehow managed to travel about nine feet, seemingly without assistance. Roll could see no way that Tina could have touched it.

Roll had been hammering the nail back in with a pair of pliers that he had found on the dresser. When he was finished, he had laid them back down again. During the few moments that his attention was focused on the traveling tape recorder, the pliers had also been flung from the top of the dresser and had landed about six feet away. Tina had been nowhere near them at the time.

Not surprisingly, as the case made national news, cries of fraud and hoax began to be raised by the debunking community. Three representatives of the Committee for the Scientific Investigation of Claims of the Paranormal (CSICOP) showed up at the Resch house unannounced on March 13, while Roll was still investigating. One of the group members was the debunker and magician James Randi, who had already publicly attacked the case in the press. The CSICOP investigators became more skeptical when the Reschs refused to allow Randi into the house. They had no objection to the other two investigators, both scientists, but would have nothing to do with Randi. Because of this, the entire CSICOP team decided to withdraw (for reasons that remain unclear) and began to issue negative statements about the case, even though they had never actually investigated it.

One of the strangest twists in the saga of the Columbus poltergeist came about when *Columbus Dispatch* reporter Mile Harden and photographer Fred Shannon, a thirty-year veteran of the *Dispatch*, visited the house. The newsmen would make national news themselves with their involvement in the case and would release a series of photographs that would shock the world.

Shannon received the first call from Harden on March 5, 1984. He phoned him directly from the Resch home and asked him to come to the house immediately. Shannon packed up his gear to leave, never realizing that he was about to embark on one of the most bizarre assignments in his career. Even the words of warning from Harden over the telephone did not prepare him for what he was about to experience. What he actually came into contact with in the Resch home happened in a short amount of time, but his later testimony about what he saw would become compelling evidence of the paranormal.

Shannon was met at the door by Harden. He was introduced to the Reschs and they began to explain to him about the strange happenings that had been taking place. The "force," as they were calling it, was hurling household objects all about the place and the majority of the disturbances seemed to be aimed at Tina. They began to show him about the house, starting in the dining room, where the chandelier had been damaged by flying wine glasses, as well as by other objects that had crashed into it. The force had almost completely destroyed the fragile long-stemmed glasses that the Reschs kept in the room. When Shannon arrived, only one wine glass remained on the portable bar in the corner.

After looking over the damage for a few minutes, John and Joan Resch went into the adjoining kitchen, leaving the photographer alone in the dining room with Mike Harden and Tina. Moments later, they followed the girl's parents into the other room and, within seconds, they heard the sound of glass shattering in the dining room. "Uh-oh," Joan Resch groaned, "there goes the last wineglass." They raced back into the dining room and found the splintered remains of the glass in the opposite corner from where it had been.

The now-perplexed photographer followed the rest of the group back into the kitchen a few minutes later and to his surprise, he found that the force again chose that moment to react. A tremendous clatter was heard in the dining room and when they returned, they found that six metal coasters (which had also been sitting on the portable bar) had sailed through the air in the same direction as the last wineglass. They now lay in a scattered pile near the broken shards of glass.

According to Shannon, they entered the kitchen uninterrupted and the Reschs told him about all of the things that had happened in the room. For example, "all hell broke loose" whenever Tina opened the door to the refrigerator. Eggs would fly out and burst on the ceiling, jars would overturn, and containers of leftovers would burst open and expel their contents onto the floor. On one occasion, a stick of butter had erupted from the icebox and had sailed across the room to become lodged between two cabinet doors. Instead of slowly sliding to the floor, though, the butter inexplicably began moving upwards toward the ceiling.

The Reschs then took Shannon into the living room. They explained about the time that a large, overstuffed chair chased Tina out of the room, cart-wheeling until it slammed into the wall and dislodged a picture. Shannon was intrigued by the story, so he decided to take a photo of the chair and the picture, the frame of which was still intact although the glass was shattered. He asked Tina to pose next to the chair and to hold the picture so that he could see it through the lens. At that same instant, when he shot the photo and the flash went off, Shannon heard a loud crash. Tina claimed that something knocked the picture out of her hand. Shannon was thinking that she had just dropped the picture and the crash when it hit the floor was what had startled him but he soon had second thoughts about this. He quickly noticed that Tina was still holding the corner of the picture in her hands, as if something had struck the picture with force and had knocked it out of her hands, leaving her holding one small corner of it.

Unnerved and upset, Tina sat down on a couch in the family room. As Shannon and Harden turned to go back into the kitchen, they heard a tremendous booming sound! Without thinking, Shannon immediately turned and snapped a photo. The developed image would later show Tina covering her head because the lamp on the stand next to her had crashed to the floor. Since his eyes were not on her at the time, Shannon was unable to say for sure whether or not Tina knocked over the lamp herself, but he was confident that she had not. "I had swung around so rapidly," he later said, "that I don't see how she would have had time to knock over the lamp and so completely cover her head. She was covering her head because she had been attacked by so many various objects. She was a badly frightened girl and her fear never left her all during the time these things were going on. At this point, I had been in the house for fifteen minutes!"

Tina sat down on the arm of a chair across the room from the couch where she had been sitting. Shannon took up a position in the doorway near a love seat, with his back to the kitchen. Suddenly, the love seat that was close to him began to move towards Tina. It pivoted on one leg and shuffled toward her about eighteen inches! Needless to say, the skeptical photographer was startled --- but not so much so that he was unable to snap a photo of the shocked expression on Tina's face. "I knew the photo wouldn't mean much to someone who wasn't there, as I was, to see what had happened," Shannon explained. "Anybody who chose to think that way would say it was just a setup. So I was looking for other things to happen. I didn't have long to wait."

Shannon and Harden decided to observe the girl more closely and took a seat on the couch, with Tina on the loveseat, facing them. On the floor in front of her was a colorful afghan, which Joan Resch had earlier explained had once risen off the floor and had covered Tina. Within a few moments of the journalists sitting down, they saw this repeated and Shannon took a photo of her with the afghan draped over her body. He had no explanation for how it could have lifted from the floor and could find no method as to how Tina could have accomplished this on her own.

Later, the three of them went into the kitchen and were talking with John and Joan, when they all heard a loud sound in the unoccupied family room. Shannon stated that it sounded, "like a cannon had gone off --- it had that much force." They went to investigate and learned that a heavy bronze candlestick (which had been on the floor to the immediate left of the loveseat and near the back door) had taken flight a short distance and had banged into the door. That door, which was made of metal, was hit with such force that two dents were left on it. The Reschs had taken to placing heavy objects like the candlestick on the floor because it seemed that items left on walls and tables had a habit of flying in Tina's direction. Once, a wrought-iron clock had flown from the wall and had hit her in the back of the head, leaving a lump.

A few moments later, another bronze candlestick took flight from the other side of the loveseat, near the kitchen. Tina was sitting in a chair in the family room and Shannon and Harden were watching her from a couch across the room. No one was anywhere near the candlestick and yet somehow, it moved. According to Tina, who had been at an angle to see the candlestick, it had flown four or five feet into the kitchen before making a ninety-degree turn and shooting down the hallway. She said that it had been turning end over end through the air. Shannon admitted that he had not seen the candlestick move, but he had certainly heard it. As it propelled itself, the object made a roaring sound, an incredible noise that he said sounded "something like a locomotive."

Everyone was shocked and when they recovered, they all got to their feet and hurried into the hallway. The first thing they saw was the hanging lamp at the entrance of the doorway. The lamp was swinging back and forth quite rapidly from what Shannon believed was wind left behind by the fast-moving candlestick. The lamp, he later reported, was swinging as if it were in a hurricane.

The incident with the candlestick was only one of the strange things that happened while Harden and

(Left) The famous photo taken by Fred Shannon of the activity surrounding Tina Resch. The second photo in the series appears above.

Shannon were watching Tina in the family room. Most of the other incidents involved telephones that were located on a stand next to Tina's chair. Usually, two telephones were kept on the stand. The reason for this was that when the outbreak began, the house was plagued with all sorts of electrical problems, including malfunctions with the telephone in the family room. Because of this, the Reschs bought a second, cheap phone and installed it next to the sturdier, original phone. Both sat on the stand next to the chair in the family room but it was the second phone that was most affected by the "force" in the house.

According to Fred Shannon, he was present on seven different occasions when one or the other of the phones flew in Tina's direction. The first two times, they hit her on the left side and fell next to her on the couch. During the other incidents, the phones flew over Tina's lap in the direction of the loveseat. The events occurred unexpectedly, usually minutes apart, but happened in seconds. This made it nearly impossible for Shannon to get a photograph of the events. At one point, he sat for more than twenty minutes with the camera up to his eye, waiting for something to happen - but nothing did. Finally, each time that he would lower the camera so that he wasn't immediately ready to take a photo --- the phone would go flying through the air!

That caused him to wonder if he was dealing with a blind force after all. Could it be aware of his presence? If this was true, he decided to devise a strategy. He brought the camera to his eye, his finger poised on the trigger, and waited, watching Tina for about five minutes. Then, without taking his eyes off her, he lowered the camera to the level of his waist, still keeping it pointed in her direction and his finger on the shutter. As he did this, he turned his head in the direction of the kitchen, where the Reschs were talking with some visitors. He waited patiently for something to happen, pretending that his attention was somewhere else.

A few seconds later, he saw a white blur out of the corner of his eye and by the time that he pressed the shutter of the camera, a phone had streaked through the air and had sailed all the way across the chair in which Tina was sitting! The resulting photo captured not only the flying telephone but also the frightened expression on Tina's face as she jerked backwards to keep from being hit. In all, Shannon was able to get three different photos of the telephone in flight but this first one was the one that got the most attention. The day after it appeared in the local newspaper, it was picked up by the Associated Press and made front pages all over the country.

The photo was immediately attacked by the debunkers, who began savaging the entire case, but Shannon was adamant about what he had seen. He emphasized in writing: "I am damned sure that she did not throw those phones. From what Mike and I observed, I would say that she couldn't possibly have thrown them - absolutely no way. We were sitting in a well-lighted room; we were looking right at her. When one of us was looking away for a moment, the other had his eyes on Tina all the time. And of course, there were some objects that took flight while she was nowhere near them --- the candlesticks, for example."

Shannon also witnessed an incident with the telephones that did not involve Tina. It occurred just a few minutes after he took the astounding photo of the phone in flight. A Franklin County Children Services caseworker and an associate arrived at the house on business and the caseworker sat down in the loveseat. Shannon warned her not to sit there, as he knew that she would be in a direct path of the telephone. She didn't take him seriously and made several comments to assure him that she thought the whole thing was a joke, but humored him anyway by moving to the other cushion on the loveseat. She stood up, shuffled sideways and sat back down again. Just as she was lowering herself to the seat, the phone shot through the air and landed hard on the cushion where she had been sitting. If she had not moved, the phone would have struck her in the chest! The incident startled her so much that she made no more light of it and she and her co-worker quickly finished their business and left.

A little while later, Harden, Shannon and Tina were standing in the middle of the family room when a box of tissues (which was also on the phone table) suddenly leapt into the air. It zipped past Shannon's leg and landed on a small table next to the couch. When it hit the table, it did not skip or bounce even though it had been moving at tremendous speed. Instead, it stopped in place as if it had been caught by a magnet or glued into position.

This was the last activity that Shannon witnessed in the family room but his experiences at the Resch house were not yet over. He decided to take some photos in the kitchen and hoped that if he got Tina to open the refrigerator door, something would fly out of it, as had been allegedly happening over the last few days. The kitchen was already a mess from these past incidents and in fact, the Reschs had been cleaning the room during most of the time that Shannon and Harden had been in the house.

Tina waited in the kitchen as he set up his camera in the corner, directly across the room from the refrigerator. Shannon ducked low to avoid being hit by any flying food and asked Tina to open the door --- but nothing happened. She repeated it three times but everything inside remained where it was. Tina decided to use the moments of inactivity to make a sandwich and Harden and Shannon decided to pack up and leave, having spent nearly four hours in the house.

As soon as the story of the Resch house, and Shannon's accompanying photo, began to appear in newspapers, the self-appointed critics of the paranormal immediately began an attack on the reality of the events that were being reported. In spite of the fact that none of them had investigated the case, nor had been to Columbus, they were convinced that the whole thing was a hoax. The debunkers managed to obtain the negatives of the photos that Fred Shannon had shot at the house. Because there were three photos of a phone in the air above Tina's lap (not just the one that appeared in AP wire stories), Shannon was immediately accused of faking the photos and having Tina throw the phone so that he could photograph it. Although Shannon explained how he managed to capture three photos, he was dismissed as a fraud. This was done without investigation of the scene, assessment of the evidence and with no regard to Shannon's thirty-year career and outstanding reputation.

The debunkers also dismissed the entire case based on the fact that Roll admitted that he believed that Tina had faked some of the less impressive activity in the house. However, he did believe that genuine activity was taking place, even when conceding there was some limited fraud involved as well. "It is certain that Tina threw a lamp down on one occasion," he said. "That's obvious. She told me that she did the same thing on two other occasions. So there's no doubt there were some fraudulent occurrences."

Roll stated that it was not uncommon for victims of poltergeists to get into the act themselves as part of the mischief making. He had been able to formulate many of the poltergeist patterns into a profile through his research. Usually at the center of the activity was a child or teenager who possessed a great deal of internal anger, usually caused by a stressful situation in the household or a mental disturbance. The PK was an unconscious, and unknowing, way of venting that hostility without fear of punishment. Because of the mental states of the agents in many of his cases, genuine phenomena and trickery often go hand in hand.

In such cases, the PK effects of the unstable person will actually cause genuine phenomena to occur. However, as the events are recorded and gain the attention of others in the household (and sometimes even the authorities and media), the agent in the case begins to receive the much-needed attention they desired. As this begins to occur, the phenomena will cease. To continue the attention, the agent will often fake the phenomena. Unfortunately, as the agent is often caught in the act of doing this, debunkers will claim the entire case was a hoax and are able to discredit any research material gathered in the early stages. Because of this, many authentic cases are never brought to public record.

Roll felt that the minor fraudulent episodes that occurred did not discredit the Resch case. "I can only say that when I was present, I couldn't find any ordinary explanation for the incidents I witnessed," he stated. "In my opinion, it is very unlikely that they were caused normally. And of course there are a number of witnesses we interviewed in Columbus who had seen things under conditions where no family members could have caused them."

Later that month, Roll took Tina back to North Carolina where he and other scientists conducted computer-based ESP and PK tests on her. The results of the tests were in no way striking, leading most to believe that she did not possess any long-term psychic abilities. As in other poltergeist cases, the mysterious happenings seemed to be confined to a short period of time. And while there were some poltergeist incidents in Roll's home and at the home of a counselor where Tina was staying, the researchers believed that her aggressive manipulations were short-lived.

What caused the manifestations? No one knows for sure and the story behind the Columbus poltergeist remains a mystery. Poltergeists in general tend to focus on disturbed children who are suppressing hostility and anger. The displacement of energy acts as a safety valve for the pent-up emotions. In Tina's case, there had been recent problems at home over the fact that Tina, against the wishes of John and Joan, had begun searching for her natural parents. Also, Tina's best friend of two years had ended their friendship just two days before the events began. To make matters worse, the Reschs had recently taken Tina out of school because she was having trouble getting along with other students. She was apparently unpopular with most of her classmates and was having difficulty with one of her teachers. Because of this, she was being tutored at home and was seemingly "cut off" from the outside world. All of this apparently combined to create an outward transference of energy.

Eventually, the activity ended and after Tina's return from North Carolina, only a few minor incidents were reported in her home. Roll was never sure of the cause of the case, but his studies pointed to the theory that poltergeist agents seemed to suffer from disturbances in the central nervous system. This may have been the case with Tina Resch, for even though the bizarre incidents ended in her home, her story was not quite over.

Many poltergeist agents have been documented to be in poor mental health, which deteriorated further in stressful situations. This might explain the findings of many standard psychologists and mental health professionals. They often discover that patients with unresolved emotional issues are associated with, or have lived in, houses where poltergeist activity has been reported. In addition, while studying the personalities of those thought to be poltergeist agents, psychologists have found anxiety issues, phobias, mania, obsessions, dissociative disorders and even schizophrenia. In some cases, psychotherapy may eliminate the poltergeist phenomena but apparently, not in all of them.

For despite counseling, Tina Resch went from being an unhappy child to being a disturbed adult. She went from one disastrous situation to another, finally to two marriages and two divorces and then to a sentence of life in prison for the torture murder of her three-year-old daughter, which occurred when the child was being watched by Tina's boyfriend. She claimed to be innocent of the crime, and was not present when it was committed. There was no trial but Tina accepted a plea bargain of life imprisonment rather than face the possibility of a death penalty. She was sent to a Georgia prison in 1994 and remains there today.

8. IN A DARKENED SEANCE ROOM... SEX AND SPIRITUALISM

There were few things that captured the attention of the nineteenth century public like Spiritualism did. And as the movement progressed through the decades, it became more galvanizing, more controversial – and definitely more fascinated with sex.

The Victorian era movement of séances, mediums and spirit contact thrilled practitioners and debunkers alike and broke all rules of decency and decorum, in spite of the fact that it was born and nurtured in the drawing rooms of proper middle-class people. Spiritualism became the faith of thousands of people for nearly a century. In spite of its strange beginnings in 1848 — a code of raps developed between a murdered peddler and two young girls --- aristocrats, scholars, and scientists, along with ordinary men and women, were converted to the belief that death was no barrier to communication. Contact with the other side was achieved through mediums who, possessed by the spirits, passed on messages from the spirit world that provided many with comfort, peace, and the reassurance of an afterlife that the social and intellectual climate of the day called into doubt.

But Spiritualism provided more than just messages from dead relatives and the thrill of seeing things flying around in dimly-lit séance rooms. During a period of history when women were considered the "weaker sex" and often treated as second-class citizens, they were actually able to become leaders in the Spiritualist movement, acting as mediums and spokespeople. They also had the chance to do things, under the cover of darkness and with the idea that possessing spirits caused their behavior, that they never would have done in polite society. Soon, séances began to involve scantily clad "spirits" and mediums were quick to disrobe in order to prove that they hid no ghostly stage props under their clothing. Spirit summonings were conducted in lingerie, filmy shifts and, in some cases, nothing at all.

It was easy to say that the "spirits made them do it," but could this have actually been true? There is a long history of spirit possession and the history that intertwines it with sex is just as lengthy.

"MOUNTED BY THE GODS"
SPIRIT POSSESSION IN HISTORY

Even though the modern day idea of "possession" seems to involve demons, spinning heads and little girls levitating above beds, the concept of being possessed by spirits has actually been with us for centuries, long before the Devil and his minions became a part of our lore. Man has long been fascinated with the thought that a person's mind and soul can be taken over by spirits, whether those of the dead or even those of the gods.

The ancient Greeks, who maintained daily contact with their gods and worshipped them in a personal manner, believed that the deities manipulated the lives of mortals every day, either by causing them to act in a specific way or by simply taking over their bodies and using them to do their bidding. Followers of Buddhism and Hinduism attribute all kinds of everyday disturbances to possession by spirits and many African tribal religions teach that possession by gods and spirits show favor on man and offer proof of supernatural powers. In the Bible, events are recounted when Jesus exorcised "unclean spirits" during his ministry. There is nothing to say that these spirits were in league with the Devil, but most Catholic theologians, and fundamentalist Christians, have come to believe this was the case. And there lurks the dark side of possession, as we explored earlier in the book.

But the state of "possession" is defined as the presence of a spirit entity that occupies and controls the physical body of the subject. The symptoms of such a possession can be many, depending on the type of possession with which one is dealing. In cases of demonic possession, symptoms can include agonized convulsions, shouting of obscenities, vomiting, excessive violence, poltergeist-like events and even a state of unnatural calm. A spirit possession is a completely different kind of situation, however. In such cases, the possession seems to be more mental than physical. Although subjects may sometimes do things and act out in ways they will not later remember, they appear to be themselves. It seems to be more of a case of having their mind taken over by the spirits than having their bodies commandeered.

The idea that spirit possession might occur is not as strange as the reader might think. There are many facets of American culture and religion that believe man can be possessed by a divine spirit. This type of religious belief is called Pentecostalism and it is a sect of the Christian church that places special emphasis on the direct experience of God through the baptism of the Holy Spirit. After the crucifixion and resurrection of Jesus, the Bible tells of what happened to his followers on the first day of Pentecost (a date that is seven days after Passover in the Jewish calendar). While gathered together, the apostles became possessed by the Holy Spirit. The Book of Acts described how small flames appeared above their heads and how each of them spoke in languages that were previously unknown to them.

The idea of "speaking in tongues" (glossolalia) became a basic tenet in Pentecostalism and it is still widely practiced today. There are several different types of the Pentecostal faith but the most conservative are members of the Apostolic branch, who are separated from many of the other "charismatic" churches. The Apostolic Christians believe that a possession by the Holy Spirit is essential to salvation. They also believe that woman should only wear skirts and dresses, should not cut their hair, should not wear makeup or jewelry and that men should always wear their hair short, should abstain from facial hair and should always wear pants, never shorts.

A Pentecostal church service includes music, prayer, laying on of hands (as shown above) and sessions of speaking in tongues. Believers are convinced that this is evidence of possession by the Holy Spirit

They also believe in what is called the "Oneness" doctrine, literally accepting the biblical instruction that all baptisms, healings and prayers should be in the name of "Jesus" only, not "in the name of the Father, Son and Holy Ghost," as most other churches believe.

Apostolic church services can be very lively, placing great emphasis on testifying, praise for the Lord, fiery sermons, and almost hypnotic music. It is during these music and prayer sessions that members of the congregation become possessed by the spirit, which can result in speaking in tongues, dancing, jumping up down, running through the church, shouting, crying, falling to the ground and passing out. I have personally witnessed some of these sessions and they can be both bizarre and a little frightening, too.

In extreme cases, divine spirit possession can even lead to handling snakes and drinking poison. Sects who take part in such behavior draw their inspiration directly from the Bible: "And these signs shall follow them that believe; In my name shall they cast out devils; they shall speak with new tongues; They shall take up serpents; and if they drink any deadly thing, it shall not hurt them; they shall lay hands on the sick, and they shall recover." (Book of Mark).

The Azusa Street Mission in 1906. The revival here lasted for three years and gave birth to the Pentecostal Movement

The Pentecostal sect can trace its beginning back to the day of Pentecost and the one hundred and twenty believers who were possessed by the spirit after Christ's ascension to heaven. In more recent times, the church as we know it today was formed. There were several incidents that occurred around the turn of the last century that led to the formation of the modern movement. The pivotal event occurred in 1901 when a woman named Agnes Ozman began speaking in tongues during a prayer meeting at Charles Fox Parham's Bethel Bible College in Topeka, Kansas. Parham, a minister with a Methodist background, created the doctrine that speaking in tongues was the "Bible evidence" of possession by the Holy Spirit. In addition, he cited the experience of the gathered disciples of Jesus on the day of Pentecost and the instructions of Peter in the Book of Acts as justification for their practices. The biblical reference stated: "Repent and be baptized, every one of you, in the name of Jesus Christ for the forgiveness of your sins. And you will receive the gift of the Holy Spirit." (Book of Acts)

Parham soon left Topeka and started a revival meeting ministry. The next significant (and controversial) event in Pentecostal history took place at the Azusa Street Revival in California. This revival was conducted by a student of Parham, an African-American man named William J. Seymour. Parham taught Seymour in Houston, Texas, but since Seymour was black, he was only allowed to sit outside the room and listen to Parham speak. Despite the racial segregation of the time, the Apostolic movement was largely accepting of African-Americans and welcomed them into the church.

Speaking in tongues was already occurring in churches across the country by 1906, but the Azusa Street Revival would be the event that would make the movement known across the country. It began on April 9, 1906 in Los Angeles, at the home of Edward Lee, who claimed that he had been possessed by the Holy Spirit. William Seymour claimed that he was possessed a few days later, on April 12. On April 18, the *Los Angeles Times* ran a front-page story on the revival with the headline, "Weird Babel of Tongues, New Sect of fanatics is breaking loose, Wild scene last night on Azusa Street, gurgle of wordless talk by a sister."

By the third week of April, the small but growing congregation rented an abandoned African Methodist Episcopal Church at 312 Azusa Street and subsequently became organized as the Apostolic Faith Mission. They would go on to achieve national fame and today, almost all Pentecostal denominations can trace their historic roots to Azusa Street.

Pentecostalism, like any other major movement, has given birth to a large number of denominations, churches, separatists and even cults with a variety of differences between them. It is a faith that is outside of the norm and even its inception was counter-cultural to the social and political feelings of the time. Record numbers of African- Americans and women, both black and white, were the initial leaders. As the Azusa Street Revival began to wane, doctrinal differences, as well as pressure from social, cultural and political events of the time, took their toll on the membership.

As a result, major divisions, separation and even the increase of extremism became apparent. Not wishing to affiliate with the Assemblies of God, formed in 1914, a group of ministers from predominantly white churches formed the Pentecostal Church of God in Chicago in 1919. George Went Hensley, a preacher who had left the Church of God in Cleveland, Tennessee, when it stopped embracing the practice of snake handling, is credited with starting the first church dedicated to this extreme practice in the 1920s. Taking up serpents, as it was called, was widely practiced in the poor, rural areas of the Appalachians. In African-American communities of the 1940s, there were Father Divine with his Peace Mission and Daddy Grace, both claiming divinity, encouraging their followers to practice the wildest forms of Pentecostalism, which many referred to as "ecstaticism." This involved manic music, dancing, shouting and an almost ritual-like session that was meant to invite possession by the Holy Spirit.

No matter what doctrines divide the Pentecostal churches, spirit possession, and speaking in tongues as evidence of it, remains a staple. Members of the Apostolic sect believe that a "baptism" by the spirit is an actual event where the person is "filled up," causing them to utter words in languages that they do not know. Critics maintain that many of these "spirit utterances" are nothing more than nonsense words and gibberish, but those who experience a possession maintain that this is a very real religious experience.

As with Apostolic Pentecostals, contact with the spirits serves as the centerpiece of religious worship for many cultures around the globe. The main difference would be that in these other cultures, it is not the Holy Spirit that people are inviting into their bodies, but various other spirits and deities. Possession by a god shows the possessed person to be worthy of that god's attention and protection. For this reason, they believe that even minor accomplishments and problems come directly from the intervention of the gods.

In India, spirit possession is a part of everyday life. In most cases, the possessed are women, who attribute personal problems --- menstrual pain, inability to conceive a child, miscarriage, death of children, marital problems, abuse, a husband's infidelity --- to attacks by evil spirits. They are often put through an exorcism by a shaman whose techniques include blowing cow manure smoke at them, pressing rock salt between their fingers, beating the victim and pulling her hair, using copper coins and candy as presents to the spirit and, of course, reciting various prayers and mantras.

Besides being female, most of these victims come from the lower classes. Possession gives these people stature and even gains them a better place in society. At the least, a placation of these gods and demons usually involves showering gifts on the victims and the promise of better behavior from their friends, husbands and employers.

Although the followers of Islam worship one god, Allah, they acknowledge the problems caused by minor spirits like djinns (genies). These spirits possess their victims, usually women, and cause sickness, martial discord, infidelity, and rebellious behavior. They will only depart if they are placated by gifts of food, clothing, liquor, jewelry or other presents for the possessed victims. At times, they also promise to leave if the men in the victim's life start treating her better. In this case, too, we can see how "possession by spirits" can cause the life of the victim to improve.

Perhaps the best-known religious experience in which worshippers literally invite the gods and spirits into their body occurs in the practice of Voodoo (or Voudon). This faith is a traditional West African religion of belief and ritual practices that made its way to the New World with the importation of slaves several centuries ago. The core functions of Voodoo are to explain the forces of the universe, influence those forces and change human behavior. It is not an evil faith, as some misconceptions would have it, but one that is based in magical rituals and a large pantheon of gods.

The number of gods within the bounds of Voodoo is large and quite complex. There are dozens of male and female gods that are related to natural phenomena and to historic and mythical individuals, as well as scores of ethnic gods that are defenders of certain clans or tribes. Some of the major gods include Legba, who takes the form of a snake, Mami Wata, who rules the water, Sakpata, who governs diseases and Baron Samedi, the lord of the dead.

Voodoo first appeared in the Americas in Santo Domingo (modern-day Haiti) where slaves were documented to be devoting rituals to the power of nature and the spirits of the dead. For many enslaved Africans, such spiritual traditions provided a means of emotional and spiritual resistance to the hardships of their lives. In time, slaves from the Caribbean were brought to America and they brought the practice of Voodoo with them.

The first American reference to Voodoo appeared in official documents written in New Orleans during the Spanish regime in 1782. In a document that tells of imports to the colony, there is a terse line regarding black slaves that have been brought from the island of Martinique. The Spanish governor, Galvez, states: "These negroes are too much given to voodooism and makes [sic] the lives of the citizens unsafe." Galvez was a soldier and was not a superstitious man, but he made an attempt to ban the importation of slaves from the Caribbean for a time for a very good reason: he feared for the lives of the colonists. Around this same time (and again in 1804), a slave revolt had rocked the island of Haiti. The revolt was based around the practice of Voodoo and would eventually end with the French being driven from the island. Many of the French escaped to New Orleans and brought their slaves with them. Tensions simmered in the city with the arrival of more Voodoo-practicing slaves.

During Voodoo ceremonies, worshippers believed they are possessed by their gods

From the beginnings of the New Orleans colony in 1718, the white colonists had been troubled by the beliefs of their slaves. Shiploads of captives came through the city on a regular basis and were bought and sold for manual labor and household work. Thousands of them were brought from Africa, packed into ships and treated like animals. There were caged and either "tamed," before being sold at auction or killed.

These slaves, most of whom spoke no French, brought their religions, charms and spells with them from Africa, but they soon learned that they were forbidden to practice their familiar religions by their new masters. Many of them were baptized into the Catholic Church and later, the use of Catholic icons would play a major role in Voodoo. The church's icons would take their place in Voodoo hierarchy and be ostensibly worshipped as if the slaves were offering prayers to the saints of the Catholic Church. The saints became "stand-ins" for important Voodoo deities. Even today, statues, candles and icons depict various Catholic images that are Voodoo symbols, as well. In this way, Voodoo became firmly entrenched in the culture of New Orleans and other regions of the American South.

One of the primary traditions of Voodoo involves the possession of the faithful by the gods to obtain true communion and protection. During Voodoo ceremonies, worshippers are overcome by the chanting, dancing and pounding drums and are "mounted" by the gods, becoming the god's own "horse." During this event, they take on the personal characteristics of the god, such as the god's preference in food, perfumes and drink; their patterns of speech; use of profanity; and even a penchant for smoking large cigars, a common Voodoo tradition.

While possessed, the worshipper may endure great extremes of heat and cold, suffer cuts and bruises with no pain, dance for hours at a time, tear the heads off live chickens that are used for blood sacrifices and even engage in ritual sex with others who are possessed. They may also issue prophecies and announcements about local affairs and while the word of the spirits is not always taken seriously, there is little doubt that the events that are occurring are real. As far as the other worshippers are concerned, the possessed person has literally become the deity and is accorded all rights and honors that would be granted to the god. Once the possession ends, though, no special treatment is given to that person. At the next ceremony, the same god is likely to simply possess someone else and the honor moves on to the next person.

But Voodoo has never been all about sex, although sexual activity often took place at many of the rituals that occurred. My late friend, Hugh B. Cave, the prolific pulp magazine writer of the golden age, sent me an essay that he wrote detailing some of his experiences with Voodoo in Haiti. Parts of his astonishing story were published in *FATE* magazine in the 1950s. Cave offers an interesting look at the rituals and the mystery involved.

(Left) My late friend Hugh B. Cave in the 1930s, when he was still a globe-trotting adventurer. Many of his pulp stories were based on the time he lived in Haiti.

(Above) Hugh at the time when I knew him in the 1990s. He passed away in 2004.

I have edited the piece slightly for length:

A while ago I attended a Voodoo service in Haiti at which a writer of Sunday features for American newspapers happened to be present.

One doesn't often find outsiders at an authentic Voodoo service. Getting into such a gathering is difficult without personal contacts, and the real thing usually takes place too far from the capital to be convenient for people spending only a short time in Haiti. There are ceremonies offered in or near Port-au-Prince for tourists, of course, but these are little more than folklore presentations staged for money. Real Voodoo is a religion, concerned not with tourists but with the invocation and worship of gods and spirits.

The service mentioned was in the seaside town of Petit Goave, about 45 miles from the capital on the Southern Peninsula. Rural slums line both sides of the main shopping district. The land is flat and dusty, except when the wet-season rains transform it into a chocolate pudding that smells rather cozily of donkey droppings. Many of the town's buildings are typically old-style Haitian, two-storied, unpainted, with wrought-iron balconies. Not the most pleasant country town in Haiti. Nor was the gentleman in question the most pleasant of visitors.

Obnoxious in the extreme, he got into trouble first with his arrogance, then with his camera. A guest at a Voodoo service is not expected to whip out a camera and start taking flash pictures any more than one at a church service in, say, New York would be expected to do so. Certainly not without asking permission first. Then because the gentleman spoke no Creole and could not understand what he was being told, he became even more arrogant and was asked to leave.

Probably nothing much would have happened to him had he refused. In five years of residence in Haiti and many return visits I have met very few violent Haitians. But he did leave, and later wrote a rather long article about what he had witnessed. A friend, happening to see it, sent me a copy. In this story our writer described the ritual dancing and singing at the Voodoo service as a "wild sex orgy." The simple offering of a chicken as food for the gods was called an "unholy animal sacrifice," with so much about blood in it that his readers must have expected the newspaper page to drip all over them. Worse, he completely missed a really dramatic event that *took place before his eyes.*

(Though he and I were the only non-Haitians present, I hadn't attempted to explain anything to him. He had come in late and seated himself across the peristyle from where I was, and then he began brandishing his camera. I thought it wise to keep my distance lest I be thought, by Haitian friends present, to approve of his behavior.)

The service was one to Cousin 'Zaca, the patron loa of the peasant farmer. Normally this means a rather uneventful evening with touches of country humor. Some fellow is possessed by 'Zaca and, with a colorful sisal handbag draped over one shoulder, goes through the motions of sowing seed. (There isn't space in an article of this length to describe any Voodoo service in detail; all I can hope to do is supply a touch of color.) My point here is that a second possession soon took place at this service, and arrival number two from the world of the spirits was the redoubtable Gede Nimbo, more often called Papa Gede, the guardian of the cemetery.

Now Papa Gede is Death, and he is at all times a jokester, which is why he often comes uninvited to a service. He likes to strut around with two cigarettes in his mouth, a top hat and black coat on, and an outthrust hand eagerly tickling female bottoms. His favorite libation, almost always awaiting him in case he does show up, is a first-distillation rum called clairin in which red-hot peppers have been steeped for weeks until it's fiery enough to sear the gullet of a granite statue.

So while our gentleman of the press was furiously taking pictures of the drummers, the dancers, the farmer who'd become Cousin 'Zaca, a boy about eight years old, sitting next to me on my bench, became possessed by Papa Gede! I had been talking to this boy. He had come with his mother from a home in the hills a few miles away. His name, he said, was Ti Bagay -- obviously a nickname, for it means "Little Thing." He was so pitifully frail that he looked as though an ounce or two of anything alcoholic would probably kill him. Keep that in mind.

When the loa mounted him -- took possession of him, that is -- the lad leaped to his feet with a wild yell and raced to the poteau mitan, the sacred central post at the base of which gifts are offered to the gods. As it happened, the houngan (priest) and his assistants at this service were people of foresight. Among the offerings was a bottle of Gede's favorite pepper-spiked raw rum. Originally the bottle had held a fifth of Haiti's marvelous Rhum Barbancourt, and it was full. Also available for Gede if he came were a top hat, cigarettes, and matches.

When Ti Bagay slapped the hat on his small head, only his protruding ears kept it from thumping his shoulders. He stuffed two cigarettes into his mouth and lit them with a flourish. Snatching the full bottle of spiked clairin off the concrete slab at the base of the post, he thumbed the cork out and began prancing around the peristyle. As I've told, Papa Gede delights in pinching female bottoms. Ti Bagay pinched away with equal enthusiasm. Gede gulps down his favorite drink -- which, by the way, when mixed this way, is called in Creole a trompe. Ti Bagay gulped it down, too.

He emptied the bottle. And all the time

he was doing this, our reporter with the camera was so busy with everyday other things that he couldn't see a genuine Voodoo mystery unfolding before his eyes. Because Ti Bagay did not get drunk. Oh, he staggered a bit -- perhaps as much from the speed of his dancing as from the trompe. And beads of sweat literally flew from him as he danced. And his eyes rolled at times. But he emptied that fifth of raw rum spiked with red-hot peppers and became neither drunk nor ill. It should have killed him, medics have told me.

When the bottle was empty, Ti Bagay returned it to the base of the post, took off his top hat and coat, and calmly walked into the sacred hounfor at the end of the peristyle. But in just a few minutes he reappeared, returned to his place beside me on the bench, and sat down.

Ti Bagay, I said, do you know what you just did?

He didn't. He was not even aware that he had left the bench. When I enlightened him, he at first seemed astonished, then delighted, that Papa Gede should have chosen him. He said he had never been possessed by a loa before.

The service over, I made my way to the poteau mitan and picked up the trompe bottle from which the boy had drunk. There were a few drops of the fiery rum left in it. I poured them into my cupped hand and touched my tongue to the stuff, just to make sure. For hours afterward my mouth was on fire.

Now if our gentleman of the press had written about that, instead of about "sex orgies" and "unholy animal sacrifices," he might have told his readers something about Voodoo. But my hunch is that he already knew what he was going to write before he ever got to the service, because he'd been reading what others like him had written and was too mired in his own preconceptions to respond to the unexpected. He wasn't the first, of course. He won't be the last.

For one thing, the observer who can't speak or at least understand Creole cannot possibly understand what goes on at a Voodoo service. Could a visitor from Outer Mongolia comprehend what goes on at a Georgia camp meeting? And along with a knowledge of Creole, a background in African and Haitian history would be a help. Voodoo came from Africa in the slave ships, and the Creole tongue of today's Haitian peasant evolved from slavery as well. Coming from many different African tribes, those ancestors of today's peasants had no common language. Creole is a result of their efforts to find one by imitating the speech of their French masters.

I have extracted a handful of exaggerations from newspaper clippings and pulp tales in my files. Here they are, with a few comments:

1. Sticking pins in Voodoo dolls to torment or kill an enemy.

I've attended many different kinds of Voodoo services in Haiti's villages and mountains and have yet to see a pin stuck in a doll of any kind. Small dolls depicting the various loa are sometimes found on hounfor altars, but these are used in ceremonies. If anyone does stick pins in dolls for evil purposes, it would have to be a bocor (sorcerer) and he would do so for a fee. The bocor has about as much to do with true Voodoo as a devil-worshipper has to do with Christianity.

2. Sex orgies.

This may be sadly disillusioning, but there is very little sex in Voodoo. Erzulie, the love loa, when possessing a female participant at a service, may command the sexual attention of a chosen male. This is a form of sex, no doubt, though ritualistic rather than orgiastic. But any other sex that takes place is likely to be between young couples who slip away from the festivities for fun and games of their own in the surrounding darkness.

3. Bloodthirsty animal sacrifices.

Chickens are frequently killed as food for the loa. Sometimes their necks are wrung; other times their heads are cut off; occasionally they are seized by the neck and whirled around the whirler's head at high speed. In two of the newspaper clippings from my files the writers claim to have see houngans bite the heads off chickens. Well, my dictionary says there are certain carnival people, called geeks, who perform sensationally morbid or disgusting acts, as biting off the head of a live chicken, and I saw it done once at a ceremony for tourists. But - sorry - I've never seen it done at an actual Voodoo service.

4. Nakedness.

This crops up time and again in stories about Voodoo. Naked dancers flinging themselves about in a frenzy are stock characters, it would seem. Well, I'm sorry. I've seen and photographed any number of naked peasant women washing themselves and their laundry in country streams (you first talk to them and make friends), but not once have I seen anyone naked at a Voodoo service. The trend is just the opposite: to flowing white robes for the women and gaudy costumes for the men.

5. The Voodoo spell or curse.

Again I say maybe. A friend of mine who taught English at the College St. Martial in Port-au-Prince once let me examine a hand-lettered volume compiled by a fellow priest whose forte was botany. This man had spent years collecting Haiti's medicinal plants so that he could describe and do watercolors of them. There were 383 such plants listed, and most were poisonous if taken in large enough doses.

Your houngan or mambo knows most of these plants and can employ them in such a way that a curse or spell might seem to have been cast upon the recipient. Really, though, that isn't Voodoo. It comes under the heading of witchcraft of sorcery again, and the bocors who practice those dark arts are loners. Zombies, for instance, are a product of the bocor, never of the Voodoo houngan or mambo.

6. People dancing barefoot on live coals.

Yes, sometimes. But more often the people who do this are walking, not dancing, and appear to be in some kind of trance. Some Pacific Islanders perform the same ritual. But some Voodooists are able to do an even more impressive thing that our people of the press don't seem to have caught up with yet. They build a fire of charcoal, plant a tall iron bar like a crowbar in it, wait for the bar to become white hot, them grasp it in bare hands and parade around the tonelle or peristyle holding it above their heads.

8. The mad, frenzied dancing.

Give the movie-makers a black mark on this one, along with the writers. I don't recall the names of the pictures, but at least three times I've sat through so-called Voodoo movies in which the dancing was atrociously "un-Voodoo." Fact is, all the dancing at a Voodoo service is ritual dancing and much of it is slow. The only time I've ever seen frenzied dancing was one, in Quartier-Morin near Cap Haitien, when more than a dozen spectators appeared to become possessed at the same time. It was probably some kind of mass hysteria, and even so, it wasn't as wild as what some of our teenagers indulge in.

9. And finally, child sacrifice.

We should at least mention this because so many sensation-seeking writers seem to feel they have to. The facts? One of the very first books about Haiti discussed the sacrifice of children at Voodoo ceremonies. I threw the book out of my library years ago because it contained so many errors; therefore I can't turn to it now to determine whether its author claimed to have actually seen a child sacrifice or merely heard about one. I tend to remember he got his information secondhand, as he did nearly everything else in his book. Later writers copied him, of course. Anything as sensational as that was bound to attract the titans of titillation. But I have never heard even a whisper about child sacrifice from anyone in Voodoo, and I doubt it ever happened.

If I seem to be overly defending Voodoo here, perhaps a bit of summing up is in order. Voodoo, again, is a religion. This doesn't mean that all houngans and mambos are saints, any more than all Protestant ministers and Catholic priests are saints. Unquestionably there are houngans and mambos who engage in extracurricular activities for whatever they can get out of it, though the Haitian peasant certainly hasn't much to be fleeced out of.

But Haiti, remember, is a poverty-stricken country with few doctors, and most of those are beyond the peasants' reach. Take away the houngan and the mambo, with their handed-down knowledge of herbal medicine, and the country people would have no one to turn to when sick. Then take away the Voodoo loa to whom they look for guidance in just about everything that touches their lives, and they would feel abandoned. That's the right word: abandoned. Few outsiders seem to understand this.

Hugh B. Cave

SEX AND SPIRIT POSSESSION

But not all spirit possessions occur by choice -- many scholars on the subject write that, in many cases, spirits can actually take over someone's life and perhaps even change it from what it once was. Wanda Pratnicka, a Polish psychotherapist, healer, and exorcist, states that one of the primary causes of homosexuality is possession of a child by a ghost of the opposite sex. According to her theory, when the spirit of a woman dominates the mind of a boy, he grows up to see out contacts with men. The same thing happens to a girl who is possessed by the spirit of a man.

According to Pratnicka, spirits remain in our world because they did not pass over at the time of death but in order to continue their existence, they have to connect with a living person to survive. After that, the ghost steals that person's energy. For some, though, it's not enough to merely drain their energy, is steals their body as well. If such a ghost then succeeds in taking over that person's mind, they can become totally possessed. The author describes that person as a "puppet" that is completely governed by the ghost.

Pratnicka adds that a ghost whose life revolved around satisfying sexual desires will likely continue this after death. As a possessing spirit, they have an obsession with seeking out sex and looking for someone to satisfy their continuing needs. Pratnicka believes that children are most often chosen and because the possession is usually by a deceased relative that the child once knew, they do not shut themselves off from the ghost. Family members are usually unaware that this has occurred and eventually may even begin to comment that the child looks like a certain relative, assuming that this is family resemblance and never suspecting a possession.

Pratnicka claims that she has encountered homosexuality as a result of possession hundreds of times out of several thousand patients. She adds that she has been successful in exorcising such possessing spirits, but they often come back.

As strange – and controversial – as Pratnicka's opinion on the subject is, she shares it with others. In August 2008, Father Jeremy Davies, a Catholic priest in England, was quoted as saying that "among the causes of homosexuality is a contagious demonic factor." He also added that even heterosexual promiscuity can open up the individual to "evil spirits" and that young people are especially vulnerable.

In 2003, William J. Baldwin, Ph.D, a Florida therapist, stated, "an attached entity of the opposite gender can cause confusion over gender orientation and sexual behavior. This confusion can lead to homosexuality, transvestism, or transsexualism, and gender reassignment surgery." He went on to say that many people who were unhappy with their sexual orientation were freed after releasing the entity that caused the problem.

Baldwin told the story of a fifty-five-year-old man who had been a transvestite for most of his life. He first became fascinated with his mother's underwear at age five and during his teen years, stole women's clothing to use in his own wardrobe. After Baldwin hypnotically regressed the man, he was able to determine that a woman who had been his babysitter when he was a young child had died in an accident and her spirit had attached herself to the man. Through "releasement therapy," the invading spirit was eventually exorcized. He also described the case of a homosexual man who was being controlled by a girlfriend of his mother's who had died in an accident before he was born. She had entered his mother's womb, Baldwin claimed, and attached herself to the unborn child. The entity was eventually released but when the man realized that the spirit was responsible for his artistic abilities, he decided to keep her attached to him.

Louise Ireland-Frey, M.D., a Tulane University medical school graduate, surmised that many medical issues, including physical, mental, and emotional disorders, can also be caused by spirit possession. She defined several degrees of attachment, beginning with temptations that would begin to be experienced by the living person after they were possessed by the wandering spirit. This would not involve an overwhelming compulsion, but thoughts of doing something out of character for the person. Second was influencing, or shadowing, where the entity begins causing mood swings, irrational moments, sudden inexplicable fears, or depression. Ireland-Frey believed that total possession by a spirit could actually push out the host's own personality entirely. Possessing souls were those unable to pass on, she stated, because they were heavy with emotion or had negative qualities like rage, greed, or lust. Such souls become wanderers and can attach themselves to living people. They are usually drawn to people with the same addictions, vices or yearnings so that they could satisfy their desires through the bodies and senses of the living.

In the early 1900s, Dr. Carl A. Wickland, a psychiatrist, dealt extensively with such spirits through the mediumship of his wife, Anna Wickland. Wickland was a respected member of the Chicago Medical Society and was affiliated with many esteemed organizations. He specialized in cases of schizophrenia, paranoia, depression, addiction, manic-depression (now called bi-polar depression), criminal behavior and phobias of all kinds, but stated without question that many incidents of mental illness that he encountered were caused by intruding spirits. "Spirit obsession is a fact – a perversion of a natural law – and is amply demonstrable," Wickland wrote. "This has been proven hundreds of times by causing the supposed insanity or aberration to be temporarily transferred from the victim to a psychic sensitive who is trained for the purpose, and by this method ascertain the cause of the psychosis to be an ignorant or mischievous spirit, whose identity may frequently be verified."

So, can possessing spirits actually cause people to do things against their will? Can they influence our mental and even our sexual behavior? A number of cases of such things have been documented but one of the strangest that I have ever run across was recorded by Hans Freimark, a German author who wrote a number of books on esoteric, occult, and sexual scientific topics in the early 1900s. The following account involved a young Czechoslovakian man, an unsuspected case of mediumship and a complicated and intensely emotional sexual spirit relationship.

The story was related to Freimark by the central character himself, who will be referred to as "Stefan." He was nineteen years old at the time, an aspiring sculptor, and an ambitious young man who had been raised by his mother, a devout Spiritualist. Stefan had never been a follower of the faith, and never had much interest in it, although he was familiar with the movement's beliefs and practices. However, his mother's death changed his outlook on things and he soon began attending lectures, reading books, and delving more deeply into Spiritualism. In the course of a séance with family members, he learned that a year before his mother's death, she had arranged with Stefan's aunt to make certain attempts at communication after she had passed away. The efforts were limited to simple things like rapping noises and the tilting and levitation of a table, which convinced the family that they were in contact with the deceased mother's spirit.

In the midst of the séances, Stefan began to experience what he called "light disturbances of consciousness." Finally, he demanded a paper and pencil and began to write in a flowery style, partly in poetry and partly in consoling messages, evidently from his mother. This was done with astonishing speed and at first, the handwriting was his own but later, as his mother brought forth other spirits to communicate through him, the handwriting changed according to the identity of the person who was speaking through him. His aunt and the other people in the séance group were amazed by what he had accomplished. Unexpectedly, the young man had discovered the power of mediumship. He described his trance states as "kind of a fog in my head." He would envision a white surface and then black letters of the words that he felt compelled to write down. He also began to feel the urge to speak some of the words and when he did, he had the feeling that he had been lifted up, as if he were sitting on his own shoulders. He avoided doing that, however, as it seemed to frighten his aunt.

Yet nothing could be as frightening as the startling events to come.

During one of the lectures that he attended, Stefan met a young man about his age named "George." Like Stefan, he was quiet, shy, and introverted. He had never had a girlfriend and the only friends that he had were acquaintances that he met at Spiritualist meetings. The two young men spoke briefly, but during a séance that evening, George went into a trance and passed on an exciting communication to Stefan about his future. Nevertheless, the friendship did not blossom and the two of them did not see one another again for more than six months. Around that time, Stefan received an expected message from George through a mutual friend, inviting him to his home for a séance. Stefan went and during the sitting, messages were received from the other side that asked for regular séances to be held in order to try and relieve George of his shyness. During the sessions that followed, the two young men became close friends. George sometimes suffered from violent nervous stomach upsets, so the spirits requested that Stefan hypnotize him and try to help him with the situation. Apparently it worked, and the two men became inseparable. Stefan later said, "If I did not find him at home I felt a terrible fear that something had happened to him. My only consolation was that I knew instinctively when he would arrive. I waited often impatiently, but was always right in knowing to the minute when he would walk in."

The two men were very attached to one another, but then things started to take a strange turn. One evening after a birthday celebration that the two men spent alone together, Stefan slipped into a trance state and when he awoke, he found George in a state of great excitement. He explained that another intelligence had spoken through Stefan and that he had been "shaken by the gentle kindness of the message." Stefan knew nothing of what had occurred, only that his head had been filled with soft whisperings while he was in the trance and he had a feeling that was something like intoxication. However, the feeling that he had of an unknown being entering into his body had sent him into a complete unconscious trance.

In order to continue the new "experiments," Stefan and George moved into the same apartment. Stefan's mediumship became more and more developed and in addition to the presence that had so impressed George, a number of other entities were also coming through. Stefan maintained that he knew nothing of the exchanges between the spirits and his friend, but they always left him exhausted. George, however, never tired of his communications with the other side and actually seemed to find a strange, obsessive pleasure in them.

Among the most prominent of the intelligences that came through were an alleged Circassian (an ethnic group, living in the northwestern part of the Caucasus Mountains) women and her brother. According to George, neither he nor Stefan spoke their language, but were gradually able to learn it. Soon, George claimed that he had fallen in love with the Circassian woman and could not bear to be without her. Tia, as she called herself, appeared almost daily during Stefan's trances and many times, George would demand that his friend allow her to come through. Tia was supposed to dance beautifully and others who saw Stefan (while possessed by Tia's spirit) confirmed this. Witnesses also stated that Stefan, who had a slight and rather delicate build, acted very girlish and gave a distinct feminine impression while he was controlled by the spirit. George began to insist that Stefan spend more and more of his days and nights as Tia.

Soon, his obsession began to spiral out of control, taking Stefan along with it. George was now speaking to Tia of marriage and wedding rites and Stefan was surprised to awaken one day and find that one room of their apartment had been converted into a "temple," where the two lovers spent most of their time. Stefan became more and more nervous and irritable during his waking moments and claimed that he was not surprised when his friend came to him one day and asked him to change places with Tia permanently. Tia wanted to take over his spirit and soul and possess him completely.

At first, Stefan refused to even consider the idea but the tension that was created between the two men finally led to him giving into the demand. The exchange of souls took place and Stefan fell into a deep sleep. When he awakened, he claimed to be Tia. He was utterly and completely different, he said, and he was now trapped inside of a body that no longer performed on command. He had no control over himself anymore, but could see what was happening around him. How long this continued is unknown, but one day, George was called away on business and had to leave the city for an extended time. While he was away, without Tia to accompany him, the weird triangle was broken. Tia went away and Stefan awakened to find that he was himself again. The possession was over – at least temporarily.

However, Tia often returned and wrote letters to George through Stefan's hand. When this occurred, he slipped into a deep trance and when he awoke, he would find letters written in a feminine script on the table in front of him. Stefan mailed the letters to his friend, who gratefully received them.

What eventually happened between Stefan, George and Tia is unknown. Hans Freimark recounted the tale in the early 1900s, a time when what amounted to a homosexual affair would not be as widely accepted as it might be today. Was Stefan really possessed by a feminine spirit? Or was this an idea that he created in his mind to make his love for his friend George more acceptable? Undoubtedly, he believed every word of his story to be true and perhaps the two men convinced themselves of the idea of a possessing female spirit as a way to overcome the societal taboo of their affair. We will never know for sure, but if the story is true, perhaps the idea of possessing spirits that can influence our sexuality is not as far-fetched as some might think.

SEX IN THE SEANCE CHAMBER

Spiritualism was born in the late 1840s, but truly came into its own during one of the most repressive periods in history: the Victorian era. During this time of scientific and literary achievements, many people turned to the belief in the spirit world as an antidote to the scholarly agnosticism that could be found each day in the newspapers and on the lips of scientists and writers. In addition, as an escape from the societal restrictions that had been placed on them, many faithful Spiritualists turned to the séance chamber as a way to express their sexual needs, wants and desires. When interacting with the spirits was not titillating enough, mixing in a little eroticism guaranteed an evening's excitement. For just this reason, we cannot underestimate the role that sex played in the practice of Spiritualism.

The movement was created in America in 1848, which seems rather fitting. Historians are often fond of remarking that America has, throughout its relatively short history, been a nation of extremes. Whether it's for the best or not, America has often been host to strong passions and great enthusiasms. They range from the vicious hysteria of the lynch mob to the ecstasies of the religious revival meeting – and even include our enthusiasm for sex. Nowhere is our great passion for the extreme as evident as it is in the history of Spiritualism. The movement swept the country, even in those days before radio, television and the Internet. People became obsessed with this alleged ability to communicate with the dead and even the most conservative, uneducated and average people became part of the new movement.

Although the idea that man was able to communicate with spirits had existed for centuries, modern belief in such a practice came about in March 1848 in Hydesville, New York. The Spiritualist movement would remain strong for nearly a century, enjoying its greatest revival after the Civil War and again after World War I.

The events that led to the founding of Spiritualism began in a cottage rented by the Fox family. John Fox and his wife had two young daughters living at home, Margaret and Kate, and they settled temporarily into the cottage. Soon after moving in, the family began to experience terrifying noises, which led them to believe the house might be haunted. John Fox, who was not a superstitious man, believed that the knockings and tappings had a logical source and one night as he was testing the walls with his knuckles, a number of raps came in reply. One of his daughters, Kate, clapped her hands together and two knocks imitated the sound. Soon, the girls devised an alphabet code to communicate with the presence and this attracted the attention of neighbors, friends and later, newspaper writers and curiosity-seekers from all over the country.

A short time later, the story of the Fox family took a more dramatic turn. Margaret and Kate Fox were both purported to have mediumistic powers and the news of the unearthly communications with the spirit quickly spread. By November 1849, they were both giving public performances of their skills and the Spiritualist movement was born. The mania to communicate with the dead swept the country and the Fox sisters became famous.

But the movement was as controversial as it was exciting. Were those involved with the movement really communicating with the dead? Skeptics, even of those times, were convinced they were not, but the public was not so easily discouraged. Seemingly overnight, Spiritualism became a full-blown religious movement, complete

with scores of followers, its own unique brand of phenomena and codes of conduct for everything from spirit communication to séances.

The Spiritualists believed that the dead could communicate through what were called "mediums." These were sensitive persons who were in touch with the next world. While in a trance, they could pass along messages from the other side. Beside these "message mediums," there were also practitioners who could produce physical phenomena that were said to be the work of the spirits. These phenomena included ghostly lights, unearthly music, levitating objects, disembodied voices and even apparitions. All of this was produced during what were called "séances" (or sittings), which were regarded as the most exciting method of spirit communication. Any number of people could attend and the rooms where the séances took place often contained a large table that the attendees could sit around, smaller tables that were suitable for lifting and tilting, and a cabinet where the mediums could be sequestered while the spirits materialized and performed their tricks. The sessions reportedly boasted a variety of phenomena, including musical instruments that played by themselves and sometimes flew about the room, glowing images, ghostly hands and messages from the dead.

While each séance was different, most had one thing in common in that they were always held in dark or dimly lighted rooms. Believers explained that the darkness provided less of a distraction to the audience and to the medium. They also added that since much of the spirit phenomena were luminous, they were much easier seen in the darkness. Those who were not convinced of the validity of the movement offered another explanation: they believed the dark rooms concealed the practice of fraud.

But while the Spiritualist movement brought the study of ghosts and spirits into the public eye, it also provided fame (and sometimes infamy) to many of those involved. Not only did the mediums gain notoriety, so did many of the investigators, and in many cases, the movement led to their ruin. Even the Fox Sisters, who had known such early notoriety, drank themselves to death and died penniless. The downfalls of many of the mediums came about because of their exposure as fakes. It was obvious that Spiritualism was riddled with cases of deliberate fraud. It seemed easy to fool the thousands of people who were looking for a miracle and many of the mediums began lining their pockets with money they had swindled from naive clients.

Of course, that's not to say that all of the Spiritualists were dishonest. Many of them, like Sir Arthur Conan Doyle, creator of the fictional detective Sherlock Holmes, truly believed in the validity of the movement. At the very worst, many of these believers were good-hearted but gullible and at best, there remain a few mediums for whom no logical explanation of their abilities has been suggested. For as William James said about the medium Lenora Piper, "To upset the conclusion that all crows are black, there is no need to seek demonstration that no crows are black; it is sufficient to produce one white crow; a single one is sufficient." Piper, James believed, was the "one white crow."

Interestingly, Spiritualism was never meant to turn into a faith or religious movement. It was little more than a popular pastime at first when the idea of communicating with the spirits was an amusing way to spend a long winter evening. There were a couple of factors that worked independently to cause Spiritualism to be inflated in importance and to be accepted as an actual religious faith. One of these was the rise of the Apostolic Church in America. The idea of speaking in tongues and being taken over by the Holy Spirit appealed to many and the Pentecostal faith (and its many offshoots) is still going strong today. Despite the fact that many ministers condemned Spiritualism as the "work of the Devil," it was not a far stretch for many to accept the possibility of strange events surrounding spirit communication and religious fervor at the same time.

Spiritualism saw a huge increase in popularity after the Civil War when many grieving people fervently hoped to communicate with their loved ones who had died in the war, but by the early 1900s, the movement had nearly died out. Spiritualism had never really been organized enough to continue, thanks to dissension in its ranks and internal politics among its leaders. The exposure of many frauds also took their toll and with science not being forthcoming about legitimizing the proof of Spiritualistic tenets, the movement began to fall apart. A little more than a decade later, though, World War I brought thousands of the bereaved back to séances when the movement went through its second heyday. Public interest soon cooled again and by the 1930s, the era of the physical medium was over. Most agree that this period was largely killed off by the continued attacks by magicians and debunkers, who exposed fraud after fraud and gave even the legitimate practitioners a bad name. Soon, the mediums no longer wanted to expose themselves to scrutiny and so they abandoned the physical effects of flying trumpets and spirit materializations and turned to mental mediumship instead, which is more along the lines of spirit possession. Spiritualism, although different than it was when it began, still exists today – as strange and perplexing as it was in the nineteenth century.

By the late 1800s, sex had infiltrated Spiritualism in ways that were largely unknown by the public. Unless someone was an actual participant in a séance, or part of an experiment to text the skills of a medium, they were unlikely to read about what was taking place in the séance room. Sex was simply not something that was discussed in public, let alone in newspapers and scientific journals.

It was quite clear, even in the early days, that there existed a strong and scientific connection between mediumship and sex, although it went carefully unmentioned. Dr. W.J. Crawford, a lecturer in mechanical engineering at the Municipal Technical Institute at Belfast, Ireland, carried out a long series of experiments that he devised for the purpose of finding out what part of medium Kathleen Goligher's body produced the mysterious psychic substance known as ectoplasm. The experiments were based on his findings that a type of powder would stick to the ectoplasm and that by placing the powder on the medium's shoes and around her legs, the track of the ectoplasm could be revealed. Careful as he was in his choice of words – speaking of the "top of the stockings" and "inside the legs of the knickers to the joint of the legs" or the ectoplasm returning "by way of the trunk" – it was clear that he was referring to the ectoplasm coming from the medium's vagina, even if he didn't come right out and say it.

For plainer language, we have to look at Baron Schrenck-Notzing's account of the mediumship of Willie Schneider, "With the increase of phenomena, the bodily movements became stronger, the clonic shakings more powerful, cramp-like, the pulse flew up and the respiration grew labored. Perspiration stood on the forehead of the medium. The whole process is very much like a birth process. Biologically, the erotic activity is unmistakable."

Another report about Schneider came from Dr. W. Osborne: "Finally, I could not fail to observe that all of the phenomena produced by an effort on the part of the medium (who perspires very strongly during the demonstration), point to happenings which hang together with the sexual sphere of the medium. It is difficult to make accurate observations in this respect, but the whole corporeal attitude of the medium during and before the phenomenon, the cramp-like increase of the totality of body energies, the rhythm of his movements, his great

Medium Willie Schneider, who many witnesses claimed had an almost sexual response during his trances.

general excitement which strives to reach a high point after the achievement of which the phenomena begin and the medium is visibly exhausted and satisfied, speak for the idea that these things somehow hang together with his sex."

General Joseph Peter of Munich also wrote about Willie Schneider: "The medium, as the phenomena was about to happen, was often in fear and excitement. Willie pressed himself trembling to me and groaned in anxiety. From time to time, however, it seemed he was possessed by erotic feelings; he stroked the hands of his controls with his cheek and began to bite me on the arm. 'Mina' [his female controlling spirit] would only desist after very emphatic requests."

The famous Italian medium Eusapia Palladino, was one of the most sexual Spiritualists of the early 1900s. She claimed that after excessive mediumistic practice, she would bleed more freely during menstruation. Her trance states were also very peculiar, especially to some of the strait-laced observers of the time. Enrico Morselli wrote, "The passing into a more advanced state of trance is truly indicated by sighs, yawns, sobs, of alternating redness and pallor of the face, perspiration on the forehead, light transparency of the palms of the hands, the alteration of voice and the quick changes of facial expression. Eusapia then progresses through a diversity of emotional states and now she is prey to a species of concentrated rage which she expresses with quick movements, with imperious commands, with sarcastic phrases directed at her critics, with smiles and loud laughter which is something diabolical. Then she passes into a state of decided voluptuous ecstasy, throwing about both her arms, squeezing us with her tensed thighs and trembling feet, resting her head and abandoning her whole body on my or Barzini's shoulders while we fearlessly resist this innocent attack against our masculine emotions."

Simply put, sex could not be disassociated from Spiritualism because mediums were human beings. They either had a normal, if somewhat impaired, sex life, or they had none, in which case something abnormal was likely to happen. If the energies bound up within the body cannot be released in a physical way, then it would certainly be expended in some other manner. In mediumship, sexual energies may have furnished fuel for the many physical, and perhaps mental, manifestations that occurred during séances.

However, sex may have also furnished even more controversy to an already beleaguered movement that was filled with scandal and questionable practices. In the accounts that follow, we will take a closer look at some of the more sexual mediums of Spiritualism's "golden age" and the reader can judge whether or not the stories that emerged helped, or hindered, the movement.

THE MEDIUM AND THE SCIENTIST

The claims being made by the Spiritualists about their contact with the dead inspired a need for the investigation of those claims. This research was not done so that the Spiritualists could be exposed as frauds (although this sometimes happened) but because the evidence that was being presented had to be questioned.

This new psychic investigation began just shortly after the birth of Spiritualism. By the 1850s, science had managed to challenge the hold that religion maintained on society, offering a new version of the truth for people to examine. Mixed into this time period was Spiritualism, with its alleged proof of life after death, and the public became fascinated by it. Not long after, however, many of the practitioners of this new faith were exposed as frauds and a division formed between those who believed in Spiritualism and those who did not.

The scientific establishment, resentful over the fact that they had managed to break the hold that religion had on society only to lose their footing to Spiritualism, encouraged the debunking of mediums and had a blatant disregard for anything that even hinted at the supernatural. In spite of this, there were a small number of scientists who had taken the time to attend séances and who believed that there could be something to the strange phenomena that was being reported. They decided to try and apply the laws of science in investigating these reports.

By the late 1800s, there were a number of scientists who investigated the claims of mediums. Many of them operated independently, while others formed groups like the Society for Psychical Research (SPR), which became one of the most esteemed investigative organizations in the world.

One of the most eminent scientists to become involved in psychical investigation was Sir William Crookes, one of the great scientists of the modern age. Crookes decision to delve into Spiritualism was greeted with wide approval. The popular press felt sure that Crookes would soon show that Spiritualist claims were nothing more than ridiculous humbug. Crookes appeared to share that view. When he announced that he was going to begin his investigations, he stated that he had no preconceived notions on the subject and then added, "The increased employment of scientific methods will produce a race of observers who will drive the worthless residuum of Spiritualism hence into the unknown limbo of magic and necromancy." This statement was taken as a disclaimer of belief in Spiritualism but if Crookes' private beliefs had been better known, it could have been interpreted that he intended only to disprove the "worthless residuum" of psychic frauds without prejudice to the basic beliefs. Crookes had first come into contact with Spiritualism in 1867 and his diary entries for December 1870 --- within months of declaring his intention of studying Spiritualism --- showed that he was already a firm believer in the possibility of the "unknown power."

Crookes was born in London in 1832 and was largely self-taught, with no regular schooling, until he enrolled in the Royal College of Chemistry at age sixteen. He graduated in 1854 and took a position as the superintendent of the meteorological department at Radcliffe Observatory, Oxford. A year later, he took a teaching position as a professor of chemistry at Chester Training College, but resigned after one year because he was not given a laboratory in which he could do research. Although he tried to find another teaching position, he was never successful and most of his later work was done in a laboratory at his home. In 1856, Crookes married Ellen Humphrey, with whom he had eight children, and from his home, he began writing and editing for scientific journals like the *Chemical News*. He also helped to found the *Quarterly Journal of Science* in 1864. In 1861, Crookes achieved the first of his scientific discoveries: the element thallium and the correct measurement of its atomic weight. This got him elected a Fellow of the Royal Society at age thirty-one.

Sir William Crookes in later years

Then, in 1867, came a turning point in Crookes' life with the death of his youngest brother, Phillip. The two men had been very close and Crookes was very disturbed by his brother's death and, like others of the time who suffered a great loss, he turned to Spiritualism for answers. At the urging of his friend and fellow scientist, Cromwell Varney, Crookes and his wife attended some séances to try and make contact with Phillip. Although the details of these sessions are unknown, Crookes believed they were successful. One of his first séances was with the famous medium D.D. Home, where Crookes was amazed to see phenomena that he never dreamed possible before. The scientist was not content to simply observe Home's manifestations, he also attempted to re-create them in the laboratory, and this was also successful.

Crookes applied strict scientific controls during his research with Home and the meticulous testing failed to find any evidence of fraud. He believed that Home possessed a "psychic force" which emanated from his body and he wrote a paper on the subject, believing it to be of scientific importance. Not surprisingly, the paper was first rejected and then met with scorn and derision when it was finally published. His critics, mainly other scientists, lashed out and stated that the phenomena Crookes reported could not have occurred, that it was simply impossible. "I never said that it was possible," Crookes replied, "I only said that it was true."

Although the scientific community frequently criticized him, Crookes continued his investigations into the spirit world, testing mediums and publishing material on the science of the afterlife. Crookes last series of sittings were experiments conducted with a medium of rather dubious reputation named Anna Eva Fay. After this, he turned away from psychic research for a time and returned to his scientific pursuits. Although he supported the foundation of the Society for Psychical Research in 1882, and even served as its president in 1886, he did not take an active part in the group's investigations.

In 1875, Crookes earned the Royal Medal for his work and one year later invented the radiometer, a device which demonstrated the effects of radiation on objects in a vacuum, and a special device called the "Crookes Tube" that went along with it. This invention would lead to the discovery of cathode rays, X-rays and the electron.

Crookes went on to serve on scientific committees, earned prestigious awards for his discoveries and invented an instrument that would be used to study subatomic particles, and yet he never wavered in his belief in Spiritualism. In 1916, after the death of his wife, Crookes attempted to communicate with her and was unsuccessful, but after a visit to a spirit photographer, he was able to obtain what he believed to be photographic proof that her presence was still with him. Sadly, this plate, under modern study, appears to have been double-exposed and is therefore a fake.

Crookes died in April 1919, never questioning that fact that the spirit world was genuine and that there were things his beloved science would never truly be able to explain.

In addition to his work with D.D. Home, there was one medium with whom Crookes was most closely linked: the controversial Florence Cook. It would be his work with this young woman, barely out of her teens, that would not only overshadow much of the important work that Crookes did in the world of psychical research, but would lead to an alleged sex scandal that would forever taint his reputation.

Florence Cook

During the heyday of Spiritualism, Florence Cook became one of the movement's most famous mediums. She was noted for her ability to produce full-form spirit materializations and became known as the first medium to do so in a fully gas-lighted room. Cook's manifestation was that of her spirit guide, Katie King. Katie already had a long history before being forever attached to the persona of Florence Cook. She first appeared during the initial Spiritualism craze of the 1850s and graced the séances of many famous mediums. Like her spectral father, John King, "Katie" was not her real name. In life, she was said to have been Annie Owen Morgan, the daughter of the pirate Henry Morgan, who had been knighted and appointed governor of Jamaica. He preferred to be known as "John King" in the afterlife, though, and his daughter adopted his name. In life, Annie Morgan had been a self-professed liar and cheat, as well as a thief and an adulteress -- and all this before she died in her twenties. Her new mission, in death, was to prove to the world the truth of Spiritualism and of course, to prove the talents of a few mediums in particular. One of these was Florence Cook.

Florence (or Florrie, as her mother called her) was born in London's crowded, impoverished East End in 1856 and as a child claimed she could hear the voices of angels. Her mother would later state that the girl had always been aware of the presence of spirits but her psychic gifts only began to manifest at age fifteen, when she levitated a piece of furniture during a table tilting session with friends. When she was still an adolescent, she began conducting séances in her home, where she became known for being able to manifest "spirit faces." To create a cabinet of the kind mediums used, Florence would sit inside a large cupboard in her family's breakfast room. A hole had been cut high up on the door and it was here where the faces would appear.

Florence would climb into the cabinet and would allow herself to be bound to a chair with ropes about her neck, waist and wrists. The door would be closed and the sitters would sing a hymn to create the proper mood. The cabinet door would be opened again to show that Cook was still tied to the chair, and then closed. A few moments later, the faces would appear in the opening. When they finally vanished, the doors would again be opened and Florence would be revealed, still tied to her chair and apparently exhausted from allowing the spirits to use her energy in order to appear. A few people noticed that the faces, which were draped with a thin white cloth, looked an awful lot like Florence. They suggested that the girl simply slipped her ropes, stood on the chair to stick her face through the hole, then tied herself back up again. Nevertheless, the audience loved her performances and she soon gained a following. Many were impressed by the fact that she never charged a fee for her séances and others came merely because she was an exceptionally attractive young lady.

With that in mind, it's no surprise that the pretty young girl quickly became famous. In addition to her looks, her séances had other appeals as well, including the fact that the spirits had a habit of tossing her into the air and -- on at least one occasion -- ripping her clothing off. While Florence basked in the newfound attention, some of her friends, and her employer, were becoming unsettled by her new gifts. Miss Eliza Cliff for one, in whose school Florence worked as an assistant teacher, was reluctantly forced to discontinue her employment. The girls in the school were unsettled by the strange happenings that seemed to occur around Miss Cook and their parents were afraid that the young ladies might become affected themselves. She was quite fond of Florrie but was "compelled to part with her."

By 1872, full-form materializations had become very popular at séances and one night, in that same year, a white face appeared in the darkness outside the curtains of Florrie's cabinet. The floating mask was announced to be the face of Katie King, who was already a spirit to be reckoned with in America. But Katie was not the mysterious and ethereal figure of Spiritualist writings --- she was a proof of the resurrection of the dead, a spirit made flesh and a young woman who could walk among and talk with the sitters. Her new body was almost indistinguishable from that of a living girl. She was a beautiful young lady in fact, and unfortunately, very close in resemblance to Florence Cook.

As with most Spiritualist mediums of the day, Florence preferred to enter her trances within the confines of the spirit cabinet, out of sight of the sitters. As long as thirty minutes might pass before the curtain would part and a figure, dressed all in white and looking quite pale, would emerge as Florrie continued to lie unconscious in the cabinet. Occasionally, while Katie was present, Florrie could be heard sobbing and moaning inside the cabinet, as if the manifestation were draining her energy. During Katie's first appearances, the spirit would simply smile and nod at the audience, but later, she began to walk amongst them, offering her (strangely solid) hand and talking to them. She was fond of touching the sitters and allowing them to carefully touch her, as well. After Katie returned to the cabinet, Cook would be found, still tied up and seemingly exhausted

It was believed that spirit forms, like Katie, were actually made up of that mysterious substance known as ectoplasm. It was generally regarded during the heyday of the movement that interfering with ectoplasm, or with the body of the entranced medium, could be dangerous to the medium's health. If this is true, then on one occasion, Florence Cook had a very close call.

While it was highly improper for sitters to grab at the spirits, or to touch the medium, during a séance, it did sometimes happen. On the night of December 9, 1873, one of the sitters at a Cook séance was a man named William Volckman. Although an invited guest, he apparently became quite agitated by the "obvious similarities" between the medium and the ghost. In a fit of anger, he jumped up and grabbed Katie by the wrist, announcing loudly that she was Florence in disguise. For a spirit, Katie put up quite a fight and managed to succeed in leaving several bloody scratches on the man's nose. Katie was finally rescued by Edward Elgie Corner, Florence's fiancée; by the Earl and Countess of Caithness and by barrister Henry Dunphy, who were friends of the Cook family and aware of the inherent danger in interfering with an apparition. They seized Volckman and a scuffle ensued, allowing Katie to make her escape. According to Dunphy, she disappeared, dissolving from the feet upward. Volckman was determined to follow up on his assault, though, and he rushed to the cabinet. There, he found no sign of Katie but he did find Florrie with her clothing in disarray, but still tied up.

Was this a case of a skeptical investigator gone berserk, or something else? It is significant that shortly after this incident, Volckman married another famous London medium named Agnes Nichol Guppy, a portly widow who was very jealous of Florence and her fame. The incident with Volckman did not immediately harm Florrie's career as a medium, but it did shake the faith of some. She suffered a slight reversal of fortune for a time and began looking for a new angle to pursue to garner some much-needed favorable publicity.

At about this same time, medium Daniel Douglas Home was undergoing testing by Sir William Crookes. Florrie quickly got in touch with Crookes and offered to add her own contribution to psychical research. Crookes was delighted to investigate the now-famous partnership of Florrie and Katie King and happily agreed to a series of private séances. Shortly after, what many consider to be the most problematical investigations of the Spiritualist

(Left) The manifestation of Katie King was achieved while Florence Cook was allegedly secured inside of her spirit cabinet. Katie was said to be very life-like and often appeared nude to the sitters at Florence's séances.

(Right) This photo was supposed to prove that Florence and Katie were two separate beings but unfortunately, Katie's face is obscured, making her impossible to identify.

era began.

Once the investigations started, Crookes invited Florence, and occasionally her mother and sister, to stay with him at his home on Mornington Road in northwest London. Crookes knew that most Spiritualists had a distrust of scientists and he hoped to rectify this by inviting the young woman into his home and befriending her. Mrs. Crookes was in the house, but was not much in evidence, as she was expecting their tenth child at the time and was usually confined to her room.

The first time that Crookes had experienced Katie had been when Florrie had initially approached him about the investigations. He had visited the Cook home and took part in a séance. He was well aware of the fact that many skeptics believed that Florence and her spirit guide, Katie, were one in the same person but Crookes took note that while watching the materialized Katie, he distinctly heard "a sobbing, moaning sound from behind the curtain where the young woman was supposed to be sitting." In spite of this, critics were not impressed.

In March 1874, though, Crookes obtained what he felt was "absolute proof" that Florrie and Katie were two separate entities. During a séance, Katie had walked among the sitters for a time and then retreated behind the curtain where Florence had been bound to a chair. In a minute, she reappeared and asked Crookes to accompany her behind the curtain. According to his account, he found the unconscious form of Florence Cook, still bound with sealed tape. Katie had vanished, leaving Florence behind. "I found Miss Cook," he wrote, "had partially slipped off the sofa, and her head hanging in a very awkward position. I lifted her onto the sofa and in so doing, had satisfactory evidence, in spite of the darkness, that Miss Cook was not attired in "Katie" costume but had on her ordinary black velvet dress, and was in deep trance." According to Crookes' account, he checked three different times to be sure that the woman on the floor, illuminated by a dim gas light, was actually Florence and he was convinced that she and Katie were separate individuals.

However, Crookes had still not seen them together. This opportunity came on March 29, he said, when Katie invited him into the cabinet after he had turned out the gaslight in the room. He carried with him a phosphorus light, which cast only a very dim glow. However, Crookes claimed to be able to see adequately. He wrote:

I went cautiously into the room, it being dark, and felt about for Miss Cook. I found her crouching on the floor. Kneeling down, I let air enter the phosphorus lamp, and by its light I saw the young lady dressed in black velvet, as she had been in the early part of the evening. And to all appearances perfectly senseless; she did not move when I took her hand and held the light quite close to her face, but continued quietly breathing. Raising the lamp, I looked around and saw Katie standing close behind Miss Cook. She was robed in flowing white drapery as we had seen her previously in the séance. Holding one of Miss Cook's hands in mine, and still kneeling, I passed the lamp up and down so as to illuminate Katie's whole figure, and satisfy myself thoroughly that I was really looking at the veritable Katie... and not the phantasm of a disordered brain. Three separate times did I turn the lamp to Katie and examine her with steadfast scrutiny until I had no doubt whatever of her objective reality. At last Miss Cook moved slightly, and Katie instantly motioned me to go away. I went to another part of the cabinet and then ceased to see Katie, but did not leave the room till Miss Cook woke up, and two of the visitors came in with a light.

Was this proof that Katie really was a ghost?

Perhaps --- but not all of the sitters at her séances were completely convinced. Many of them insisted on extreme measures to prevent Florence from practicing trickery. Customarily, before the séance would begin, Florrie would be bound with a cord or sealed with tape. Each time, the bindings were found to still be intact at the end of the evening. And although the indignities that were later inflicted on mediums, such as filling their mouth with fruit juice to prevent ventriloquism and checking all of their orifices for secreted ectoplasm, were never pressed onto Florrie, her hair was nailed to the floor on at least one occasion. Believe it or not, Katie still appeared.

In 1874, Crookes began test Florence and he produced a number of photographs of Katie King and was allowed to test her appearances with Florence in plain sight. During the test, Florence reclined on a sofa behind a curtain and wrapped a shawl about her face. Soon, Katie appeared in front of the curtain. Crookes checked to be sure that Cook was still lying on the sofa and he saw that she was --- although incredibly, he never moved the shawl to be sure that it was really her.

Crookes created fifty-five photographs of Florence and Katie but only a handful of them remain today. The rest were destroyed, along with the negatives, shortly before his death in 1919. Crookes used five cameras, two of them stereoscopic, operating simultaneously during the sessions. Many of the photos were both poorly shot and questionable in authenticity and while many of them purported to show both Katie and Florence at the same time, they mainly played right into the hands of the debunkers.

Crookes was called into question about his testing methods but he rushed to the defense of his subject. He stated that Florence agreed to every test that he submitted without question and that he had never seen the slightest inclination on her part to try and deceive him. "Indeed, I do not believe that she could carry on a deception is she were to try," Crookes wrote, "and if she did she would be certainly found out very quickly, for such a line of action is altogether foreign to her nature."

Crookes may have been convinced of the genuineness of the Cook-King collaboration but his critics were not. Katie looked so much like Florrie simply because that's who she was, the skeptics said. It was not simply good enough to cite Crookes' integrity and his stature as a scientist to convince someone of the authenticity of the séances. They also say that it was possible that Crookes might have had a sexual relationship with Florrie, which would explain his willingness to help her perpetrate fraud. And while no evidence of this exists, it would be naive of us not to consider the possibility of it.

There are five possible explanations for the seemingly unexplainable events that occurred between Crookes, Florence and Katie:

1. That the scientist became embroiled in an affair with Florence under his wife's nose and that he colluded with her to manufacture fraudulent results for the Katie King investigation. This sex scandal followed Crookes to the grave. Not only was the suggestion made during his lifetime but many years later it has re-surfaced as a possible explanation for his seemingly naïve acceptance of Florence's fraud.

2. That Crookes was enamored with the girl, or her alter ego of Katie, and that he kept up the pretense that he believed her act to save face and to keep her close to him. It has also been suggested that perhaps Crooke fell in love with the girl, but the affair was a one-sided one. The brilliant scientist is believed by some to have immediately seen through Florence's fraud but, because he was infatuated with her, he chose to ignore it.

3. That Florence employed a double to pretend to be Katie King. This is not as outrageous as it might sound. During the investigations, a young medium named Mary Showers stayed in the Crookes' residence while Florence was there. She performed a double act with Florrie as the two of them would go into trances together and would create two materializations, one of Katie and one of "Florence Maple," who bore more than a passing resemblance to Mary. Would it not have been possible for Mary, or even for Florence's sister, to have simply stepped in and pretended to be an unconscious Florrie, slumped over and usually covered, while Florrie walked about as Katie King?

4. That Florence truly believed that she was manifesting a "spirit," while she had actually created a split personality, which she called Katie King. To most modern readers, the accounts of Katie's manifestations contain many clues about the nature of Florence and her possible alter ego. Katie flirted and teased, wandering about the darkened room and sitting on laps, touching and being touched and, on one occasion, even stepping out of her robes to reveal her naked form. "Now you can see that I am a woman," she said. Could Katie have been a way for the repressed young lady of the Victorian era, as Florrie undoubtedly was, to act out her innermost desires? And if so, was she doing it consciously --- or had she actually convinced herself that the manifestation of Katie was real?

4. Our final explanation: that Florence was a genuine medium, that Katie was real and that Crookes' investigations were completely genuine. Although Crookes behaved strangely for a man with a scientist's regard for detail --- such as omitting names and addresses of witnesses from his record --- this may have been in regard for Florrie's strict rules of secrecy.

In addition, we can look to the eyewitness accounts of the séances that survive. According to Mrs. Ross-Church, who was better known as the novelist Florence Marryat, Katie resembled Florrie in some ways but was remarkably different in others. She stated that Katie was taller and heavier than Florence and that Katie had red hair, while Florrie's hair was dark and almost black. Crookes had also noted a number of differences between the two young women. Katie was taller, heavier and broader in the face, had a fairer complexion and longer fingers. Florrie had pierced ears, Katie did not. On one occasion, Florence had a large blister on her neck but when Katie appeared, her neck was as fair and smooth as usual. Another time, Katie's lungs seemed to be clear while Florence was under treatment for a severe cough.

Unbelievably, though, as when he failed to check under the shawl, Crookes took no comparison photographs to show the pierced and unpierced ears or the length of the girls' fingers. Or if he did, he left no record of them. This seems amazing in that Crookes was investigating a phenomenon that could theoretically change the way the world believed.

But not everyone was so careless. Cromwell Varley, the famous electrician who worked on the Atlantic cable, believed that he had proof that Katie and Florence were not the same person. Varley, an ardent Spiritualist, designed a test to prove that Florence was still in the cabinet while Katie walked about the séance room. Florence was placed in an electrical circuit with wires connected to coins that were placed on her arms so that a small current was running through her body. A large galvanometer --- an instrument that detects and measures small electrical currents --- was placed ten feet away from the cabinet. It was placed on a mantelpiece in full view of the sitters so that the flow of electricity could be monitored. If the medium broke the circuit in order to leave the cabinet dressed as Katie, the galvanometer would register wild fluctuations. Katie appeared as usual and there was no change in the current. Crookes asked Katie to plunge her hands into a chemical solution that would cause a change in the current flow if Florence had managed to dress as Katie and still get out of the cabinet. Again, the galvanometer showed no fluctuation in the current.

Did this prove that Katie and Florence were not the same person? Perhaps, but it still didn't prove that Katie King was a spirit. It's still very possible that she could have been Florrie's sister or her friend, Mary Showers.

In 1875, Katie sadly announced that she would soon be leaving Florence and that her time visiting Earth would soon be at an end. Crookes later wrote of a scene that he witnessed when Florence and Katie said their final goodbyes. According to his account, Katie made one last appearance in the séance room and then walked over to where Florrie was lying on the floor. She touched the medium on the shoulder and implored her to wake up, explaining that she had to leave. They talked for a few moments until "Miss Cook's tears prevented her from speaking." Crookes was asked to come over and hold Florence in his arms, as she was falling to the floor and sobbing hysterically, and when he looked around, the white-robed figure of Katie was gone.

With Katie now gone, there was no point in Florrie staying on for further investigations. In fact, she told Crookes for the first time, she had been married about two months before to Edward Corner. Florence went into a sort of retirement for six years but then returned to the Spiritualist scene manifesting a new spirit, this one named Marie. This new spirit partner managed to provide even more entertainment that Katie had, singing and dancing for the sitters at her séances and providing contact with the spirit world.

But there was something about "Marie" that was beginning to bother people. At a séance in 1880, Sir George Sitwell noticed that Marie's spirit robes covered corset stays, so he reached out and grabbed hold of her. He held on tightly to her and when he pulled aside Florrie's curtain, he found that the medium's chair was empty. He was not surprised to discover that he was holding onto Florence, clad only in her underwear.

After that, Florence would only perform if someone were tied up in the cabinet with her. On at least one occasion, Florence Marryat participated and she later testified that during Marie's appearance, she was firmly tied to Florence in the cabinet. This wasn't enough to keep her audience, though, and Florence vanished into relative obscurity as a housewife in Monmouthshire. She gave her last séance in 1899 and passed away at age forty-eight in 1904.

SPIRITUALISM'S MOST OVERSEXED MEDIUM

Toward the end of the nineteenth century, the rise of Spiritualist organizations caused a relative decline in the sort of mediumship practiced by some of the early members of the movement, who were often exposed as frauds. The organized groups were now taking steps to examine the claims of their own members and they did so with such thoroughness that mediums began to act with caution. This is not to say that physical mediumship began to disappear from the scene, but the emphasis began to shift in 1880s away from tipping tables and tooting horns to a more serious attempt to examine those proofs of spirit existence that took the form of messages and information. Commercial mediumship suffered for a time.

And then along came Eusapia Palladino. This Italian peasant woman became almost single-handedly responsible for restoring the prestige of physical mediumship and went on to became perhaps the most famous medium of the period --- and one who more than made up for the lack of controversy that surrounded the more respected mediums of the day.

Eusapia Palladino was born near Bari in southern Italy in 1854. Her mother died shortly after she was born and her father was murdered in 1866, leaving Eusapia an orphan at the age of twelve. Even then, it was later reported, she had experienced many strange and supernatural events, such as rapping sounds on the furniture, eerie whispers and unseen hands that would rip the blankets from her bed at night.

Friends and relatives sent Eusapia to Naples, where it was hoped that she would find a position as a nursemaid. Things did not go well. The family that hired her was disturbed by the fact that the eerie events continued to occur around the young girl and also by the fact that Eusapia refused to conform to life in the city. She had a stubborn streak that ran through her character, which often showed itself in her refusal to bathe, comb her hair or learn to read. She was soon dismissed from her position.

She took shelter with some family friends who dabbled in Spiritualism. Eusapia attended a séance one night

Eusapia Palladino

and almost as soon as she sat down at the table, it tilted and then rose completely into the air. She began to act as a medium to reportedly avoid being sent to a convent, although she claimed that she was afraid of her powers and avoided using them. The family she was staying with asked Eusapia to stay on with them, and continue holding séances, but with her typical independence, she moved out and began to work as a laundress. She later married a merchant named Raphael Delgaiz and worked in his shop for a time before starting to offer séances on a professional basis.

In 1872, a wealthy and influential Spiritualist couple named Damiani sought Eusapia out. They had heard good things about the séances that she had been conducting and wanted to introduce her into society. Unfortunately, the coarse and rude young woman was no more interested in education and social polish than she had been years before and her introduction was a disaster. The Damianis' efforts to develop and study Eusapia's powers proved thankless and she lapsed back into a life of ordinary mediumship, virtually unknown outside of a small circle in Naples.

In this way, Eusapia would have lived out her entire life if she had not come to the attention of Ercole Chiaia, a doctor and occult buff, who sought her out in 1886. Acting almost like a manager, Chiaia took upon himself to publish an open letter to the famed Italian psychiatrist and criminologist Cesare Lombroso. In the letter, which he wrote as if describing a patient, Chiaia gave a summary of Eusapia's mediumistic abilities and urgently requested Lombroso's help in determining whether or not she possessed some sort of new physical force. The letter turned out to be a stroke of genius for Eusapia's career. Even though Lombroso ignored the letter (at that time), her livelihood saw an immediate boost.

In Nandor Fodor's *Encyclopedia of Psychic Science*, he quotes from Chiaia's letter:

She is 30 years old and very ignorant; her appearance is neither fascinating nor endowed with the power which modern criminologists call irresistible; but when she wishes, be it day or night, she can divert a curious group for an hour or so with the most surprising phenomena. Either bound to a seat or firmly held by the hands of the curious, she attracts to her the articles of furniture which surround her, lifts them up, holds them suspended in the air like Mahomet's coffin, and makes them come down again with undulatory movements, as if they were obeying her will. She increases their height or lessens it according to her pleasure. She raps or taps upon the walls, the ceiling, the floor, with fine rhythm and cadence. In response to the requests of the spectators something like flashes of electricity shoots forth from her body, and envelops her or enwraps the spectators of their marvelous scenes. She draws upon cards that you hold out, everything that you want --- figures, signatures, numbers, sentences, by just stretching out her hand toward the indicated place.

If you place in the corner of the room a vessel containing a layer of soft clay, you will find after some moments the imprint in it of a small or large hand, the image of a face (front view or profile) from which a plaster cast can be taken. In this way portraits of a face at different angles have been preserved, and those who desire so can thus make serious and important studies.

This woman rises in the air, no matter what hands tie her down. She seems to lie upon empty air, as on a couch, contrary to all the laws of gravity; she plays on musical instruments --- organs, bells, tambourines --- as if they had been touched by her hands or moved by the breath of invisible gnomes. This woman at times can increase her stature by more than four inches.

She is like an India rubber doll, like an automaton of a new kind; she takes strange forms. How many legs and arms has she? We do not know. While her limbs are being held by incredulous spectators, we see other limbs coming into view, without her knowing where they come from. Her shoes are too small to fit these witch-feet of hers, and this particular circumstance gives rise to the intervention of a mysterious power.

This letter, which turned out to be her first real introduction to the glare of the public spotlight, would be typical of Palladino's entire career. It described incidents in the séance room that were both common Spiritualist manifestations, along with events that were much more rare --- and much harder to explain. What, for example, was to be made of the bowls of clay where handprints appeared and yet were out of reach of the bound medium? And what of the phantom feet and limbs that appeared and could not be explained? Nearly the entire history of Palladino's next thirty years was devoted to accounts of the committees and investigators who sought to answer these, and other, mysteries about her.

The first major researcher to seek out Eusapia was Cesare Lombroso, the same man who had ignored the letter from Chiaia two years before. He came to Naples in 1890 and arranged to hold a number of private séances with Eusapia at his hotel. Most of these initial sessions were below the level of Eusapia's usual impressiveness, with one exception. At the close of one séance, the lights had been turned up and the observers were discussing their impressions while Eusapia was still tied to a chair, about eighteen inches in front of the curtain that formed her spirit cabinet. Suddenly, sounds were heard from the alcove behind her, the curtain began to swing and billow forward and then a small table emerged from behind it and began to slide across the floor towards the medium. Lombroso and his associates hurried into the cabinet, convinced that a confederate must be hiding inside, but it was empty, save for a few musical instruments. The observers were stumped and Lombroso dismissed any previous doubts that he had about Eusapia's abilities. He had no explanation for what he had seen.

Lombroso published a report of his findings and it was greeted with shock and surprise by many. Other investigators began contacting the medium and in October 1892, Eusapia was asked to sit for a scientific committee in Milan. Among its five members were Lombroso himself and Professor Charles Richet, a noted student of psychic phenomena and a winner in 1913 of the Nobel Prize in physiology and medicine. He would also go on to publish a number of books about psychic phenomena and investigate other mediums during his career.

The séances that were held for the Milan committee were the first of which there were relatively reliable records concerning the manifestations of Palladino. They are also the first to not only make note of unexplained occurrences but also of something else that would shadow the career of the medium: Eusapia cheated.

There was no question whatsoever, even among her most ardent supporters, that she took advantage of every lapse in attention or muscular relaxation on the part of those who were supposed to "control" her movements, in order to produce touches, raps, or movements of objects in places where they should have been impossible. Sometimes her tricks were clumsy and obvious and at other times, subtle and clever but it could not be denied that she cheated. It seemed to make no difference to her that she might be exposed in these activities (as she repeatedly was). Given the slightest opportunity, Eusapia cheated.

One of her most common ruses was to convince the two people assigned to hold her arms that each had continued to keep contact with a separate limb, when actually one of them had transferred his hand to her other arm. This was possible because Eusapia constantly moved about while in her trances, thrashing restlessly back and forth. In the course of her tossing her head and waving her arms about, it took great skill on the part of the handlers to be sure they were not both controlling the same hand. This was especially true as the handlers were usually allowed only to follow the medium's hands by touch but not to restrain her movements in any way. Because of all of the excitement, it was also nearly impossible to decide whether or not Eusapia's feet were where they were supposed to be.

And while the reports from the Milan sittings made it clear that Eusapia would cheat whenever she could, there were also manifestations that occurred that could not be explained. During the sessions, which were held by a dim red light, members were able to see and feel what were apparently a number of spectral hands that groped outward from behind the cabinet curtain while the medium remained plainly visible in front of them. Even given the fact that Eusapia was not above faking certain effects, was it possible for anyone (let alone a semiliterate peasant woman with no knowledge of applied mechanics) to bring about such happenings through trickery? That is the exasperating problem that haunted the scientific minds of the time and still haunts us about Eusapia Palladino today.

Eusapia continued to baffle scientists and investigators. She performed for Russian zoologist N.P. Wagner in Naples in January 1893 and then did so again later in Rome. She sat for Polish psychologist Julian Ochorowicz in Warsaw at the end of the year and at the beginning of 1894. During every session, the results were mixed. Some of the effects that occurred were plainly the result of cheating. Some of them could have been produced by cheating, although witnesses were prepared to state that no cheating had taken place. And some of the effects were judged to be inexplicable in terms of any of the methods of deception that Eusapia had so far been known to use ---- and possibly inexplicable in any way whatsoever.

A more revealing series of séances was held in 1894 at the home of Professor Charles Richet in France. Almost every member of this group of sitters was major name in the fledgling field of psychical research. In addition to Richet himself, the earlier mentioned Dr. Julian Ochorowicz, and the German researcher Baron von Schrenck-Notzing, there were also four highly influential English investigators. They were Sir Oliver Lodge, Professor and Mrs. Henry Sidgwick and Frederick William Henry Myers, all of whom had been founders of the Society for Psychical Research (SPR) in 1882.

The entire group was well aware of the medium's tendency to cheat and the need for suspicious watchfulness. In spite of this, they observed the cabinet curtain billowing when there was no breeze, they experienced repeated "spirit touches" at times when all were certain that Eusapia could not have been responsible and saw and heard objects being moved around the séance chamber. One of these items was a stalkless melon that weighed more than fifteen pounds. It somehow moved from a chair behind the medium to the top of the séance table.

Even if Eusapia had managed to get a hand (or foot) free on this occasion, it's difficult to guess how she could have grasped an object as smooth as a melon, somehow moved it from a chair behind her to a table and managed to do it before the eyes of a group of trained observers. It seems impossible and because of this, alternate theories emerged to explain the incident. Some suggested that the observers had simply hallucinated the "magic melon." Others claimed that one or more of the committee members had been in league with the medium, which seems even more unlikely given the reputations of those present.

So, how did this bizarre event occur? No one knew then and no one knows now. This is why investigators came to realize that there was a need for the more extensive use of recording devices and photographs during investigations. That way, the control of the medium and the occurrence of the phenomena would not be subject to errors in human perception. Unfortunately, even after this important series of séances, such improved methods of investigation were not used with Palladino until a later period, and even then, were not as thoroughly applied as they should have been.

After the sittings in France, the next important sessions with Eusapia took place in England and were generally regarded as a disaster. Of the four English participants in the investigations of Professor Richet, only Sir Oliver Lodge had found himself completely satisfied that Eusapia's phenomena were in part supernatural. The others, Myers and the Sidgwicks, wanted further trials before they could reach firm opinions. They invited Palladino to sit for them at Myer's home in Cambridge, where she went in the late summer of 1895.

Unfortunately, no detailed record of the Cambridge séances was ever published by the SPR and so we have no way of knowing what led up the conclusions reached by those involved. We only know that in October 1895, Professor Sidgwick announced at the society's general meeting that nothing had been witnessed at Cambridge that could not be put down to trickery. He then went on to withdraw what limited support that he had for Palladino, based on the French sittings, and to state that he had come to believe that all of her manifestations were fraudulent. Myers joined Sidgwick in rejecting the Cambridge séances, although he did choose to reserve judgment on what he had seen in France, which he claimed was more impressive.

No one knows for sure what occurred in Cambridge that summer but it is clear that there were things about Palladino that would have likely offended the Sidgwicks and their friends, regardless of the quality of her mediumship. In fact, had it not been for her inexplicable abilities, it is highly unlikely that these highly cultivated English people would have ever associated with a person like Eusapia. Regardless of her reputation as a medium, she did not fit into the mold of previous major mediums. She had none of the social graces or charm of many of the mediums and certainly none of the sober, upright character of others. Instead, she was almost everything that her Cambridge hosts were not: poorly educated, coarse, emotional, loud and quite uninhibited about her interest in the opposite sex. She tended to wake from her trances hot, sweaty and sexually aroused. On many occasions, she tried climbing onto the laps of male sitters at her séances. She was not shy in making in clear that she was looking for intercourse, or that she wanted it immediately. Despite her weight and unattractive appearance, she had no shortage of men who were happy to volunteer – all for the good of the spirit world, of course.

Needless to say, Eusapia's overtly sexual behavior was considered quite unacceptable in Victorian England. In spite of this, the Cambridge investigators did try and make Eusapia as comfortable as possible so that she would be in a receptive state for the séances. Professor Myers' wife took her shopping, allowed Eusapia to cook Italian meals in her kitchen and listened to her incessant chatter, even though Mrs. Myers spoke only a few words of Italian and had no idea what Eusapia was talking about. The Myers' young son, Leo, was recruited to play croquet with her on the lawn, but the boy complained that she cheated during every game.

Even after all of these efforts to please her, Eusapia was unhappy. She hated the climate in Cambridge, the cool summer weather, the polite conversation and cultured people. She fell into an ill-tempered sulk that carried over into the sittings. She became indifferent about the entire situation, refused to be tied in place, sometimes wouldn't allow her feet to be held and performed poorly. Because of this, little happened. Tables tipped a time or two, but that was about all. It's not surprising that Sidgwick and Myers had enough of the troublesome medium and withdrew their support of her after that summer.

A denunciation by the SPR should have damaged Palladino's career but as it turned out, her work was far from over. She left England and returned to the continent, where she had always felt most comfortable. She presided over numerous séances in private homes and the sitters were apparently satisfied, for she continued to be in great demand. It was not until November 1898 that Eusapia consented to be examined by another scientific committee. This time the investigation was held in Paris and the organizer was Camille Flammarion, an eminent astronomer and a student of the paranormal. One of his chief assistants was Professor Richet.

The Paris séances produced a number of manifestations that were familiar --- and some that were decidedly strange. During one session, Eusapia was seated at one end of a table, and controlled in the usual way, when the sitters were stunned by the sight of a series of semi-transparent female half-figures that seemed to glide out of her body and down the length of the table.

Richet apparently felt the Paris séances were so interesting that they ought to be extended, and when the sittings sponsored by Flammarion had ended (and Flammarion himself had declared that he was satisfied that trickery could not account for what had occurred), Eusapia consented to continue the sittings. Richet quickly organized a new series of séances and invited the attendance of Myers, as a private individual and not as a representative of the SPR. According to their individual accounts, these further sittings were truly remarkable. But as with the Cambridge séances, it is unfortunate (and more than a little mystifying) that no official records exist to tell us why they were so exciting.

Whatever occurred, it led the formerly skeptical (and hostile) Myers into declaring before the general meetings of the SPR for December 1899 that he was now convinced of Palladino's gifts. He had just witnessed, he told the group, phenomena "far more striking" than the séances that he had attended by Eusapia in 1894. However, neither Myers not Richet ever published any notes on these sittings, though in the case of Myers the continuing negative attitude of his friends in the SPR was apparently responsible for this.

The only surviving account comes to us from the unofficial notes of Professor T. Flournoy of the Faculty of Sciences at the University of Geneva, who was also present at the séances. Flournoy was an experienced observer of the Spiritualist movement but does not go into enough detail about what he saw to permit any sort of strict analysis. Regardless, there is no reason to doubt his overall description of the conditions of the séances. It's interesting to note that this time Eusapia not only agreed to produce her phenomena in a light that, while dim, was more than sufficient for her movements to be seen by the sitters, but she also allowed her wrists and legs to be firmly held rather than just followed about.

Under these conditions, which were more satisfactory for scientific observation than the medium usually allowed, the manifestations that took place were of familiar kinds but could hardly be dismissed when so many were at a loss to explain them. The curtains of the spirit cabinet blew about, as if in a strong breeze, although the closed séance room was still and quiet. A zither that lay on the floor of the cabinet, well out of the medium's reach, was first to repeat a single note over and over again and then began to thump up and down on the floor. Finally, the instrument was seen leaving the cabinet and landing on the table in front of the sitters. During these and other happenings, the witnesses felt themselves pushed, pinched, patted and even struck by what they described as a "large hand." All agreed that Eusapia's hands were not only tightly held, but were clearly visible at all times.

In spite of there being no records for these séances, word spread of the results and Eusapia's fame increased once again. Judging from the fact that she had allowed the test conditions in Paris to be much stricter than normal, she must have seen these sittings as a way to recover ground that she had lost when the SPR withdrew its support of her. If this was her plan, then she succeeded. Even in England, the Cambridge disaster was all but forgotten and it seemed that every scientist in Europe was anxious to have a séance with Eusapia Palladino.

The next investigations were carried out in Genoa in 1901, under the sponsorship of a society called the Minerva Scientific Circle. This time, careful records were kept and published but the manifestations were far below the level usually carried out by Palladino. It should be noted though. that Professor Enrico Morselli, the group's leading investigator, though fully aware of Eusapia's continued cheating, calculated that at least seventy-five percent of what occurred during the sittings was genuinely paranormal.

Over the course of the next few years, Eusapia sat for one committee after another but time was wearing on her and she was growing old. Her strong face had begun to sag and lines etched her features. Sometimes, she was unable to perform and sometimes she found herself so exhausted after a séance that she was barely able to walk. The feeling of constantly being put to the test was starting to irritate her and it manifested itself as contempt for her sitters. She was tired but she could not stop. The séance room was her workplace and she had no other way to make a living.

She was studied by Professor Bottazzi of the Physiological Institute of the University of Naples in 1907 and by Jules Courtier of the Paris General Psychological Institute at intervals from 1905 to 1908. In every session, the same problems occurred again and again. Eusapia made all of the rules as to what kind of control of her movements would be allowed. Any attempt to overstep these rules resulted in an absence of any phenomena. On the other hand, the kind of control that she permitted remained far from foolproof. She was not only adept at the substitution of hands (described earlier) but she could also sometimes slip a foot out of a shoe in such a way that the handler never realized the shoe was empty.

The one innovation implemented by Courtier was the fairly extensive use of recording devices during the séance. Measurements were taken of the temperature, humidity, barometric pressure and electrical conditions in the room. Courtier also measured Palladino's pulse and respiration rate and also the decrease in weight of various objects that levitated in the séance room. Nothing astonishing was shown by these tests but they did serve to provide evidence that, at least on this occasion, the phenomena was real and was not merely caused by hallucinations on the part of the witnesses. While much more progressive than any other investigative methods used up to that time, the sensors still did reveal anything about what caused the manifestations, whether it was Eusapia or some "unknown physical force."

In 1908, Eusapia performed in Naples for a three-man committee that was likely the most formidable that she had ever encountered. One of the men was Hereward Carrington, an American researcher who, though only twenty-seven at the time, had been engaged in exposing fraudulent mediums for eight years and had written a book on their methods called *The Physical Phenomena of Spiritualism*. Carrington had persuaded the SPR (despite their continued misgivings about Palladino) to send with him its secretary, the Honorable Everard Feilding, a man with little experience in the séance room but also a man who was hard to convince of the supernatural. The third member of the committee was William Wortley Baggally, who had been investigating the paranormal for more than thirty years. He stated that he doubted that he had ever actually met a genuine medium and was an accomplished amateur magician who amused his friends and colleagues by duplicating the tricks of fraudulent Spiritualists.

These men were not your average believers and Palladino would have an uphill battle on her hands to convince them she was genuine. They planned to document everything to the letter. The séance records were taken by a shorthand stenographer and appeared in detail in Feilding's later book *Sittings with Eusapia Palladino & Other Studies*. The records gave a minute-by-minute account of the researchers, extensive descriptions of the séance room and its furnishings, diagrams and measurements and even careful notes on any changes in lighting. The phenomena witnessed were not only noted but were classified and discussed in separate sections. In addition, each investigator was given ample space to note any disagreements he might have and to state his individual conclusions.

Throughout the sessions, the investigators reported movements and levitations of the séance table; movements of the cabinet curtains; bulging of the medium's dress; raps and bangs on the table; noises inside the cabinet; the plucking of a guitar; movements of a small table from the cabinet onto the séance table and movement and levitation of the small table outside the curtain; transportation of other objects from the cabinet; touches by unseen fingers and hands; appearances of hands from behind the curtain; appearances of heads and objects that looked like heads from the curtain; lights; sensation of a cold breeze issuing from a scar on the medium's brow; and the untying of knots.

The investigators were perplexed. These were highly skeptical, yet open-minded men. They could find no easy explanation for what they had witnessed. In their notes, they wrote:

It was only through constant repetition of the same phenomenon, in a good light and at moments when its occurrence was expected, and after finding that none of the precautions we took had any influence on impeding it, that we gradually reached the conviction that some force was in play which was beyond the reach of ordinary control, and beyond the skill of the most skillful conjurer.

The investigators offered only two explanations. One, that they were under some sort of hallucinatory trance that had been caused by Palladino or two, that there was some sort of unknown, unascertained force at work.

The men reluctantly adopted the latter explanation. They wrote:

We are of the opinion that we have witnessed in the presence of Eusapia Palladino the action of some telekinetic force, the nature and origin of which we cannot attempt to specify, through which, without the introduction of accomplices, apparatus, or mere manual dexterity, she is able to produce movements of, and percussive and other sounds in, objects at a distance from her and unconnected with her in any apparent physical manner, and also to produce matter, or the appearance of matter, without any determinable source of supply.

The report turned out to be a tremendous victory of Eusapia. In light of it, the SPR specifically withdrew its ban on Palladino and reasserted her place among mediums meriting serious investigation, in spite of her continued cheating. Most investigators, familiar with the medium and her trickery, felt that she was psychologically unable to discontinue it. Easily identified, they chose to ignore it in light of what they felt was the genuine phenomena that she continued to produce.

One can only hope that Eusapia enjoyed this small bit of glory for the rest of her story is bitter and tragic. It was almost as if she managed one last spectacular series of séances before she began to crumble into obscurity. In spite of the success of the Naples sittings, Eusapia's health was breaking down and with it, her power to create her acclaimed phenomena. Hereward Carrington was anxious to have her visit the United States so that his American colleagues might have the opportunity to witness her performances. So, she agreed to come to America, despite her failing health. The trip lasted from November 1909 to June 1910, a period of constant disasters for Eusapia.

In her younger days, Eusapia would have loved the raw vibrancy and excitement of America. She would have seen it as a challenge but by 1909, she was aging, tired, in poor health and used to being taken seriously. However, the American press did not treat her as a visiting celebrity or even a scientific enigma. Instead, they saw her as a carnival sideshow and treated her more as an oddity than as a person who had stumped scientists in the major cities of Europe. She received many requests to perform but most of them came from music hall managers rather than from scientific committees. The prevailing attitude, from both the general public and other mediums, seemed to be one of suspicion and hostility. Eusapia was very unhappy and soon became angry and difficult to work with.

The investigators at Cambridge could have predicted what would happen next. When Eusapia was unhappy, her séances suffered. Feeling undervalued in America, she became irritable. She recognized immediately that most of the sitters who were coming to her séances were inexperienced; so when the phenomena were slow in coming, Eusapia cheated. She was caught repeatedly (she underestimated the America sitters) and each time the press reported the incident as "exposure," leading many of the American Spiritualists to wonder if the woman had ever produced anything genuine at all.

When Eusapia finally left America, she went into retirement. The time for the world to learn about the mysteries of the great medium had run out. She was a sick and tired woman by this point and she vanished into history. Eusapia Palladino died on May 16, 1918 and left to the scientific community an exasperating legacy. It's doubtful that the questions raised by her mediumship will ever really be answered. As Hereward Carrington once wrote, the question of Eusapia leaves us with a choice "between two improbabilities" ---- either at least some of Eusapia's phenomena were genuine or human testimony in such cases is without value.

There was no experiment that was conducted with her for which any other method of control or observation would have been more complete or with sitters who might have been better qualified to judge the results. Some may criticize what was done but can never agree on exactly what, given the technical limitations of the time, should have been done differently. There is no debate over the fact that she cheated. The scientists both recognized and accepted this. Her supporters maintained that she used trickery only when the phenomena were slow in coming or that she did it to save herself from illness and exhaustion. But should her trickery nullify all of the séances that she conducted, even the ones in which learned experts swore that no cheating took place?

Could Eusapia Palladino have been the "real thing"? Was she truly a person who was able to harness that "unknown force"? Or was she merely a clever hoaxer who managed to turn the tables on scores of observers who she saw as her intellectual and social betters? Did this common peasant woman have the last laugh?

Doubtless, we will never really know for sure, leaving us with one of the greatest unsolved mysteries of the heyday of the Spiritualist movement.

THE STRANGE CASE OF "MARGERY"

Mina Crandon, best known as "Margery," was a Boston medium who found herself embroiled in one of the most bitter controversies in American psychic research. Her followers claimed that she was one of the greatest mediums who ever lived, while her critics called her a fraud and blamed her for almost bringing paranormal research in America to an end. Her heyday came about during the decline of mediumship in America and perhaps for this reason, more blame has fallen on her than she deserves. Regardless, though, she was perhaps the greatest rival of magician Harry Houdini while he was involved in his crusade against fraudulent mediums and their bitter sparring and acrimonious debates almost damaged his career beyond recognition, as well.

The controversy over Margery will forever be linked to Houdini, who, at the time he met her, had been involved with debunking fraudulent Spiritualist mediums for years. His bitterness toward the movement began after his numerous failed attempts to find a legitimate medium who could contact his late mother. As he found fraud after fraud in his search, he began an all-out attack on the movement in general. He wrote books about how fake mediums managed their effects and traveled coast to coast on a lecture and stage show circuit, showing audiences how the frauds managed their "ghostly" effects. He began to be considered one of the greatest – and toughest – psychical investigators in the country. He was also a man of enormous ego and arrogance who rarely admitted to being wrong.

Houdini's collision course with Margery began in 1923, when he joined a panel that was put together by *Scientific American* Magazine, which offered a reward for any medium who could prove his or her psychical gifts were genuine. Medium Nino Pecoraro (who would later be publicly exposed by mentalist Joseph Dunninger) applied for the *Scientific American* prize money while Houdini was still on the road with his lecture tour. A telegram from publisher Orson Munn brought the magician from Little Rock, Arkansas, to New York to attend a test séance. Fellow committeemen planned to tie the Italian medium with a single long rope and Houdini literally exploded. Even amateur escapologists could free their hands when trussed up in such a manner, he told them. Houdini slashed the rope into short lengths and secured the medium himself. After that, the medium produced no manifestations.

Houdini returned to his lecture circuit, only to hear three months later that the investigative panel had deadlocked over medium Mina Crandon, who used the stage name Margery. They stated that they believed Crandon to be genuine and were prepared to give her the $2,500 reward. J. Malcolm Bird, an associate editor for *Scientific American*, was a supporter of Crandon's and was eager to give her the magazine's endorsement. He allowed word of the panel's favorable findings to reach the press. "Boston Medium Baffles Experts," one headline announced. "Houdini the Magician Stumped," cried another.

Houdini, who had not been present during Crandon's investigations, much less stumped, was stunned to think the magazine would even consider approving a medium that he had never seen. Munn called him in for a consultation and he publicly told *Scientific American* that he would forfeit $1,000 of his own money if he failed to expose Margery as a fraud. Mina Crandon seemed to welcome the opportunity to test her mettle against Houdini. The prize money meant nothing to this wealthy woman but the opportunity to win the approval of such a prestigious committee --- at the expense of the mighty Houdini --- proved too great a temptation for her to resist.

Houdini traveled with Munn by train to Boston and on the way, he reviewed the findings of his colleagues on the investigative panel. To his way of thinking, the investigation had

Mina Crandon, a.k.a. "Margery"

Houdini with Margery, *Scientific American* publisher Orson Munn (left) and editor J. Malcolm Bird lurking in the background.

been badly bungled from the start. Margery did not perform under the same stringent test conditions as the other mediums. She was allowed to hold her test séances at her home in Boston, which opened things up widely for the possibilities of fraud. Most of the committee members had availed themselves of the Crandons' generous hospitality during the proceedings, staying in their home, eating their food and enjoying their company. Houdini believed that this had badly compromised their objectivity and later, it was learned that accepting food and a bed from the Crandons were the least of the problems. One investigator had actually borrowed money from Margery's husband, while another hoped to win his backing for a research foundation.

Worse yet, the "distinguished" panel was not unaware of Margery's physical attractions. Years later, at least one committee member would tell of his amorous encounters with the celebrated medium. Margery had a very clever method of dealing with her detractors and those who investigated her: she seduced them. Years later, claims would be made that Margery also tried to use her erotic charms on Houdini, in hopes that he might ignore some of her more obvious fraud, but if this was the case, Houdini was apparently not impressed.

The sexual hijinks that occurred during Margery's séances created a firestorm of controversy in the 1920s, but in truth, she was a rather unlikely medium.

Mina Stinson had been born in Ontario in 1888, the daughter of a farmer. She moved to Boston when she was sixteen so that she could play the piano, coronet and cello in local bands and orchestras. After working as a secretary, an actress and an ambulance driver, she married a grocer named Earl P. Rand, with whom she had a son. They remained happily married until a medical operation introduced her to Le Roi Goddard Crandon, a prominent surgeon and a former instructor at the Harvard Medical School. She divorced Rand in 1918 and married Crandon a short time later.

Mina had no psychic experiences early in life and in fact, had no interest in the spirit world at all until her husband became interested in the subject in the early 1920s. One evening in May 1923, Dr. Crandon invited a number of friends over for a "home circle" meeting. The group gathered around a small table and soon had it tilting in response to the sitters' questions. Crandon suggested that they each remove their hands from the table, one at a time, to see which individual was responsible for the paranormal activity. One by one, each of them took their hands away but the table only stopped rocking when the last of the sitters lifted her hands. Crandon had solved the mystery: the medium was his own wife.

At first, the idea of being a medium seemed like a lark to Mina. Throughout the summer of 1923, the Crandons held one séance after another at their home. Each time, Mina seemed to exhibit some new ability. It seemed that Crandon only had to read about some new spirit manifestation before his wife could duplicate it.

Within a month of her first official séance, Crandon announced a plan to place his wife under hypnosis so that they could try and make contact with the psychic control who would serve as her spirit guide. At first, Mina resisted this idea, claiming that she didn't want to miss any of the "fun" while she was under hypnosis. Eventually, though, she gave in to her husband's wishes and soon, a male voice made itself heard to the Crandon home circle.

The voice turned out to belong to Mina's brother, Walter Stinson, who had been crushed to death in a railroad accident in 1911. From this point on, Walter's spirit was a regular presence in the Crandon séance room. He proved to have a strong personality, a quick wit and was given to using rough language. Many visitors to the séance room became convinced of what they heard simply because they could not imagine that such coarse and vulgar language would come from the mouth of the doctor's pretty wife. A number of observers noted that Walter's voice did not seem to come from Mina at all. The sound seemed to emanate from another part of the room and would continue even when Mina was in a trance or had a mouth filled with water. The effect seemed so remarkable that one skeptic, searching for a plausible explanation for what he had experienced, wondered if perhaps Mina were able to speak through her ears! Walter became well known as Mina's spirit guide and, along with his sister, began to find fame all over the world.

But Mina hardly needed Walter's help to become a popular medium – especially among her male sitters. Unlike old and ungainly mediums like Eusapia Palladino, Mina resembled nothing so much as a light-hearted flapper. Even Houdini conceded that she was an exceedingly attractive woman, and one psychic researcher warned his colleagues to "avoid falling in love with the medium." She usually greeted her sitters wearing nothing but a flimsy dressing gown, bedroom slippers and silk stockings. This attire, leaving almost nothing to the imagination, was intended to rule out the possibility of trickery or concealment, but it also tended to distract male visitors. Mina's slender figure, fashionably bobbed hair and light blue eyes made her, in the words of one admirer, "too attractive for her own good." To make matters more titillating, it was rumored that it was not uncommon for her to hold sessions in the nude and according to some, she was especially adept at manifesting ectoplasm from her vagina.

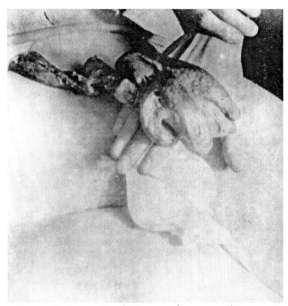

A close photograph of Margery's vagina (discreetly covered by a handkerchief) as it allegedly exudes strangely colored ectoplasm.

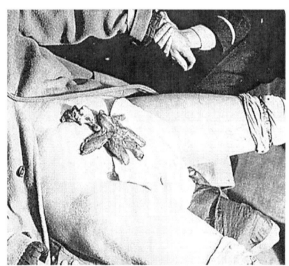

Another photo of Margery with her dress pulled up and her stocking rolled down, again exuding ectoplasm.

Dr. Crandon believed that his lovely wife was a "remarkable psychic instrument" and her took her abroad to build up a consensus of favorable opinion from European experts. One of these was Sir Arthur Conan Doyle, who declared her to be a "very powerful medium" and said, "The validity of her gifts was beyond all question." J. Malcolm Bird, from *Scientific American*, shared Doyle's opinion and wrote a series of articles extolling her virtues. It was Bird who gave her the name "Margery" in an effort to protect the Crandons' privacy. Under this name, her fame steadily grew.

By bringing Margery to the attention of *Scientific American*, Conan Doyle had inadvertently started the most controversial episode of her career. With the urging of Bird, the panel had deadlocked over whether or not genuine phenomena were occurring in Margery's presence. No one would commit to anything without Houdini's opinion, which was why Orson Munn brought him back into the investigation. Not everyone was happy about this, however. J. Malcolm Bird who (unbelievably, given his opinions about Margery to start with) had been assigned to observe, organize and record the investigations. Bird wanted Houdini disqualified from the panel and for this reason, started the investigations without him.

Houdini traveled to Boston, though, anxious to see the medium for himself.

On July 23, Houdini called at the Crandon house. He wanted to see Margery perform under the same circumstances that his colleagues had experienced. The medium, meanwhile, relished the idea of converting the notorious debunker to her cause. Some observers saw the séance as an acid test --- not just of Margery's authenticity, but of Spiritualism itself.

Houdini watched as a spirit bell rang, a voice called out to him in the darkness, and a megaphone crashed to the floor at his feet. If these manifestations impressed him, he gave no sign of it. When the lights came back on, Houdini politely thanked his hosts and left. On the drive back to the hotel though, he finally spoke about what he was feeling. "I've got her," he said. "All fraud."

Houdini was impressed by what he had seen at the Crandon home and very impressed with the famous Margery --- though not by her supernatural powers, he quickly assured Munn. At his hotel that night, he explained how and why his conclusions about Margery differed from those of some members of the panel. One feat that had puzzled the panel was the ringing of a "spirit bell box," a small, wooden clapper-box that sounded an electric bell when pressed on the top. Although sitters on either side of her held Margery's hands, and her feet were in contact with theirs, the bell box rang many times during the séance, a happening that she attributed to Walter.

Usually, the bell box sat on the floor between Margery's legs, but Houdini had insisted that it be placed on the floor at his own feet. Regardless, the bell rang repeatedly anyway. Houdini had a ready answer for this: "I had rolled my right trouser leg up above my knee. All that day, I had word a silk rubber bandage around that leg, just below the knee. By night, the part of the leg below the bandage had become swollen and painfully tender, thus giving me a much keener sense of feeling and making it easier to notice the slightest sliding of Mrs. Crandon's ankle or flexing of her muscles... I could distinctly feel her ankle slowly and spasmodically sliding as it pressed against mine while she gained space to raise her foot off the floor and touch the top of the box." In other words, Margery's foot, and not a spirit, had been responsible for the ringing of the bell.

Another of the evening's mysteries had involved a megaphone that, according to the spectral voice of Walter, had levitated in the air above the sitter's heads. Walter commanded that Houdini tell him where to throw the object and the magician instructed him to throw it in his direction. Moments later, the megaphone crashed to the floor in front of him.

Houdini had an explanation for this, too. Earlier in the evening, when one of Margery's hands was free, she had snatched up the megaphone and had placed it on her head like a dunce cap. In the total darkness of the séance room, no one could have seen her do this. She later made the megaphone fly across the room by simply snapping her head forward. Houdini said: "This is the slickest ruse that I have ever seen..."

In the wake of his first séance, Houdini refused to speak publicly about Margery. He did not reveal his opinions over what had occurred that night. Instead, he asked that more stringent tests be performed. It was rumored that Margery had somehow outwitted Houdini -- and rumors also flew that perhaps her powers were genuine after all.

Houdini ignored all of this and set about making plans for additional séances. To assure proper control at future sittings, Houdini designed a special "fraud preventer" cabinet, a crate with a slanted top that had openings at the top and sides for the medium's head and arms. Once inside, Margery's movements --- and her chances for deception --- would be severely limited. Reluctantly, Margery agreed to conduct the séance from inside the cabinet, but not before Houdini and Dr. Crandon exchanged such harsh words that they nearly came to blows.

The first séance with the cabinet was not a success. Shortly after Margery entered her trance, Walter came through, and the committee asked that the spirit ring the bell box, which had been placed into the cabinet with her. Almost immediately, Walter exclaimed that Houdini had done something to the bell so that it would not ring. An examination of the bell revealed that a piece of rubber had been wedged against the clapper so that it would not ring. Outraged, Dr. Crandon accused the magician of trying to sabotage the proceedings, a charge that Houdini repeatedly denied.

A short time later, Houdini was accused of cheating again. A collapsible carpenter's ruler, which could have been used to manipulate the bell box and other apparatus from within the cabinet, was discovered at Margery's feet. Walter's voice echoed in

A poor photograph of Margery trying to conduct a séance from Houdini's fraud prevention box for the first time.

the séance room, "Houdini, you god-damned bastard, get the hell out of here and never come back!"

In Houdini's opinion, the folding rule had been planted in the box in order to make him look bad. He swore that he had not placed it there and the Crandons made the same claims. They blamed Houdini for the ruler and he blamed them. He resented anyone who would take their word --- an especially the word of Walter, the spirit guide --- over his.

There were many, including some members of the panel, who believed that Houdini had been the one who was caught cheating this time. He was widely discredited for it, leading some to doubt the integrity of some of his earlier investigations. In any case, *Scientific American* finally declined to grant the prize to Margery, in large part because of Houdini's exposure. The confrontational magician had quarreled, often violently, with every member of the committee. J. Malcolm Bird, whom Houdini suspected of active collusion with the Crandons, resigned as secretary of the panel. He was angry with Houdini and he continued to insist he should have been disqualified at the very beginning.

Houdini further outraged Bird, the Crandons and their supporters by publishing a small book called *Houdini Exposes the Tricks Used by the Boston Medium Margery*. He was adamant about the fact that Margery was doing nothing more than offering clever ruses. In his final verdict on the medium, he wrote: "My decision is, that everything which took place at the séances which I attended was a deliberate and conscious fraud..."

From the other side, Walter chimed in his final words about Houdini. He ended them with a prediction: Houdini would be dead within a year. Houdini managed to defy this prophecy, but not by much. He died in 1926 and in an interview with the press, Margery had only good things to say about the magician, praising him for his virile personality and great determination.

Despite Houdini's exposures, Margery emerged from the debacle relatively unscathed. She continued her séances and by the end of 1924, she had begun to produce even greater manifestations, including "spirit arms" that rang the bell box and caused things to fly about in the séance room.

In 1925, J. Malcolm Bird published a book that supported Margery and as the research officer of the American Society for Psychical Research, he was able to sway many other ASPR members to her side. They became her greatest supporters and devoted hundreds of pages in the ASPR journal to her séances.

Eric J. Dingwall, an officer of the SPR in England, read of his American colleagues' support, and decided to investigate the medium for himself. Dingwall was an anthropologist and a psychical investigator who traveled expensively throughout the world. He published many books, among them, "*Studies in the Sexual Life of Ancient and Medieval Peoples*" and "*The Girdle of Chastity: A Fascinating History of Chastity Belts.*"

Dingwall's friends jokingly called him "Dirty Ding," referring to his unpaid position as honorary assistant keeper of the infamous Private Case. This was a secret collection of erotica and outright obscene printed material owned by the British Museum. The collection was generally unacknowledged and, until the 1930s, uncatalogued. Dingwall used his own money to purchase books for the collection, three of which were said to be pederastic works by The Reverend Alfred Reginald Thorold Winckley, who, when he wasn't writing child pornography, was an assistant curate of the parish of Buxton in Derbyshire.

Dingwall wanted to see the ectoplasm that Margery was manifesting and Dr. Crandon allowed him to view the proceedings by the light of a red lamp, which Crandon flashed on and off to reveal quick glimpses at the phenomenon. Too much light, Crandon said, would have an inhibiting effect on the ectoplasm. Halfway through his investigations, though, Dingwall began having doubts. Crandon's red lamp never allowed him to see the ectoplasm actually emanating from Margery's body. He had only seen it after the fact. Odder still, many of the photographs revealed that a large number of the emanations seemed to be hanging from slender, almost invisible threads. Others who looked at the photos said that the "hands" looked suspiciously like animal lung tissue, a substance that Crandon could have obtained through his work at Boston hospitals. Dingwall's final report on the case was inconclusive. As usual, Margery was unconcerned. Sitters continued to file into the séance room at the Crandons' Lime Street home. One investigation after another raised allegations of fraud but no one was ever able to make the accusations stick.

In 1928, Margery began to develop a highly unusual manifestation that made her even more widely known in Spiritualist circles. On the table in front of her during a séance would be placed two dishes, one containing hot water and the other cold. In the first dish was a piece of dental wax. When the wax was softened, it was claimed that her spirit guide, Walter, would make an impression of his thumb on it. Then, the thumbprint was put into cold water to harden. The prints appeared mysteriously on the same night that Margery obtained the wax from her dentist. A so-called fingerprint expert that was called in by the Crandons stated that the thumbprint matched one that was taken from an old razor that once belonged to Walter Stinson.

Margery had confounded the skeptics and believers were enthralled by this new manifestation. It was almost as if the spirit was leaving a calling card, even better. The excitement was soon to a crashing end, however.

Psychic researcher E.E. Dudley set out to compare Walter's wax print with those who were regulars at the Crandon séances and made a surprising discovery. Walter's thumbprint was identical in every way to that of Margery's dentist, Dr. Caldwell. Someone had apparently used a sample thumbprint that Dr. Caldwell made for Margery to create a metal die-stamp that was suitable for making impressions in wax.

This was the end of the ruse. Many of Margery's most devoted followers drifted away. J. Malcolm Bird, once her staunchest defender, admitted that, at times, he had been guilty of elaborations and half-truths about Margery's so-called "wonders." The scientific community let it be known that Margery's séances were no longer of interest.

Margery's decline was quick and tragic. After the death of Dr. Crandon in 1939, Mina grew depressed and turned to alcohol for consolation. She began to look older than her years, gained weight and watched as her beauty faded away. She continued to hold séances, finding people who still believed in her, and during one sitting, she grew so distraught that she climbed to the roof of her home and threatened to throw herself off. She died at the age of fifty-four in 1941.

Many researchers today believe that some elements of the paranormal were present in Crandon's séances, but just what was genuine and what was not remain unknown. Crandon and her husband were known for baiting investigators and trying to fool them if possible. And then there were the always-present rumors of the sexual favors that Margery granted to those who either supported her, ignored fraud during their investigations, or simply looked the other way. Just what secrets did Mina Crandon hold? We'll never know – she took them with her to her grave.

9. PHANTOM LOVERS AND EROTIC ENTITIES
SEXUAL HAUNTINGS IN HISTORY

I was about twelve years old when I realized that it was possible to have sex with a ghost. While I can't say that it happened to me – I was greatly unschooled in the mechanics of sex in those days – I did run across a first-hand account of an erotic entity in a book that I was reading at the time. Needless to say, this soon became my favorite chapter of the book, which explains a lot about the mindset behind the book that you are now holding in your hands.

According to the account, a young American man took a summer trip to England in the late 1970s. He spent the first few days of his vacation seeing the sights in London and then, because he wanted to experience the British countryside, took a room at a charming old inn in Devon. The ancient place allowed him to soak up the ambience of the region and he found the other guests quite friendly, not minding an American in their midst.

His first night at the inn was uneventful and he spent the day roaming the countryside. He spent the second day in the same way and when he returned to the inn that night, he was exhausted. He ate dinner and then was sound asleep in his bed by 11:00 p.m.

In the middle of the night, he was coaxed out of his sleep by what he described as "a rustling of leaves." Something told him that he was not alone in the room. He could hear his heart pounding as he looked around, seeing only the curtains billowing in the breeze. It was dark and eerily silent – until the rustling sound came again. This time, it was much closer, nearing the bed. Then, goose bumps covered his body as he saw a pale, shadowy apparition appear. He recognized the shape as a faint, female form but he was unable to make out any details. The young man violently shook his head from side to side, convinced that by doing so he could rouse himself from what he was sure was a dream. Soon, he realized that it was no dream. He was wide-awake, his hands clenched at his sides, wondering what was going to happen next. He recalled later that he never felt panic and that it never occurred to him to be afraid. He seemed to be mesmerized by what was taking place.

Suddenly, the young man felt a pair of soft lips press against his own. He could see nothing – no face, no body. He brought his hands up from the bed and felt for the woman who had to be there, but there was nothing! A warm tongue slid into his mouth and entwined itself with his. The kiss soon ended and the tongue and lips moved away from him, only to begin moving down his chest, to his stomach and beyond. He then went on to describe what he called "the most erotic experience of his life" adding, "I had to pinch myself to prove that I wasn't dreaming. My eyes strained in the darkness to discern a recognizable feature, a face, hair, anything. I reached toward the apparition. I moved my hands back and forth where her body had to be. Nothing but air. I gave up trying to figure it out and surrendered to the pleasure."

The man was unable to explain how he was unable to reach out and feel the apparition's body, but was able to physically experience the fleshy body of a woman making love to him. However, he was unable to deny that it was happening. The ghost moved slowly at first, with a steady, unhurried rhythm that spoke of her experience. Then, gradually, the tempo increased until the young man had what he called "the climax of my life." After his unbelievable orgasm, he waited expectantly, hoping that since it was over, the spirit would speak, explain, or at least show herself to him. But nothing. The shadowy form left the bed and the soft rustling sound of leaves accompanied her as she floated off toward the wall. As he watched in utter disbelief, she disappeared into the wall.

He reached down and felt the sheet, fully expecting to find evidence of their eerie coupling on the bed but was shocked to find that it was dry. "What happened to my ejaculate – where had it gone?" the man asked, then realized, "My ghost girl had obviously taken it with her."

The young man didn't sleep at all for the rest of the night. When morning came, he hurried downstairs, bursting to tell someone, anyone, about what had happened to him the night before. He found one of the men whom he had met on his first day at the inn sitting at a table drinking coffee. He rushed over to him, sat down, and blurted out the story. When he finished, the man laughed. The young American was distraught that his new friend didn't believe him.

"But I do believe you," the man replied. "That sexy bitch must have been in the mood for a handsome American. I only wish that it had been me with her last night."

Thoroughly confused, the young man asked for an explanation. His friend explained that the inn was haunted. Apparently, a married barmaid had worked there many years ago and had a habit of sleeping with the guests. One night, her husband caught her in bed with someone and in a fit of rage, murdered her on the spot. The man went on, "But her spirit lives on, you see, and from time to time, she selects a guest and gives him the time of his life. Men come from miles around just to spend the night here, all in hopes of making it with her – most of them, though, don't stand a ghost of a chance with her."

That was the end of the story but I never got tired of it and read and re-read it for years after. Later, as I began writing about ghost and hauntings, I tried in vain to track down the name and location of this British inn – all in the interests of research, of course. So far, I haven't had any luck, but I'll keep my fingers crossed.

But not all visitations from spirit lovers are welcome ones, as in the case of Daniel Van Oppen, a wealthy young man who was visited by the ghost of a woman he had known before death but did not have an intimate relationship with. She had always been a quiet, spinsterish woman and had died quite young. Van Oppen was startled to be visited by her spirit – but not as shocked as he was when he realized why she was there. Not only did she seduce him in his bed, but she also demanded that he should not become involved with any other woman. The threats that she made filled him with terror. During some of the episodes, the spirit was visible not only to Van Oppe, but also to others, including his brothers, who, as Daniel was planning to get married, encouraged him to disregard the ghost's warnings. The result of this was that the spirit came to his bedroom in the night and caused a disturbance that roused the whole household. This time, there were witnesses to the fact that she was trying to have sex with Van Oppen by force. Restrained with difficulty, the ghost vanished with the threat that his first child would be stillborn and this in fact was what happened.

The ghost continued to prey on Van Oppen after his marriage and he began suffering from seizures and convulsions brought about by the repeated attacks. Eventually, Van Oppen's marriage failed, partly because of his wife's distress following the death of their child. In time, his health improved and after his illness was gone, the torment from his phantom lover finally ceased.

So, does love exist beyond the grave? Does lust? Theories abound as to what ghosts are, why they manifest themselves in the manner in which they do, and why they choose to remain behind in this world at all. It seems to be the general consensus with most ghost buffs that spirits largely stay behind because of some of sort of unfinished business. It's possible that their emotional attachments to people who are still living may act as a type of unfinished business because they are unable to let go of the feelings that they had. In addition, ghosts that remain behind in the physical world are usually bits of the personality of the individual who once lived. An unusually passionate or lustful person is liable to maintain those same qualities as a ghost.

For this reason, it's no surprise that we often run across hauntings that are sexual in nature. Over the years, I have personally been involved in cases where people claim they have been touched or groped by unseen hands, molested by a spirit or have been repeatedly unnerved by the presence of someone unseen crawling into bed with them. Such incidents are usually isolated cases, but they do happen. Unfortunately, many such cases have been thinly reported in years past, often because researchers felt the accounts were inappropriate or because the general public frowned on such things.

But there are cases that have been revealed in the light of day and I promise not to hold it against the reader if he occasionally wonders why some of these things don't happen to him!

THE GHOST LOVER OF MACHATAS

Stories of phantom lovers date back over the centuries, often finding a place in the earliest records of human history. One such account from the second century was provided by Phlegon of Tralles, the Greek writer and freedman of the emperor Hadrian. The story was told of a young woman named Philinnion, who had fallen in love with a handsome youth named Machatas. Her parents, possibly for social reasons, did not approve of the young man and forced their daughter to accept a man named Krateros as her husband instead. In the depths of her despair, the young woman went into a decline and her health soon broken, she died within a year.

The story does not tell us how Machatas felt about the loss of his lover, but five months later, when he was staying in the home of her parents, he was awakened in his bed by a nocturnal visitor. He looked up to see the spirit of Philinnion, who came to his bedside to declare her love for him and her grief at their separation. Whatever Machatas' fears at seeing his dead love, she found the means to not only reassure him, but to prove that a spirit could materialize to the satisfaction of a living person and they spent the night together. During the next night, the visit was repeated and the happy reunion might have become an ongoing association if not for a distressing intervention.

A maidservant, whose presence near the door of Machatas' bedroom might well suggest an amorous interest in the young man, peered into the bedchamber and saw him embracing his spectral lover. The sight of the well-remembered form of Philinnion sent her hurrying to arouse her master and mistress from their beds and give them the terrible news. However, the reacted angrily and sent the girl away, admonishing her for having drank too much wine at dinner.

Early the next morning, the maid was vindicated. Philinnion's parents, questioning Machatas, were shaken to find that he readily admitted the truth of what the girl said: their daughter had returned from the grave. He even had the audacity to show them a gold ring that Philinnion's spirit had left for him the night before. At this, the grieving mother broke down and wept. Machatas, moved by her tears, promised that he would let her see her lost daughter if she came back again.

And she did return, the following night, in fact. Machatas' lovely phantom was in a happy mood and they ate and drank wine together like a normal couple, which, in fact, they were – no matter how wide the distance between the worlds to which each now belonged. In this blissful atmosphere, Machatas found the courage to keep his word and called her parents in to see her. Doubts and concerns vanished as they raced to embrace the girl, but their visit was short and was not meant to last. That night, the living phantom disappeared.

Later, they visited the family crypt and Philinnion's vault was opened in their presence. It contained nothing but the golden ornaments that she had left with her lover and evidently retrieved before her spirit departed forever. Her physical remains had vanished, but not for long. When her parents returned home they made the awful discovery of their daughter's body in their house, awaiting reburial. Machatas, inconsolable, died a short time later. Perhaps he was reunited with his lover at last.

CHARLES DICKENS' PHANTOM LOVER

The esteemed British novelist Charles Dickens, who brought the world some of the most famous literary ghosts in history, had his own encounters with the spirit world. He wrote of how he awakened one morning to see the apparition of his father sitting next to his bed. The image vanished when Dickens reached out and tried to

Charles Dickens

place his hand on the specter's shoulder.

But Dickens' most remarkable supernatural experience came to him after the death of his beloved sister-in-law, Mary Hogarth, in 1837. Dickens had married Catherine Thompson Hogarth, the daughter of George Hogarth, editor of the *Evening Chronicle*, in April 1836. After a brief honeymoon, they set up home in Bloomsbury and went on to have ten children. Catherine's sister, Mary, joined the Dickens' household to offer support to her newly married sister and brother-in-law. It was not unusual at that time for an unmarried female relative to join the household of a newly married couple. However, many of Dickens' biographers believe that the author had much more than just a brotherly interest in his wife's sister and became very attracted to her. Some believe the feelings were mutual and that the two may have become involved in an affair. Mary died in Dickens' arms after a brief illness in 1837. She went on to become the inspiration for characters in many of his books, and her death is fictionalized as that of Little Nell in *The Old Curiosity Shop*.

Shortly after the young woman's death, Dickens began receiving nocturnal visits from Mary's spirit. The attractive phantom invaded not only his dreams, but his bed, as well. The lovely spirit became, in Dickens' own words, "… as inseparable from my existence as the beating of my heart is."

When she first appeared to him, he was unable to make out her features, but soon became convinced that it was Mary. He wrote, "I was not at all afraid, but in a great delight, so that I wept very much, and stretching out my arm to it, called it 'dear.' I entreated it, as it rose above my bed and soared up to the vaulted roof to answer me a question, touching the future life. My hands were still outstretched towards it and it vanished."

THE OCTOROON MISTRESS

Located in New Orleans' famous French Quarter is a building that serves as home to one of the city's most enduring ghostly legends. It is that of the "Octoroon Mistress," a beautiful mixed-race spirit who only appears here on the darkest nights of December. It is a time of year when even the warmth of the Deep South is tempered by cold winds, icy rains and sometimes even freezing temperatures.

They say that she walks on the rooftops of this building, completely naked and unprotected from the cold. She ascends an old, narrow staircase that leads up from the attic and then steps out onto the roof. As the wind slices around the eaves, this breathtaking phantom huddles in misery with her slender arms wrapped about her as if they can somehow shield her from the elements. The stories say that she huddles here throughout the night, only to fade away as dawn begins to color the sky. Those who have seen her, and have come to search for her in the night, will find no trace of her in the darkness and yet the apparition will return to the rooftop the following evening. She seems doomed to repeat these actions, but only on the coldest nights of the year.

According to the legends of the French Quarter, the mournful figure's name was Julie, the octoroon (one-eighth African-American) mistress of a wealthy Creole man who "kept" her in an apartment on Royal Street. In the early 1800s, it was common for many rich young white men to keep attractive black women as mistresses in the city. These wealthy sons of plantation owners sometimes supported these one-fourth or one-eighth mistresses in addition to their "legitimate" white families. Even though some of these young women carried only a trace of African blood, marriages and open relationships with them were considered forbidden.

These women were not prostitutes but proper, educated young women. They were all free women and widely known for their beauty. The Creole gentlemen who kept these young ladies would support them in fitting style, usually giving them the deed to a small cottage or paying the rent on an apartment in the French Quarter. Many of these arrangements would last for years, or perhaps for a lifetime. In addition, many of the ladies became well known for their business establishments, while other simply enjoyed the fineries the arrangements allowed them.

They were unhampered with jobs or families and were content to enjoy whatever being a white man's mistress would allow them in the segregated world of that time period.

This was certainly the case with Julie. Her life was pleasant and filled with plenty of food, fine clothing, expensive jewelry and more. She was content with such things, until she made the mistake of falling in love with the man who gave her such a lavish lifestyle. Such an emotion would not seem so terrible in a different time and place but because of the fact that black blood ran through her veins, a more permanent arrangement than what she already enjoyed could never take place. When Julie would explain to her protector that she loved him, he would always reply that he loved her, as well. He did everything that he could to try and make her happy. He gave her gifts and new dresses and made sure that she had enough money so that she would never want for anything. The only thing that he was unable to give her was legal status as his wife.

But it was this one thing that Julie wanted more than anything else. She begged and pleaded with him, sometimes angry and sometimes despondent, but each time, his answer remained no. In those days, even a drop of African blood was unacceptable in New Orleans society. The young man's very livelihood depended on the generosity of his family. No matter how much he loved Julie, he could not shame the family by marrying a black woman.

A group of Octoroon women in New Orleans in the late 1800s. Although considered to be some of the most beautiful women in the city, they could never be accepted into white society because of their bloodlines.

Julie's anger turned to despair and soon, her lover was not so eager to come to the Royal Street apartment. His fine gifts, and even his love for her, did not seem to be enough and so finally, he agreed to her demands -- but under conditions that he never dreamed that she would try to meet.

"I will marry you, Julie," he told her, "but only if you do one thing to prove your love to me. You must take off all of your clothes and go up onto the roof until morning. I know that it is cold, but if you love me enough, your love will keep you warm. If you will not do this, then our marriage can never be and we will go on in just the way that we are."

The young man must have spoken these words in the belief that Julie would never do such a reckless and foolish thing. It was the middle of December and New Orleans was suffering under a cold spell. Rain and sleet were pelting the windows even as he spoke. He was sure that Julie would laugh at his demands and see the ridiculousness of them being married. Then, he believed, their life could get back to normal.

To his surprise, Julie agreed to do what he asked, although he was sure that she would never go through with it.

During the short time they spent together that evening, darkness fell on the city and the cold rain and monstrous winds battered the house. But a fire blazed in the apartment's fireplace and the young couple remained safe and warm in each other's arms. There would be no more talk of marriage this evening.

Later on in the night, there was a summons at the front door and the young man admitted a friend who had planned to come by and play chess with him. Together, they sat down in the parlor and began drinking and laughing over a chessboard. Soon, all talk of weddings, and perhaps even Julie herself, was briefly forgotten.

But Julie did not forget. As midnight approached, she removed all of her clothing and slowly climbed the steps

The building where Julie died -- and where her ghost lingers today.

to the roof. As she reached the outer door, she began to shiver uncontrollably. Icy tendrils of air slipped in around the doorframe and danced over her naked flesh. She bit her lip and pushed on, intent on enduring the price that her lover demanded of her. She pushed open the door and walked out into the cold and menacing blackness.

What happened next we can only imagine. The young gentleman remained with his friend until nearly dawn. Bleary-eyed, he made his way back up the stairs to climb into bed for a few blessed moments of sleep. Curled up next to his beautiful Julie, he knew that time would pass sweetly. He must have pictured her warm and supple body as he opened the door to her bedchamber.

The stories say that he was stunned with horror at what he discovered there. The bed was empty and her night clothes lay in a heap on the floor. The room itself was silent and deserted. A cry left his lips as he ran for the attic staircase. He never thought she would go through with it. As he made his way out onto the roof, he spied the crumpled body of his lover -- cold, frozen and lifeless.

And every December, Julie still walks that lonely rooftop. Her naked body bends to the force of the freezing wind and as dawn approaches, she falls limply to the roof and then vanishes into the ether.

The occupants of the building today maintain that strange things do not only occur on the rooftop. For many years, previous tenants claimed that, when the house was quiet and deserted, footsteps would sound in the chamber that once belonged to Julie. They also stated that a young man playing chess would often materialize in the one of the rooms. Perhaps this is Julie's lover, paying an eternal penance for his role in her death.

Today, Julie apparently tries to make her presence known in various parts of the brick townhouse. Occupants claim to have heard tapping sounds that they cannot identify, along with a ghostly perfume that comes and goes without explanation. They have also seen her spectral reflection in a fishpond in the building's courtyard and once spotted her apparition rounding a corner.

Many feel that Julie has never left this place. Could the memories of the past be holding her here? Perhaps -- for in addition to being the scene of her horrible death, this building holds her most treasured memories of love, as well.

THE RETURN OF "BERTIE"

Many cases of supernatural lovers have been recorded as highly personal experiences, sometimes resulting in deep emotional and psychological damage. The case of Christian Reimers is one such case.

Reimers was a musician who, because of a nervous ailment, was unable to continue performing. Thanks to his wealth, he was able to pursue whatever interests struck his fancy, including Spiritualism. In the late 1880s, he began to experiment with séances and spirit contact and became so emotionally affected by what he saw and experienced that he was unable to remain an objective observer -- he was soon a full-fledged believer. He visited many mediums over the course of the next few years and eventually began to develop his own mediumistic skills. He was contacted one night during a séance and began to speak in the voice of a female spirit that was to profoundly influence his life.

When Reimers made contact during the séance, the entity, which called herself "Bertie," claimed to have lived as a lady-in-waiting in fifteenth and sixteenth century London. She showed herself helpful and accommodating toward Reimers, who accepted her as a sort of spirit guide for the small private circle of Spiritualists that he hosted. After that, in all of the séances that he led, Bertie became the controlling intelligence. It soon became too much for Reimers, who was still only a beginner, to handle. He contacted a medium named Mrs. A. H. Firman, whose spirit control was John King, aka Henry Owen Morgan, spectral father of Katie King, the spirit manifested by Florence Cook. Mrs. Firman took over the leadership of the group. Soon after, during a séance that was presided over by her, Reimers received a letter. It appeared in the darkness and allegedly, had not been received through any sort of "automatic writing" on the part of the medium. In other words, it simply appeared in the séance room! The letter began, "Dear friend, think of us only as spirits which hover around you in order to encourage you to feel freed of all mundane worries." After complimenting the medium, it went on to assure Reimers of "their" happiness at his "burning enthusiasm for their mission" and "their" concern for his physical welfare. He was to control his zeal and not let his profession suffer by sacrifices in "their" cause. It was signed, "loyally on your side, Bertie."

The unusually considerate tone of the letter from the spirit greatly excited Reimers and his enthusiasm for the deceased lady-in-waiting rose from séance to séance. His query through another medium to Bertie as to "why sublime spirits sometimes demean themselves by manifestations through low and even shady mediums" was answered by Bertie in a long speech "which was like a beautiful garland of flowers and thought, breathing the love of humanity." Reimers later stated, "The increasing intimacy drew me closer and closer to this mysterious being and I felt as if a dead loving sister had approached me, carefully hiding her relationship so that words of consolation should not be drowned by emotional excitement." It was obvious that Reimers was falling in love with the spirit, in the proper custom and manner of the Victorian era.

During a séance, Bertie promised him her photograph and Reimers promised his own. He visited a spirit photographer named Frederick Hudson and received a photograph that he accepted with great joy. The female image with the pretty face and flowing robes was alleged to be Bertie. As séances continued, Reimers began receiving spirit writings and poems that were signed by Bertie. They caused him "intense delight". Later, during a séance with Mrs. Firman, which was joined by Hudson the photographer, Bertie made her presence known by tapping almost instantly when the séance began. The sitting became like a "tea party, during which the charming invisible guest seasoned us with gay messages."

A series of séances followed during which Reimers used every conceivable precaution against cheating by the medium. The measures included binding and tying her in various ways and them examining the room and it furnishings before settling down to await Bertie's presence. Before her arrival, Reimers became aware of a strange sense of "flooding" in his left side. It was followed by the first of Bertie's visible materializations.

At first, Bertie only appeared a little at a time; a hand here, a head, her breast, and then her full figure. Reimer's reports were aglow with admiration. He wrote, "She showed me her enchanting little hand, as delicate as wax and pale, so that secretly I was doubtful until the fingers began to move playfully and she disappeared, throwing me a kiss. I felt, I still feel now, as it had been a greeting and a joyous signal, a hint of the mountains of doubt which those angelic hands were preparing to remove. I did not dream how soon that same lovely hand, shaped in plaster, would lie before me on the table after the basin of liquid wax had been removed."

To obtain an even stronger sense of the reality of his beloved, Reimers asked for casts of both of her hands, which were obtained by using pouring hot, liquid wax into a basin on the table. Bertie then plunged her spirit hands into the wax and when she withdrew them, forms had been made from which Reimers could make his plaster casts.

Reimers' feelings became deeply emotional and at Christmas, he presented her with a small gold cross, which disappeared with her when the séance ended. After that, she always appeared with it and once, it was visible in a hand cast that she made. Once when he asked her if he could have it back, she refused, "It is much too dear to me."

As the relationship grew more intimate and tender, she began to appear to him in his home, as well as at séances. After a session during which spirit flowers had appeared to the participants, Reimers found a small flower on the pillow in his bedroom. He imagined that it was a little joke by Mrs. Firman, who rented rooms in the same house, but she denied leaving it there. To secure himself from tricks, he sealed the doors and windows of his room and left secret markings on the tape. In spite of this, flowers continued to appear, even though the seals remained unbroken. He also found a note from Bertie referring to a letter that had been left in his room, which later disappeared. Reimers was now lost in a dream world with his beloved ghost. "I was not secretly exchanging letters and flowers with a spirit," he wrote, "and the hullabaloo of daily life struck almost cruelly upon my ears."

The events became more and more mysterious. After the letters and flowers, it seemed destined that Reimers and Bertie would become lovers. He came home late one night, exhausted from lecturing, to find that Bertie had spirited wine and cakes into his sealed bedroom. Soon, Bertie herself followed. Reimers described her, "She showed a heavenly face which I could not attempt to describe. A charming bosom, with delicate flesh color melting into the white satin of her light dress, with brilliant eyes under the long lashes and the most charming posture. All this has surpassed her former appearances and I must open confess my posture began to falter."

These experiences were related in Reimers' own accounts but the ensuing events were pieced together by a friend of Reimers' who was also a psychical researcher. Bertie's latest visit to Reimer's bedroom caused him to forget her spirit nature and the two of them made love. After that, Bertie became more and more pressing and her nocturnal visits were not enough. She began to pester her lover during the day with her sexual demands. Reimer's initial eagerness was quelled by the constant drain on his body because Bertie had become a creature of insatiable lust. He got to the point that he fell into a state of terror before each of her visits and was so desperate to escape from her that he took a friend's advice and accepted an offer for a speaking engagement in Australia. But his hope that a change of location would free him from her was not fulfilled. Bertie left him alone during his long sea voyage, perhaps because he was not involved in any séances while on the ship, but she appeared once again when he reached Australia. His remaining writings made it clear that there was no stopping her from visiting his bed each night.

Eventually, Reimers was able to free himself from the once-beloved spirit – by death. Only at that point was he able to escape from her persistent attentions. Or was he? We have to wonder if Bertie was waiting for him on the other side.

THE HEADLESS LOVER

Until recent times, the ghost of Ronald Travis' sweetheart was said to haunt the place where Britain's old Midland Railways Brooke End signal box once stood. Her sighs, moans and orgasmic groans were reported on many occasions, despite the fact that her spirit appeared to have no head.

The story began in the early 1900s with the meeting of Ronald Travis, a young railroad worker, and Marion Gorman, the daughter of one of his co-workers. Travis was working at the Brooke End signal box when Marion visited the box one evening looking for her father. An attraction grew between the two young people, who were both roughly the same age and from country family upbringing.

At first, Marion's parents approved of the romance, but before long, the young woman began spending more and more time with her sweetheart. Her parents' resentment over her frequent absences grew and soon, her father decided to confront Travis in an effort to bring some peace to his household. Travis was unhappy after being visited by Marion's father and told the older man that she was old enough to make up her own mind about whom she wanted to spend her time with. The two men, who had always been on good terms in the past, began avoiding each other when they had to work together.

One autumn evening, Gorman remembered that he had not posted the signal box duty roster for the next day, as was his normal practice. He left home and journeyed back to the signal box, only to find it apparently empty. Climbing the wooden stairs to the signal box door, he looked into the window, expecting to see the signalman resting on the floor. What he saw though, was his daughter and Travis, naked, and making love on the floor. Although Marion was certainly of age, Gorman was furious. A tremendous argument broke out between the three of them, ending with Marion being dragged away by her father, who vowed that he would never let the couple meet again.

After that night, Marion became almost a prisoner of her parents. Weeks passed and she was never allowed to leave the house unless in the company of her father and mother. Before long, though, the attraction between the two young people prompted Marion to plan a secret meeting and she slipped out of the cottage one night while her parents were sleeping. She hurried to the signal box, where Travis had night duty.

Marion hurried across the tracks as the night train sped down the railway toward her, taking a risk in trying to beat it to the crossing point just down from the signal box. She was spotted by the engineer and succeeded in crossing the line safely, but her shoes slipped on a muddy patch on the steep embankment and, to the engineer's horror, he saw the young girl fall beneath the locomotive's wheels. The engineer quickly applied the brakes but it was much too late to

Old Signal Box on the Midland Railways line

stop. Once the train finally slowed, the engineer found a horrific scene. Marion's body had been badly mutilated by the wheels of the train, which had run over her neck, completely severing her head.

A coroner's inquest found a verdict of accidental death, but the jury's findings did nothing to alleviate the guilt felt by Travis or by Marion's bereaved parents. All of them moved away from the area in an attempt to escape from the terrible tragedy that had scarred their lives. Marion, however, was not quite ready to depart. Soon after her death, a series of strange hauntings occurred.

A train guard named George Marsh was the first to spot the ghost of the girl. He was drinking a cup of tea while sitting on a freight train and waiting for another train to pass and clear the line so that his train could move on. As the second train approached, Marsh saw a young woman in a white dress run across the tracks in front of the engine. Terrified that she might fall on the tracks, he called out to her – and then watched as she tumbled under the wheels! Others who had heard his cry turned to look and saw the girl fall to her death. They rushed to the scene with Marsh only slightly ahead of them. When he arrived, he looked down at the decapitated body of a young woman in a white dress and then was shocked to see the figure disappear in front of his eyes.

Another incident was reported by Jan and Alice Marshall in the early 1950s when they were picking blackberries in the area. One quiet summer afternoon, they were approaching the old signal box and began to hear the sounds of a young woman in the act of making love with her partner. They were startled and embarrassed to hear her throaty cries and ecstatic groans and feared they were about to interrupt a couple in the throes of passion. With a knowing look at one another, Jan and Alice began to walk off in the opposite direction of where the sounds seemed to be coming from. However, this had no effect. The sound of the girl's thrashing and moaning seemed to follow them wherever they went. At last, the Marshalls had had enough and Jan beckoned to his wife to cross the railroad tracks to the other side of the line. At that same moment, the sound of a train could be heard approaching and Alice, without speaking, grabbed Jan's arm in an effort to hold him back from crossing the tracks until after the train had passed. By now, the sounds of the groans and cries were muffled by the sound of the approaching train. Immediately, and out of nowhere, the couple noticed a young girl in a white dress almost opposite them on the line, obviously intending to cross. Shouting together to try and stop her, the Marshalls were shaken to see her dart across the tracks and barely make it safely to the other side. Jan gave a sigh of relief and shook his head at his wife in disbelief.

As the train thundered past, however, the couple saw that the girl had not made it across the tracks, as they had first believed. To their horror, they saw her bloody body sprawled across the tracks. Her head had been severed and blood was splashed all over her dress, the railroad tracks and the surrounding earth. Alice began to scream and Jan ran over to see if there was anything that he could do for the injured woman, too stunned to consider the fact that she had been decapitated. He turned to his wife and shouted at her not to come any closer, but to run and get help. Almost as soon as he spoke the words, the ghostly body disappeared, leaving the distressed couple completely baffled.

After the Marshalls' experience, many others reported hearing the moans and gasps of a woman making love, followed by a spectral figure that tried to beat the train across the tracks at Brooke End. Remarkably, engineers never reported an accident at the spot, other than the terrible tragedy that claimed the life of Marion Gorman, but many saw the phantom re-enactment of the girl's last attempt to see her lover. The ghostly figure and her sad sounds of love had not been seen or heard for a number of years now and it seems that Marion Gorman is finally resting in peace. Perhaps she and Ronald Travis have finally been reunited on the other side, where their spectral lovemaking can continue for eternity.

THE PHANTOM GROPER OF BORLEY RECTORY

In the annals of supernatural history, there is no house that is as famous as Borley Rectory, a rambling mansion that once stood in Essex, England. Made famous by ghost hunter Harry Price, the rectory burned to the ground in 1939, bringing an end to an era of ghosts and legends that has never been rivaled.

Many tales were told of the strange happenings in this building, from moving objects to the phantom nun who strolled a garden path near the summer house. Poltergeists threw items across the room; objects vanished; fires started with no explanation; and ghostly footsteps were heard both day and night. Experiments with automatic writing were undertaken after mysterious messages were found written on the walls and noises manifested themselves regularly, while ringing bells, chanting voices, and eerie music were often heard at night.

Although hundreds of people were terrified by these strange events over the years, starting in 1863, no one was ever really harmed. However, there was one bedroom in the house where a ghost was known to sexually molest sleepers during the night.

The first such incident occurred in 1892. At that time, a headless man was reportedly being seen wandering in the garden of the house. Guests staying with the Bull family, who had built the house in 1863, were given a small bedroom, which, until that time, had been free from the hauntings. Harry Bull, the son of the original owner, The Reverend Henry Bull, had taken over the house and made light of the building's spooky reputation. He advised his unsettled guests that they were in the safest room of the rectory. Unfortunately, that designation did not last for long. Soon, both male and female sleepers began to complain that they had been visited in the night by a ghostly presence – one that made intense and persistent sexual advances.

Borley Rectory

In every situation, the story was the same. Guests would climb into bed, only to be awakened by a whispering voice. As they struggled to light the closest lamp, the flame would mysteriously be blown out and the whispering sounds would cease. Later in the night, the bed covers would be lifted and a ghostly hand would start caressing their legs and their genitals. After freezing with fright, the sleeper could come to his or her senses and jump from the bed, sure that the whole thing had been some sort of unsettling dream. When the guest got back into bed, though, the ghostly hand would begin stroking, rubbing and grabbing once again. Every guest left the house the following morning, or at least demanded another room in which to spend the night.

Those who tried to get to the bottom of the situation (so to speak!), with the belief that worldly hands were responsible for the nocturnal groping, found their efforts at investigation to be thwarted. They searched in vain for practical jokers, hidden passages and secret panels, but found nothing. Volunteers who were locked in the room all night failed to come up with any conclusion other than that the "phantom groper" was indeed a supernatural one.

No one ever saw the ghost (or the ghostly hand, in this case) and it was found that guests sleeping anywhere else in the room, other than the bed, were not subjected to the unwelcome advances. Only one clue was ever given that might shed light on the molester's identity. This came in an otherworldly message that mentioned the name "Marie," together with the French word *lait*, which means milk. The ghost came to be known in later years as "Marie the Milkmaid." And while this name appeared to be insignificant at the time, it was later discovered that a French nun had been reputedly strangled by her lover in a building that once stood on the same site as Borley Rectory. One of the spirit messages that appeared mysteriously on the rectory's walls in the 1930s stated that her body was still buried in the building's cellar. Excavations in the ruins later discovered pieces of a human skull that were believed to have belonged to the murdered nun.

The nun's name was said to have been Marie Lairre.

THE WEDDING NIGHT MONK

The Augustan house of Newstead Priory in England's Nottinghamshire has been the home of a number of Lord Byrons, including the famous poet, George Gordon, Lord Byron, who actually wrote a lyrical account of the building's malicious monk. The monk is said to haunt the occupants of the priory upon their deathbeds --- and on their wedding beds, as well. The eerie black figure gained infamy when it began menacing newly married couples as they spent their first night together in the manor house.

The poet Lord Byron inherited the house when he was just a boy and it has been said that he spent a very happy childhood there. Much of the imaginative young man's delight came from the tales of dark events that occurred during the four hundred years when the Black Augustan monks occupied the building. According to legend, when King Henry VIII confiscated the monastery and its surrounding acerage, a number of the monks placed a curse upon anyone who took over the abbey lands. For just this reason, it was said, owners of the house began to report the presence of a sinister-looking monk in a black cowl prowling about the place. He was seen lurking at a

Lord Byron

number of christenings and gloating at the bedside of those who breathed their last within the confines of the abbey walls. Weddings, too, did not escape the monk's attentions and Lord Byron himself was said to have seen the ghost at his own marriage ceremony.

But those who seemed to earn the greatest attention from the monk were newlywed couples, usually in the midst of their first sexual encounter. Following intercourse, a young man reportedly found himself streaming blood from his sexual organs. Rushing to find the source of the hot, sticky blood that he felt streaming down his legs, he would be amazed to find no trace of it whatsoever. And yet, in the flickering light of the candle, he would see the scowling face of the monk staring at him from a shadowy corner of the room. The phantom would smile

Newstead Abbey in Nottinghamshire, home of Lord Byron -- and the phantom monk

menacingly and then disappear.

On another occasion, newlyweds were said to have found themselves bound together and unable to move apart, "as if bound by unseen tethers," and they also saw a black figure looking over them. The man remained trapped within his wife's flesh until their cries caught the attention of a servant, whose presence seemed to break the spell and the couple were able to move about normally again. The dark shadow of the monk once again moved across the bedchamber.

On only one occasion, several monks were seen. As a young man and his wife undressed on the second night of their marriage, the black monk appeared in the corner of the bedroom, bringing with him a sickly smell and a strange pool of sticky, white substance that seemed to bubble on the floor. Frozen with fear, the couple watched as another monk appeared from out of the wall at the other end of the bedroom. He was dressed in the same manner as the original monk but was not wearing a hood and was carrying a large crucifix, as if he were leading a procession. He was followed by another monk, and then another, until a stream of them began to cross the room, walking two abreast. Although the procession of monks did not acknowledge the presence of the original ghost, he was obviously extremely distressed by their appearance. Immediately, the bubbling mess on the floor faded away and carried the original monk with it, apparently dragging him down into the floor.

This strange event did nothing to curb the haunting by the spectral monk and he continued his appearances at family events hosted by the owners of the house. His menacing presence continues to be reported in bedchambers at the manor house to this day. Why he haunts the place, aside from the curse, and what his fascination is with newlywed sex remains a mystery.

THE GHOSTLY ENCOUNTER

A young attorney named Nicholas Prior once told of a strange experience that he had in London in June 1930. At the time, Prior had a wealthy client who lived in London and who insisted that Prior take care of all of his legal affairs. This usually meant that the attorney would travel from Birmingham to London for a week or two, carrying out his legal duties during the day and "doing the town" on his expense account at night. Prior was a single man and when he returned home, he would treat his colleagues at the firm with tales of his various sexual exploits in the city.

That June, when Prior returned from one of these trips, he appeared to be far from his normal self. His friends begged him to tell them of his sexual antics, but this time, Prior remained silent and only stated that he had a good time. Eventually, a few weeks later, a friend of Prior's managed to draw out of him a experience that had shaken him so badly that he resolved never to return to London again.

One evening in the city, Prior dined at an expensive West End restaurant, where he enjoyed a large dinner and a number of cocktails. Afterward, he took a cab to one of the areas of the city known for its "better quality of good time girls," where he wandered about, surveying the scene and deciding which bar he wanted to visit. Having been propositioned a number of times, he decided to move on to another area and looked for a

London's West End has long been home to theaters, nightspots and clubs

passing cab. As he waited, he was approached by a attractive, respectable-looking girl, who seemed to come out of nowhere. She walked up to him and asked him for a light for her cigarette. Prior confessed that he didn't know if the girl was a prostitute or not, for she was dressed very well. She was of medium build, had long, silky hair, wore a ring on her wedding finger and a broad-brimmed hat. Her long dress was covered by a dark, heavy coat with a short attached cape, of the kind that was then worn by nurses. Prior's most distinct memories were of her piercing blue eyes and bright smile.

They talked for several minutes, but the question as to whether or not the girl was a prostitute was never brought up. Finally, Prior suggested that they have a drink and the girl agreed. Just then, a strangely painted cab with a blue and white checkered door pulled up and took them to a bar at a nearby hotel. During the trip, the girl never spoke and Prior assumed that she was embarrassed at being picked up in such a manner. His attempts at light conversation fell short with the cramped interior of the cab.

When they reached the hotel, they climbed out onto the curb and the vehicle drove off. But before they could go inside, the young woman reached for Prior and pulled him close. She kissed him with such passion and ferocity that even this adventurous young man was taken aback. When he did respond, the girl became more and more passionate, begging him to book a room at the hotel and take her upstairs.

It was at this point that Prior realized that she was indeed a prostitute and he asked her how much the night was going to cost him. However, the young woman insisted that this was her night off and she would not charge him anything. Prior now began to suspect, thanks to her accent and fine clothing, that she was likely the wealthy daughter of some notable family, and despite her claims, she was not actually a prostitute, but was acting out the fantasy for her own sexual satisfaction. But the young man was not about to ruin what he knew would be an amazing night and he left the girl waiting as he went and booked a room. He returned to her and passed along the room number. She told him that she would be upstairs right away.

The attorney went straight to the hotel room and waited for the girl to join him. He found it hard to believe that such a beautiful, exciting stranger was about to share his bed. The girl arrived moments later and during the hours that followed, Prior was treated to lovemaking like he had never experienced before. The insatiable appetite of his partner left him exhausted, but even when he protested that he was too tired, he was sweetly persuaded to perform again and again. Finally, unable to go on any longer, he fell into a deep and satisfied sleep.

Prior next remembered being awakened by the teasing hands of his companion, at which time he muttered that he was unable to go on. He avoided her hands and slid to the side of the bed, quickly attempting to get dressed. It had been a wonderful night, he thought, but enough was enough. However, the girl was not willing to stop. Sensing that her partner was leaving her, her mood very quickly and violently changed. To Prior's horror, her beautiful face contorted into that of a raging lunatic. She spit and cursed at him, then dragged him back onto the bed. As she hovered over him, she began to tear at her own flesh with her fingernails, dragging at the pale skin. Her eyes turned red and bloodshot and then her entire form began to change before Prior's eyes. As he lay under her, frozen with terror, the girl's skin became old and wrinkled and her thick, dark hair turned white. The young woman soon transformed into an ugly, old hag – then reverted back to the pretty girl again. Prior was sure about what he had seen, however, his beautiful lover had changed into something ghastly!

As the girl looked down at him, her eyes seemed amused by Prior's shock. He opened his mouth to speak, but he was silenced as she pressed a finger to his lips. The girl did not talk to him and instead, began to slowly fade away. Even though he could still feel the pressure of her finger, he could barely see her as she disappeared. Finally, only the outline of her face and her lips could be seen and her mouth opened to utter her last words -- "only a ghost."

With this, she vanished completely, leaving Prior to hurriedly throw on his clothes and try to understand the strange events that had just occurred. He practically stumbled out of the hotel toward the street, hailing down a passing cab. It was the same strangely painted taxi that had brought him to the hotel hours earlier. The driver remembered him and greeted him cheerfully, to which Prior responded by asking him if he knew the young woman who had been with when he had earlier picked him up.

The driver looked at him with confusion. "There must be some mistake, sir," he said. "You were alone when I picked you up."

Assuring the man that he must be mistaken, Prior described the girl who had been with him.

The driver looked serious when he replied. "Some around here might laugh, sir, but that's the second time that someone had said the same thing to me. Only three days ago, I picked up a young gentleman at the same place as you, and brought him back again. He must have had a lot to drink, though, said she'd turned into an old witch while he was in bed with her."

Prior tipped the cab driver and asked to be let out. He decided to walk back to his hotel and give himself some time to think and pull himself together.

Over the course of the next few days, Prior investigated the matter, asking other cab drivers in the area if they had seen anyone who looked like the young woman with the wide-brimmed hat. None of them had. Stranger still, none of them had ever seen a cab with a blue and white checkered door and in fact, knew of no company in London that used a cab that was painted that way. Prior found out they were right -- finally believing that the driver had also come from the ghostly realm.

To his dying day, Prior repeated his belief that if he had taken the return journey in the blue and white cab that night in June, he would have never been seen again to tell his tale.

THE VENGEFUL LOVER

In September 1950, a man named Harry Wagner had a startling story to tell his sister, Virginia Santore. According to his nerve-rattling story, he has being haunted by the ghost of a woman who had been dead for twenty years – a ghost who wanted to kill him!

Virginia assumed that Harry was joking with her when he first blurted out the story while sitting at the kitchen table of her home in Youngstown, Ohio. Harry had come to visit and they were having coffee when he finally gathered the courage to ask her if she believed in ghosts. Without waiting for her reply, he told her that he had a story that he needed to tell someone and that when he finished, she was not to tell it to anyone else. He didn't want his wife to know because she would be worried sick. "The ghost," he said, "means to kill me."

Wagner explained that the haunting began in July. One night he found it too hot to sleep and after his wife, Mary, and the children went to bed, Harry stayed up reading. When the temperature finally cooled down, he went to his bedroom. He turned off the light and climbed into bed next to Mary. Suddenly, although it was still warm in the room, Harry felt a chill creep over him, making him shiver and shake. He was unable to describe the intensity of the cold, except to say that it was so frigid that his teeth began to chatter.

When the cold was nearly unbearable, he looked up to see an unusual sight near the bedroom door. There, suspended in the air, was a glowing ball of light. He watched in shock as it moved toward him, misting and swirling about as it changed form into a luminous, human-like shape. As the light intensified and became solid, Wagner realized that it had formed into the presence of his first wife, Alice.

He could not have been more surprised. Alice had died in 1933 and although Wagner never discussed the marriage with anyone, his sister knew that it had been an unhappy and bitter one. He had been eighteen years old when they were married, and Alice twenty, and she had died just four years later. Wagner's mind told him that the woman was dead, and had been for many years, but he could plainly see her in every detail. She was dressed in a flowing white gown and her dark hair tumbled down over her shoulders. She was just as beautiful as she had been in life and she stood next to Wagner's bed, smiling calmly. He later realized that the bitter coldness of the room had been forgotten.

Moments later, the apparition began to move. With a twisting movement, she turned and spun as her body rose into the air. Seconds later, Alice was hovering above him and then began to slowly descend down onto his body. As he lay there paralyzed with fear, Wagner could feel her solid weight as she settled down onto him. Gripping his shoulders with both hands, she smiled at him – but then her face began to change. Her pretty face became a chalky mask and her eyes blazed red. Wagner opened his mouth to scream but at that moment, Alice's face darted forward and she fastened her mouth over his in a grotesque kiss. Wagner was pinned beneath her, feeling the entire weight of her body, which seemed to grow heavier with each passing second. He was terrified and unable to breath since it felt as if Alice was literally pulling all of the air out of his lungs.

When he felt that he couldn't bear it another moment, Wagner was suddenly released. Gasping and choking, he swung his feet over the side of the bed and then fell to the floor. His heart was thudding in his chest as he struggled to pull air into his body. The apparition had vanished, but Harry was sure that he heard mocking laughter in the distance, which gradually died away. Several minutes passed before he was able to breathe normally again.

Somehow, he managed to get through the rest of the night, although he was unable to fall asleep until it was nearly dawn. In the morning light, he was able to convince himself that the whole thing was a nightmare, a terrible nightmare, but a nightmare nonetheless --- but then it happened again. Alice returned to him several times, becoming more insistent and more sexual with every visit. She came two times a week for the rest of the summer and by September, he told his sister, he was drained and unable to make her leave him alone. "I am really afraid," he told Virginia, "because I know that if these episodes don't stop, I'll die. But I don't know what to do to stop them."

Virginia was stunned by her brother's story, and impressed by his sincerity, but was sure that the incidents were merely a recurring bad dream. It was clear that Harry was suffering from some sort of physical ailment, she believed, and that his subconscious mind was trying to bring attention to this in a very unorthodox manner. But that was all that it was – he was letting his imagination run away from him. He needed to seek medical help and the sooner that he did, the better off he would be. Finally, even though he still insisted that the nocturnal visits were not dreams at all, he did agree to see a doctor.

Several weeks passed and every medical test that was performed on Harry came back normal. Finally, Virginia asked him if he had told the doctor about the dreams that he had been having. He said that no, he hadn't, and she begged him to do so. He promised he would, but by now, it was the third week of October and everyone in the family was worried about Wagner's health. His weight had dropped alarmingly and he was so weak that walking, or even driving his car, was becoming an effort.

On his next visit to the doctor, Wagner told him about his recurring dream. The physician was sympathetic, but quick and to the point – Harry needed to be hospitalized as soon as possible for psychiatric tests. He believed that Harry's illness was psychosomatic. He made immediate arrangements for Wagner to be admitted to the Woodside Receiving Hospital in Youngstown, Ohio.

Harry and his wife stayed with Virginia on the night before he was to be admitted to the hospital. Mary's sister watched the children overnight and Virginia picked up the Wagners early in the evening. They were in good spirits, convinced that Harry would be helped by his hospital stay, and after dinner they retired to bed. Harry took the front bedroom and Mary and Virginia turned down the bed in the rear of the house, hoping to talk some more after Harry went to sleep. But Harry was nervous and tossed and turned for hours. The two ladies took turns bringing him water, hot tea and aspirin, until finally, about 3:00 a.m., he dropped off to sleep. Virginia and Mary were exhausted by this time and went to bed a short time later.

Virginia tried to relax but an odd sound startled her to alertness. She slipped out of bed and hurried down the long hallway toward Harry's room. As she walked in, she switched on a lamp and was horrified by what she saw! Wagner was lying rigid on the bed, his face flushed a deep red. His eyes were wide open and seemed to be popping out of their sockets. And while his mouth was gaping open, Virginia was unable to see any sign that he was breathing. She was terrified that he was either dead or dying. She ran to the bed and got another horrible shock. She felt a cold chill sweep over her and she felt frozen to the spot. It took everything that she had to push her body forward and to throw herself over the prone form of her brother. Grabbing him by the arms, she pulled him into a sitting position and she realized that something invisible was writhing and twisting between them. Whatever it was, Virginia could feel it as an actual physical presence. She saw nothing at first and then recoiled as a misty, gray, vaporous mass appeared and flowed upward toward the ceiling!

Now free from whatever was strangling him, Harry began gulping in huge, choking mouthfuls of air. The glazed expression left his eyes and he looked at his sister. She relaxed as she could see that he recognized her and was recovering from the attack. She was just about to speak when he heard wild, muted laughter coming from the distance. She didn't realize that she was still holding Harry's arms until she felt a twinge of pain in her knotted hands. "My God, Harry, what was that?" she cried.

Weakly, Harry replied, "I've been trying to convince you all this time…" And then he closed his eyes and fell back onto the bed.

Somehow, they got through the rest of the night. Virginia left all of the lights on until dawn, sitting in a chair and watching over Harry while he slept. When her brother awakened, she finally admitted to him that she had been wrong about his dreams. Virginia begged him for forgiveness and then pleaded with him not to go to the hospital.

But Wagner was adamant, convinced that perhaps there was something that the doctors could do to help him. Later that morning, as planned, Virginia and Mary delivered Harry to the hospital. When she checked later, Virginia was told that Harry was in good health and that his mental condition was perfectly normal. He was overly nervous, perhaps, but he had been given medication to help with that. That afternoon, Virginia picked him up at the hospital and drove him home.

A few days later, on Wednesday, November 1, Virginia picked up her sister, Evelyn, and they went to visit the Wagners. They arrived to find Mary very upset and Harry, his lips ringed with blue, waiting for a doctor to arrive. The doctor arrived a few minutes later, took one look at Harry, and immediately summoned an ambulance. During the early morning hours, Harry had suffered a heart attack, which turned out to be fatal. By the time the ambulance reached the hospital, Harry Wagner was dead.

Virginia later recalled that she would never forget her brother's farewell gesture to her that morning as paramedics carried him out to the waiting ambulance. He nodded his head at her several times and she knew exactly what he meant – his ghostly visitor had paid him one last call.

Until the day that she passed away, Virginia pondered the mystery of Harry's unwanted lover. Why did the vengeful spirit of Alice return to prey on her former husband? Why did she blame him for her death and why did she wait so long to come back? Virginia would never know the truth and the strange riddle of Alice Wagner will never be solved.

BIBLIOGRAPHY AND RECOMMEND READING

Barton, Blanche – *Secret Life of a Satanist* – Los Angeles, Feral House; 1990

Bayless, Raymond – *Enigma of the Poltergeist*, New York, Parker Publishing, 1967

Black, Candice – *Satanica Sexualis*, Oakland, CA, Wet Angel Books; 2006

Carrington, Hereward & Nandor Fodor – *Haunted People*, New York, Signet; 1951

Chambers, Paul – *Paranormal People*, London, Blanford; 1998

Ebon, Martin – *By Lust Possessed*, New York, Signet, 1980

-------------- - *Demon Children*, New York, Signet, 1978

-------------- - *Devil's Bride*, New York, Harper, 1974

-------------- - *Exorcism: Fact Not Fiction*, New York, Signet, 1974

Fate Magazine

Fodor, Nandor – *The Haunted Mind*, New York, Signet; 1959

Glut, Donald F. – *True Vampires of History*, New York, HC Publishers, 1971

Guiley, Rosemary Ellen – *Encyclopedia of Vampires, Werewolves & Other Monsters*, New York, Checkmark Books; 2007

Hall, Trevor – The *Medium and the Scientist* – New York, Prometheus Books, 1984

Hill, Douglas – *History of Ghosts, Vampires & Werewolves*, New York, Harrow; 1973

------------- & Pat Williams, *The Supernatural*, London, Aldus Books; 1965

Holzer, Hans – *Love Beyond the Grave*, New York, Barnes & Noble; 1992

Houdini, Harry – *A Magician Among the Spirits*, New York, Harper; 1924

Hurwood, Bernhardt – *Vampires, Werewolves & Ghouls*, New York, Ace, 1968

Jackson, Herbert G. – *The Spirit Rappers*, New York, Doubleday; 1972

Kendrick, Walter – *The Thrill of Fear*, New York, Grove, 1991

LaVey, Anton – *Satanic Bible*, New York, Avon, 1969

-------------- - *Satanic Rituals*, New York, Avon; 1972

-------------- - *Satanic Witch*, New York, Avon,; 1970

McHargue, Georgess – *Facts, Frauds & Phantasms*, New York, Doubleday; 1972

McNally, Raymond T. – *Dracula Was a Woman*, New York, McGraw-Hill, 1983

Mannix, Daniel P., *History of Torture*; New York, Dell, 1964

Pearsall, Ronald – *The Table Rappers*, New York, St. Martin's; 1972

Pratnicka, Wanda – *Possessed by Ghosts*, Self-Published, 2006

Robson, Peter – *The Devil's Own*, New York, Ace; 1966

Roll, William – *The Poltergeist*. New York, Signet; 1972

-------------- & Valerie Storey, *Unleashed*, New York, Pocket Books; 2004

Smith, Michelle & Lawrence Pazder, MD, *Michelle Remembers*, New York, Congdon & Lattes, Inc; 1980

Steiger, Brad – *Haunted Lovers*, New York, Dell; 1971

-------------- - *Sex and Satanism*, New York, Ace, 1969

-------------- - *Sex and the Supernatural*, New York, Lancer; 1968

-------------- - *Strange Guests*, New York, Ace, 1966

Taylor, Troy – *Devil Came to St. Louis*, Decatur, IL, Whitechapel Press, 2006

-------------- - *Ghosts by Gaslight*, Decatur, IL, Whitechapel Press; 2007

-------------- - *The Possessed*, Decatur, IL, Whitechapel Press, 2007
Waters, Colin – *Sexual Hauntings Through the Ages*, New York, Dorset Press, 1993
Welleslet, Gordon – *Sex and the Occult*, New York, Signet; 1973
Wheatley, Dennis – *Satan & All his Works*, New York, American Heritage Press; 1971
Wikipedia References
Wilson, Colin – *The Occult*; New York, Random House; 1971
-------------- - *Poltergeist,* St. Paul, MN, Fate; 1993
Winer, Richard & Nancy Osborn – *Haunted Houses*, New York, Bantam; 1979
-------------- - *More Haunted Houses*, New York, Bantam; 1981

Personal Interviews & Correspondence

Acknowledgements
Jill Hand – Editing and Proofreading Services
Ken Melvoin-Berg
Rosemary Ellen Guiley
Anton LaVey
Dennis Wheatley
Barry Downard
Hugh B. Cave
& Haven Taylor 🐢

ABOUT THE AUTHOR

Troy Taylor is an occultist, supernatural historian and the author of nearly 60 books on ghosts, hauntings, history, crime and the unexplained in America. He is also the founder of the American Ghost Society and the owner of the Illinois and American Hauntings Tour companies.

Taylor shares a birthday with one of his favorite authors, F. Scott Fitzgerald, but instead of living in New York and Paris like Fitzgerald, Taylor grew up in Illinois. Raised on the prairies of the state, he developed an interest in "things that go bump in the night" at an early age and as a young man, developing ghost tours and writing about haunts in Chicago and Central Illinois.

He began his first book in 1989, which delved into the history and hauntings of Decatur, Illinois, and in 1994, it spawned the Haunted Decatur Tour -- and eventually led to the founding of his Illinois Hauntings Tours (with current tours in Alton, Chicago, Decatur, Lebanon & Jacksonville) and the American Hauntings Tours, which travel all over the country in search of haunted places.

Along with writing about the unusual and hosting tours, Taylor is also a public speaker on the subject of ghosts and hauntings. has appeared in scores of newspaper and magazine articles about the subject and in hundreds of radio and television broadcasts about the supernatural. He has also appeared in a number of documentary films, several television series and in one feature film about the paranormal.

Troy and his wife, Haven, currently reside in Central Illinois in a decidedly non-haunted house.

ABOUT WHITECHAPEL PRESS

Whitechapel Productions Press is a division of Dark Haven Entertainment and a small press publisher, specializing in books about ghosts and hauntings. Since 1993, the company has been one of America's leading publishers of supernatural books and has produced such best-selling titles as "**Haunted Illinois**", "**The Ghost Hunter's Guidebook**", **Ghosts on Film, Confessions of a Ghost Hunter, Resurrection Mary, Bloody Chicago, The Haunting of America, Spirits of the Civil War** and many others.

With nearly a dozen different authors producing high quality books on all aspects of ghosts, hauntings and the paranormal, Whitechapel Press has made its mark with America's ghost enthusiasts.

Whitechapel Press is also the publisher of the acclaimed **Ghosts of the Prairie** magazine, which started in 1997 as one of the only ghost-related magazines on the market. It continues today as a travel guide to the weird, haunted and unusual in Illinois. Each issue also includes a print version of the Whitechapel Press ghost book catalog.

You can visit Whitechapel Productions Press online and browse through our selection of ghostly titles, plus get information on ghosts and hauntings, haunted history, spirit photographs, information on ghost hunting and much more. by visiting the internet website at:

WWW. DARK HAVEN ENTERTAINMENT.COM

Writing is not necessarily something to be ashamed of, but do it in
private and wash your hands afterwards.
Robert A. Heinlein

LaVergne, TN USA
25 August 2009

155918LV00004B/21/P